THE
ALBERT ELLIS
READER

THE
ALBERT ELLIS
READER

A Guide to Well-Being Using
Rational Emotive Behavior Therapy

Edited by Albert Ellis
Founder of Rational Emotive Behavior Therapy
and Shawn Blau

A CITADEL PRESS BOOK
PUBLISHED BY CAROL PUBLISHING GROUP

A Citadel Press Book
Published by Carol Publishing Group
Citadel Press is a registered trademark of Carol Communications, Inc.

Editorial, sales and distribution, rights and permissions inquiries should be
addressed to Carol Publishing Group, 120 Enterprise Avenue, Secaucus, N.J. 07094.

In Canada: Canadian Manda Group, One Atlantic Avenue, Suite 105, Toronto,
Ontario M6K 3E7

Carol Publishing Group books may be purchased in bulk at special discounts for
sales promotion, fund-raising, or educational purposes. Special editions can be
created to specifications. For details, contact Special Sales Department, Carol
Publishing Group, 120 Enterprise Avenue, Secaucus, N.J. 07094.

Manufactured in the United States of America
10 9 8 7 6 5 4 3 2 1

Library of Congress Cataloging-in-Publication Data

The Albert Ellis reader: a guide to well-being using rational emotive
   behavior therapy / edited by Albert Ellis and Shawn Blau.
      p.   cm.
   ISBN 0–8065–2032–9 (pbk.)
   1. Rational-emotive psychotherapy.   2. Sex (Psychology)
RM489.R3A4   1998
616.89'14—dc21   98–38654
                                                         CIP

To Janet L. Wolfe and Georgia Panagopoulos

Contents

Introduction by Shawn Blau

I'll never forget the sense of excitement I felt when I first began reading some of these articles on my own back in the late 1980s. I had read Albert Ellis's and Robert Harper's *Guide to Rational Living* much earlier in college, in the seventies. While it seemed creative and interesting, Ellis's "rational-emotive" model appeared to be just another of the bewildering assortment of personality theories which we students were forced to soak up in freshman psychology class. Although I remember trying to picture how Ellis's theory might help me make sense of my own problems back then, it didn't really "click" for me.

Fortunately I kept Ellis's book around, and when I picked it up again as an adult in the eighties, I had a completely different reaction. This time, his ideas rang perfectly true. The second time around I was so impressed with Ellis's writing that I began searching for a real live Rational Emotive Behavior Therapy (REBT) therapist to see privately. I finally located one by calling around, and luckily he turned out to be one of Ellis's long-term disciples and a true REBT purist. I explained my interest to him, and the problems I wanted to work on, and he analyzed everything just as I had read about in Ellis's books.

At first, though, even though the words made theoretic sense, I still couldn't *feel* that the theory could help me solve my own practical problems in life. Then, by chance a few weeks later, I had a bad fight with my wife right before I was scheduled to meet with my REBTer. In retrospect it wasn't that serious, but it was our first year together and the fight shook me up. I was so upset that I almost decided to cancel my appointment. When I walked into my therapist's office, I was still preoccupied by the fight and still in the grip of overwhelming feelings about it—anger, anxiety, shame, depression, and so forth. It turned out to be one of the luckiest days of my life.

That day I finally discovered that I really had the power to change my own feelings just by changing how I thought about the fight. It wasn't easy, but it really worked. I poured out my story about the fight, and we tried to dissect each emotion according to Ellis's A-B-C model, and then to look for which irrational beliefs might be making me so upset. It seemed like magic, because in a few minutes I felt myself calming down, and I could see that *I* was the one who had caused my own emotional turmoil, and *I* had the power to "uncause" it.

This kind of experience happens so fast, and the changes are so subtle, that it's always a challenge to describe the interior phenomenology, but I vividly remember the fight, and feeling overwhelmed by feelings of anxiety, depression, and anger. These were what Ellis calls my Cs (emotional consequences). We tried to infer what my Bs (evaluative beliefs) might be. Surprisingly, we didn't even question *if* I were really blowing the whole thing out of proportion, or if I were taking on too much of the responsibility for the fight. (which, in hindsight, I was doing on both counts). On the contrary, he told me, "Let's assume the very worst." In compressed form, here's the argument that worked so dramatically for me, as nearly as I can recall it:

1. If I feel depressed, maybe I'm telling myself that this marriage is the most important anchor of my life, and if I were to blame for screwing it up, then I'd be a real loser! Now let's just *suppose* that you're the one who's entirely to blame for this fight. It's probably not 100 percent your fault, but for the sake of argument let's just suppose it is. How could that make you a total loser? By a stretch, it might conceivably make you a crummy husband, but could even being a crummy husband make you 100 percent no good? And even in this marriage, aren't there *good* things you've done?

2. If I feel angry, maybe I am telling myself that my wife is being unfair and unreasonable, and she has no right to treat me like that. Let's suppose she is 100 percent responsible for the fight, and that she is totally unreasonable. Again, she probably isn't, but let's just suppose she is, for the sake of argument. Would that make her a completely rotten, bad person? How could it? Didn't she have other good qualities, or why would you still be with her?

Suddenly, in a flash, I felt better about the fight, myself, my wife—everything. My emotional turmoil stilled, and I was able to see things in perspective. At that moment, which really felt like an epiphany, I became hooked. I had somehow begun to feel palpably better and more in control, and the relief was so intense that I wanted to get it back again and again.

Apart from this particular fight, and even apart from my marriage, I found that being able to free myself from the ever-looming burden of having to give or receive blame was extremely liberating.

Whenever I felt upset, Ellis's mantra "Look for the 'must'! Look for the demand!" played in my mind. For when I had gotten upset over that fight, I discovered that I had turned my *preferences* that I behave well and that my wife behave well, into *demands* that unless I behaved well I'd be damnable, and unless she behaved well she'd be damnable. Inevitably, whenever I could locate a "must" in my thinking, and then succeed in changing it, however briefly, I would feel my emotions change.

At this point some readers may start to feel suspicious, as I myself felt when I first read about this stuff in college. How could calling something a "must" or not make any difference in your feelings? After all, *must* and *demand* and *blame* are just words, and this is the part of REBT which is such a challenge to explain. It's not changing the names you call your beliefs that is so powerful, rather, it's being able to change your internal evaluations, from "demands" to "desires" inside your head, which so powerfully affects your emotions. The best way that I know for a reader to become convinced of this is to experience it yourself by reading Ellis's chapter on Rational Emotive Imagery in this reader, and then trying to follow Ellis's instructions with your own images. If you succeed, you'll feel a palpable, physical shift in your emotions, and a visceral change in your gut. This is a reflection of the organic, neurophysiological change in your brain which occurs when your evaluations change.

That day, I knew that somehow I'd made a change in my feelings by working on my beliefs, but for the life of me I wasn't sure exactly how I'd done it. It had all been so ephemeral that I almost thought it might have been an illusion or a coincidence. The next time I was upset, I tried to calm myself as I'd done before, but the thinking was too subtle and I couldn't get it back at first. But slowly, with practice, I became better able to identify and chip away at the irrational beliefs behind my feelings when I became upset, and slowly *I* became more in control of my own emotional fate. I also discovered that all of my concerns about blame, and my "musts" and "demands" themselves, were really illusory creations of my own mind and had nothing at all to do with my practical problems in the world. I said to my wife, "This guy [Ellis] is really on to something important. This is not just another pretty *theory* about the mind. This is a practical method which anyone can use on themselves to straighten out their own thinking and feeling."

"How come every one doesn't know about this?" she replied.

Good question. Why wasn't Ellis more widely known among the general public? As I began reading more, I found that despite his enormous reputation and influence, Ellis was still considered very controversial in the field, and even those clinicians who approved of REBT often thought of his theory as only one among several useful ones. I pored through every piece of Ellis's work I could find, and discovered—as I hope the reader of this volume will discover—that Ellis has consistently and honestly applied his theory of emotional disturbance to an extremely wide range of human experiences. I was continually impressed by his straightforward, relentlessly logical approach to life's most difficult problems. Ellis's writing seemed so cogent I was anxious to meet the man in person.

Albert Ellis the Man

Meeting Ellis wasn't hard, because he is probably one of the most accessible psychologists there is. I got my chance at one of his famous weekly Friday night workshops in New York City. Since 1965, Ellis has given a weekly demonstration of REBT to the public every Friday night at his institute. I'll never forget the first time I attended one of these demonstrations. The Friday night workshop is open to anyone who pays the five-dollar admission fee, and Ellis picks two people who volunteer from the audience. That night Ellis called for each volunteer from the audience to join him up on stage, asked them to describe an actual personal problem they were experiencing, and then proceeded to give each one a live therapy session right there.

It quickly became apparent to me that Ellis, the man, was as much a product of his own ideas as his ideas were a product of him. He clearly tried to apply his theories to himself as honestly as he could, and had become almost a living embodiment of his own philosophy. What impressed me most was that he really tried to take his own medicine—as completely and as elegantly as humanly possible.

Several things jumped out. First was Ellis's complete lack of defensiveness. While he obviously believed that his theories were superior, he just as obviously wasn't equating his own values with those theories. So if someone called him to task on a mistake, he had no problem admitting it; in fact, he seemed to welcome it and enjoy it if someone found him in error. I had never met anyone like that, and it really blew me away. Second was the completely straightforward and unaffected manner in which he expressed his ideas. Even though parts of his presentation were subtle, he worked at explaining things so that they were just as clear to the janitors who worked in the building as to the professors of psychology who were, along with lay people, in the audience.

This also came across in the way he fielded questions. Since five dollars is pretty cheap Friday night entertainment in New York City, the audience always has its share of scruffily-dressed street people. Ellis would listen just as respectfully to one of their questions as to anyone else's, and answer it just as thoughtfully. He was interested only in what *ideas* came up, not *who* they came from—and sometimes some of the scruffy questioners did come up with good ideas!

Ellis has been among the most prolific contributors in the history of psychology. In addition to treating more individual and group clients than probably any other clinician in history, he has published well over a thousand articles, and sixty-five books. In terms of sheer quantity of work, there is little question that Ellis has been the most productive psychologist ever. In addition, he has trained hundreds of therapists at his clinical institute and been a tireless ambassador for REBT, giving speeches, workshops, and seminars around the world.

Surprisingly, he came to the field relatively late in life. Ellis was born in 1913, in Pittsburgh, the oldest of three children of Henry and Hettie Ellis. He had a younger brother, Paul, and a younger sister, Janet, both of whom are now deceased. Ellis got his bachelor's degree from the City College of New York in business administration in 1934. He graduated during the Great Depression, and wanted to make as much money as possible in business so that he could pursue his dream of becoming a full-time fiction writer by age thirty. In his spare time he produced mountains of fiction, plays, and belles lettres, but never got anything published.

In his twenties, Ellis worked for a gift and novelty distributor. Since his fiction and plays couldn't find an audience, he decided to try his hand at writing nonfiction. Doing research at the New York City Public Library and several private libraries, he began work on a massive study of sex, a decade before the first Kinsey report came out.

Fortuitously, because of his scholarly research on the subject, Ellis became known among his family and acquaintances as something of an authority on sex, and some of them began to seek him out for help with their own love and marital problems. He set up an informal counseling practice under the acronym LAMP (Love and Marriage Problems) Institute. Ellis's attorney advised him that he was asking for legal trouble by giving psychological advice without a license, so at age twenty-eight, he enrolled in the clinical psychology program at Teachers College of Columbia University. He resumed his marriage and family counseling practice after completing his M.A. in 1943.

In 1947, after getting his Ph.D., Ellis took a job as a psychologist at the Northern New Jersey Mental Hygiene Clinic in Morris Plains, New Jersey. He decided that psychoanalysis was the deepest form of psychotherapy, so he underwent a personal training analysis with Charles Hulbeck of the Karen Horney Institute in New York.

Ellis worked for the state of New Jersey for four years, becoming its Chief Psychologist in 1950. He began to publish widely in the professional journals, kept up a part-time private practice in Manhattan, and commuted between New Jersey and New York. In his private practice, Ellis experimented with psychoanalysis, psychoanalytic psychotherapy, and then with the more active approaches of Ferenczi and Adler. However, he became disenchanted with the lack of efficiency of psychoanalysis, and formally abandoned it in the early 1950s.

At this time, Ellis returned to his hobby of philosophy, and reading his favorite philosophers helped him to come up with the basic foundations of REBT in 1955, which he first presented in a paper at the American Psychological Association Convention in Chicago in 1956.

Ellis and Self-Help

In many ways REBT is the most self-helping of psychotherapy theories. Unlike Freud and B.F. Skinner, who saw more or less involuntary forces as causing neurotic behavior, REBT hypothesizes that humans, even when they behave stupidly or neurotically, are not usually under the control of outside forces. Rather, even though they may once have been influenced by external forces and by their thoughts about them, they mainly continue their bad behavior by thinking their own irrational thoughts. Since they're the ones who keep telling themselves these self-defeating ideas, they also have the power to stop conveying it to themselves. Thus, Ellis hypothesizes that people have within themselves enormous capacity to improve their thinking, feeling, and behavior.

I am pleased that some of the following articles demonstrate how Ellis mainly learned to help other people solve their emotional problems, by first learning to help himself overcome some of his own early handicaps. Many parts of REBT grew out of Ellis's own attempts to overcome his own problems of anxiety and shyness in his youth. When he was in his teens, Ellis suffered from a crippling fear of public speaking. At the time, this really put a damper on his ambition to make a career as a professional revolutionist and propagandist. So he pushed himself to follow the behavioral techniques of John Watson and desensitize himself, in vivo, to speaking in public. Using Watson's techniques of in vivo desensitization was so effective that Ellis made a 180-degree change, from abject fear of public speaking to really revelling in it. Since the age of twenty, he has been an entertaining and unflappable public speaker.

Encouraged by his success with public speaking, Ellis decided to try to cure himself of his shyness with women. In 1933, in his famous escapades at the Bronx Botanical Gardens, he pushed himself to attempt to pick up one hundred women, even though he was rejected all one hundred times. The pick-ups themselves didn't succeed, but Ellis did succeed in getting over his own fear. Later on, he pushed himself to overcome his tendency to be ashamed of being poor. He deliberately forced himself to do things which he knew other people would put him down for, such as going into a restaurant to use the rest room without ordering anything, just to teach himself how not to take criticism personally. Ellis later incorporated these "shame attacks" into his REBT practice with clients. Later on, with his first wife Karyl, Ellis pushed himself to make a sharp distinction in his own heart and mind between healthfully loving another person and unhealthfully believing that he *needed* her and couldn't live without her. His discovery of "love without need" later became a cornerstone of his counseling and therapy practice.

So, for better or for worse, Ellis became a living laboratory for his own psychological theories.

The ABCs of REBT

Ellis's enduring insight is that, unlike Skinner's animals, we humans can give ourselves emotional problems just by thinking about our practical problems. Just because we are human, we all tend to escalate our strong preferences and desires—about the world, ourselves, and others—into demands in our own minds. Ellis coined his own neologism for this tendency: "musturbation."

In REBT, Ellis has devoted himself to figuring out how to peel away the emotional problems from the practical problems which lie under them, so that people can focus more efficiently on working on their practical problems. REBT analyzes emotional disturbances in terms of Ellis's A-B-C model. *A* represents the "adversity" or "activating event." *B* represents one's evaluative "beliefs" about *A*. *C* is the emotional "consequence" generated by both *A* and *B*.

REBT hypothesizes that people *create* both rational beliefs (RBs) and irrational beliefs (IBs) when they come up against As which block their goals. Human beings, especially, are prone to escalate their rational preferences (RBs) about the As into irrational beliefs (IBs), by insisting that they *must* have something which they want very much, or that they *must* avoid something else which they very much *don't* want. It's these demands, Ellis explains, which lead to paralyzing and crippling emotional upsets.

REBT shows people how to "dispute" their own IBs at point D, in order to come up with a new effective philosophy at *E*. If people can successfully persuade themselves that one of their irrational beliefs is false, they'll feel a release from whatever emotional disturbance was crippling them, and be freer to attack their practical problems as effectively as possible.

REBT and CBT

Ellis started using REBT in his private practice in New York in the early 1950s, and introduced it publicly at the American Psychological Association convention in 1956. In the 1960s, REBT was joined by a host of other cognitive-behavioral therapies (CBTs). REBT still has some unique features,[2] which I should point out:

1. REBT teaches an explicit and coherent philosophy for thinking and living more rationally, rather than a cookbook of therapeutic techniques.
2. REBT discourages the kind of self-esteem which is conditional on doing well at something, and instead encourages both unconditional acceptance of oneself and other people.
3. REBT often encourages people to focus first on their secondary disturbances, that is, their disturbance about being disturbed.
4. REBT often accepts, for the sake of argument, people's negative and distorted inferences about the unfortunate facts of their own lives. It encourages people to focus first on philosophically disputing their explicit and implicit "musts," "shoulds," "com-

mands," and "demands." REBT hypothesizes that it is this "demandingness" which leads people to make distorted and negative inferences about their lives in the first place.

5. REBT strives to help people really *get* better, rather than just *feel* better. People are encouraged to make pervasive and long-lasting changes in their general philosophies, in addition to simply ameliorating their current emotional upsets.

6. In addition to disputing their "musts" about their own and about other people's performances, REBT often encourages people to fight against their tendency to upset themselves about hassles because of their human propensity for "low frustration tolerance," or "discomfort disturbance."

7. REBT makes a qualitative distinction between two different kinds of negative emotions—first, those which are healthy, despite being negative, because they help you achieve your goals (such as regret over making a bad mistake), and second, negative emotions which are *unhealthy* because they hinder you from going after your goals (such as depression after making a bad mistake).

Rational Revolutionary

I hope the reader will notice the iconoclastic and combative tenor of many of the following articles, for this reveals something important about REBT, and especially about Ellis the man. Like many in his generation, he was drawn to the romantic ideal of being a revolutionary. However, Ellis was always a peculiar sort of revolutionary, one who was mainly interested in freeing people's minds and intellects from their ideological chains. In fact, REBT represents the third revolution which he has sought to wage.

When he was twenty, Ellis worked as a (poorly) paid revolutionist for a radical political group in New York for a year. The group was called New America, and was dedicated to a collectivist economic system, but was against Soviet communism because of its totalitarian nature. Ellis soon became disillusioned with communism in general, and also discovered that many of his fellow revolutionaries were really drawn to political action mainly because of their own personal psychological problems. Later on, in Ellis's first career as a psychological sexologist and sex therapist, he wrote first-rate scientific articles in many of the professional journals, but was mainly interested in propagandizing for his liberal views on sex, love, and marriage. He was willing to forego a lot of respect and professional acceptance in order to teach people about what he thought was wrong with the mores of the time.

Finally, in his third attempt to spread revolutionary ideas and practices, Ellis sought to apply the power of cognitive-behavioral theory and practice to the fields of psychotherapy and counseling through REBT. In many ways, this revolution was even more difficult than his earlier attempt to promote sexual freedom in the 1950s and 1960s. With REBT, Ellis deliberately attacked most of the common "wisdom" of psychotherapy and academic psychology. That he was eventually vindicated in the psychotherapeutic marketplace is a tribute to his persistence, and especially to his own use of REBT on himself.

In all three revolutions, Ellis was mainly trying to overthrow inefficiency and irrationality. He often says that he was born "with a gene for efficiency." I don't know whether he's right about that, but it does seem to be the most constant characteristic in his professional career. Even in his first job in the gift and novelty business, Ellis distinguished himself by coming up with more efficient ways to organize the business. He was able to convince his boss to let him work fewer hours than the other employees because he was so much more efficient at his job. Likewise, in his writings on sex and later on REBT, Ellis often inveighed against the inefficiency of traditional ways of looking at things.

Taking His Case to the People

Ellis has also seen his role as a popularizer of new ideas as being at least of equal importance to his role as a creator of these ideas. In his twenties, he wrote a popularization of all three volumes of Karl Marx's *Das Kapital* in simple question-and-answer format, to show Marx's errors. Likewise, many of Ellis's early publications on sex were written for the layman, and his 1960 book *The Art and Science of Love* was so popular that it enabled his institute to purchase its current building. Even his first book-length treatment of REBT, *How to Live With a Neurotic* (1957), was written for a popular, rather than a professional, audience.

Ellis sees REBT as playing just as great a role in popular education as in clinical therapy, and I agree. That's why I'm so pleased that Dr. Ellis and I can offer this volume to the general, nonpsychologist reader. These articles span the past forty-five years and cover Ellis's thinking on a very wide range of subjects. He has personally revised and updated each of the articles in this volume.

For the sake of convenience, I've broken them down into three parts. Part I covers problems of sex and love. For those readers interested in Ellis's current REBT model, Part II contains his latest thinking about how to use REBT to help yourself with personal problems like anxiety, depression, and hostility. Part III covers larger social problems, including problems in the workplace, substance addiction, efficient psychotherapy, and some larger philosophical issues. The breakdown is somewhat arbitrary, but it helps to organize the breadth of his concerns. Within each of the three main sections, the articles are arranged in order of their first appearance.

These twenty-nine articles were chosen from among over a thousand Ellis has written since 1945. I was mainly interested in selecting those which show ordinary people how they can apply rational-emotive behavioral principles to their own lives, and also in articles which give some insight into how Ellis came up with these principles in the first place.

It has been a pleasure for me to read over some of the older articles again. I envy those of you who may be discovering them for the first time. There are many important topics we haven't included, which we just didn't have space to cover. The problems of procrastination and anger especially come to mind. But if this reader gives people an overview of Ellis's way of showing individuals how they can become better able to cope with their own problems, then we will have done our job.

REBT is certainly no panacea. Even Ellis himself, who practices what he calls "super-elegant" REBT on himself, still has lapses into "demandingness." Human reason is certainly not infallible, but it does seem to be the best and most reliable tool we have. I hope readers will find at least one article in this volume that resonates with their own experiences.

In my own case, it took me fifteen years from the time I first read about REBT until I understood it enough to begin incorporating it into my own life. If this reader helps to shorten that journey for some, it will have accomplished its goal.

PART I

Sex, Love, and Marriage

Introduction to Part I

Ellis has become so closely associated with Rational Emotive Behavior Therapy that many people may not remember that he originally made his first major professional contributions as a psychologist in the fields of sexology and sex therapy back in the 1940s, '50s, and '60s. Since he hasn't written much about sex since the 1970s, I'll have to admit that I myself was mostly unaware of Ellis's contributions in this area. I got a chance only recently to review his early writings on sex and love, but as the reader will see, they still hold up remarkably well.

Ellis began his study of sex in 1939, about a year after Alfred Kinsey began his landmark study in Indiana. Ellis had previously tried and failed to get the earlier nonfiction manuscript published in which he simplified and critiqued Marx's *Das Kapital*. Switching fields, he then began research for a large book, *The Case for Sexual Promiscuity*, a part of which was published much later, in 1964, as *The Case for Sexual Liberty*. Then, in his doctoral work at Columbia, Ellis's first Ph.D. dissertation proposal was on the love emotions of college coeds, but the faculty rejected his topic as too daring for the time.

Many of Ellis's early scientific papers were on sexual topics, as were his first several published books. He became very controversial because of his outspoken views on sex in the 1950s and 1960s, and still attributes much of the controversy surrounding him and REBT to his earlier writings on sex.

Many of Ellis's most radical views in the 1950s have now become part of the common wisdom of the 1990's. But here are some of his unique contributions:

- He was one of the first researchers to come out in favor of masturbation, petting to orgasm, and premarital sex as positively beneficial activities, and not merely as being unharmful.
- In marital counseling, he helped couples to "desacredize" the primacy of intercourse so that they could also feel free to enjoy whatever noncoital sexual pleasures they chose.

3

- From the beginning, Ellis not only wrote about sex but was vitally interested in the interrelationship between sex and love. He helped couples work against their catastrophizing and self-defeating tendencies simultaneously in feelings of both sex and love.
- He taught people with sexual problems not only to practice the kinds of behavioral exercises which Masters and Johnson also recommended, but advised them to look carefully at the implicit self-statements with which they indoctrinated themselves *while* they were experiencing sex difficulties, and then to work on improving these inner self-statements as well as their outer behaviors.
- He was one of the first to firmly oppose the notion that certain sexual practices were in and of themselves deviant or immoral, or that people who practiced them were somehow morally defective or damnable.
- As the first chapter in this section illustrates, Ellis was among the very first psychologists to come out against the Freudian notion that clitoral orgasm in women was somehow an inferior or less mature experience than the so-called vaginal orgasm.

In addition to the above contributions, in reviewing Ellis's writings on sex for this book I was surprised to learn that many of his later innovations in REBT had their roots in his earlier studies in the psychology of sex. The following paragraphs on jealousy from his second book, *The American Sexual Tragedy*, are particularly revealing.

> It may be asked whether, from the standpoint of reducing inane and insane jealousy, it would be best to favor a thorough-going romantic or monogamic pattern of living. That is indeed a difficult question to answer, since both sex-love romanticism *and* monogamy encourage the height-scaling growth of jealousy....Being somewhat loath to give up romanticism entirely, despite my clearly seeing its short-comings, and probably because of my culturally-instilled bias in its favor, I find myself thinking in terms of some possible compromise solution. Exactly *what* solution I am frankly not as yet prepared to say.
>
> When I first wrote the preceding paragraph, in the year 1953, I honestly knew no good solution to the problem of romantic love and jealousy—nor, for that matter, to many of the other main sexual-emotive problems that are, after many

thousands of years of civilized living, still plaguing mankind. At that time, I was a psychoanalytically-oriented psychotherapist and still, quite naively, believed that giving human beings insight into the origins and development of their disturbances would eventually help them overcome their sex-love and other difficulties; but I did not quite know *how* this semimagical solution to human disturbance could actually be effected in many or most instances, and was already beginning to see that in innumerable cases it could not be.

Within the next two years I fortunately broke radically with my psychoanalytic background and developed a new system of personality evaluation and therapy called Rational Emotive [Behavior] Therapy, which largely arose from my own clinical experience and which owed more to the writings of philosophers such as Epictetus, Marcus Aurelius, and Bertrand Russell, and to psychologists such as Adler, Horney, Fromm, and Sullivan than to Freud and his more orthodox followers.

The devotee of Rational Emotive [Behavior] Therapy comes to realize that it is *not* his beloved's possible rejection of him that is terrible, frightful, or ego destroying, but simply his illogical *interpretation* of that rejection.

As the above selection suggests, several key concepts of REBT may have been inspired, at least in part, by Ellis's earlier work in the study of sex:

- The concept that it's self-defeating for a person to rate his or her entire *self* based on any individual aspect, trait, activity, or behavior.
- The practice of combining behavioral rehabilitation with changing *what people tell themselves* while they perform the behaviors. It's not only what you do that's important to your psychological health, it's what you *believe* while you do it.
- The idea that catastrophizing about the possibility of failure just makes failure more likely. Catastrophizing is just an unrealistically exaggerated prediction of what bad things might happen, and it usually makes people too anxious to focus on the task at hand.
- The concept of "secondary disturbance," that is, people becoming *disturbed about their own disturbance.*

- The benefits of *unconditional* self-acceptance as opposed to self-esteem (which is always really conditional on some presumed accomplishment or strength). This concept of unconditional self-acceptance—choosing to accept oneself regardless of one's actions or traits—may have been inspired by Ellis's practice of teaching his clients not to damn their entire selves for their sexual failures or unconventional sex practices.
- The concept of "discomfort disturbance," or experiencing anxiety or depression about the *prospect* of future discomfort, may have been inspired by Ellis's treatment of couples in marital counseling. Ellis found that husbands and wives would often exaggerate in their own minds how damaging the effects of their partners' misbehaviors actually would be.
- The idea that you can *choose* to respond to adversities with two different kinds of negative emotions. Some negative emotions (such as anxiety, depression, shame, and anger) stand in the way of your achieving your goals, while other negative emotions (such as concern, sadness, regret, and annoyance) are more helpful in adverse circumstances because they help you achieve your goals.

Many of Ellis's outspoken notions regarding sex and love may still strike people as somewhat radical and controversial. However, readers who follow the logic of his arguments cannot help but be struck by how provocative and cogent they still are.

—Shawn Blau

1

Is the Vaginal Orgasm a Myth?

This paper was written in 1952 and first published in the *International Journal of Sexology*. It was revolutionary for its day, especially because it was written when I was a psychologist who' was still practicing psychoanalysis. Virtually all analysts, including psychologists, followed the Freudian notion of the primacy of the vaginal orgasm in women. Not I! I was never an orthodox analyst and always leaned toward the neo-analysts—such as Erich Fromm, Karen Horney, and Harry Stack Sullivan—who were really largely neo-Adlerians. More importantly, I was a sexologist even before I became a psychotherapist in 1943, and I always realized that Freud, whose sex life seemed to include only his wife, Martha, was a very poor sexologist and knew little about women's sexuality from personal experience. So I respected Havelock Ellis, who also disagreed with Freud, and was very happy when Alfred Kinsey brought out his first report and confirmed many of my anti-Freudian sex views.

This article was followed by several of my bestselling sex books—especially *Sex Without Guilt*, *The Art and Science of Love*, *Sex, and the Single Man*, and *The Intelligent Woman's Guide to Dating and Mating*—and brought to millions of men and women the sensible message that orgasm was orgasm, however experienced, and released them from the sexual drivel of Freud and his followers. To this day, almost a half century after they were first published, as I make the rounds giving talks and workshops throughout the world, scores of people tell me that my books of the 1950s and '60s first turned their sex lives around and released them from enormous feelings of guilt and inhibition. Welcome to the fold.

Today, almost all mental health professionals and sex therapists endorse the teachings of this article, and my later books on sex and my position has been experimentally vindicated. This pioneering article needs very little revision. The Freudians have been routed in the vaginal primacy war. I hope that they gracefully stop their nonsense and go home.

For many years, the orthodox Freudian viewpoint has claimed that there are two distinct kinds of sexual orgasms in women: the so-called clitoral and the so-called vaginal orgasms. According to this viewpoint, the clitoral orgasm is an immature reaction of girls and young women, which normally should give way to a more mature reaction, or a vaginal orgasm. Recently, this Freudian theory has been seriously challenged by psychologists, psychiatrists, and sexologists, who hold that the vaginal orgasm is something of a myth, and that female orgasm, however achieved, is a legitimate and perfectly mature reaction. The recent literature on both sides of this controversial issue will now be reviewed.

The orthodox Freudian view on vaginal orgasm has been forcibly restated by Edward Berger and E. Hitschman. According to these authors, vaginal orgasm is the *only* legitimate type of sexual climax, and they categorically state that "frigidity is a neurotic symptom and sign denoting the inability of a woman to experience vaginal orgasm during intercourse." G. Bychowski, another Freudian, backs up Bergler and Hitschman with this statement: "As a manifestation of feminine sexuality, the difference between the vaginal and the clitoral orgasm is of paramount importance. In cases where only the latter is possible there is always a deep denial of the feminine role and a morbid masculine identification." M. R. Sapirstein concurs: "The girl's original genital sensations are probably almost exclusively derived from the clitoris, and in adult life have to be transferred to the vagina."

Sandor Lorand has an interesting variation of this view of vaginal orgasm. He believes that vaginal sensations are always primary, and that even female infants resort to vaginal and labial, as well as clitoral, masturbation. States Lorand: "The theory that the clitoral sensations are primary and have to be transferred to the vagina cannot be substantiated. In analysis the clitoral sensations lost their importance because the woman rediscovers and relearns early infantile sensations in the vagina which were repressed, forgotten, and could not be enjoyed. The vagina can now be accepted and does not have to be denied because it is 'an evil and dangerous organ like the mouth, which wants to devour everything and everybody,' as Ernest Jones has pointed out."

In emphasizing the importance of vaginal orgasm, some writers concomitantly stress the importance of involuntary muscular contractions in the pelvic regions as the one objective sign of female orgasm. This is stressed, for example, by Lena Levine, who contends that "by accepting involuntary, perineal contractions as the criterion for the female orgasm, we would have a definite standard for evaluation of the reaction of the female, which can be used in diagnosis and in treatment. These involuntary contractions must not be confused with the voluntary contractions, which the female will sometimes consciously produce during sexual intercourse." Hitschmann and Bergler posit a similar view: "The only objective sign of frigidity is absence of *involuntary* muscular contraction, which can be felt by the penis at the end of the act and cannot be simulated."

A rather opposing view of the primacy of vaginal orgasm is taken by several other writers. Kinsey, Pomeroy, and Martin have especially thrown cold water on this notion. They state: "The most common error which the male makes concerning female sexuality is the assumption that stimulation of the interior of the vagina is necessary to bring maximum satisfaction to the female. It is certain that most of the physical stimulation which the female receives from actual coitus comes from contact of the external areas of the vulva, of the areas immediately inside the outer edges of the labia, and of the clitoris with the pubic area of the male during genital union. There is a great deal of anatomic and clinical evidence that most of the interior of the vagina is without nerves. A considerable amount of surgery may be performed inside the vagina without need for anesthesia. Nerves have been demonstrated inside the vagina only in an area in the anterior wall, proximate to the base of the clitoris."

Clellan Ford and Frank Beach in *Patterns of Sexual Behavior* have also presented some interesting evidence against the theory of the primacy of vaginal orgasm. They point out that studies have shown that only about three percent of lesbians use their finger or some substitute to stimulate the interior of the vagina, and note that "it is probably significant that the clitoris was reported to be by far the most frequently stimulated region during homosexual relations."

Ruth Hershberger, writing from a woman's point of view, insists that males in our culture have for many years tried to ignore the obvious primacy of the clitoris in female orgasm because they, the males, could not face this fact squarely. She notes that, in our society, the very word *clitoris* has come to be consistently mispronounced (with a short *i* taking the place of a long *i* in the first syllable) because men unconsciously desire "to reduce by phonetic magic the actual frequency of the organ." She contends that "if the clitoris were allowed to act and react with the full conviction of its nerve centers, the myth of woman's diffuseness in sex might evaporate."

Clara Thompson, again writing from the woman's standpoint, flatly contradicts the Freudian notion that girls first discover the clitoris and then later transfer their sexual pleasure to the vagina. She states: "Nor does the girl ever renounce her interest in the clitoris. It remains one of her natural sex satisfactions throughout life."

Other evidence against the hypothesis of the primacy of vaginal orgasm has recently been presented by me, Edwin Hirsch, and Helena Wright. Hirsch contends that "woman's destiny is largely controlled by the clitoris" and that "stimulation of the clitoris is positively essential for the experience of sexual pleasure and the ultimate climax or orgasm." Wright claims that "it is my contention that ease and confidence in the use of the clitoris is the natural and quickest method of awakening sensation in the vagina."

An intermediate position, which does not deny the existence of a vaginal orgasm but which insists on equal or equivalent status for a clitoral orgasm as well, is taken by several other recent writers, including G. L. Kelly, Joan Malleson, and Helen O'Hare. Kelly points out that "orgasm in woman is felt chiefly in the clitoris," but he also notes that vaginal intromission heightens a woman's voluptuous sensations in many instances and accentuates her pleasurable feelings. He further contends that "orgasm is orgasm, however won."

Malleson holds that vaginal or vulval contractions are not necessarily equivalent to orgasm, and that when they do arise they may be the result of clitoral manipulation. She refers to a patient who has complete vaginal anesthesia but who still gets vulval contractions through clitoral stimulation. On the other hand, some women have only vaginal or cervical desire, with complete clitoral anesthesia. Consequently, she insists, we must accept the existence of *both* vaginal and clitoral orgasms, and must not arbitrarily set up one type as being better or more mature than the other.

In two remarkably frank communications of her own sex life, O'Hare presents some highly interesting evidence in favor of the thesis that both vaginal and clitoral orgasms exist and that both may be perfectly satisfactory and mature. She states that in her own case she first experienced vaginal orgasm with her mate after reading a sex encyclopedia; then, three years later, after the birth of her first child, she experienced her first orgasm via the clitoris. Since the birth of her second child, clitoral orgasm has tended to predominate, but she prefers vaginal ones. She notes that "I sometimes have one kind, sometimes the other, and sometimes fail altogether." She insists that "the difference in clitoral and vaginal orgasms is unmistakable in feeling." Her vaginal orgasm produces a pronounced and prolonged tonic state of the deeper placed vaginal muscles, while the orgasm itself often seems to involve deep-seated organs, such as the uterus and rectum. Her clitoral orgasm is more shallowly placed and seems to be localized in the anterior wall of the vagina not far from the clitoris itself. She also notes that clitoral stimulation may contribute to her vaginal orgasm.

Mrs. O'Hare's reference to the clitoral orgasm being localized in the anterior wall of the vagina is interestingly corroborated by Ernest Grafenberg and L. H. Levie, both of whom seem to feel that what is ordinarily called a vaginal orgasm usually takes place because of the sensitivity of the anterior wall of the vagina (or the part of the vagina which is immediately below the vulva and clitoris). Grafenberg states that physical evidences of female orgasm can actually be felt as contractions in this area (rather than the more often described contractions of the levator muscles of the pelvic floor). Levie contends that the fitting of a woman with a diaphragm that is too large may lift up the anterior wall of the vagina too much and thus interfere with coital pleasure. LeMon Clark, however, throws doubt on this view of the sensitivity of the anterior wall of the vagina and points out that when this wall is surgically incised, little lessening of vaginal sexual sensation seems to occur.

On the point raised by Kinsey, Pomeroy, and Martin to the effect that the vagina is a relatively insensitive and nerve-deficient organ, Joan Malleson partly agrees that this is true, but she points out that while one can *cut* the vagina without pain, one cannot *stretch* it without sensation. She therefore holds that vaginal intromission, aside from leading to clitoral, vulval, and introital stimulation, may induce other sensations which result in a vaginal orgasm. As noted previously, however, Malleson does not give any special primacy to the vaginal orgasm, as do the Freudians. LeMon Clark takes a somewhat similar position, and states that "I am convinced that, whether or not the cervix has end organs of sensation, the movements of intercourse can knock the cervix up and down or forward and backward so that this motion is transmitted to the muscular and ligamentous attachments at the side of the pelvis or to the peritoneum to such an extent that a woman does get some sensation from it."

Several authors, while pointing out that there may be such a thing as a vaginal orgasm, seriously question the advisability of psychologists, psychiatrists, and sexologists stressing the importance of this particular kind of orgasm and thereby making millions of women who never or rarely attain it feel that they are sexually deficient or neurotic. Conrad Boas, Lena Levine, and A. P. Pillay particularly speak out in this connection. Levine notes that "those women in whom orgasm results from clitoral stimulation only frequently are greatly concerned about it and bring that problem for solution. We should take away the emphasis from the need of a complete response in a normal woman and advise satisfaction in whatever manner is possible, while we pursue our task to discover the basis of this lack of complete satisfaction through more clinical and laboratory investigation." Pillay concurs: "If clitoridian orgasm in itself helps toward relief of sexual tension of the woman and toward marital harmony, why call lack of vaginal orgasm, which is difficult of achievement by most women, pathological? Then again, why add to the burden of frigid women who often are distressed at their condition and have already an inferiority complex, by calling them neurotic?"

What, then, is the final answer to the problem of the so-called vaginal and clitoral orgasm? Is there actually such a thing as a vaginal orgasm? If there is, are women who rarely or never achieve it neurotic or immature? After due consideration of the recent evidence and opinion in this connection, I would like to make the following observations:

The so-called vaginal orgasm seems to be misnamed, and instead should normally be referred to as orgasm obtained through intercourse (or through other methods of intravaginal stimulation). When orgasm is obtained as the result of intravaginal contact, there is no conclusive evidence that it results *only* from such stimulation, nor that it *uniquely* involves vaginal contractions or other vaginal effects. It seems more probable that intravaginal contact *also* normally involves vulval and clitoral stimulation, and that this latter stimulation enhances or leads to orgasmic release of sexual tension. The so-called clitoral orgasm may also be badly misnamed, since sexual sensations which are aroused by clitoral stimulation may be experienced in or may lead to sensations in various other parts of the body, including the vagina.

The real issue seems to be: Is orgasm or release from sexual tension that is obtained through intercourse (or through other methods of intravaginal stimulation) essentially different from orgasm that is obtained through clitoral or other extra-coital manipulations? There seems to be little doubt that most women can experience an orgasm through clitoral stimulation, and that some women can also experience an orgasm through intercourse that is not accompanied by special clitoral stimulation. The question is whether orgasms experienced in these two ways are essentially different.

The present facts would appear to indicate that many women experience two kinds of orgasm, but that these two kinds are not necessarily vaginal and clitoral orgasm. Instead, many women seem to have a relatively mild orgasm and a relatively intense orgasm. Still other women seem to have sexual satisfaction without any culminating orgasm, while some women (apparently, a small minority) seem to have no sexual satisfaction and no orgasm.

All women who have intense orgasm by no means obtain this through intercourse or other intravaginal stimulation. It is possible, however, that women who are able to experience orgasm through intravaginal stimulation more often or more easily obtain intense orgasm than women who are able to experience orgasm only through clitoral stimulation. However, no conclusive evidence in this connection is yet available. What does seem to be clinically evident at present is that some women who experience the most intense kinds of orgasm imaginable experience it only or mainly as a result of clitoral (or other noncoital) stimulation.

Some women undoubtedly receive additional organic sensations from coitus that they do not obtain through clitoral or other noncoital manipulation. Some women who do not receive additional organic sensations from intravaginal stimulation do experience additional psychological or psycho-physiological sensations from intravaginal stimulation that they *interpret* as organic sensations. Still other women receive no additional organic sensations, or receive unpleasurable sensations, from intravaginal stimulation.

Although the vagina itself is rather insensitive to sexual stimulation in most women, semivaginal or quasi-vaginal sensations may be obtained by many women through intercourse or other intravaginal stimulation. Thus, the passing of the penis through the introitus, or entrance to the vagina, which is well supplied with nerve endings, may lead to intense sensations. Or, the hitting of the penis against the vaginal walls, which in turn may set in motion the cervix, uterus, or surrounding body parts, may add sexual sensations. Or, the stretching of the vagina may sometimes enhance sensation. These semivaginal sensations, while they may not often lead to orgasm by themselves, may frequently help to bring it on.

In most women, intense sexual sensation in general, and sexual orgasm in particular, is probably obtained, during their whole lives, largely but not exclusively through the clitoral nerve endings and their branchings. Some women may be clitorally insensitive and may be able to have an orgasm only through intravaginal stimulation, but they are probably well in the minority. Many more women, probably, may never experience an orgasm solely through intravaginal stimulation. There is certainly no evidence that women who may have an orgasm only through clitoral manipulation are emotionally immature or disturbed, and there is considerable evidence that they are no more disturbed than are women who may only have an orgasm through intravaginal stimulation. However, as a result of our falsely teaching that women who do not have orgasms through intravaginal stimulation are missing something essential in their sex lives, or that they are immature, we may easily help make such women emotionally and sexually disturbed.

There is no factual evidence whatever that there are fixed stages of orgasm development for most women, from clitoral to vaginal channels, or from extra-coital to coital manipulations. However, since puritanical sex teachings in our society encourage many women to have much more guilt about vaginal than about clitoral stimulation, it is easy to see why many women consciously or unconsciously will not permit themselves to have as much sexual satisfaction through intravaginal stimulation as they will permit themselves through clitoral stimulation. This means that many of our women may, because of our antisexual teachings, turn out to be relatively insensitive to intravaginal excitation, but it hardly means that *all* women who have little or no vaginal sex sensitivity are rendered thus insensitive by emotional blockings. Most women with relatively little intravaginal sensitivity seem merely to be the heirs of physiological tendencies that endow normal women with greater clitoral than vaginal sex sensitivity.

Orgasm is orgasm, however experienced. Each woman should preferably try to obtain the deepest and most intense type of orgasm (or nonorgasmic sexual pleasure) that she is capable of experiencing, and she should try to obtain it through those means that are best suited to her—whether vaginal or extra-vaginal. When we dogmatically assert that any method of obtaining orgasm is "better," "more mature," or "less neurotic" than any other, we are likely to do immense harm and little good—particularly when the method we label as immature is the one commonly employed by many women. Moreover, for men, to try to impose upon women those techniques of inducing orgasm or sex satisfaction which happen to be best suited to male pleasures is certainly presumptuous and pernicious.

Intensity of orgasm in women does not, of course, depend merely upon clitoral or intravaginal stimulation but on a host of other physiological and psychological factors. Women, for example, are likely to experience more intense orgasms, either through intravaginal or extravaginal stimulation, when they have had considerable sexual experience, when they are emotionally attracted to their sex partners, when adequate sexual foreplay has taken place, and when they and their male partners are relatively released from antisexual attitudes and blockings.

Orgasm is hardly the only form of sexual satisfaction, and in the case of some women it is not even the major one. Many women appear to obtain considerable, and perfectly sufficient, sexual pleasure without experiencing a culminating orgasm, and there is no reason they should not continue to do so for the rest of their days. Most women attain intense orgasms when they are sufficiently sexually and emotionally liberated, but there is no reason to believe that *all* normal women can do so. Those who cannot achieve orgasm can usually attain other, and quite satisfying, sexual sensations and should have no hesitation in trying to attain these.

The woman who always obtains an orgasm, or who almost always obtains the most intense orgasm of which she is capable, seems to be exceptional, and she should never be used as a standard against which to measure the sexual satisfactions of other women. Orgasmic and nonorgasmic sexual sensations vary enormously among humans, and the range of normal reactions is unusually wide.

It should be the object of sexological research to discover and publish more information about female orgasm before existing speculation continues to run away with itself.

2

Sex Fascism

Sex Without Guilt, in which this chapter was included, first appeared as a series of articles in 1956, in Lyle Stuart's free-speech periodical, the *Independent.* Paul Krassner, who was then working for Lyle, read my books *The Folklore of Sex* and *The American Sex Tragedy,* and thought Lyle and I would hit it off. We did. Paul and Lyle resonated to my liberal views on sex, and I became a regular columnist for the *Independent.* Lyle subsequently published *Sex Without Guilt* and many of my other books.

I began thinking about intellectual fascism and sex fascism in 1955, soon after I began to use Rational Emotive Behavior Therapy. From the start, it includes the idea that people are "good" or "worthy" just because they are people—because they are human, alive, unique, and capable of enjoyment. This, as I say elsewhere in my writings and in this book, is an existential idea which I largely got from Paul Tillich's *Courage to Be.* It is an idea which you can *choose* to follow.

If, on the other hand, you choose to severely restrict your thinking, which is typical of fascism and other forms of authoritarianism, you unduly find yourself in cognitive, emotional, and behavioral chains. As I show in this chapter, intellectual fascism and sex fascism—which overlap—are narrow and bigoted systems that create anxiety, depression, and rage. Read this essay and you shall see.

Although relatively few Americans could be legitimately labeled as political or economic fascists today, probably the great majority are sex fascists. What is perhaps even more surprising is that the sex fascists tend to be just as prevalent among the politico-economic liberal groups as they do among the social bigots and reactionaries.

Sex fascism is a major subheading under what I call intellectual fascism—which I find, among my clients and friends, to be perhaps the most pandemic and virulent psychosocial disease of our times. So before I discuss sex fascism in particular, let me briefly say something about intellectual fascism in general.

Fascism, essentially, is the arbitrary belief that individuals who possess certain "desirable" traits are intrinsically superior to those who possess certain "undesirable" characteristics. Thus, people who are white, Aryan, or Christian are defined as being "good" or "worthwhile," and those who are black, non-Aryan, or Jewish are defined as being "inferior" or "worthless."

Intellectual fascism capriciously points to a group of human characteristics and dogmatically declares that they are "better," and that only individuals who possess this mark of distinction are truly worthwhile. The traits that are arbitrarily glorified by intellectual fascists are usually intelligence, culture, esthetic taste, achievement, success, etc. Where intellectual fascists often make a great to-do about how democratic they are in hobnobbing with blacks or intermarrying with Jews or ignoring economic class distinctions in their friendships, the attitude they take toward anyone who is "stupid," "incompetent," or "unartistic" is one of extreme condescension or scorn.

What intellectual fascists, exactly in common with politico-economic fascists, find it impossible to see is that their definitions of "superiority" and "worthwhileness" are arbitrary and definitional. "But intelligence and competence," they will insist, "definitely *are* better than stupidity and incompetence. Why, then, should we not prefer a bright and capable person to a dull and incapable one?" In this insistence, they confuse several important issues.

First of all, such traits as intelligence and artistry, although good *for some purposes,* are not necessarily good *in themselves.* Thus, intelligence is fine for problem solving and artistry is most useful in decorating a home, but high intelligence may be a handicap in driving a truck or working at a monotonous job, and artistic sensitivity may be a disadvantage to someone who works in a coal mine or is stranded on a bleak desert island.

Second, politico-social fascists could argue, with equal logic, that a man's possessing blue eyes and blond hair gives him a more "esthetic" look than one who has brown eyes and black hair, or that Aryans are superior to Jews because they suffer less frequently from certain diseases, such as diabetes. The fact that individuals possess some traits which are "better" or more advantageous than those possessed by others hardly makes them superior beings *generally*.

Third, a man's *preference* for a given characteristic should never be confused with the *intrinsic worth* of that characteristic. If I prefer twelve-toed or ivory-haired women above all others, that hardly proves that you and everyone else in the world have similar preferences. And even if the majority of us esteem twelve-toed women for, let us say, our wives or mistresses, that does not constitute valid evidence that ten-toed women are not good for any other purpose, nor that they cannot be worthwhile to themselves.

Fourth, assuming that the possession of certain characteristics may be preferable to the person who possesses these traits as well as to others, does this mean that those who do not possess these traits are utterly worthless, criminal, and ready for the trash can? Granting that tallness, high intelligence, or physical strength may be useful for most humans, should those who are short, of average intelligence, or unmuscular be induced to commit suicide or be led to the gas chambers?

Fifth, in the final analysis, any trait that is "good" or "superior" must be satisfactory or excellent for *something*—for some purpose. And that purpose must, to some extent, always be an arbitrary prejudice or value judgment. Thus, even a trait such as good health, which almost everyone accepts as being "good," is only good for living, for leading an enjoyable life. But anyone could question—as indeed many have—the intrinsic value of life and enjoyment, and could claim that it would be better if human living ceased. Consequently, *all* human characteristics are to some extent "good" only by arbitrary definition—good for some purpose which some individual or group has stipulated as being "beneficial" or "fine."

Intellectual fascists, then, exactly like politico-economic fascists, arbitrarily define certain human purposes and traits as being "superior," and, in one way or another, they scorn and discriminate against those who do not possess these traits. Although they often claim to be super-democrats, they are actually exceptionally oligarchic or authoritarian in their basic beliefs about human value. What is more, where the political fascist mainly judges others by his arbitrary standards, considers himself worthwhile for adhering to them, and deems others worthless for not possessing the "elite" traits he demands, the intellectual fascist tends to judge herself as well as others by the perfectionistic esthetic-intellectual criteria she establishes, and to condemn herself, too, when she fails to measure up to these ideals. She is thus in the unenviable position of being undemocratic and overdemanding toward everyone, including herself.

What has all this to do with sex fascism? A great deal. For sex fascism is based on both politico-economic and intellectual fascism, and has some of the worst features of each.

First, let us consider the side of sex fascism that largely stems from the political authoritarianism of the Mussolini- and Hitler-type brands. One of the fundamental tenets of Nazism is that not only Jews and blacks, but women as well, are second-class citizens whose main role should be to cater to males and the preservation of the race, rather than to the development of their own personalities. This is what the sexual fascist believes too.

More specifically, the sexual fascist firmly upholds the double standard of sexual morality. He thinks that women are radically different from men in their sexual desires; that they can invariably get along with less sexual activity than males; that it is not too important if they do not achieve orgasm when they have sexual relations; that when they do climax, they should be able to do so exactly as males do, in the course of coitus rather than in extracoital ways; that if noncoital methods of sex relations are employed, it is all right for the female to engage in fellatio but that no real male would ever participate in cunnilingus; that a woman should remain an absolute virgin until she is married while a male should have as many sexual adventures as possible; that it is a far greater crime for a female to have a child out of wedlock than it is for a male to father such a child; and that if a wife commits adultery it is a heinous offense against morality, while if a husband is adulterous he is merely following his natural human bent.

All these beliefs of the sexual fascist, precisely like those of his politically fascist brother, are arbitrary and scientifically groundless. Women are not radically different from males in their sexual desires, and when they are, they are sometimes *more* rather than *less* highly sexed than men. It is usually important that they achieve regular orgasms, and it is more important, in many instances, that they achieve their orgasms by extracoital techniques than that the male enjoy noncoital sex play. Literally millions of women find it virtually impossible to come to climax during intercourse, while they can fairly easily do so through clitoral manipulation, cunnilingus, and other noncoital methods.

The notion that a woman should remain a virgin until marriage, and is a far greater criminal than a male if she has a child out of wedlock or commits adultery, is an antiegalitarian view that largely stems from the patriarchal customs of biblical days and has no place in a democratic society. Women, of course, are the child-bearing sex, but they obviously cannot bear children without male collaboration, and should therefore assume no more and no less responsibility for premarital or extramarital "illegitimacy" than their paramours. To discriminate against females for their sex acts because they carry the biological burden of childbirth makes as much sense as punishing female thieves or murderers more severely than male criminals because the former, as potential or actual mothers, have greater responsibilities and presumably should therefore know better than to commit crimes.

The second major facet of sexual authoritarianism also stems almost directly from politico-economic fascist ideologies, namely, the demand for rigid conformity to a single, all-encompassing sex code for many different kinds of individuals. Politico-social fascism almost always goes in for monolithic moral codes. The grand patriarch or monarch of a tribe or nation usually decides that what is right for *him* is right for *all,* and, willy-nilly, he crams his preferences down the throats of his adherents.

So, too, the sexual fascist. Either he is raised to abide by a straight and narrow set of sex mores and laws, and, in doing so, never practices any other mode, or for a period of time he tries various sex acts that do not conform to the code under which he was raised. Then, as age and diminished sexuality take their toll on his proclivities, he finally reverts to rigid rules of sexual morality. In either event, he dogmatically decides that what is good enough for him is good enough for everyone—and they'd damned well better agree with him or else.

This means that the sexual fascist arbitrarily defines other people's worth in direct proportion to the extent to which they conform to certain sex codes he has unthinkingly adopted as "good" ones. If these other people conform to these codes closely, or agree with what *he* thinks they should do sexually, they are accepted as "good," "moral," "worthwhile" humans; if they do not conform to the codes he deems to be correct, they are condemned as "wicked," "immoral," or "worthless."

Here again, he is following the fascist philosophy of measuring people's worth not in terms of their humanity, of what they are, but in terms of how well they do—or in this case do *not* do—certain things.

Forcing human beings to conform to almost any constricted pattern of living is an authoritarian and antidemocratic procedure because the very first law of human behavior is that of individual difference. Living things differ from inanimate objects in several basic ways: they have some freedom of choice or movement, some ability to reproduce themselves, and some individuality or uniqueness. To the extent that their individuality is ignored or restricted, men and women become that much less human.

In regard to their sexuality, people are notably different. Some have enormous sex drives, some little or no erotic impulses. Some enjoy the same kind of sex play or coitus almost all the time, while others demand a large variety of sex acts and positions for their maximum satisfaction. Some find more and more enjoyment with the same partner, while others find monogamous relations dull and boring.

The hallmark of emotional health for most human beings is their maintaining a reasonable degree of flexibility and freedom from fixation in the major aspects of their lives. A few individuals may be truly happy if they rigidly stick to one limited job or a few basic foods all their lives, but many people who are "content" to limit themselves in these ways may be compulsively or fetishistically driven to do so by conscious or unconscious fears. These individuals are generally afraid to try to get out of their vocational or dietary ruts—irrationally afraid that they might fail in a new job or be nauseated by novel foods. Out of their irrational fears, they surrender a good deal of their potential life space, and taste only a minority of the pleasures and adventures of living that theoretically might be theirs.

So, again, with sex. The emotionally healthy individual wants more than the limited satisfactions she happened to hit upon fairly early in her sexual development. At the same time, she is not a person who compulsively has to try every possible sex variation, in and out of the books, because she cannot enjoy sexual participation for its own sake. No, the healthy sexual participant is one who open-mindedly and unfearingly tries a wide variety of practices and finally ends up favoring a few which she has, through personal experience and observation, found to be maximally satisfying to her.

The philosophy and practice of the sex fascist, however, does not permit the sex adventurousness and experimentation that is normal for most people. It attempts to force all persons into a single, invariant mold. In our own society, this one-sided brand of legally and socially allowable sex conduct has consisted of heterosexual coitus in one or two "natural" positions between a man and a woman who are formally married to each other. All other forms of sexual behavior, such as masturbation, petting, premarital intercourse, or noncoital relations between husbands and wives have been encrusted with guilt, or, as in the case of such acts as adultery and homosexuality, often been subject to persecution.

Fascist ideologies have particularly prevailed in the areas of sex while they have been relatively milder in many other aspects of social "misbehavior." Thus an individual is considered to be unmannerly or impolite if he does not follow certain rules of etiquette, such as eating or dressing in a decorous way. And a man or woman is looked upon as vice-ridden if he or she is seriously addicted to, say, smoking, drinking, gluttony, or slothfulness. But in regard to most forms of so-called impoliteness and vice only minor criticism or social sanction is leveled. In regard to sexual "vice," however, people have been savagely proscriptive and penalizing—just as political fascists, when they have power, generally are against the "vices" of individualism and nonconformity to their views.

The whole philosophy of excoriating and punishing human beings for their "sins" is, in fact, a fascist attitude that stems directly from primitive patriarchism. If a patriarch, monarch, or primitive deity lays down a set of rules for behavior, and someone in his jurisdiction flouts them, he never thinks in terms of the real problem—which, simply stated, is: How can I induce this rebellious individual to desist from breaking my rules in the future? Instead, he tends to be so personally aggrieved that he only thinks in terms of: How can I punish that dirty so-and-so for his past and *present* impiety?

In other words, the fascist is not really interested in inducing people to avoid repeating their mistakes or to change their future behavior for the better. She is interested not in *them* but in *herself*—in her own arbitrary beliefs and how she can force people to conform to her dogmatisms. Similarly, the sex fascist is not in the least interested, really, in what modes of sex conduct would be best for people to follow—meaning, least self-defeating and most satisfaction-producing. She is egocentrically concerned with what codes she *insists* they should follow.

In consequence, the sex fascist can only think in terms of how different from *his* recommendations are the actions of those who masturbate, fornicate in ways not traditionally accepted, and pet to orgasm. And instead of, at most, legislating against certain sex practices—such as rape or the seduction of minors—which would be harmful when perpetrated by one individual against another, he legislates against many sex modes which are matters of personal taste and preference, and which are not in the least antisocial as they are normally practiced.

A third significant aspect of sexual fascism is that which stems directly from and is linked inextricably to intellectual fascism. As we previously noted, the intellectual fascist is an individual who insists that human beings are only worthwhile in relation to how well they perform—how competent, effective, and achieving they are. The sexual fascist applies this yardstick of intrinsic human worth to sex, love, and marital relationships.

More specifically, the sexual fascist views anyone—including, ironically, himself—as a worthless, valueless individual unless he or she is perfectly sexually competent. In the case of a male, this means that the "worthwhile" individual has to be able to achieve an erection without any difficulty, to maintain it for a long period of time, and finally to be able to have an orgasm exactly at the same moment that his female partner has her climax. In addition the male should be able to become sexually aroused again shortly after he has had his initial orgasm, and be capable of several climaxes a night. He should be able to arouse even the most recalcitrant female by his adept technique of sexual foreplay, and continue to arouse her so that she has several orgasms in quick succession and considers him the greatest lover in the world.

According to this intellectually fascistic view, the sexually adequate female can be aroused to a fever pitch of excitement in short order, can easily have an orgasm after a brief period of intercourse, can hold off her climax, if necessary, to match the moment when her male partner has his, and can enjoy every conceivable kind of sex play and all kinds of noncoital techniques, especially fellatio. Such a woman is able to have many terrific orgasms per evening and is satisfied only when her lover is finally surfeited.

This fascistic view of sexual adequacy is completely unrealistic in that, like some of the other authoritarian views we have been examining, it ignores the basic facts of individual human differences. It fails to take into account that many men and women are not great sexual athletes;

that sexual lasting powers differ enormously; that many sexually competent females do not have orgasms during coitus and many males are normally rapid firers in their sex actions; that some individuals who are excellent lovers are not unusual responders, and that some who respond beautifully have little interest in making active love themselves.

More importantly, this perfectionistic view of sexual adequacy contains the basic fascistic assumption that if one is *not* uncommonly good at coital and noncoital sex play, one is essentially a nincompoop and a louse, and might just as well curl up and die. It utterly ignores the truth that no man or woman can be competent or effective in all respects, and that many "worthwhile" humans have little or no sexual desire, technique, or capacity.

Let us consider a specific case, to examine the results of this kind of sexual fascism. Several years ago I saw for psychotherapy a young man whose main occupation in life appeared to be having affairs with females. He was unusually handsome and articulate, so he had no difficulty in finding one partner after another.

Whenever he described his sexual adventures to me, he invariably spoke in a highly deprecating tone about his girlfriend of the moment. This one looked fine when she was all dressed up, but she was "disgustingly titless" when she took off her clothes. That one was "absolutely beautiful, from tip to stern," but "she must have had a chunk of lead in her ass, and just lay there on the bed without even a wriggle, expecting me to do all the work." This new woman "stunk like a carload of pigs"; the one before "was so inhibited that she couldn't be oral with a lollipop"; the one before her "was so bad in bed that a board with a hole in it would have been more exciting," and so on.

With rare exceptions this young man always described his sex partners in highly negative terms as far as sexual proclivities went, and he gave the impression that since these women were coitally or extra-coitally inept, they were perfectly worthless as human beings and could drop dead for all he cared. He had no interest in educating his partners so that they might become better bedmates, or gave any thought to nonsexual traits that might somewhat redeem their erotic deficiencies.

As it happened, this deprecator of young womanhood eventually met a woman who could give him cards and spades in nocturnal gymnastics and kept coming back for more. Whether lightly caressed or vigorously taken, she had no difficulty achieving one tremendous orgasm after another, and there seemed to be no sexual practices which she did not thoroughly enjoy.

After seeing this paragon of feminine sexuality for a period of a few weeks, my client began to notice a serious decrease in his own desires and powers. He frequently found himself unable to maintain an adequate erection to complete copulation; at other times, when he was sufficiently potent, he found coitus to be joyless and nonclimactic. His increasing sexual incompetency began to acutely depress him and it was only by forcing him to face and question the innermost roots of his intellectual and sexual fascism that I was able to help him overcome his neurotic condition.

Like the typical intellectual fascist, this young man tended to define *all* human inadequacy and imperfection, including his own, as horrible and frightful. Needing to appear superior to others, he felt continually impelled to belittle the women with whom he had affairs—and whom, unconsciously, he often picked just because he could eventually focus on their deficiencies and show them up. When he finally met his own sexual match, he could no more tolerate her competence than he could previously tolerate the ineffectuality of his earlier girlfriends. For, according to his fascist-based ideology, he *had* to be best, *had* to be supreme himself, and no effective competition to his grandiose claims could be borne.

The more my client began to see that he was not sexually peerless, the more he began to hate himself for his own inadequacies, and the more he focused on how horrible it was for him to be impotent or inept, the more incompetent he became. This kind of vicious neurotic circle can be broken when the afflicted individual is able to see the fundamental irrational assumptions or beliefs that underlie his behavior. In this instance, when I finally was able to induce this young man to question his fascistic, perfectionistic ideas of sexual adequacy, and to stop measuring his and others' intrinsic value as human beings in terms of his or their sexual prowess, he stopped trying to keep up with his high-sexed partner, and his potency returned. He also started to question his entire attitude toward women and their sexual propensities, and to see them more as human beings than as mere bedmates.

Until we consistently acknowledge the intrinsic merit of ourselves and our fellows just because we are human, because we are alive, politico-economic and intellectual fascism are bound to survive—and with them, their sexual fascist derivatives. Until we accept people for *being* rather than being *something*, for *doing* rather than for doing *well*, all our vaunted liberalism and democracy will be babble. At bottom, we will still be fascists.

3

Adventures With Sex Censorship

Sex censorship is still very much with us, despite the fact that today one can view R-rated movies on television and many bookstores are full of pornographic books. Yes, things have let up considerably in that respect, and I may be given some credit for this. As this chapter from the revised edition of my book *Sex Without Guilt* shows, various censors gave me a hard time in the 1950s and 1960s, leaving my head fairly bloody but unbowed. Often, I won out over the censorship in the end, and my book *Suppressed: Seven Key Essays Publishers Dared Not Print* included several essays that were previously banned.

But as I show in this article, censorship still plagues me. Although I am probably the most famous living American psychologist and counselor, have published more books and articles than any other therapist, and have won more awards from leading professional associations than any other person, restrictions are still placed on me.

I am "too controversial" to be nominated for or elected to the presidency of practically all national psychological associations, though I am probably more qualified than most other psychologists. I practically never get invited to write articles for the most respected popular magazines, or have my articles accepted by them. Many American universities have refused to hold lectures or workshops by me. Some have arranged for them and canceled them at the last minute because members of their board of directors or prominent professors have objected to me.

Although I have appeared on scores of popular radio and TV shows, some of the most respectable prime-time shows refuse to let me appear. Again, some of the shows that I have been scheduled for have been canceled at the last minute after protests from advertisers or high officials of the network.

Why all this fuss? First, although I have not published books on sex or popular articles for almost twenty years, my early writings on sex are remembered and deplored. I am renowned as the first psychologist to liberally use four-letter words at professional conferences (in 1950 at the American Psychological Association Convention in Chicago) and at many other gatherings. God forbid that I might do so again!

I have little hesitation in calling a spade a spade, and have often disparaged the writings—but not the person—of some of the most respected psychologists, such as Freud, Jung, Reich, and Perls—you name them. Very specifically and severely, and in plain English.

I often present the principles and practices of Rational Emotive Behavior Therapy (REBT) with no holds barred, and vigorously oppose—and expose—aspects of other popular therapy systems that are firmly entrenched in many universities and training centers.

I am one of the country's leading atheists. I don't oppose people having religious views and leanings—and am collaborating on a book with two Christian psychologists on how REBT can be used with religious clients. But I am not merely skeptical about God and other supernatural entities. I say that the chances are one in several billion that anything supernatural exists, and therefore I believe, on the basis of probability, that no angels, fairies, devils, or gods exist. If they do, they do, but until I have some evidence of them, I'll assume that they don't. Religionists and their followers are horrified by my frankness in this respect, so they often hate my views—and me for having them. *Does all of this opposition stop me? Yes, it stops me from publishing some of my views and appearing in public to present them—but not from thinking or writing them!*

When I began my series for the *Independent* with a column titled "New Light on Masturbation," Lyle Stuart wrote an editorial about the difficulties I had previously had trying to publish that material. Let me now recount some of my other firsthand adventures with sex censorship. My serious encounters with restrictions on the publication of sexual material began when I contracted to write my first book, *The Folklore of Sex.* Charles Boni asked me to do this book for him, and since he did not directly publish books himself, he said that he would arrange to do so through one of the large publishers.

He accordingly submitted the outline of the book to Simon and Schuster, with whom he had excellent relations. He was told that they had got into some difficulties over a sex book they had published some twenty years earlier, and therefore it was their policy to steer clear of this field. Shortly thereafter, however, Simon and Schuster contracted to publish Abraham Franzblau's *The Road to Sexual Maturity*—surely one of the most reactionary books on sex brought out in years.

Undaunted, Mr. Boni took the outline of *The Folklore of Sex* to the world's then largest publisher, Doubleday, who was quite enthusiastic about it and immediately offered me a contract. They were equally delighted with the manuscript and were so eager to send it to press that they arranged to do some of the retyping in their own offices.

Everything was set for publication in the fall of 1950, and galley and page proofs were speedily printed and corrected. The imprint on the title page was that of Doubleday and Company, and on the back of the title page was the usual statement found in all Doubleday books: "Printed in the United States at the Country Life Press, Garden City, N.Y."

Then something happened.

"Certain people" at Doubleday began to get quite distressed about the nature of the book when they were shown the page proofs. Their distress appeared to stem from the fact that the book took a (rather mildly) liberal attitude toward sex; that it quoted from the most popular American newspapers and magazines, whose editors might object to having their sexual proclivities exposed; and that it also ruthlessly revealed the frankly sexual underpinnings of numerous best-selling novels and nonfiction works, many of which were either published by Doubleday or distributed by one of the several book clubs owned by Doubleday.

After several frantic conferences were held, publication of *The Folklore of Sex* was delayed; Doubleday's name was taken off the title page and Charles Boni's name substituted instead. Publication was still further delayed, and the book finally appeared almost half a year after its originally planned publication date.

It was still printed at the Country Life Press and was distributed by Doubleday, but although editorial enthusiasm for it was sustained and Mr. Boni did everything possible to aid its sale, promotional initiative at Doubleday noticeably dimmed. Few reviews or publicity stories appeared in leading newspapers and magazines. The *New York Times* and the *Chicago Tribune* were not seriously opposed when they refused to publish any ads whatever for the book, and it was remaindered with unusual alacrity. Only when Grove Press published a revised edition of the book in paperback form a decade later, did it begin to attain real popularity.

So much for *The Folklore of Sex.*

My second book, *The American Sexual Tragedy,* was something of a sequel to the first book, but Doubleday, who had an option to publish it, didn't even want to look at the manuscript. It was then accepted by Twayne Publishers, who had no vested interest in well-known authors or book clubs, and who were unusually liberal in their editing of the manuscript.

Where Doubleday had insisted that I take out several references to bestselling writers or famous personalities—such as my highlighting of several sadistic passages in Frank Slaughter's novel *Divine Mistress*— Twayne wielded no blue pencil in this respect. They did, however, object to my dedicating the volume "to John Ciardi, one hell of a fine editor," insisting that this was not a dignified remark for a Ph.D. in psychology to make. I disagreed, but they won. Again, Lyle Stuart and Grove Press later came to the rescue by including the original dedication in the revised edition of the book.

My third book, *Sex Life of the American Woman and the Kinsey Report,* also ran into serious censorship trouble. Greenberg contracted to publish the work and then arranged with Popular Library to bring out a paperback edition simultaneously with their hardcover edition. When Popular Library saw the manuscript of this anthology they first rejected two of the chapters, one on masturbation and another on prostitution, both written in collaboration with Dr. Harry Benjamin. Then, after further hemming and hawing, they reneged on their contract to publish the whole book, even though they had to sacrifice a substantial down payment in doing so.

Although Popular Library's objections, like those of Doubleday, were not explicit, it appeared that they particularly disliked the fact that *Sex Life of the American Woman* was largely pro-Kinsey and they were afraid that, as a paperback publisher, they might run into official censorship of the book.

Doubleday, motivated by similar fears, had overpriced *The Folklore of Sex,* the argument being that official and semiofficial agencies are less likely to ban a book that is high-priced. Actually, for all the publishers' caution in this regard, none of my publications has as yet aroused any official action, except when a paperback edition of *Sex Without Guilt* was banned, along with ninety-nine other books (including novels by Faulkner, Steinbeck, and O'Hara) in one county in Southern California.

Sex Life of the American Woman and the Kinsey Report was finally published in cloth by Greenberg, a firm that took a highly liberal attitude toward the publication of sexual subject matter. As a result of legal advice, however, Greenberg omitted the same two chapters of the book that Popular Library had first banned. My opinion, and that of my collaborators on the book, was that these chapters were not objectionable or censorable. We lost.

My fourth book, *Sex, Society and the Individual,* ran into no censorship problems as far as publication and editing were concerned, for the simple reason that the book was published by Dr. A. P. Pillay, the coeditor of the work. For several years, however, the *New York Times* refused to publish advertisements on this or any of my sex books, even if the ad contained nothing more than the title of the book and the name of the author. At first, large advertisers like Marboro Books, who include scores of titles in each ad, were able to squeeze mentions of some of my volumes into their *Times* displays. But later even this privilege was denied all of my books on sex. When queried in this respect, the *Times* never came up with a satisfactory explanation— especially in view of the fact that it frequently published advertisements for more conservatively attuned volumes on sex. More recently, the *Times* has run ads for several of my books on sex, but has often insisted on cutting out large chunks of the ads submitted for *The Art and Science of Love, Sex and the Single Man,* and other books of my authorship.

Most of my subsequent works on sex, love, and marriage have been published by Lyle Stuart, Inc.—largely because, after this firm brought out the first edition of *Sex Without Guilt,* I discovered that the same freedom of speech that permeates the columns of the *Independent* similarly prevails in the books Lyle publishes. Although he has personally disagreed with some of my ultraliberal views (after all, he has raised a teenage daughter of his own while publishing my books on sex!), he has never red-penciled any of my frank expressions or expletives, and so far both of us have managed to stay out of jail.

In any event, my most controversial books—including *A Guide to Successful Marriage, Reason and Emotion in Psychotherapy, If This Be Sexual Heresy...*, *Sex and the Single Man, The Intelligent Woman's Guide to*

Manhunting, The Art of Erotic Seduction, and my hard-hitting sex manual, *The Art and Science of Love*—have all been published by Lyle Stuart, Inc. Even though reviewers have frequently uttered anguished screams about my ideas and language, my censorship problems have been absolutely nil, all of which tends to show, I am convinced, that the American public and our gendarmerie are not our worst censoring agencies; the publishers themselves are.

To make this point even more convincing, I had the same censorship problem again when I arranged to have some books on sex brought out by other publishers than Lyle Stuart. Bernard Geis commissioned me to do *The Intelligent Woman's Guide to Manhunting,* liked the manuscript very much, but found my language "too rough." When I reluctantly agreed to tone some of it down so that the book would not be inordinately delayed in going to press, he finally decided that his main business associates (including *Esquire* magazine and Art Linkletter) would never tolerate the liberal sex views I included in the book, especially those outlined in a section, "The Fine Art of the Pickup." Although he predicted (accurately, as it turned out) that the book would sell very well, he forfeited the advance royalty, returned the manuscript, and agreed to let me have Lyle Stuart publish it.

A little later on, I took another chance and let Julian Messner, Inc., talk me (and my coauthor Edward Sagarin) into doing a book called *Nymphomania: A Study of the Oversexed Woman.* Much to our chagrin, some of the material in the manuscript was bowdlerized as it was being rushed into print, and the sexiest chapter, "How to Satisfy a Nymphomaniac Sexually," which had been specifically requested by the original editor, was deleted because it was "too provocative." Subsequently, arrangements were made to include this chapter in another of my books, whose publisher, this time, thought it perfectly fine and proper. With still another of my books—the massive, two-volumed *Encyclopedia of Sexual Behavior,* which I edited in collaboration with Albert Abarbanel and which was published by Hawthorn Books, Inc., the articles were not censored by the publisher (except, I believe, in some of the foreign countries where the *Encyclopedia* has been translated and republished). However, great effort was brought to bear on me and my collaborator to include in the volumes several ultraconservative articles, since a number of our contributors were (without my instructing them to be) quite liberal in their presentations.

By 1965, I had published fifteen books on sex in fifteen years. I had had considerable experience with a variety of publishers, editors, reviewers, and advertising managers, and was inclined to take a somewhat less than enthusiastic view of the many friends and fellow writers who greeted me with some variation of "My God, aren't you lucky to be writing in the sex field? Such a popular area! And so much money to be made in it!" Actually, this is largely bosh. It is my experience that today's author who writes an honest book on sex will have difficulty in finding any publisher for his work. Then, if he does find a publisher, he will usually have to fight his way through censorship difficulties with the publisher and his editors and lawyers. Then he will find that the reviews he receives are rarely commensurate in quantity or quality to those of volumes on nonsexual subjects which he may have published.

To make matters still worse, an author will often find that her book on sex has been deliberately overpriced just because it deals with sex. She may be shocked to note that some of the finest bookstores refuse to display it prominently, especially in their windows. Many libraries will refuse to purchase the book, or, when they do purchase it, put it behind locked shelves and discourage reader interest in it. Finally, her books may run into official or semiofficial disapproval, and may be banned from advertising columns, the mail, public sale in certain communities, or, in extreme cases, any further printings.

In view of these facts, I am inclined to paraphrase the famous advice that *Punch* over a century ago gave to men about to be married. Say I in this latter-day version: "Advice to authors who are about to write a book on sex: Don't." Time and again I have been called upon to prepare or outline articles by editors of mass-circulation magazines, such as *Redbook* and the *Ladies' Home Journal*. But even though I may safely say that I am generally considered to be one of America's outstanding authorities on sexual subjects, for many years not a single one of my down-to-earth essays in the field appeared in a large national magazine. My efforts were somehow always found to be "too realistic," "too bold for our readers," or "overly controversial." In 1962 *Esquire* was about to break the sex barrier by accepting one of my articles, "The Case for Polygamy." However, after paying me generously for the article they first delayed its publication, and finally, at the behest of one of the chief editors, who found it "too strong," returned it to me.

When I finally did break into print in a small popular magazine a few years ago, largely because the editor was a good friend to whom I had given several ideas on what kind of periodical he might publish, he enthusiastically accepted my article and vaguely said that he might change it around a bit. Naturally, I thought, that he would consult me about these changes. To my surprise, he blithely changed some of the salient points of the article without consulting me, and each change was a distinct toning-down of any liberal views on sex I may have included. For example, in the course of a discussion of sexual freedom in marriage, I asked, "Can the average American couple practice sex freedom in marriage and still have a good marital relationship?" And I replied: "The answer is, alas, no." My editor friend changed this to: "The answer is, of course, a resounding no."

Since the publication of the first edition of *Sex Without Guilt*, I have had more success than usual in publishing material in national magazines. *Pageant* has been the most liberal periodical in this respect, and has actually asked me to write and has printed four articles on sex by me. Mass-circulation magazines such as *Cosmopolitan, This Week,* and *True Story* have also included pieces by me. More often than not, however, such publications have been more interested in my nonsexual than my sexual writings, and when they have run the latter they have commonly deleted or changed significant passages where I was exceptionally frank about copulatory or noncoital procedures.

Even the highly sexy men's magazines have at times proved to be quite prissy in this regard. Thus, after I had written, on request, an article on nymphomania for *Gent* (which is normally one of the sexiest of the men's publications), the editor apologetically told me that because of strict post office regulations, I had to delete all explicit references to sexual relations. And an article I wrote for another men's periodical, *Saga*, on "How to Have an Affair and End It With Style," was seriously cut and bowdlerized, without my consent, before it was printed.

After I wrote the first edition of *Sex Without Guilt*, I began to make more frequent radio and TV appearances, and I quickly began to run into censorship trouble in sensitive media. When I spoke in favor of premarital sex relations on Channel 5 in New York, such a hue and cry was raised that many years after that my appointment as a consultant in clinical psychology to the Veterans Administration was temporarily blocked because I had advocated "free love" on this particular program.

I appeared many times on the old Long John Nebel show on WOR, New York, and the programs on which I appeared were very popular and were normally tape-recorded and rebroadcast at a later date. The program I did on *Sex Without Guilt*, however, in which masturbation and fornication were specifically mentioned as desirable sex acts, was forbidden to be rebroadcast by the station management.

On the radio station WINS I debated the virtues of premarital sexual relations with the editor of a magazine who stoutly opposed such relations (although she was unmarried at the time and showed up at the studio with a man who was obviously her lover). When I vigorously stated that to be mentally healthy, a woman had damned well better stop caring too much what her associates thought of her reputation, there were hundreds of protests to the station; the Federal Communications Commission took the program off the air until the station explained that it had not specifically invited me to say what I said, and that previously I had made similar statements on many other radio and TV shows. The next day the management of the station humbly apologized to its audience for my appearance.

On the David Susskind Open End TV show, I appeared with Max Lerner, Hugh Hefner, Ralph Ginzburg, Maxine Davis, and Rev. Arthur Kinsolving in a two-hour program entitled "The Sex Revolution." When David Susskind asked me what I would do if I had a teenage daughter, I candidly answered that I would encourage her to pet to orgasm rather than to have intercourse (because of the danger of pregnancy involved in coitus). But when I went on to say that if she insisted on having full copulatory relations I would fit her up with a diaphragm or birth control pills and tell her to have fun, the program was banned from the Metropolitan Broadcasting syndicated TV network, and the two-hour TV tape was never played anywhere. Ironically enough, on the same show, Max Lerner had previously remarked that the mere fact that we were doing this program that night showed how liberal in its sex attitudes TV was becoming! When I did a daytime radio performance on WCBS New York in which I directly answered listeners who phoned in, I clearly stated that premarital sexual relations were fine and that the Bible was hardly a good guide to sane sex conduct. The result: more than a thousand listeners jammed the telephone lines to complain to the station about my sexual liberality, and the Federal Communications Commission again considered suspending this program from the air. When I said similar things on the telephone-answering shows on radio stations in Philadelphia, Boston, Los Angeles, and other cities, complaints were voluble and vociferous, and in consequence I am now persona non grata with several of these stations.

In recent years, a pernicious form of precensorship has been applied to me by several radio and TV outlets. Thus, producers of some open-discussion programs will call me and arrange to have me be on the air a week or two later. Then, just before the program is about to be recorded or to go on live, they will call me again and give some lame excuse why they cannot use me on the show, or will honestly admit that they have been told that I am "too controversial" a figure. As a result of these various types of censorship, my participation in radio and TV programs in New York City and throughout the country has been seriously curtailed, and I sometimes wonder if eventually practically all the large and respectable outlets will be barred to me. If so, I shall just have to keep writing more books and articles than ever!

So it has gone, and so, by and large, do I expect it to go in the future. Frankness on sex breeds suppression of sex. This, I dare say, will not stop me from continuing to express views on sex and convey facts that should assuredly be communicated. But—to be utterly realistic—I will definitely be curbed and limited in this connection.

This is too bad, but, fortunately, not fatal.

4

Sexual Intercourse: Psychological Foundations

After writing a number of articles for the public and the profession on sex-love techniques, I decided to do a sex manual summarizing my ideas and practices. The result was *The Art and Science of Love,* in 1959. I avoided using the word *sex* in the title because I found that the bestselling books in the field used words like *marriage* or *love* or *relationship* but rarely openly used *sex*. Why? Because, in those days, readers were ashamed of buying sex books and putting them on their shelves for friends and relatives to see.

I was apparently right about selecting my title, for both in hardcover and paperback form *The Art and Science of Love* sold exceptionally well and was translated into many foreign languages. Royalties for it, as usual, went to the Albert Ellis Institute and not to me personally, and in 1964 enabled the institute to purchase the six-story building where we have a psychological clinic, train therapists, and conduct many workshops, lectures, and courses for the public. At the time of its publication the uniqueness of *The Art and Science of Love* was that it showed people, in simple English, that sex with a consenting adult was permissible in many forms, coital and noncoital, while most sex manuals of the day were restrictive and narrow. In turn, it influenced many other books on sex and sex therapists to take an open-minded approach and, along with *Sex Without Guilt* and my other writings, helped spark the Western sex revolution of the 1960s. Today, some of its messages may seem mild and uncontroversial, but not in the

1960s! Millions of readers were, I am happy to say, enormously liberated by this book and it contributed to their first real sexual awakening. Its influence still continues.

Healthy Attitudes Toward Intercourse

Assuming that initial intercourse has been completed and that you are having regular coitus with your partner, there are several attitudes which are important as a foundation for maximum fulfillment. I shall now review some of the main attitudes for having regular intercourse in a manner that is mutually satisfying.

Absence of Coital Fetishes

First and foremost, it is advisable for you to adopt the philosophy that if you are intent on having fine coital relations there is nothing sacred about intercourse itself, it is only *one* of the main ways by which couples may enjoy themselves and come to climax. As soon as you conceive copulation as the *only* method of achieving satisfaction, you make a fetish of it.

Husbands and wives do not owe each other intercourse, even though some of our marriage laws state or imply that they do. As part of the marital partnership, what they are responsible for, if anything, is some form of sexual satisfaction, usually leading to orgasm. That is, assuming that one mate desires to achieve climax and that his or her demands are not unreasonable, the other mate should preferably go out of his or her way to satisfy these desires. Otherwise, monogamy does not make much sense and becomes an onerous restriction on the unsatisfied mate.

Satisfying one's mate, however, does not necessarily mean fulfilling oneself at the same time, nor does it mean pleasing the mate through coitus. Thus, a wife may ask her husband to gratify her sexually when she is aroused, but it is silly for her to demand that he also receive simultaneous gratification. If he is not in an aroused mood, he can still bring her to climax.

Similarly, a husband may ask his wife to help him achieve

orgasm—but not necessarily in intercourse. If, for the moment, she is indifferent or averse to coitus, it may become too directly involving an act to request of her.

By the same token, if she has serious objections, temporarily or permanently, to oral-genital relations, then this also becomes too directly-involving an act to demand. But, out of several possible ways in which the husband may achieve a climax, it is hardly unreasonable for him to want his wife to help him achieve it in one of these ways—such as, for example, by massaging his penis with her hands—that will be a relatively uninvolving method for her to employ when she herself is not aroused. Otherwise, if the wife does not satisfy her husband in *some* manner (and, of course, vice versa) continuous frustration will result, usually leading to poor marital relations and perhaps to extramarital affairs.

If and when intercourse is seen not as a fetish or a necessity but simply as one of the possible satisfying sex acts, even low-sexed or inhibited partners often become aroused spontaneously in the course of extragenitally satisfying their mates. Under these circumstances, coitus is likely to become more frequent.

Under other circumstances, where only coitus is conceived of as "proper" or "good," lack of desire on the part of one of the mates may lead to frustration, anger, and anxiety; sex may become more and more laden with negative emotion; both the desiring and the desireless partner may tend to avoid irritation-provoking sexual relations, and in a period of time active copulation may cease.

Differentiating Sex Competence From Worthiness

A second psychological attitude about intercourse is that it should never be taken as proof of masculinity or femininity, nor should sexual competence ever be confused with an individual's essential worth. The fully masculine man is not necessarily the one who can last indefinitely at intercourse, or who easily gets an erection, or who is gymnastically adept at many coital positions. On the contrary, many of the most masculine men are rather poor at intercourse, for the simple reason that they are so easily aroused that they quickly ejaculate and never learn to be coitally adept. Also, many other men, who are masculine in that they are strong individuals, with self-confidence and a powerful belief in themselves—just happen to be physically deficient and inept at intercourse.

Moreover, a man who is not, for one reason or another, the best coital partner may still be one of the best sex partners. For intercourse is only one way to satisfy the average female, and frequently, one of the lesser ways. The main sources of sexual sensitivity in the female are not usually deep within the vagina, but in the clitoral region and the inner lips and vestibule of the vagina, which are well supplied with nerve endings, while the vaginal canal itself often is not. A man may therefore be an excellent *lover* without necessarily being an excellent *copulator*, since it is easy for him to stimulate a woman's most sensitive parts with his fingers, lips, tongue, or other parts of his anatomy if his penis is not erect. Indeed, as I often tell my marriage counseling and psychotherapy clients, a man who had no penis whatever could be an excellent lover, just as a woman who had no vagina could be a satisfactory sex partner for a man—if the two did not have overpowering procoital prejudices. And a woman with a normal vagina can be relatively inept at or uninterested in copulation and still be an excellent lover, since, like the man, she has hands, lips, and other organs which are in many ways capable of giving exquisite pleasure.

Once again: the fact that a male or female has trouble enjoying and giving enjoyment through penile-vaginal coitus has nothing whatever to do with this individual's worth as a person. Many of us are inadequate at playing basketball, bridge, or the stock market, but that inadequacy hardly makes us a loser, a fool, or a bad person. We may be adequate in other areas, and even if we are not, we may still be perfectly kind, nice, and lovable.

Therefore, if your marital partner is not a good coital bedmate and you happen to enjoy copulation immensely, that is certainly too bad, and you hardly have the best of luck. But this does not prove that your mate is a poor spouse. If you stop viewing his or her coital limitations as criminal, you may still be able to have a remarkably good relationship, including even a good sexual relationship, with this mate. Deifying the coital act, or making it appear that your partner is weak, incompetent, or worthless because he is not adept at it, will tend to sabotage rather than encourage coitus. For once he begins to worry about how good he is at intercourse, his ability to perform almost immediately tends to become impaired. This is not necessarily because of profound psychological reasons—such as unconscious hatred of the mate—but more often because of distraction and anxiety.

Humans usually find it impossible to focus on two things at exactly the same time. If they are reading a book and listening to music simultaneously, they are not able to pay as much attention to either the book or the music as they would if they were doing either act separately, and they actually keep shifting their main attention from one to the other. This is especially true when people are doing two similar things at once—such as two kinds of thinking. If you concentrate on a math problem, you will find it almost impossible to figure out the solution to a business or love problem at the same time. Similarly, if you focus on *how* you are doing at a given problem you will find it difficult to focus, at the same time, on *what* you are doing. Thus, if you are worrying about how well you are reading a paragraph, or how much time it is taking you to read it, or whether you will remember most of what you read, you will find your reading rate noticeably slower and you may actually read the entire paragraph without comprehending it.

Similarly with intercourse. If you concentrate on how well you are doing at coitus, or on how long you may last at it, or on whether you are going to have an orgasm, you cannot help detracting from the act of intercourse itself and your enjoyment of it. In consequence, it will hardly be surprising if you lose your excitement or achieve only a mild orgasm. Worry, fear, or panic—all of which are created by convincing yourself that it is awful to fail at anything—will help a public speaker forget his speech, stutter, or say sheer nonsense. Why, then, should it not make a sex partner perform at a worse level than he or she would without this handicap?

The more, then, you demand that your mate be good at intercourse, the more you look upon him or her as weak, incompetent, or worthless for not being coitally adept, the less likely that he or she will perform satisfactorily. But the more you let your partner feel at ease—feel that it would be nice, but not absolutely necessary, for coitus to be energetic or prolonged—the more he or she is likely to fulfill your fondest hopes.

Interest in the Partner

A third attitude for successful intercourse is: be vitally concerned about your partner's succeeding for his or her sake rather than merely for your own. This is the same kind of attitude you might well apply in all your relations with close associates. No matter how strongly you tell people that you want to do something for *their* good, if they become convinced, in their own minds, that you really want them to do this for *your* good, they often rebel and (albeit often unconsciously) decide that this is the *last* thing they will do. But if you convince the same people, that you are out for *their* good—because it is true—and that you want them to do something because you honestly feel that *both* of you will benefit, you have a good chance of inducing them to do this thing. This means that you should preferably want your mate to succeed at intercourse because you love her and, through love, want her good. By love, I do not necessarily mean romantic, obsessive-compulsive devotion—which often is a mask for the unconscious dire need to *be* loved—but the mature wish for another individual's growth and development for *her* sake, even when her desires do not precisely jibe with yours. Although this kind of love is not absolutely necessary for the achievement of satisfactory coital relations between you and your partner, it distinctly helps—especially when your relationships are enduring.

In any event, people who feel that they are loved and approved of by their mates, and that they will continue to be even if their coital performance is not super-excellent, will tend to have more confidence in their ability to perform, will not overexaggerate the significance of possible failure, and will focus more adequately on the act of copulation rather than the supposed horror of failing at it. Under these circumstances, coitus will tend to be maximally proficient and enjoyable.

Deemphasizing Simultaneous Orgasm

A fourth attitude helpful for having successful intercourse is to place less emphasis on the achievement of simultaneous orgasm. It is all very well when husband and wife, in coitus or extracoital play, are able to have exactly as many orgasms as each other and to have them precisely at the same instant. This, however, is a goal that relatively few can achieve because of the enormous range of orgasm capacity among different normal individuals. Thus, a man or woman may be capable of having one climax every two or three weeks, or may be able to have three to four every day (in the case of a man) or twenty to thirty a day (in the case of a woman). One individual may have an orgasm after a few seconds of active copulation or manipulation, another only after a solid hour of active sex participation. One person may have one climax and then be totally uninterested in sex for anywhere from a few minutes to several weeks, while another (especially a female) may have strings of climaxes, or multiple orgasms, which may continue for many minutes at a time.

Under these circumstances, with individuals differing so widely in their sexual desires and capacities, it is most unusual for a husband

and wife to be so perfectly matched that they can achieve simultaneous orgasms all or most of the time. Moreover, even if they experience such simultaneity in the early years of their relationship, there is an excellent chance that later on they may change in their sexual proclivities, so that their old timing is no longer possible to achieve. It should also be realized that even when a couple makes a successful effort to achieve orgasm at the same moment, their achievement may detract from rather than add to their pleasure. For each partner may be concentrating so mightily on hastening or holding back his or her climax that orgasm is never properly focused on and enjoyed.

A more realistic goal, then, is *mutual* rather than *simultaneous* orgasm, with each partner trying to satisfy the other in *some* way at *some* time during the sex act. Even this goal should never be overstrictly sought, as many partners do not desire a climax at a given time, but are most willing (as loving mates often are) to help their husbands or wives attain one or more climaxes. In any event, the false ideal of two spouses always achieving simultaneous orgasm will frequently result in distraction, frustration, disappointment, self-blame, hostility, and other unfavorable thoughts and feelings. A greater saboteur than this concept of coital "fulfillment" can hardly be imagined, and the sooner this ideal is realistically toned down and relegated to the realm of mild preference rather than obsessive demand, the more likely are partners to have the kinds of satisfactory coitus of which most of them are quite capable.

Effective Intercommunication

A fifth psychological attitude for achieving successful intercourse is that of down-to-earth and no-nonsense-about-it talking and signaling between the married pair. When intercourse is about to start, the partners should preferably signal or tell each other that they are ready. Similarly, after coitus has ended, the mate who wants to break apart first should signal the other to this effect.

If one mate wishes to remain united for several minutes after intercourse, the other should preferably cooperate to maintain the interlocking position. But this maintaining of the coital position for a long period of time can also become onerous to one of the mates— especially the one who may be lying under the other. Or other aspects of coital positions, such as the manner in which one's arms or legs are uncomfortably bent, may tend to be irritating to one of the mates if such positions are held too long.

If for any reason either of the partners feels physically uncomfortable before, during, or after coitus, he or she should speak up and ask the other to change to a more comfortable position. Sometimes one mate desires sex or love talk before, during, or after coitus, and the other should preferably make a point of saying the desired words. Here again, however, the super-romantic or sexually fetishistic demands of one partner may become onerous and should be held in check or psychologically investigated if they seem to be unduly imposing on the reasonable preferences of the other mate.

Coitus as Part of a Whole Relationship

Still another psychological attitude relating to intercourse is that coitus is not isolated from the rest of a couple's life, but is part and parcel of the pair's whole relationship. Occasionally, I see husbands and wives who have nothing in common except sexual attraction and who manage to keep having excellent coital relations in spite of the fact that there is no love between them. These, however, tend to be the exceptions rather than the rule. Usually, if no love exists between a couple, or either or both mates are shirking their financial, companionable, parental, or other major responsibilities, their sex life will also suffer. In cases where one or both mates are sexually unenthusiastic because of general marital difficulties, the basic causes of their incompatibility should be squarely faced and met—often with the help of a trained marriage counselor or psychologist.

The husband who is puzzled about his wife's sexual unresponsiveness can first ask himself whether he is generally a good partner, and the wife who feels sexually unsatisfied should try to discover whether she and her husband have a specific sex problem or whether it is part of a broader setting. Only when the total relationship of two mates is honestly faced is it possible to see whether an actual *sexual* difficulty exists.

The Setting for Intercourse

Although some individuals, particularly males, are able to enjoy coitus under almost any conditions—in a semipublic place, for instance, or a cold room or on an uncomfortable sofa—others are more sensitive and require a proper setting for their maximum enjoyment. Even though you yourself may be rather insensitive in this connection, it is well to discover the preferences and sensitivities of your mate and try to cater to them to any reasonable extent, in order that he or she may feel fully relaxed when having intercourse.

It is often better to have coitus in a lighted room rather than in complete darkness. For one thing, nudity is often arousing to one or both of the partners, and certain coital positions require sight as well as touch for their successful completion. It should be pointed out, however, that if one of the mates has serious objections to having sexual relations in a well-lit room, the other can willingly accept this at least temporarily, while gradually trying to reeducate the mate so that they are finally overcome.

In all instances where one mate has strong prejudices in favor of or against certain sexual practices, the other partner should preferably try to be unusually understanding and uncritical, even if the practices that are favored or disfavored seem to be outlandish. If the presumably more reasonable mate will at least give the "outlandish" procedures an honest try, he or she may find that they are really not as bad as they seem to be. Or, if they are found to be unsatisfactory, the more "normal" mate will then have a better basis for refusing to participate in this kind of "peculiar" behavior.

If a very clear-cut difference exists in this respect, with one mate insisting upon sex practices that the other mate finds completely distasteful, it is usually best for the first mate to drop his insistence and seek alternative outlets with the mate who finds particular acts most unpleasing. In extreme cases of disagreement, professional help should be sought fairly early during married life. One or both of the spouses may have a serious psychological problem that, if it were cleared up, would remove the existing sexual incompatibility.

5

The Facts of Female Sexuality as Learned From My Personal Sexual Experiences

This article was written for a national magazine and was liked very much by the editors, who wanted to publish it quickly. But the publisher of the magazine got into censorship trouble with other ventures and, at the time I submitted it, his case in court was still pending so he decided against publishing it.

I was then asked to present it at a special conference on female orgasm sponsored by the American Association for Marital and Family Therapy, but since I was unable to attend that conference, one of my colleagues agreed to read it for me. But he was allowed to present only a few pages of my conclusions—and none of the detailed experiences on which they were based. Finally, all the papers of this conference, including my essay, were never published because they were "too intimate." Only one innocuous review of the literature was published; the rest of the papers were quietly buried.

The article was finally published in my book, *Suppressed: Seven Key Essays Publishers Dared Not Print* (1965).

Now that I have published over fourteen books and 150 articles on sex, love, and family relations, I suppose I am considered to be something of an authority on the subject. One of my books, *The Art and Science of Love*, has been the fastest selling marriage manual in the United States, and several of my other books, such as *Sex Without Guilt* and *Sex and the Single Man*, have also been bestsellers. Apparently the public gives some credence to my views on sexuality in general, and particularly to my opinions on female sexuality and the problem of orgasm in women.

Assuming that I know something about why and how women do and do not fulfill themselves sexually, the pertinent question may be asked: Exactly how did I gain this information? Obviously—as one can easily see from the many references included in many of my writings—I learned a good deal of it from the publications of other authorities. My first teachers in this area were Havelock Ellis, August Forel, Iwan Bloch, and many other outstanding pioneers in the field of sex, who from their own clinical observations and from studying earlier writers, recorded considerable salient sexological information. Later on, I gained immeasurably from the observational data presented by G. Lombard Kelley, LeMon Clark, Alfred C. Kinsey and his associates, Robert L. Dickinson, and many other modern students of sex. For having access to all this material, I am duly grateful.

Then, beginning in 1943, I began to do my own clinical and experimental studies in the area of sex-love relations. My first Ph.D. project at Columbia University was on the love relationships of American college women, and even though I was forced to abandon this study by some of my more prudish professors, I continued it on my own and published several scientific papers on it. I also did library and firsthand sex research on hermaphrodites, gay men and women, convicted sex offenders, the sexual preferences of psychologists, the sexual attitudes and behavior of the American public as revealed in popular mass media, and various other sex and marital subjects.

Finally, as a psychotherapist and marriage and family counselor, I began to see literally hundreds of people who had sex-love problems and to report on my treatment of these individuals. Included in these reports were examples of examining and treating scores of women with orgasm difficulties or other sexual problems. Not only have I, as a clinician with more than fifty-five years experience, often expressed my view of the causes of female disorders, but I have also written about and presented tape-recorded sessions with women who were apparently cured of their sexual problems by my particular Rational Emotive Behavior Therapy approach.

All this evidence that I have gained about female sexuality, and that other clinicians and experimentalists have likewise presented during the last century, has its distinct limitations. As many critical appraisers have pointed out, this kind of information is usually gathered from untypical and nonrepresentative kinds of subjects, and the clinical material, especially, is clearly obtained from disturbed individuals who may not in any way be a good sample of women. Thus, Dr. Meyer Maskin, in an NBC radio debate with me on my book *Sex and the Single Man,* charged that much of the "evidence" presented by me and other sexologists has been gained from generalizing about problem-centered patients who are not likely to be typical of average males or females in our society. I had to agree with Dr. Maskin that this has often been true, from Krafft-Ebing's and Sigmund Freud's day to the present.

There is, however, a body of empirical evidence I have amassed during the past six decades about female sexuality; I have used it in my writings on sex, and I am going to employ it in the present chapter. This evidence is gained from my personal sexual experience with several score female partners. During the past sixty years I have had two wives, a couple dozen long-term paramours, one woman with whom I have lived for thirty-three years, and many other short-term bedmates. Naturally, these partners have hardly been a random sample of the American female populace, but they probably are somewhat representative of bright, college-level, cultured females in our society.

My partners have ranged from eighteen years to seventy; have included those who are single, married, widowed, and divorced; have held jobs as secretaries, clerks, teachers, nurses, clinicians, and professionals; have come from various parts of this country and the rest of the world; have been raised in a variety of religious faiths; have tended to be physically attractive, but have also included some decidedly homely women; and have ranged from the highly conservative and conventional to exceptionally liberal and unconventional individuals. Most of them have come from middle-class families, but some have come from wealthy and some from lower-class backgrounds. A minority of these partners has been seriously emotionally disturbed; the great majority has been moderately disturbed (as practically all people in our society seem to be); and another minority has been unusually well-adjusted.

The only unusual thing about these women seems to be that they have been better educated and brighter, on the whole, than the average American woman. Otherwise, they do not seem to have been unusual or atypical. There was, however, one exceptional thing about my contacts with these females—practically all my intimacies with them took place after I had reached the age of twenty-four and when I was already well embarked on the road to becoming a sexologist and a clinician. In fact, I became a sexual scientist as a direct result of my attachment to the first of these women.

This is a rather interesting story in itself, which is too long to go into in detail at the present time, but which I can relate briefly. In my early twenties, when I finally became truly involved with a woman, after having previously lusted after females to the nth degree but managed only to have many mild and fleeting petting relationships with them, I quickly found that I knew nothing about sex. In order to fill in my knowledge, I went to the New York Public Library, where I had previously always gone to gain knowledge in other areas. Much to my surprise, I found the circulating branch of this library a fine source of sexual information, while the reference branch was much more restricted because many of the better books were kept on closed shelves and not even listed in the catalogue that was open to the public. But by taking advantage of central circulation and interlibrary loans, I was soon able to acquire, and to keep at home for two weeks or a month, some of the finest books on sex printed up to that time.

I became so engrossed in this material that I determined to do research in the field. I started to do a large-scale study that would have eventually been a kind of Kinsey report if I hadn't learned that just a short time before Kinsey and his associates had already started their own study. Anyway, I still continued my research. I became interested in my women friends of that day (and later) not only because of the pleasures I experienced in being with them, but also because I wanted to learn, firsthand, certain things about which the best sex books were often indefinite, vague, or inconclusive. So for the last sixty years I have, in addition to being psycho-physically intimate with a good many women, talked with most of them at great length about their sexual responses, desires, and problems, and gone out of my way to discover things about them that the average lover does not too often bother to ask about.

My interest was initially given impetus by some erroneous information that I at first accepted from one of the scores of sex books I kept poring over at the age of twenty-four. The woman with whom I was going at the time was a virgin and intended to remain so for the present, even though she would spend the night sleeping in the same bed with one of her sex partners and do just about everything that could be done sexually except engage in actual penile-vaginal copulation. When she gave me my first opportunity to spend part of a night with her I muffed my chance; just the day before I had read in one of these "highly authoritative" books on sex that giving a woman an orgasm by clitoral manipulation helped fixate her only on this kind of satisfaction, and frequently prevented her from going on to have vaginal orgasms. So I dutifully explained this to my would-be sex partner, and told her I was not going to arouse her too much, much less make an attempt to bring her to climax, since that would not be healthy for her. Rather, I lovingly declared, I was going to wait until she felt ready for full intercourse; then I would be most happy to have sex with her.

Well, I certainly picked the wrong woman for *that* line! Although she somewhat passively and sweetly let me get away with my great sacrifice for that evening, she didn't let me hear the end of it for the next several weeks; unfortunately it was not until a long time, and several intervening boyfriends later, that she let me make up for the error of my ways. Meanwhile, my faith in the dogmatic Freudian statement about the perniciousness of clitorally induced orgasm was immediately shaken. I also began to seriously question much of the presumably authoritative sex information that I was voluminously ingesting. I began to understand that whether Sigmund Freud liked it or not, some women did get the most powerful orgasms of which they were capable through clitoral massage, and that many of these same ones were actually helped to reach climaxes through penile-vaginal intercourse *because* they had first practiced masturbatory or petting relations of a purely clitoral nature.

This early eye-opener led me to question many other dogmatic statements, some of which were repeated in almost all the sex books of that day. And the more I questioned, and the more open-mindedly I experimented with my sex partners, the more I seemed to discover the facts of female sexuality. For one thing, I soon discovered that even when females had what seemed to be vaginal sensitivity (which, according to Dr. Robert L. Dickinson and his fellow sex anatomists, they were not technically supposed to have, since the vagina is a relatively insensitive organ that does not have the kind of nerve endings that the clitoris, inner lips, and introitus have) and could fairly easily have an orgasm during copulation, they still did not always require intercourse in order to achieve their greatest and most satisfying climaxes.

Thus, there was a little Greek waitress with whom I had an affair for awhile who enjoyed almost all aspects of sexuality but insisted that she only got a "real" orgasm during intercourse. I doubted this but made no attempt to argue. We enjoyed both precoital and coital relations. One night, when we had copulated for about ten minutes, in the course of which she appeared to have a terrific orgasm, we talked for awhile afterward and had a fine time together. Then, more out of curiosity than anything else, I began caressing her clitoral region, and got her exceptionally aroused.

Because she seemed to want me to do so, I then entered her vagina with my fingers and began to massage it internally. This produced a violently pleasurable reaction in her. I then went further, found an unusually sensitive spot, where her cervix and her posterior vaginal wall seemed to coalesce in a kind of cone, and where my two massaging fingers were practically caught and held. As I continued to massage this area, she began a series of ecstatic pelvis thrusts, and soon had what she described as the most powerful orgasm she had ever experienced in her twenty-eight years of existence, even though during the decade just passed she had been fairly promiscuous and had experienced orgasms with about thirty different lovers.

Still later that evening, I began to massage this woman's clitoral region, and again produced powerful involuntary pelvic contractions, soon leading to a series of orgasms that she described as being not quite as strong as the digital-vaginal induced orgasm but distinctly greater than most of the penile-vaginal orgasms she had previously experienced. Quite obviously, in this case, although she was clearly prejudiced against orgasms induced by other methods, she was able to let herself go in noncopulative ways and to broaden and deepen her sexual satisfaction.

Curiously enough, I had something of the opposite experience with still another woman. This twenty-five-year-old person enjoyed intercourse, as well as various extravaginal means of sexual participation, but always seemed to have her greatest and most exhausting climaxes through direct stimulation of her clitoral region. In fact, she could go on almost endlessly in this manner, and experience forty or fifty orgasms a night, until she literally became too tired to continue and then would fall into an almost immediate and profound sleep. She also normally experienced better orgasms when she was copulating in the female-surmounting position, since she then had greater leeway to rub her clitoral region against my pubic bone, and thereby to bring on violent climaxes. On a few occasions, however, when I was mounting her in the conventional face-to-face position, when there had been relatively little preliminary love-play and when intercourse lasted only a few minutes, she insisted that she had "utterly astounding" sexual sensations, culminating in the "weirdest and most powerful orgasms" she had ever experienced. She believed, though she wasn't sure, that my deep and powerful pelvic thrusts had something to do with these extra-special orgasms. But she also believed that there was some special readiness about herself at these times that produced such unusual sensation, and that mere technique alone could not easily reproduce it.

Then there have been a number of other women with whom I have had sex-love relations who insisted that they practically always got exactly the same kind of orgasms, and usually fairly powerful ones, no matter whether we copulated, engaged in clitoral massage, had oral-genital relations, or tried anything else in or out of the sex books. One woman with whom I had a long affair not only would have strong climaxes, and often strings of climaxes that would last for several minutes at a time when I caressed the usual sexual parts of her body, but would also have them when I touched her shoulder, or merely hugged her closely to me, with my forearms exerting vigorous pressure against her shoulder blades. This same woman could often get equally strong orgasms when I had not yet touched her, but was obviously on the way to touch or kiss her shoulders.

The opposite extreme, unfortunately, has been much more frequently represented in the sample of women with whom I have been sexually intimate—the women who can only have an orgasm, even a light one, if they are specifically stimulated in the clitoral region, and sometimes even more specifically stimulated in a certain rhythmic manner and for a long length of time. I originally went along with the Freudian hypothesis that such clitorally-triggered females are not truly sexually mature, and that they will never be emotionally stable or sexually fulfilled until they learn to experience so-called vaginal orgasm. The more women I went to bed with, however, the less sound that hypothesis appeared to be. If Freud had copulated with a number of women besides his wife Martha, I am reasonably sure that he would have given it up too!

For one thing, I soon noticed that the women who had orgasm only as a result of clitoral stimulation were frequently among the highest and most adequately sexed ones I was encountering. Many of them would just about always have climaxes, no matter at what point of their menstrual cycle they happened to be, while some of the women who had orgasms during intercourse reached sexual summits more infrequently. These clitorally-triggered women, moreover, would often be able to achieve multiple orgasms in a given day or evening, and the next day they would be eager to start all over again. In contrast, some of the women who achieved orgasm through penile-vaginal copulation would have a single explosive climax, much as many men have, and then would have no further interest in sex for that day or several days thereafter.

At the same time—and this is a consistent finding from my own experiences with a number of different women—I also found pretty much the opposite kind of result. That is to say, I have been with several who could have orgasm only through direct clitoral manipulation, and sometimes only after twenty or thirty minutes of such manipulation, and when they finally did achieve climax they were finished for the evening and had no interest in sex for from one to several days. I have also had sexual relations with a number of women who easily could have orgasm during intercourse and who were among the most highly sexed women I have ever met and could have one sexual peak after another within a short period of time. In fact, I became convinced that some of these women could have so-called vaginal orgasms precisely because they were highly sexed, and because almost *anything* would set them off— including the relatively inefficient method of penile-vaginal coitus!

The evidence I have found in regard to the puritanical upbringing of women and its effect on their sexuality is also conflicting. On the one hand, I have been with those who clearly were traumatized by accepting the puritanical dictates of their parents and their society and who consequently were unable to enjoy various aspects of sexual intimacy. In many instances, I was able to help these women overcome their prudish indoctrinations and to broaden the scope of their sexual participation. In one particular case, I met a woman at an annual meeting of the National Council on Family Relations (a rather prim professional group, many of whose members frown severely on my sex writings and clinical orientation), and become friendly with her partly because I listened sympathetically to her tale of woe about her ex-husband. She had recently divorced him largely because he insisted on having oral-genital relations, which completely disgusted her. After spending most of a wintry weekend in bed with this woman and literally getting up only to eat and go to the john, she voluntarily started to use her tongue on every possible part of my body, and apparently enjoyed herself immensely in the process. From this and several similar experiences I have had with inhibitedly raised women, I am able to say that through a combination of activity and talk with a cooperative partner, they can begin sexually to "swing."

But the other side of the coin is equally interesting. I have had affairs with women whose rearing was of the most puritanical quality and who were thoroughly frightened by their parents, Sunday school teachers, and girlfriends, about the dire things that would certainly ensue if they masturbated or had heterosexual relations. Yet these girls were always highly arousable and easily sexually satisfied. Even when they were terribly guilty about their sexual activity they still reached orgasm quickly and easily, and often had many orgasms on a single evening. One of these women had such a good time in bed with me one night, including at least five explosive orgasms, that she became terribly guilty about what she had done, ran to a priest to confess, and refused to see me again. A few months later, however, she was fornicating with a new boyfriend, and in spite of her continued guilt and self-castigation, she was still having orgasms all over the place. Obviously, her sex guilt did not interfere with her sexual performance, and neither, according to my personal observation, does the extreme sex guilt of many other women.

I found a somewhat similar phenomenon in regard to extreme emotional disturbance. According to most of the marriage counseling texts, and especially to nearly all the psychoanalytically-oriented literature, severely disturbed women are not able to relate adequately to members of the other sex and therefore invariably have all kinds of sexual difficulties, including orgasm blocks. My personal experiences with women indicate that although this hypothesis is not entirely false, it is unmitigated hogwash when it is applied to *all* neurotic and psychotic females. Two of the best sex partners I have ever had were exceptionally disturbed young women. One was a clear-cut paranoid schizophrenic, spent some time in two different state hospitals, lived on huge quantities of tranquilizers when she was not hospitalized, and committed suicide several years after our relationship ended. Yet she was a fantastically good bedmate, was often imaginatively preoccupied with inventing new forms of sexual engagement that we might try, and could fairly easily have orgasms through regular intercourse, digital manipulation of the anterior wall of the vagina, clitoral massage, anal copulation, and various other forms of excitation. If there was any form of sexual participation that this woman did not employ and enjoy, I can't imagine what it could be. I lived with her for about six months, and although she was usually a bore and a zombie in many respects, as schizophrenics often are, and although she was flooded with anxiety almost every minute of every single day, I hardly remember a night when it was not a sheer delight to be with her in bed.

My second great sex partner was an unusually bright and beautiful woman with a borderline personality disorder. She, too, could achieve orgasm in a variety of different ways, although she particularly favored clitoral massage. She was the most promiscuous girl I ever met, since she would have as many as forty or fifty different lovers a year, and when she was alone for an evening, which was rare considering how many men she usually had around, she would use an electric vibrator to give herself several orgasms. She also excelled in demonstrating to her sex partners that they could do much better in bed than they thought they could do, and she thoroughly enjoyed being with many men, especially those with whom she could have intelligent conversations as well as have good sex. Yet, like so many borderline personalities, she was generally bored with life, unable to maintain lasting attachments, incapable of keeping a steady job, and operated on a level far below her considerable intellectual capacities.

On the other hand, I have also had experiences with women whose severe disturbances clearly interfered with their potential sexual functioning. One divorcée I knew would, on a given day, be exuberantly immersed in incredible sex forays and could flail away wildly for hours at a time in glorious orgasmic paroxysms. On another night, however, she would be so absorbed in some minor problem that had arisen during the day, and so depressed about her ability to cope with the world, that no amount of stimulation would awaken her sexually. A twice-divorced woman of thirty-five with whom I once had an affair was even more erratic in that only about once every few weeks would she come out of her shell long enough to become interested in any kind of human relationship, including sex. The rest of the time she was withdrawn, terribly fearful of being dominated, and apparently determined *not* to engage in sexual relations because she felt that they somehow might bring her out of her shell and violate her integrity. Still another severely disturbed woman I knew had little interest in sex with a partner at any time, but she herself was convinced that this was a form of emotional blocking, since she was frequently aroused by reading sexy novels and masturbated regularly to orgasm.

This is not the place to go into the orgiastic details of my entire sex life. Besides, I must save some material for my eventual memoirs.

The instances I have been citing are merely examples of the wide range of sexual responsiveness that I have found among the several-score women with whom I have been personally intimate and whose activities I have clinically and scientifically, as well as often quite warmly and relatedly, observed. But along with these differences I have also found some surprising uniformities. Although women are notoriously supposed to be masochistic and love physical pain, I have found that when fully aroused, a number of those I have slept with have quite spontaneously resorted to violent biting, pinching, nail-digging, kicking, and other kinds of presumably "sadistic" behavior that they would never employ in their nonsexual moments.

As a result of my sex-love involvements with a wide variety of young women, I have come to some tentative generalizations about female sexuality and orgasm capacity. Since my days are hardly ended, I may yet modify these notions, or even reverse some of them completely. But for the present record, here are some of my conclusions:

Orgasm capacity in women seems largely, though by no means entirely, inherited. It does not usually seem to be mainly the result of early conditioning. On the contrary, early conditioning itself is highly influenced by inborn sexual tendencies. Thus, the highly sexed young woman practically forces herself to masturbate at an early age, while the low-sexed one easily keeps herself from doing so, and then both these women become partly conditioned, as a result of biologically influenced thoughts and social experiences, to favor subsequent kinds of sexual behavior.

In most women of all ages, the clitoris is the main instigator of orgasm. This again is not because these females have been conditioned to respond in this clitorally-triggered manner, but largely because they are anatomically and physiologically constructed so that it is much easier for them to do so than to bring on orgasm in other ways. Consequently, the most efficient and quickest manner of giving the average woman an orgasm is to provide her with some kind of steady friction around the clitoral area.

A large percentage of females is also able to achieve full orgasm through penile-vaginal copulation, but many of these women do so with difficulty, take quite a long time to obtain it, or do so only on occasion. Moreover, a large minority of females who almost always obtain clitoris-triggered orgasms are practically never able to climax during intercourse alone, no matter how long coitus is prolonged or how effective a lover her male partner may be.

Of the women who achieve orgasm through regular coitus, a sizable percentage (but probably less than half) has greater sexual pleasure, and often a more powerful orgasm, when in this manner than when achieving it through extravaginal massage. The psychological factor of these females wanting to be penetrated by the male organ may have something to do with their greater satisfaction during coitus, but there also seems to be some anatomic reasons for this difference. Perhaps the fact that the contraction of the vaginal muscles, which takes place as a result of orgasm, has a penile object on which to impinge and thereby is more kinesthetically felt or prolonged has something to do with this greater pleasure, which often occurs as a result of coitally induced climax.

The great majority of women, probably like the majority of men, has a much greater capacity for sexual excitement and orgasm than this majority thinks it has when left to its own perceptions. Most women who would be highly content to stop sexual relations after experiencing one or two orgasms can be led, by proper male stimulation of their genital regions, to go on to three, four, and often many more orgasms—and some of these later orgasms are more powerful and satisfying than the earlier ones. Some women, in fact, seem to be able to get vaginally-induced climaxes only after they have a series of clitorally-induced ones, and some start with the later kind of orgasms but then seem to want to continue largely with the former kind.

The main psychological blocks to orgasm are rarely closely related to childhood or adolescent experiences, but are more closely connected with contemporary irrational thinking. The female is afraid to let herself go sexually when she is blocked, usually because she is ashamed to do so with her present partner, is overly worried about not getting an orgasm, or is inefficiently focusing on nonarousing stimuli that easily come to mind at the time she is having sexual relations. Consequently, psychological blocks against orgasm can frequently be removed if the woman's partner behaves sensibly and freely with her, and shows her that in the present moment, there is nothing for her to be afraid of, and that he will not despise or dislike her if she is not fully orgasmic.

The main physical blocks to orgasm are usually the result of the male's failure to be a good lover and the female's neglecting to instruct him to give her precisely the kind of stimulation she requires. If both partners will stop dwelling on trying to achieve orgasm through intercourse and experiment instead through several different kinds of genital stimulation, they are likely to discover some particular method of bringing the woman to climax.

Many women who are quite normally sexed and who achieve orgasm can regularly through one means or another still find the sex act not necessary for a happy existence, and can tolerate sexual abstinence for fairly long periods of time. Their interest is in a total loving relationship between themselves and their partners, not in sex for its own sake. When they are not in a relationship they become relatively cold and do not actively look for sexual satisfaction. Although this kind of blocking is emotional in the sense that it results from a psychological frame of mind, it is not necessarily a symptom of pathology; it is closely tied to the anatomic and physiological fact that many women can easily live without orgasm, while the average male has a more imperious urge that keeps driving him to sexual activity.

The foregoing observations are hardly startling. I believe that most of them are at least partly confirmed by other evidence, such as that gathered by the Kinsey investigation and William H. Masters and Virginia E. Johnson in their research. They are also confirmed by much clinical data, including those I have gathered from hundreds of my own clients. The main point that I want to emphasize is that sex research does not *only* consist of gathering interviews, doing laboratory experiments, or observing individuals under a cold scientific light. It may also stem from firsthand observation on the part of individuals who themselves are actively and enjoyably involved in sexual activities.

A final word on the role of personal sexual experience in sex and marriage counseling and in the profession of psychotherapy. I do not hold that all marriage counselors must themselves be married, nor even that all psychotherapists must undergo prolonged and intensive experiences of psychotherapy. I do think, however, that such personal involvement is highly desirable for the individual who is going to spend a considerable part of his or her time practicing therapy on others. By the same token, I have no intention of suggesting that all marriage counselors, sexologists, and psychotherapists be required to undergo a good many sex-love affairs themselves before they are allowed to practice. But I do believe it would be highly desirable if they did, and that as a result they would be saner, less dogmatic, and more efficient practitioners. I am very grateful for the many short-term and long-term affairs I have had with women outside the state of legal matrimony. In my own case, I am certain that these affairs have helped me immeasurably as a sexologist, counselor, and psychotherapist.

6

Unhealthy Love: Its Causes and Treatment

I wrote this article in 1972, after almost a lifetime of making the study of love my great hobby. I began to become intrigued with the study of sex, love, and marriage in 1939, when I was twenty five. I planned massive research in these areas, but a few years later discovered that Kinsey had already begun his famous sex studies, in 1938. So I decided to focus on what he largely omitted, the study of love. Kinsey, with whom I met, was quite interested in my research, particularly in my study of the love emotions of college level women, which I planned as my Ph.D. dissertation in psychology—but which Columbia University stopped me from finishing.

Undaunted, I finished my studies of love myself, as I note in this paper, and published some pioneering articles on the studies. When Mary Ellen Curtin invited me to do a chapter on unhealthy love for her book *Symposium on Love,* I had had almost thirty years treating it as a therapist, and also almost twenty years of treating unhealthy love relationships with Rational Emotive Behavior Therapy. So I gladly agreed to her request and in this chapter summarized the REBT treatment of love problems. We made a pamphlet of this article and have given it to our clients at the Albert Ellis Institute since 1973. A good many of them have reported that they have received considerable help from reading it.

Let me start out with a few of my own prejudices. I have been engaged in research on the subject of love—and I mean love, not just sex—since 1939—that is, almost sixty years ago. My first attempt at a Ph.D. thesis was on the love emotions of college girls, and although Columbia University did not let me proceed with this particular topic (*because* it was on love, and hence closely related to sex), I nonetheless completed the study myself and published it in a series of papers in psychological and sociological journals.

Then I became a psychotherapist and a well-known sexologist. In the latter capacity, I dealt partially or obliquely with love and published a good many articles and books on the subject. In the former capacity, I have dealt with problems of love almost every day for over a half century. For it is the basic problem of love—how much do I accept and respect myself and how much do you care for me?—that makes the world go 'round, and even the so-called sex problems (such as those of sexual inadequacy and sexual disturbance) are usually problems of human worth and worthlessness (or self-love), as I have shown in many of my writings on psychotherapy.

There are many healthy or normal aspects of love, as a great many authorities on the subject have pointed out; it also has many unhealthy or abnormal aspects. I shall deliberately focus on some of the unhealthy aspects, for love is a huge subject, and there is never time or space to cover all its ramifications. Erich Fromm has incisively analyzed some of the self-defeating elements of "in-lovedness" and loving. Starting from a highly unpsychoanalytical framework and sticking largely with clinical data, I shall now give my own analysis of unhealthy love, as well as what can be done to help individuals who have love addictions.

Most human disturbance is a form of *demandingness*. People who love "neurotically" do not merely want or prefer to be involved intimately with another person; they demand, dictate, insist, or command, in a highly absolutist manner, that (1) they find an attractive individual, usually of the opposite sex; (2) that they act exceptionally well and impressively with this person; (3) that this individual love them completely, devotedly, and lastingly; and (4) that they love this person in an intimate, deep, and abiding fashion. They may, in addition, have various other demands, such as that this person whom they discover and whom they intensely love be available, live nearby, have values and goals similar to their own, and be a great sexual partner. If the individual's goals, aims, and purposes about loving and being loved are *wishes*, that is fine and healthy. But if they are, as they ever so often are, absolutist dire needs or mandates, if they are incorporated in the utter necessity that love *should, ought,* or *must* be achieved, then that is not fine or healthy. *That* is one of the essences of emotional disturbance.

Let me illustrate with the case of a woman I saw who, in spite of her unusual comeliness and intelligence, had a long history of failures in love and insisted that she never had a reasonably good affair for any length of time and was sure that she was incapable of achieving or maintaining a lasting relationship. She was consequently anxious, depressed, and angry. I was quickly able to demonstrate to this woman, Roseann, that her emotional problem—that is, her anxiety, depression, anger, and inability to maintain the kind of deep emotional involvement that she said she very much wanted to maintain—could probably best be understood within the A-B-C model that is used in Rational Emotive Behavior Therapy. At point A (adversity), she was finding great difficulty in relating intensely and enduringly to a suitable man; at point C, she felt the emotional consequence of despair, panic, anger, and hopelessness. As is almost universal in cases like this, she flatly stated during our first session, "Because I am having so much trouble in achieving a long-term relationship with someone I really respect and love, and because I am convinced that I probably never will, this has made me very depressed." "Oh, no," I immediately interrupted as I frequently do in instances of this kind, "that's not true. You have just made a magical jump—from an external situation to an inner feeling. And, since there is, as far as we know scientifically, no magic in the universe, your statement is a non sequitur. It just isn't so."

"What do you mean?" she asked.

"Well, you're saying that an adversity, at point A—the fact that you're having trouble achieving a long-term relationship and the possibility that you will never achieve the kind of relating that you want—is causing a feeling in your gut, an emotional consequence, at point C. But how could this be? How could *any* adversity, or noxious stimulus that is happening to you, cause you to feel something inside you—unless, of course, it were a physical force impinging on you? And even then it would only cause, directly, physical pain; and you would still have to react, emotionally, to that pain."

"Do you mean that A doesn't directly cause C, and that virtually *nothing* can upset me emotionally?"

"Yes, that's just what I mean. *You* largely directly upset yourself. And you do so by convincing yourself something at B, your belief system. What's more, when you're intensely upset—feel depressed, for example—you invariably convince yourself of some irrational belief, at B."

"And what is that?"

"Oh, I think I know exactly what that is—for most of the time I can figure it out on the basis of my therapeutic theory. But first let's see if you can guess what sane or rational belief you convinced yourself of at point B, just before you thought of the irrational belief."

"Rational belief?"

"Yes, rational belief about what is occurring at point A. It's on the order of, 'I am having a great deal of difficulty in achieving and maintaining a long-term involvement with the man I care for, and that is...' That is what?" I asked.

"That is awful!" replied my client.

"No, that's your irrational belief! It's interesting how so many people just as intelligent and educated as you are tell me their irrational belief and think that it's rational. But we'll get back to that in a minute. First, what *rational* belief, rooted in social reality, do you think you tell yourself immediately *before* you gave vent to this irrational one?"

"Mmm....I really don't know."

"You do know. You're just not thinking about it. You're probably telling yourself, right now, another irrational belief that's blocking your thinking."

"You mean, 'Isn't it awful that I can't think of this rational belief he wants me to locate!'"

"Exactly! But let's get back to the rational one. What would anyone in your position tell herself if she wanted very much to establish a long-term involvement and she was having great trouble doing so? 'I have great difficulty relating permanently to a man, and that is...'?"

"Disappointing?"

"Right! That is disappointing; that is unfortunate; that is deplorable; that is disadvantageous; that is too bad! All these kinds of things. And if you stuck rigorously only to that kind of rational belief— that it is disappointing and unfortunate to be unable to relate to a man *but not more* than that, how would you feel?"

"I...suppose I'd feel, well, terribly sad."

"Right again. You'd feel quite sad, sorry, regretful, annoyed, or inconvenienced. For it is, we could justifiably say, most unfortunate if you don't relate well to a man and perhaps never will, and you'd better feel healthfully sad and annoyed about that. But, of course, you feel much more than that: you feel very depressed. Now what *irrational* belief do you probably have, again at point B, for you to create this unhealthy feeling?"

"Why is it *un*healthy for me to feel depressed?"

"For several reasons. Although sorrow over not relating might prod you to do more to relate, depression normally won't: it will cause you to be inert, to give up, and to feel that you *can't* possibly relate. Hence, it is dysfunctional or self-sabotaging. Moreover, depression almost always includes self-downing or self-pity. Just answer my question about what your irrational beliefs are, and I think you will see."

"You mean my irrational belief about not relating?"

"Yes, in addition to your rational beliefs that it is unfortunate and disappointing not to relate."

"Well, uh, I guess, uh, that I never will be able to relate."

"Yes, that's right. That is an irrational belief, because it's unprovable. You can prove that you haven't ever related well, and that you *may* never be able to do so. But how can you prove that you can't possibly, under any conditions, *ever* relate?"

"Mmm....I guess I can't."

"But what else are you irrationally believing? There's something else even more important than 'I never *will* be able to relate.'"

"Let me see. Uh....Oh, yes—and it's *awful* if I never do so!"

"Right! That's the main villain: that *awfulness* that you are creating in your head. Because you could rationally believe that you haven't related and you most probably never will, but not believe that it is awful. When you believe that anything you do (or don't do) is awful, it's highly irrational. Why?"

"I don't know. It certainly *seems* awful! Especially if I find out that I never do, actually, relate to any man."

"Yes, but just about anything that you *think* is awful will *feel* awful to you. That's the way the human being works: whatever she very strongly thinks or believes she tends to feel. That doesn't prove a damned thing except that she has a feeling. But why is it awful if you never relate to a man?"

"Mmm....I can't really say."

"Nor will you ever! Because this is an unrealistic hypothesis. For when you say, 'It's awful (or horrible or terrible) if I never relate,' you mean: 'It's very inconvenient or handicapping,' as we've already stated, and 'It's one hundred percent inconvenient or handicapping! It's as bad as it could possibly be.' Is that realistic? Is it really one hundred percent bad?"

"No, I guess not."

"And, again, when you call a thing awful you mean: 'It's very inconvenient'; and 'Because it's very inconvenient, it shouldn't exist!' Well, is there anything in the universe that because it is terribly inconvenient to you, should not, ought not, *must* not exist?"

"No, not if it *does* exist."

"Exactly! Whatever exists exists. No matter how displeasing failure to relate is for you, if that's what always occurs that's what always occurs. It's silly and grandiose to say that it *shouldn't* occur."

"Are you saying, then, that if I give up all *awfulness* and accept the reality that when obnoxious things exist, there's no reason why they *must* not exist? Will I stop being upset about being rejected by males I like and fail to relate to?"

"No, I'm not saying you won't be bothered *at all*; I'm saying that under these conditions you won't be bothered unduly, irrationally, self-defeatingly. You'll still be extremely sad and sorry about not relating, but you won't depress yourself about it. And you'll work your head off to rid yourself of this annoying condition—because you are bothered about it and want to eliminate it—and do your best to relate."

At the same time I was showing Roseann that her lack of relating was not causing her to be severely depressed, but that *she*, with her irrational beliefs about this deplorable state of affairs, was depressing herself, I also showed her that her anxiety and anger were similarly self-caused. To make herself anxious, she was rationally, again, saying that it would be most unfortunate if she failed to relate, but, irrationally, that she *had* to relate and was an utterly worthless person if she didn't. She was risking her entire worth as a human, her respect for herself, on the possibility of her not relating, and naturally, with so much at stake, she was making herself inordinately anxious.

In regard to self-created anger, she was sanely telling herself, "Isn't it too bad if a man doesn't appreciate my good qualities and refuses to keep relating to me on an intimate level?" and irrationally telling herself, "Isn't it horrible if he doesn't appreciate my good qualities? What a turd he is for being so benighted."

To sum up: In the case of depression, Roseann was *demanding* that she get what she wanted in the way of an intimate relationship, and was making herself feel hopeless and suicidal when her demands were not being met. In the case of anxiety, she was *insisting* that she succeed in relating well to every man she wanted to relate to, and was putting her entire self, her personhood, down when she didn't. And in the case of anger, she was *commanding* that a man in whom she was vitally interested be equally appreciative of her, and was thereby hating him in toto because of his unappreciative qualities.

This, I hypothesize, is what almost invariably happens in the case of unhealthy love. Like my unrelating client, people dogmatically *order* that the world conform to their love goals. By this kind of Jehovian fiat, they make themselves unusually insecure, anxious, or jealous when they may not be loved by someone they have selected; they induce feelings of depression, despair, hopelessness, and suicide when they're not adequately loved; and they frequently direct anger, hostility, and rage at specific people who refuse to give them the love they demand. Does super-romantic idealization, which I describe in *The American Sexual Tragedy,* also stem from the same kind of demandingness? As far as I can see, in large part it does. For one thing, it is compensatory. Humans do not merely denigrate themselves for failing to have good love affairs, but for many other things as well, for example, failing to achieve notably in the realm of business, art, science, or social relations. When they foolishly rate themselves (instead of merely sensibly rating their traits or performances), they feel exceptionally inadequate, inferior, or rotten. Consequently, if they could ideally fall in love with a member of the opposite sex and he or she did gloriously love them in turn, this marvelous romantic feeling would (they imagine) at least partly perfume their shithood, and they would (at least temporarily) feel much better about themselves. So they have considerable incentives to believe that their beloved is the greatest thing since Eve and that her acceptance of them makes them the greatest thing since Adam.

There are, however, several other reasons why humans tend to idealize a member of the other sex (or in the case of homoeroticism, a member of the same sex) and to fall madly, and sometimes irrevocably, in love with someone whose qualities may be highly questionable, particularly if they are contemplating marrying this person. These other irrational reasons include:

Misperception. The beloved is actually a person with fairly ordinary traits but is misperceived as having remarkable characteristics. Lovers may need (or think they need) their beloveds to be memorably intelligent, beautiful, sexy, or sincere; hence, they may actually observe them to have these unpossessed features.

Fixation. The lover is treated very well by a member of the opposite sex (such as a father, an uncle, or a brother) during her early years and keeps falling in love, for the rest of her days, with other members of this sex who have traits somewhat similar to those of the original person (e.g., blond hair, green eyes, or high intelligence).

Magical Identification. The lover desperately needs to be strong or good-looking (often because of his own feelings of inadequacy) and keeps falling in love with someone (often a member of his own sex) who has these traits, magically believing that he will come to possess them if this other person can be induced to love him.

Narcissism. The lover really likes some of her own qualities (such as her good posture) and only becomes highly enamored of individuals with these same qualities, no matter what their other characteristics are.

Hostility. The lover hates his parents or other authority figures and consciously or unconsciously becomes infatuated with individuals who possess those features that would tend to be most offensive to the persons she hates.

Security. The lover cannot stand any form of rejection and thinks she needs to be loved totally and forever; consequently she only becomes enchanted with partners who seem to be utterly safe in this respect and will presumably adore her forever.

Romantic Illusions. The lover believes that "true love" lasts forever and only permits himself to become passionately endeared to a person who has the same romantic illusions and who swears undying devotion.

Caretaking Needs. The lover believes that she cannot stand on her own feet and that the world is too hard for her, so she becomes enormously attached to individuals who will presumably take care of her and make things easy for her for the rest of her life.

If we examine in detail these various kinds of idealized love, it can be observed that they are all forms of demandingness. The lover wants some advantages of an intimate relationship; he or she then arbitrarily establishes, absolutely, some characteristic that *must* exist if an ideal love relationship is to exist; this characteristic is then either discovered or invented in another person, and the lover may become utterly convinced that the beloved: really possesses this exemplary characteristic; will continue to possess it forever; will use it for the advantage of the lover; and will have a glorious ongoing relationship with the lover in spite of any other disadvantageous characteristics the beloved may possess or handicapping conditions under which the relationship will probably exist.

Because it is highly unlikely that, especially in the long run, these insistences and absolutist predictions of the lover will be realized, the unhealthy lover almost always winds up with several kinds of disturbed feelings. For example:

Anxiety. The lover is incessantly overconcerned about whether he will find the "right" beloved, win her, and always keep her completely attached to him in the exact manner that he demands she be attached.

Jealousy. The lover is frequently intensely jealous of the beloved, believes that this beloved is overweeningly interested in other potential beloveds, can't stand the idea of sharing him to any extent, tends to spy on him, nag him, and paranoically believe that he no longer loves her and instead is devoted to someone else.

Depression. The lover thinks that his beloved does not love him sufficiently or at all; that she never will; that no one whom he wants to love him intensely ever will; that this is a horrible state of affairs; and that he will be able to obtain practically no joy in life from any source unless he is truly beloved by some enchanting person whom he loves.

Inertia. The lover is convinced that it is too hard for her to get what she wants in a love affair, that it shouldn't be this hard, and that she might as well give up and do nothing about trying to arrange and develop the kind of an affair that she thinks she has to have.

Hostility. The lover thinks it is terribly unfair that he is not loved the way he should be loved by the person he selects; that it is horrible that this kind of injustice exists; and that this person is therefore rotten for being so unfair to him.

Worthlessness. The lover imagines that she is unloved by the person she selects because she has some exceptionally rotten traits and that therefore she is a totally rotten person who doesn't deserve to be loved by anyone.

Erotomania. Occasionally, the lover obtains considerable evidence that the person he loves does not care for him and even detests him, but he refuses to accept this evidence and convinces himself that this person really does care, and perhaps is even madly in love with him. Assuming that unhealthy love usually stems from dogmatic demandingness or absolutist insistence that the world be the way the lover wants it to be, and is a distinct pattern of emotional disturbance that includes elements of anxiety, depression, worthlessness, and hostility, what can be done to ameliorate this condition? An answer, though not necessarily the complete or only one, is intensive psychotherapy. This may take two major forms: a palliative or curative method. Unfortunately, most therapy today is of the former variety.

In addition to palliative or inelegant methods of therapy, there exist a number of curative or more elegant methods. These are concerned with making clients aware that they are errant demanders— showing them why this philosophic outlook will not be effective in helping them get what they want, and persuading, educating, and training them to give up their basic commandingness and to work for those goals they strongly *desire* rather than those they think they absolutely *need*. In Rational Emotive Behavior Therapy in particular, some of the more elegant methods that are regularly employed include the following:

Antidemandingness. The therapist shows the client, in accordance with the A-B-C theory of symptom-creation, that his emotional disturbance is not created by the influence of external situations or adversities (A), but largely from his own belief system (B), and particularly from his irrational beliefs that he should, ought, and must achieve the love goals he desires. The client is also shown how to analyze, attack, ameliorate, and extirpate these irrational beliefs by realistically and logically disputing them (at point D).

Unconditional Self-Acceptance. The therapist shows the client unconditional positive regard—that he or she can accept the client no matter what she does or how she fails. Moreover (and often more significantly), the therapist shows her how she can give herself unconditional positive regard or self-acceptance, that is, by *always* refraining from rating her self, her being, while still rating her deeds, traits, and acts. The therapist teaches the client, by work and example, tolerance of herself and others.

Higher Frustration Tolerance. The therapist indicates to the client how he can raise his frustration tolerance and thus helps the client convince himself that he doesn't *need* what he *wants*; that he can stand losses and rejections even though he'll never like them; that frustration may be annoying and irritating but that it's never awful, horrible, or catastrophic.

Emotional Education. In order to show the client how to be tolerant of herself, others, and the difficulties of the universe, and how to stop childishly demanding that her desires be immediately gratified, the therapist uses a variety of dramatic-evocative approaches such as role-playing, assertion training, authentic self-disclosure, and various kinds of emotive-relating methods. However, these techniques however, are not merely used as ends in themselves but also as means of philosophic restructuring, or of revealing to the client what her self-defeating values are and how she can change them.

Behavior Therapy Methods. The therapist who uses the REBT approach usually employs in vivo activity-oriented homework assignments. Thus, he or she gives graduated assignments whereby the client takes the risks of meeting, dating, and relating to potential love partners; the client is helped to stay with frustrating conditions (such as an affair which is going badly) in order to learn how to tolerate these conditions before he finally (rationally and with determination rather than irrationally and with anger) leaves them.

In many ways, then, the REBT practitioner uses a combination of cognitive-emotive-behavior methods to reveal to the client what her fundamental self-destroying and antisocial philosophies are and what she can do to change them. The goal is to help the client accept social reality (even when she doesn't like it), stop whining and wailing about it, stop foolishly exacerbating it, and persist in trying to actively change it for the better. The therapist tries to show the client how to surrender her dictatorialness, with its concomitant compulsiveness, fixation, and fetishism, and to maximize her freedom of choice and be able to fulfill her human potential for growth and happiness.

Love is one of the greatest forces and influences in human life. It can bring enormous benefits and gains. But when people turn it from a powerful desire into a presumed necessity, they unrealistically endanger and minimize it. Moreover, they usually create gratuitous anxiety, depression, feelings of inadequacy, and hostility. But all is not lost. They have the capacity to reverse their childish demandingness, to grow up, and to love in a nonobligatory manner. One of the main purposes of effective psychotherapy is to help them love compellingly but uncompulsively—a difficult but hardly impossible goal!

7

Sex-Love Adventuring and Personality Growth

I wrote this chapter in 1972 for Herbert Otto's *The New Sexuality*. At this time the sex revolution of the 1960s was in full swing, aided by my *Sex Without Guilt* and bestselling paperbacks of that decade. Nena and George O'Neill's *Open Marriage* and Terry Garity's ("J") *The Sensuous Woman* were runaway bestsellers. My essay was meant to summarize my liberal writings on sex and love, and to tie up adventuring in this area with personality growth.

I had originated Rational Emotive Behavior Therapy in 1955, after I was already a well-known sexologist, and through it had developed concepts of healthy and unhealthy personality development. In this essay, which I revised slightly in 1991, I attempted to show how an enlightened view of sex-love relationships is conducive to emotional health and how healthy personality growth also leads to liberal sex attitudes and actions. This interactional effect, and my pointing it out in 1972, is still important as we are now ready for the twenty-first century.

⚜

To define sex-love adventuring is not very hard. But who really knows what personality growth is? A great many words have been spoken and written on this subject during the last quarter of a century—the cynical say *too* many! But the results are hardly definitive. Authorities differ as to what "growth" really is. For example, leaders of the existentialist movement in the field of psychotherapy, such as Ronald Laing and Rollo May, have stressed such personality virtues as openness, authenticity, caring, and acceptance of our basic irrationality. Those in the forefront of the encounter movement, such as Bernard Gunther and William Schultz, have emphasized physical contact, sensory awareness, expression of deep feelings, and relatedness. Those on the level of reality therapy, such as William Glasser, have seen personality growth largely in terms of ruthless reality-facing and self-discipline. And those in the vanguard of cognitive-behavior therapy, such as Aaron T. Beck, Donald Meichenbaum, and myself, have insisted that fundamental personality growth rarely takes place without conscious and concerted philosophic restructuring. Quite a potpourri of theories!

Therefore, for the purpose of the present chapter, how can we characterize personality growth? I have already given a great deal of thought (not to mention clinical practice) to this topic and have come up with some reasonably satisfactory answers. In a paper on the subject of religion (also reprinted in this reader), I have outlined what I consider to be the main goals of emotional health or personality growth, and it seems to me that these are at least as good as those outlined by various other theoreticians, researchers, and clinicians.

The important elements of personality growth are probably the achievement of enlightened self-interest, self-direction, tolerance, acceptance of ambiguity and uncertainty, flexibility, acceptance of reality, commitment, risk-taking, and self-acceptance. It is my thesis that just about all these goals may be abetted and enhanced by sexual adventuring. And by sexual adventuring I mean the individual's engaging in a good many sex-love relationships before he (or she) settles down to any form of monogamous mating, and even then, if the spirit moves him (or her), continuing to engage in some further sex-love experimentation and varietism. However, in this era of AIDS and other sexually transmitted diseases, sexual adventuring after steady mating with one person had better be done with full knowledge of the mate.

Let me go through the traits that I listed above as being associated with personality growth, define them more precisely, and indicate why I think each of them is usually aided by sexual adventuring.

Enlightened Self-Interest

People who are well-adjusted to themselves and to the social group with which they live are primarily devoted to being happy, gaining satisfaction, and avoiding truly noxious, painful, or depriving circumstances. At the same time, they are also devoted to seeing that their fellow humans also survive and are reasonably happy. While they are most interested in their own life and pleasure, they realize the importance of not needlessly stepping on others' toes and unduly restricting their living space. Consequently, they try to be nonharming to practically everyone, and select a relatively few individuals (because their time is limited) to actively befriend and care for. They do not dishonestly pretend to be purely altruistic; but are authentically and realistically self-interested *and* socially interested, and therefore impose certain social restrictions on themselves.

Sexual-amative adventuring encourages and aids enlightened self-interest because adventuring people keep asking themselves, "What do I really want in regard to this relationship? I realize that she wants to begin or maintain this affair, but is that what *I* really desire? How much time is likely to be involved? What will I probably learn about myself and others? What other satisfactions will I get if I choose another relationship, or even no relationship at all? Granted that the union may or may not work out well, what, in either eventuality, am I and my partner likely to gain and lose?"

Adventuring of any kind tends to be healthfully self-seeking. I may travel, climb mountains, search a library for new books to read, go to a party to find new friends mainly because I am curious, venturesome, and absorption-bent. If someone will accompany me on these experiments, and especially if that someone can share my delight and converse with me about it, that is great—sometimes truly glorious. However, there are times I deliberately want to go alone, since that makes the outreaching still more adventurous.

In sex-love adventuring, I almost always require a partner (for the limits of masturbatory experimentation are usually quickly reached!). But I still don't know what is going to happen with or to that partner— and that's one of the main reasons why I find the relationship, as long or as short as it lasts, exciting. I do know, however, that almost anything can happen; that the two of us are taking some real risks; that the final outcome of the affair—whether it be a one-night stand or marriage—is pretty much in doubt. Therefore, I often recognize that sex-love adventuring is one of the remaining major explorations of life that is left to me now that it is difficult to pursue the kinds of physical and social risks that were available in earlier times.

I therefore make a decision on whether or not to have an affair. If I decide yes, then I recognize I am choosing to relate to another human being and that even though she has voluntarily agreed to become involved with me, she has her own desires, ideals, and vulnerabilities. Moreover, because she may be emotionally involved with me and her wishes may be father to her thoughts, she is exposed to the possibility of disappointment and disillusionment. Consequently, out of empathy and enlightened self-interest, I do not wish to needlessly mislead her. So I lean over backwards to be honest with her, to define the kind of relationship, whether it be mere sex or grand passion, that I would like to have with her, and I honor her acceptance or rejection of my offer. As I point out in some of my writings, I may try to "seduce" my partner into having an affair with me. But I try to do so by showing her that it is probably in her own best interests, as well as in mine, for her to give up any arbitrary, puritanical ideas about refraining from affairs and to make her decision on the basis of true choice and some risk-taking rather than compulsion.

Self-Direction and Independence

People who have a mature and growing personality assume responsibility for their own thinking and living. They are able to work independently at most of their problems, and while at times *wanting* or *preferring* the cooperation and help of others, do not *need* their support to create an inner sense of worthiness. The sexually adventuring person tends to fall into this self-directed framework in several ways:

1. He rarely accepts traditional and conventional sex-love views merely because he was taught them during his childhood or because they are the majority views in his culture. He intently considers, weighs, and asks for the evidence backing these opinions and accepts them only when he has arrived at good reasons why he should personally follow them.
2. She enters into relationships knowing full well that she may easily fail at them and that she has no one but herself to fall back on in case she does fail. By being adventuresome, she gives herself plenty of practice at failing and learns that she can easily survive such mishaps.

3. In between relationships, he usually spends time, being on his own. He does not convince himself that he absolutely must have a date every weekend (and therefore maintain a long-term relationship with a partner whom he considers rather inferior), or that he must sleep with someone during weekday nights (and therefore is often with someone who actually bores him). Because of his relative independence, he remains distinctly selective rather than cowardly compromising in his choices, in spite of his desire to keep having interesting and absorbing sex-love relationships.

4. Because of her independence and selectivity, she is usually able to pick partners on the basis of common interests and love rather than sheer sexuality. Knowing that she can be happy alone, and knowing that she can afford to break with a safe and steady partner she no longer finds exciting, she tends to select someone she truly cares for and with whom she can have a deep and more profound relationship.

Tolerance

Emotionally stable and growing people are highly tolerant of the desires and behaviors of other human beings, even though these may differ significantly from their own. Even when others behave in a manner they consider to be mistaken or unethical, they acknowledge that because of people's essential fallibility, others have a right to be wrong. While disliking or abhorring some of their partners' acts, tolerant people do not condemn them, as persons, for performing these unlikable acts. They tend to accept the fact that all humans are remarkably error-prone, do not unrealistically expect others to be perfect, and refrain from despising or punishing others even when they make mistakes.

Sexually adventuring people tend to forgive themselves and others for their failings. They try a variety of sex-love behaviors, including some that may be considered aberrant, and consequently can understand and tolerate others' idiosyncracies. If he is a male, he freely and fully has sex-love relationships with a number of women and consequently tends to adopt a single rather than a double standard of morality and to avoid being sexist. If this individual is a female, she is more likely to have sexual affairs in less restricted and less arbitrarily inhibited ways: to have them, for example, spontaneously, with or without love, within or outside the institution of legal marriage. Relatively few sex-love adventurers maintain the rigid, puritanical, damning codes of sex practice that have been prevalent in Western civilization for many centuries. And even in nonsexual ways, few of them tend to be as moralistic and proscriptive as sexually unadventurous individuals often are.

Acceptance of Ambiguity and Uncertainty

People who allow themselves room for growth tend to accept the fact that we all live in a world of probability and chance, with no absolute certainties. They demand no surefire predictions about the future and realize that it is not at all horrible—indeed, it is in many ways fascinating and exciting—to live in a distinctly probabilistic, variable environment.

The sexually adventurous male clearly does not demand that he meet some perfect woman early in his life, that he immediately get into a fine relationship with her, and that this remain intact forever. Nor does he demand that one mate be everything to him and that because he likes her traits and finds it beneficial to be with her, she completely fulfill him, sexually, companionably, emotionally, and otherwise. He realistically accepts the point, which Brian Boylan incisively posits, that infidelity is a natural human desire, if not everyone's actual habit, and that giving in to this desire, preferably in an honest and above-board manner, is not horrible.

Just because she is a varietist, the sexually adventurous woman is able to accept the imperfections of each of her partners, to be unterrified by their inevitable ambivalences (knowing full well that she has her own), to face the fact that even the most intense loves may be somewhat ephemeral, and to be unhorrified at the thought of losing a beloved through his moving away, becoming ill, dying, or otherwise being unavailable. Since, by accepting ambiguity and uncertainty in sex-love areas and resolving to live happily in spite of these realities, she can hardly be thrown by anything that happens to her in these aspects of her life, she generally tends to take an equally realistic attitude toward other aspects of living and to tolerate life's ambiguities.

Moreover, sexual adventurousness, almost by definition leads to maximum experiencing. Unadventurous, incurious individuals will always exist, but in many ways they live restricted lives. Venturesome people, on the other hand, do many more things, have a greater number of relationships, enjoy themselves *and* suffer more, and in many ways are more alive. They tend to realize that existence is many-faceted, that everything does not fit into one neat-niched arrangement, and that practically nothing is utterly certain. When things do not rigidly conform to some of their preconceived notions, they do not become upset.

Flexibility

The opposite of intolerance and the need for certainty is flexibility. The emotionally growing individual consequently tends to be intellectually and emotively labile, to be open to change, and to view without bigotry the infinitely varied people, ideas, and things that exist in the world. The disturbed person, on the other hand, tends to be exceptionally narrow, rigid, and overly constrained. Personality growth, in particular, would seem to be almost impossible to achieve if the individual is not open and flexible, for how can growing and remaining closed to change be compatible?

Sex-love varietism and pluralism tend to abet human flexibility. People who think that they must only go with one member of the other sex at a time before marriage, that they must remain absolutely faithful to their partners after marrying, and that they must never contemplate divorce, remarriage, communal forms of marriage, or any other diversion from strict monogamic ways are not likely to be marked by flexibility and openmindedness. The chances are that, like the members of ultraconservative groups, they are going to be just as uptight about general license as about sexual license, and that their nonsexual and sexual views are going to be significantly correlated. Similarly, a significant relationship has been found to exist between sexual liberalism and social-personal liberalism. Not that this is always true. Many members of the Rene Guyon Society, which is unusually sexually liberal in some ways, and which espouses full sexual relations between young children, are very conservative politically and socially. But in general, sexual adventuring is itself a form of open-mindedness that encourages other forms of flexible thinking and emoting, and that thereby enhances personality growth.

Scientific Thinking

The longer I practice Rational Emotive Behavior Therapy, the more I am convinced that what is usually called emotional disturbance and interference with personality growth stems largely from an unscientific, magical way of thinking—thinking that is particularly involved with irrational, dogmatic, and absolutist hypotheses such as, "My deeds are sometimes not only wrong and inefficient, but I am an awful person for performing them." "You *absolutely must not* treat me unfairly, and you are a thorough louse and should be eternally condemned for doing so!" "The world is not only a rough place in which to survive and live happily, but it is *too hard* for me to get along in, and I can't *stand* its being the way it completely *must* not be!" If people would largely follow the scientific canons of thinking in their personal lives, and would stop dogmatically musturbating, awfulizing, and whining about the many kinds of hassles and frustrations to which, as fallible humans, they are inevitably heir, they would not only rid themselves of much of their deep-seated feelings of anxiety, depression, guilt, and hostility, but give themselves leeway to discover, with lack of prejudice, what they really enjoy in life and how they can truly grow as human beings.

Reason is indeed a limited faculty and may never quite solve all the mysteries of life. But for maximum emotional functioning, people had better be fairly flexible, open, and scientific, and be able to apply scientific thinking not only to external people and events but also to themselves and their interpersonal relationships. Sex-love adventuring, though hardly a guarantee of rationality, abets scientific thinking in several important ways:

1. The sexual varietist, as noted above, is undogmatic and unconventional. Like the scientist, he is out for discovery, satisfying his own curiosity, and devising new solutions to old problems.
2. She is, above all, an experimentalist. She does not know what will occur when she leaves an old love or takes on a new one, but she is more than willing to find out. Although she cannot, like the typical physical or social scientist, normally do a well-controlled study of her behavior, she usually does less rigorous, less controlled studies of her own thoughts, feelings, and experiences as she samples first one affair and then another. She may not come up with startling truths about sex and love in general, but she frequently does arrive at profound truths about her own sex and love propensities.
3. The sexual adventurist is relatively objective and nondefensive about his and others' amorous ways because he has a good deal of firsthand information about love at his disposal; he uses larger rather than smaller samples to observe; and he uses his latter-day knowledge to correct more erroneous earlier impressions.
4. She is usually more rational and nonmagical about sex-love affairs than are those whose sex lives are much more restricted, because

she strives for greater human pleasure and less pain, and not for fictional, super-romantic visions of what sex and love presumably *should* be like in some hypothetical heaven. She tends to be more of a realistic and hardheaded empiricist than a softheaded visionary.

Commitment to a Large Plan or Goal

Emotionally healthy individuals are usually committed to some large life plan or goal—such as work, building a family, art, science, or sports. When they have steady personality growth they tend to be vitally absorbed in some large goal outside of themselves, whether it be in the realm of people, things, or ideas. And they frequently have at least one major creative interest, as well as some outstanding human involvement, which is highly important to them and around which they structure a good portion of their lives.

In terms of vital absorbing interests, at first blush many monogamists would seem to do better than do sexual varietists, because they so frequently absorb themselves in finding one mate and then for thirty years or more build a strong sex-love-family relationship with him or her. I think that this is one of the strongest points about monogamy, and one of the principal reasons that it has survived over the centuries. Sexual adventuring, however, is not necessarily incompatible with this kind of marriage-building goal, because today it is very possible for varietists to agree with their mates, when they are first settling down to a long-term relationship, that they will devote most of their time and energy to remaining attached to each other and the children they bear and rear, but that they will also allow each other a reasonable amount of sexual adventuring on the side. In this way, they may reap the main advantages of security and novelty, and maximally fulfill themselves in their sex-love relations.

Sexual commitment, moreover, need hardly be to a monogamous marriage, as there are other possibilities. Thus, two or more couples could decide to live in a communal or tribal marriage and dedicate themselves to building, on a long-term basis, that kind of sex-love relationship. And even varietist adventuring in its own right can become a vital absorbing interest—as indicated by a well-known writer who has arranged mate-swapping affairs for himself and his wife to participate in while they have, at the same time, reared three healthy, happy, highly creative children.

Monogamous commitment, moreover, often has its severe limitations, because it is often done in an obligatory rather than a truly voluntary basis. Thus, a man sexually and amatively devotes himself exclusively to his wife and children not because he truly enjoys doing so but because he believes, for conventional or religious reasons, that he ought to do so. In so doing, he frequently prevents himself from being committed to art, science, his work, or something else (such as a string of intense love affairs) to which he may have been more genuinely and intensely attached had he not believed that he had to be absorbed only in monogamous marriage.

The question is: If people were more honest with themselves and their sex-love partners, would there be fewer obligatory absorptions in a single relationship and more voluntary absorptions in various kinds of nonmonogamous or quasi-monogamous relations? I am inclined to think that there would be, and I am also inclined to think that such a state of affairs would be more emotionally satisfying and healthy.

Commitment, while a most important part of human existence, had better be to each of the partner's *individual desires* as well as to their preferences for pairing. It is questionable whether devotion to a coupling arrangement is often very good or healthy if it is not based on the premise that each of the partners is truly self- *and* other-interested, and finds, because of this double interest, that he and she can be authentically devoted to the union. As Herbert A. Otto has noted, "The lack of commitment of self-realization, together with the lack of framework and opportunity for self-realization, are responsible for much of what is labeled as pathological or asocial behavior." Therefore, for those who enjoy sexual adventuring, commitment to realizing themselves through this kind of activity may be one of the most healthy and self-actualizing acts they can do.

Risk-Taking

Emotionally sound people are able to take risks: to ask themselves what they would really like to do in life and then endeavor to do it, even though they risk defeat or failure. They try to be adventurous (though not necessarily foolhardy), are willing to chance almost anything once to see how they like it, and look forward to some breaks in their usual routines. In this connection, it is interesting to note, that even some of the most self-actualizing and creative individuals spend so much of their time in routine, unadventurous pursuits that it takes something drastic, such as near death from a heart attack, to jolt them into a new sense of vital living and a greater degree of risk-taking to savor their existence.

Sexual adventuring almost by definition is one of the major, and I would say one of the most exciting and pleasurable, forms of risk-taking. In my own life, for example, I have found that no matter how sorry I was about the breakup of an affair or marriage (and, contrary to silly rumors that circulate about me, I have had many affairs but only two marriages), my sorrow was always significantly attenuated by the adventurous thought: "Ah! I wonder what kind of person I'll become involved with next. How great to look forward to a relationship that is almost certain to include several important elements that I have not yet experienced!"

Adventurousness in sex-love affairs virtually forces the individual to take notable risks of defeat or failure. For the security-minded individual cannot be very adventurous, and the adventure-headed individual cannot be terribly security-bound. Sexual varietism, moreover, normally proves to the adventurers that they can definitely survive defeat; that they need not crack up when they are rejected; that even a host of love failures is generally tempered by a few outstanding successes; and that the loss of a potential or an actual beloved is indeed an inconvenience, but it is never truly a horror.

Concern and caution are wise and valuable human characteristics, but humans, alas, are born as well as reared with a tendency to escalate these feelings into those of overconcern and panic, thereby cruelly constricting a vast amount of their potential living space. Sexual risk-taking occurs in a lovely area where the individual, unless she is incredibly foolish, will rarely suffer bone-breaking physical injury or death (as she may, of course, in highly respectable sports like skiing and autoracing!). The main thing she risks, sexuo-amatively, is rejection and loss of approval. But it is precisely by taking these emotional gambles that the individual learns how to stop caring too much about what others think of her and to start truly accepting herself. If sexual adventuring can give her repeated practice in this important area of her personality growth, as it often can, it may render her one of the most valuable services of her lifetime.

Self-acceptance

Above all else, emotionally healthy and sane people are glad to be alive, and to fully accept themselves just because they are alive, because they exist, and because (as living humans) they almost invariably have some power to enjoy themselves. If they assess or rate themselves at all, they do so not on the basis of their extrinsic achievements or their popularity with others, but on the basis of their own existence—on their propensity to make an interesting, absorbing life for themselves. As I have shown in my other writings, they preferably do not rate their self, or give their total being a report card, at all. Instead, they only rate their deeds, traits, and performances, and refuse to play any of the usual self-rating ego games. Consequently, instead of deifying themselves (appraising themselves as being better people than others) and instead of devil-ifying themselves (appraising themselves as being worse than others), they more modestly strive for self-acceptance. Self-acceptance, which is much less noble and ego-inflated than self-esteem, merely means that the individual accepts the facts that: she is alive for a certain length of time; she is able, while alive, to experience pleasure and pain; and she chooses, merely on the basis of her bias in favor of living and enjoying, to stay alive and to have a hell of a good and growing time.

The individual who has full self-acceptance lives without any absolutes, without any rigid shoulds, oughts, musts, have-tos, or got-tos, but with a whale of a lot of it-would-be-betters. He ceaselessly experiments and explores to discover what he truly likes and dislikes, and uses this knowledge for his own maximum growth and enjoyment. Although, as Alan Watts indicates, he is not likely to experience sheer ecstasy for more than a few moments a day, he does his best to have those moments and to make them count. He is totally unashamed of his own hedonism, though he often strives for long-term and well-disciplined rather than short-range and undisciplined kinds of satisfaction.

What better than flexible sex-love adventuring to help people strive for unconditional self-acceptance? Very little, as far as I can see. For in the realm of experimentally and spontaneously embarked-upon sex-love affairs, they are likely to find almost innumerable harmless and knowledge-amassing intellectual, emotional, and physical delights. Sigmund Freud, who in spite of his overemphasis on the presumably sexual origins of emotional disturbance was something of a prude and a sexist, and who created one of the most inefficient systems of psychotherapy still extant, was wise enough to see that the two main sources of personal stability and growth are love and work. Occasionally, maximum sex-love fulfillment can be achieved by the bright and cultured individual within a strict monogamic framework, but if we are ruthlessly honest about it, this seems to be far more the exception than the rule. Consequently, if many (though not necessarily all) of us are to continue to grow, it is unlikely that we will achieve our maximum personality potential, especially in terms of our loving and being loved, in a lifetime of minimal sexual adventurousness.

In other words, maximum openness, tolerance, and self-acceptance, are much more likely to be achieved when people truly acknowledge all their thoughts, emotions, and physical urges and when they refrain from condemning themselves for *any* of them. Of course, this includes the pluralist as well as the monogamous, the ephemeral as well as the lasting, the inconstant as well as the steady sex-love inclinations and experiences. Not that all sexuality, nor even feelings of love, are wise and good for every individual. Both sexing and loving can in many instances interfere with what some persons find are, for themselves, "deeper" and "better" pursuits—such as artistic and scientific endeavors or philosophic contemplations. But none of us really knows what we want and what will be best for us until we widely experiment and experience. None of us knows what our own potential for personality growth is until we take many risky bypaths and wrongly enter a number of blind alleys. Trial—and error—is still the road to maximum self-knowledge and growth, and that goes for sexuality and love as well as for virtually every nonsexual aspect of living. Sex-love adventuring, therefore, is at least to some degree an almost necessary step to greater personal and personality advancement.

Does sexual freedom have its disadvantages and limitations? Of course it does! In the essay "Group Marriage: a Possible Alternative?" I point out that this form of varietist relating is, at the present time, "a logical alternative to monogamic and to other forms of marriage for a select few." In another essay, "Healthy and Disturbed Reasons for Having Extramarital Relations," I show that what I call "civilized adultery" (that is, honest adultery engaged in with the consent of one's marital partner) is highly beneficial to some individuals, but that there are not as yet many couples who can accept it with equanimity. All new and less limiting forms of mating tend to be difficult for most people. It requires a good deal of emotional stability and intellectual wisdom on the part of those who attempt to engage in these sex-love modes.

Herbert Otto, in commenting on my somewhat cautious approach to group marriage, notes that "jealousy and interpersonal conflict in the group are some of the main reasons why Ellis believes group marriage faces great difficulty. [But] group dynamic techniques, or the encounter group approach, with the help of competent professionals, might go a long way toward resolving some of the problems inherent in a group marriage structure."

I agree with Otto that efficient group (and individual) therapy can help couples be saner and happier in both regular and less regular forms of mating, and I have specifically shown how Rational Emotive Behavior Therapy can help people remain rationally jealous but surrender their irrational, insecurity-based jealousy. I still hold, however, that humans are exceptionally human. They are and probably always will remain incredibly fallible. They tend to be enormously different from each other and variable in their own right. Moreover, practically all kinds of sex-love relations have their intrinsic difficulties and their flawed aspects. Consequently, even the healthiest personalities are going to have to work their way through various kinds of sexual arrangements until they find what works for them. Perhaps this is not an inevitable fact of life, but it certainly seems to be one that is highly probable.

Because of the above-mentioned human fallibilities and widespread individual differences, personal experimentation and risk-taking in sex-love affairs is still highly desirable. As noted in the body of this chapter, sex-love adventuring gives maximum leeway for this kind of experimentation. I therefore contend that it is one of the sanest and most enlightened paths to sexual, marital, personal, and love growth.

8

The Nature of Disturbed Marital Interaction

This paper was written for presentation at the Annual Convention of the American Psychological Association in Los Angeles, September 7, 1974. It was published as a pamphlet by the Albert Ellis Institute for Rational Emotive Behavior Therapy.

I had been realizing for some time that ego problems or issues of self-worth were crucial to most emotional disturbances, but that often discomfort disturbances were also involved. Especially in marital interactions, people followed their own rules rather than the agreed-upon rules of the relationship.

Then they made themselves disturbed by ranting and raving against their partner's supposed goofing. They then saw, by themselves or in therapy, what they were personally doing badly—but they still refused to work at changing. They had LFT (low frustration tolerance) to a high degree. [LFT is synonymous with discomfort disturbance.] So I wrote this paper on marital interaction, and I later developed my ideas on LFT in an article I presented at the Annual Conference of the American Association for the Advancement of Behavior Therapy, in November, 1979, "Discomfort Anxiety: A New Cognitive-Behavioral Construct."

Of course, it is the individual who decides to upset himself or herself with the three major musts emphasized by REBT: (1) "I *absolutely must* do well and be approved by significant others", (2) "You *absolutely must* treat me kindly and fairly", (3) "Conditions *absolutely must* be the way I want them to be." So in a sense all human disturbance is ego-oriented, but the third of these musts, which leads to various kinds of low frustration tolerance, is important in its own right. This paper shows how important it is in individual human affairs and marital interactions.

Let me begin with a typical example of disturbed marital interaction; then I shall try to show what the essential nature of this kind of interaction is; and finally, I shall try to indicate some of the remedies that can be taken to interrupt and minimize it.

Richard, the thirty-two-year-old husband of a couple I saw for marriage counseling, was very bright and artistically talented. His ideal was to have a mate who would be stimulating to live with and who would give him sufficient time to be by himself when he was pursuing his writing. His thirty-year-old wife, Anne, was warm and beautiful, but far more interested in close ties with her husband and two children than in intellectual pursuits. She also wanted more intimate, sensual sexual relations, while her husband was perfectly satisfied to have a brief interaction centering around intercourse once every two or three weeks.

Richard was so unhappy over Anne's persistent demands for companionship that he constantly criticized her, belittled her in front of others, neglected his relations with his children, and became so depressed on numerous occasions that he only sporadically worked at his writing. Anne, in her turn, carried on side affairs with men for whom she had little love or liking, frequently complained to the children about what a poor father they had, and found excuses to keep interrupting Richard on those days when he finally did come out of his depressed moods and began to do some work on the novel he was desperately trying to finish. Both mates frequently argued over sex and had highly unsatisfactory intercourse on those relatively rare times when they did manage to have it.

Both these individuals were obviously disturbed in their own right. Richard was needlessly condemning himself for not consistently buckling down to his writing, and was consequently making himself more and more depressed and doing less consistent writing. Anne was so desperately in need of being loved in order to sustain her own worth as a human being that she was having affairs to reaffirm her attractiveness and desirability. In other words, both mates were foolishly sabotaging their own life goals and needlessly creating self-hatred and hostility toward each other.

They were neurotically interacting in their marriage because, frustrated as they were in some of their main marriage goals, instead of stoically facing and trying to minimize their disappointments, they were raging against these frustrations and thereby sabotaging themselves all the more. By denigrating Anne for not being more self-sufficient and for demanding so much of his time, Richard was encouraging her to be still *less* able to be by herself and to be more upset about his wanting more time to himself. By angrily interrupting Richard's writing, Anne was helping increase his desire for solitude, and by excoriating him for being a poor father and bedmate, she made fatherhood and having a regular sexual relationship even less desirable to him.

In other words, disturbed marital interaction arises when one mate reacts badly to the normal frustrations and the unusual and unrealistic demands of the other, and in the process helps accentuate these frustrations and demands. Then the other mate, in his or her turn, also reacts poorly to the sensible requests and the unreasonable demands of the first mate. As a result, increasing low frustration tolerance and outbursts of temper on the parts of both ensue. Disturbed individuals often respond anxiously or angrily even to relatively good life situations, because their philosophic assumptions are basically irrational. When external pressures are difficult they react more neurotically.

Disturbed people often respond particularly badly to marriage or living together, because monogamic mating is never easy and our expectations in regard to it are often unrealistic. It seems obvious that while friends, lovers, and business associates are often on their best behavior and consequently will treat one politely and noncritically, spouses and children are not likely to be able to maintain the same kind of urbane pretense for any length of time. Consequently, domestic partners are almost certain to be frequently irritable, short-tempered, unresponsive, and difficult.

Yet the average husband thinks that just *because* he is married, his wife should be consistently kind and mannerly, and the average wife thinks that just *because* her husband is married to *her*, he should be invariably sweet and responsive. The same is often true of other living together relationships, whether they are between same-sex or opposite-sex partners. Thus, if they were realistic, two people who would occasionally expect the very *worst* kind of behavior from their mates are irrationally demanding the very best conduct from the other all the time. The result of these highly untenable assumptions about what the coupled state *should* be usually leads to deep disappointment and disillusionment. This is especially true for disturbed individuals who tend to invent and cling to unsound premises in the first place, and then give themselves a pain in the gut when social reality proves their assumptions unwarranted.

A foremost cause of disturbed marital interaction, then, is the unrealistic expectations that partners tend to have not merely about themselves and others (as is the case with nonmaritally upset individuals), but also about the relationship itself. They senselessly cling to the supposition that their mate absolutely *should* be continually loving and forgiving. Then, after constructing and internalizing this self-defeating belief, couples usually do one more thing that insures their neurotic interaction: they pigheadedly cling to and utterly refuse to work at eliminating their unrealistic demands on each other.

This is the real tragedy, and one of the main causes of neurosis: avoiding work and effort that is in one's best long-term interest. Although humans acquire and create major self-defeating philosophies and destructive patterns of response usually early in their lives the fact remains that they are capable of changing these philosophies and reconditioning themselves. But they usually don't. This is why we usually refer to irrational people as neurotic or disturbed rather than as stupid or incompetent: because they presumably *can* behave better than they currently do. Neurosis, as I pointed out in my book *How to Live With a "Neurotic,"* is essentially stupid behavior by a *non*stupid person. Neurotics can do better, but they often don't. Rather, they tend to drift along, continuing their pattern of self-defeating conduct.

Take Richard, for example, the husband I mentioned earlier. He was unusually bright, well-educated, and artistically talented. Nevertheless, he easily surrendered to several forms of self-defeating thinking and behavior in his relations with himself and his wife Anne. First, he uncritically accepted, and refused to actively dispute, the hypothesis that he *had* to succeed as a writer and that he was a worthless individual if he didn't. Second, when he became depressed about his sporadic attempts at writing he allowed himself to wallow in his depression for days or weeks at a time without making any real effort to see what dysfunctional beliefs he was telling himself to cause his depression and to vigorously challenge and question these ideas. Third, even though he expected to remain married indefinitely, he made little effort to strive for true interaction with his wife and children, but instead largely tried to do exactly what he wanted to do, just as if he had no marital responsibilities. Fourth, he refused to make any allowances for the fact that marriage *is* the kind of a relationship where one is often not responded to by one's wife and children the way one would like, since they may well be preoccupied with problems of their own. Fifth, when his wife acted badly, he failed to let any of her mistakes go by, but felt constrained to open his big mouth and angrily point out all of them in considerable detail. Sixth, when he observed that Anne was using his negative barbs against her to feel hurt and demeaned, he stubbornly stuck with the belief that his defamation of her would somehow, magically, do good rather than harm. Seventh, when he could have pacified his wife to some extent by having the kind of sexual relations that were satisfying to her, he vindictively chose to have less sex than even he desired.

In many ways, then, Richard acted ineffectually in his relationships with himself and his wife. Moreover, when his main premise—that he *should* be happy with his wife no matter how great their differences and extensive their emotional hang-ups were—proved unworkable, he did nothing to examine or change this premise. On the contrary, he rigidly held onto it and preferred to believe that it was solely his wife's fault that his life and marriage were not working out well.

The more disturbed people and negative interpersonal behaviors I see in my psychotherapy and marriage counseling practice, the more I am convinced that *most* forms of disturbance are largely perpetuated by various kinds of avoidance of the hard work required to change oneself. Human disturbances, as I began to point out in the mid-1960s, are emotional disorders that are largely sparked by crooked thinking. The origin of this irrational cognizing is interesting, but plays a relatively small part in its treatment. Many clients, even before they come for psychotherapy, know full well just how they originally started having crazy thoughts and what they must do to give them up—just as most cigarette smokers know how they started smoking and what they must do to discontinue it. But in spite of their insight, they continue their irrational demands that stopping must be easy, and refuse to do the hard work required to give it up.

This is particularly true in marriage, and other sex-love relationships, where one partner, such as the husband mentioned above, may see that his treatment of his mate is shortsighted and foolish, but nonetheless stubbornly continues this relationship-sabotaging behavior. In the case of Richard, I was able to show him that his expectations about marriage in general and Anne in particular were highly unrealistic and that he had little chance for a happy home life if he maintained them. Somewhat to my surprise, he quickly went to work to challenge and question his own assumptions, began to reduce his rage and hold his tongue when his wife and children behaved badly, concentrated more on solving his writing problems than on demanding that Anne change to suit him, and made real efforts to provide his wife with the kind of affection and sexual stimulation she enjoyed.

Richard's concerted work on his marriage soon began to pay off. Anne stopped her outside affairs, encouraged the children to be more respectful and affectionate toward Richard, and got absorbed in her own painting rather than badgering him about the time he spent at his writing. Although Anne did not significantly change her own basic assumptions that she desperately needed his love to consider herself worthwhile, and hence remained somewhat neurotically needy, she was at least able to live more successfully with her disturbance—largely because Richard tackled his own neurosis and stopped blaming her for being disturbed. Hard work on Richard's part, therefore, led to a considerable reduction in his own disturbance and in the disturbed marital interaction, while some, though limited, work on Anne's part led to a better marriage in spite of the maintenance of many of her own negative premises about herself.

Similarly, I find that whenever I can induce any of my psychotherapy or relationship counseling clients to *work at* changing their underlying neurosis-creating assumptions, significant changes in their interactions with their mates, families, or other intimate associates often ensue. This work usually consists of helping partners: (a) fully face the fact that they themselves are often doing something wrong, however mistaken their intimates may also be; (b) clearly see that behind their neurotic mistakes and inefficiencies there are important irrational, unrealistic philosophic assumptions; (c) vigorously and continually challenge these assumptions by examining them critically and actively doing acts that prove they are unfounded; (d) make appropriate allowances for the intrinsic difficulties and frustrations of certain human relationships, such as monogamous marriage; (e) learn to keep their big mouths shut when their partner is clearly behaving badly, or else unblamefully point out the other's mistakes while constructively trying to show him or her how to correct them.

Above all, continually remember that a relationship *is* a relationship, that it rarely can progress spontaneously in a super-smooth manner, and that it had better be actively worked at to recreate and maintain the honest affection with which it often starts.

To sum up: Disturbed marital and sex-love relationship interactions arise when partners are neurotic in their own right and when they consequently have unrealistic expectations of what their mate's behavior *should* be. Whatever the original source of these irrational premises, people usually do not clearly understand what they are, and even when they do, they stubbornly refuse to work to give up their irrational beliefs. Basically, therefore, they lazily avoid the hard work involved in changing. Their disturbed relationships will usually continue until they realize that lazy thinking simply does not pay, and that usually there *is* no way out of individual and relationship dilemmas other than work, work, work.

9

How I Became Interested in Sexology and Sex Therapy

As this chapter shows, I was a "natural" sex researcher from childhood onward, as well as a "natural" writer. Put the two together and that made me—and still does—a writer on sexology. I became a professional psychologist in 1943, so "naturally" I specialized in sex therapy. Then, when I originated Rational Emotive Behavior Therapy in 1955, I became the first major cognitive behavior sex therapist. I have continued in this direction for many years.

My history as a sexologist and sex therapist up to the present time is summarized here. Also included are some general advances in the fields of sex research and therapy.

My keen interest in sex began, at the very latest, at the age of five, when I was caught by my parents trying to pour some milk through a funnel into the vagina of Mary J., a blonde and blue-eyed five-year-old bombshell with whom I was madly in love. I don't remember that I considered this act sexual—but both our sets of parents certainly did! So Mary, my beloved and my friend, was abruptly whisked out of my life. I continued sexual—or at least nude—exploration at the age of seven when I spent ten months with nephritis in New York's Presbyterian Hospital and used a flashlight to explore the nude bodies of the other children in my ward, and to let them see how scrumptiously I was hung. Still curiosity—no real sex.

However, I soon graduated, and just about got my first degree in sexual pleasure, when I discovered that if I pressed my genitals against the rails of my hospital crib I could get a semiorgasm—a real sexy thrill. So I made myself slightly addicted to crib-rail sex. Later on, when I went back to school, I found that climbing ropes in gym could also lead to genital joy. So, although I generally hated gym, I became quite a rope climber!

My first feeling of shame about sex was at the age of twelve, when I found that I had an almost constant erection and was afraid that other people—especially the girls in my class whom I obsessively loved—would notice it and despise me. Oddly enough, however, I was still so ignorant about sex that I didn't start to control my perpetual erections by masturbating until I was fifteen. Then I really went to town!

I masturbated twice daily and wasn't guilty about it until I figured that maybe I was too uncontrolled. So I rushed to the public library—to which I was also addicted—and found a few books that said masturbation was okay, even when frequent. Pretty good books for the 1920s!

From the age of sixteen onward (in 1929), I read many books by Freud and his followers, but I could see that Sigmund was especially obsessed with the sexual "origins" of disturbance, especially with the ubiquitousness of the Oedipus complex. I could also see that he was an overgeneralizer and a dogmatist, and therefore a poor scientist. But psychoanalytic details about sex helped to loosen me up; I came to consider practically all forms of noncoercive sex permissible. In fact, at the age of fifteen, I had my first and only homosexual episode—with my thirteen-year-old brother no less! I saw that I could easily come to orgasm in that way, too, and didn't feel one bit guilty. Realizing, however, that to seek out gay sex would probably get me into trouble—especially in those days!—I continued to obsess about and to try to have sex only with women. That was both easier and safer.

About fifteen years later, when Alfred Kinsey interviewed me for his first report and discovered that I was highly heterosexual, he seemed delighted to find that I had had an early homosexual encounter. I think that he was determined to discover that a large percentage of males had at least one homosexual episode in their lives. So fortunately I fulfilled this quota!

My accompanying obsession to sex was writing. At the age of

twelve, I decided I would be a writer, and between my eighteenth and twenty-eighth years I wrote no fewer than twenty book-length manuscripts—novels, plays, poems, and nonfiction works. Many of them, especially my novels, were very sexy, in fact, probably too sexy to be published, for I described sex play as few published writers other than James Joyce had previously done. I got a number of fine rejection letters, and some near publications, but not an actual contract. So at the age of twenty-six I decided that nonfiction writing on sex, love, and marriage would be my best bet. Why? Because I was quite interested in these fields, and presumably because they sold well.

As usual, I went to the New York Public Library, and to two special private libraries of which I was a member. Using all three, I could borrow ten books every day, which I did at least five days a week. On Saturdays and Sundays I went to the main reading room at the 42nd Street Public Library and devoured from thirty to fifty books each day. That I am a fast reader is an understatement. Without having taken any Evelyn Woods courses, I skim magnificently, especially when the books are on sex, love, and marriage, and most of them are nauseatingly repetitive.

For two years I read hundreds of books and thousands of articles and began writing my "masterpiece": a thousand-page single-spaced tome titled *The Case for Promiscuity*. Did I get any publication offers on it? Not one. Some great feedback from editors, but the unanimous view was that it was just too liberal for the early 1940s. Years later, I published the first volume of it.

My notable library endeavors, however, catapulted me into becoming a sexologist and a sex therapist. My friends and relatives, hearing that I was studying sex, love, and marriage so intently, started to ask me how they could deal with their personal problems in these important areas. To my surprise, I was able to give them some good answers. In one or a few (unpaid) sessions of avid and often highly intimate conversation, I dispelled their ignorance, gave them realistic suggestions, relieved their anxiety, and helped a number of them to lead happier sexual, marital, and love lives.

My subjects and I both benefited. I discovered much additional sex-love information, and I greatly enjoyed doing this kind of counseling, so much so that at twenty-seven I founded the Love and Marriage Problems Institute, devoted to helping and researching sexual, marital, and love difficulties. The problem was, I had no status in the field, so my lawyer for my first divorce strongly advised me to get some. At that time, graduate schooling in sex therapy and even in marriage and family therapy did not exist. The closest thing to it was a Ph.D. degree in clinical psychology. I applied for that. But because my bachelor's degree was in business administration, which I took to make money and support myself as a writer, I had trouble getting into graduate school at NYU and Columbia. I did so well in taking three trial courses during the summer term at Columbia, however, that they broke down and let me enroll in the clinical psychology program at Teachers College in the fall of 1942.

A piece of cake! Within a year, by not letting Teachers College know that I was working full-time, I received my M.A. with honors and was soon matriculated for a Ph.D. degree. There came a hitch, however! When it was time to work on my doctoral dissertation, I had the good sense to avoid doing one on any overtly sexual subject; that would have been verboten. So I thought I skirted this ticklish issue by doing one on *The Love Emotions of College-Level Women*. At first everything went well and I was about to write up my interesting data on this subject when—wham!—Teachers College, most unusually, forced me to attend a special seminar that would decide whether my topic was acceptable.

All thirteen members of the clinical psychology department then got together with the provost of the college. The provost? I didn't realize that we even had one until my main adviser told me that we definitely did—for administrative but not academic purposes. He never sat in on a thesis seminar, but this time he had heard about my topic, was afraid that the Hearst newspapers would make a federal case out of it, and called this special seminar to see if I was to be allowed to polish it off.

Undaunted, I presented my research to the assembled professors and the provost, they politely listened, and then voted twelve to two in my favor. They agreed that I had a great topic, that I was a fine person and a scholar, and that I was proceeding scientifically with my study. Marvelous! But as my adviser, Professor Goodwin Watson, sadly told me, the two (anonymous) dissenters were going to adamantly oppose this and *any* dissertation on love·that I could come up with. They would be sure to show up at my final thesis orals and knock me for a loop, no matter *what* I did.

Well, that ended that. Not being a whiner and wanting my degree, I picked another topic that had nothing to do with love, sex, or marriage, and quickly polished off a safe, highly statistical dissertation,

A Comparison of the Use of Direct and Indirect Phrasing in Personality Questionnaires, which was nicely accepted. My poor orphaned thesis on love? I turned it into seven pioneering articles on the subject, which I published in several psychological and sociological journals. So I fixed Teachers College.

Soon after this I began writing on sex with a vengeance. By 1954 I had published no fewer than forty-six articles on sex, love, and marriage, in addition to two books and two anthologies. I was also the American editor of the pioneering *International Journal of Sexology.* I had a wide psychotherapy practice and specialized in seeing hundreds of clients with sex, love, and marital problems.

Although I was well known in the psychology profession as a sexologist in the 1950s, my public fame mushroomed in the early 1960s when several of my books appeared in paperback and became bestsellers. Thus, millions of copies were sold—and more millions borrowed from libraries—of my books *Sex Without Guilt, The Art and Science of Love, The Intelligent Woman's Guide to Man-Hunting, Sex and the Single Man,* and *Nymphomania: A Study of the Oversexed Woman.* Although at this time my name was not exactly, like Kinsey's, a household word, my books were avidly read as well as bought while his were widely bought and not read. Thirty years later, I still meet many individuals who enthusiastically tell me that they were first catapulted into enjoyable and guiltless sex by reading my books. I think that I can say without immodesty that the sexual revolution of that decade was largely sparked by the writings of Kinsey and Ellis.

All this notoriety at first did me little good professionally. To be sure, I received many referrals for sex therapy from psychologists and sexologists whom I had never met and who knew about me only from my publications. But I also received much opposition from professionals who were against popular writings by psychologists and who therefore hated my guts.

The opposition to my work as a sexologist also significantly spilled over into my reputation as a theorist and practitioner of psychotherapy. In 1955 I started to do Rational Emotive Behavior Therapy, the pioneering form of cognitive-behavior therapy, and since then I have spent the majority of my time as a therapist, writer, and workshop presenter dealing with general psychotherapy, not just with sex therapy. But my reputation as a sexologist followed me into the general field of therapy, and I have often been savagely criticized for my "controversial"—meaning, largely sexual—perspectives.

Even friends and associates who follow much of my therapeutic teachings have often tried to induce me to tone down my sexual writings and presentations. Thus, Rollo May, who used to send me his "difficult clients" for REBT when he practiced in New York in the 1950s and 1960s, opposed my becoming president of the American Academy of Psychotherapists because I was "too controversial." And many other "respectable" psychologists have used my therapeutic teachings without giving me due credit, or have even gone out of their way to criticize me largely because of my reputation as a liberal sexologist.

Some other prominent sexologists have also vigorously opposed my sexual liberalism and widespread popular publications on sex. My good friend Hans Lehfeldt, who helped me found the Society for the Scientific Study of Sex in the 1950s, opposed my being nominated as its first president because he felt that I was "too controversial." Fortunately for me, the other members of our board of directors, including Harry Benjamin and Henry Guze, did not go along with Hans. So I was renominated and elected.

In spite of this kind of opposition, I continued to absorb myself in the field of sexology as well as psychotherapy, largely because I took my own counsel as a therapist and firmly taught myself that it is great to be loved and approved by other people, including members of one's own profession, but that it is far from necessary. This is one of the main tenets of REBT. Without following it myself, I might well have given up being a sexologist and merely have stayed with the safer aspects of psychotherapy and counseling. On the other hand, clinical sexology definitely has its rewarding aspects, which kept me interested in working within it despite the disadvantages it also entailed. Let me mention some of the rewards that I have found by being absorbed in it for over half a century.

First, sexology is the science of sexuality. I greatly enjoy the discovery aspect of science. Thus, in 1943, I was doing a term paper for a clinical psychology class on the various "causes" of homosexual behavior when I accidentally discovered that most hermaphrodites whose sexual direction was known were heterosexual in spite of their physiological and hormonal anomalies. This led me to publish my first scientific paper, "The Sexual Psychology of Human Hermaphrodites," which appeared in *Psychosomatic Medicine* and created quite a stir. It showed that although the power or strength of the human sex drive is strongly influenced by biological factors, its direction is largely influenced by familial and cultural teachings.

This was a very exciting discovery; I enjoyed the article's being cited in a great many articles and books, and its influence on the work of some other outstanding sexologists, including Harry Benjamin and John Money. Almost any kind of discovery—including artistic, political, and economic findings—can be uplifting. Of course, this also goes for sexological discovery.

Second, I have always found that my absorption in clinical sexology has important practical aspects. From my earliest consultations with my friends and relatives to my later sessions with thousands of clients and my writings for therapists and the public, I have apparently helped innumerable people with their sexual, love, and marriage problems, and others in general. This has been, and still is, most gratifying. The hundreds of voluntary endorsements that I have received from readers in every major country in the world have been especially satisfying. Conveying my knowledge to these people has often produced splendid results.

Third, I have personally benefited from my sexological findings. As noted above, not only did I overcome my own guilt and shame about sex largely as a result of my reading—not from conversations with mentors or therapists—but I also tackled some of my own problems, such as the fast ejaculation that I was plagued with early in my life, and significantly helped myself through my sex research. In addition, I helped quite a number of my sex and love partners to decrease their anxiety and increase their pleasure. And that has been great!

If I had my life to live over again, I would still choose the field of sexology as one of my major pursuits. I have always disagreed with Freud's notion that sexual problems, including incestuous thoughts and actions, are the major causes of general emotional problems such as anxiety, depression, self-deprecation, and rage—one of the causes or contributions, yes, but hardly the only one. On the contrary, as I have said for several decades, general human disturbance is much more likely to lead to sexual disturbance than vice versa. The two actually tend to be interactional.

Humans, as I keep preaching in REBT, are both born and reared to be easily disturbed, and their emotional and behavioral disorders are both nonsexual and sexual. The solutions to their problems, moreover, are complex and involve a number of important cognitive, emotive, and behavioral insights and methods. But sex is an exceptionally important aspect, and anything that we can do to minimize its disorders and enhance its fulfillment is meaningful and of great consequence.

The twentieth century has so far been the outstanding period of general psychotherapy and of sex therapy. In the latter area we have the pioneering findings and ideas of a number of unusual scholars and clinicians, including Havelock Ellis, Alfred Kinsey and his associates, William Masters and Virginia Johnson, Joseph LoPiccolo, and many others. I am delighted to have been on friendly terms with and worked with these pioneering sexologists, and to have made some significant contributions myself.

I will now risk mentioning what I consider my main contributions to the field of sex, love, and marriage:

1. I was probably the first prominent psychologist to unequivocally point out that masturbation is not only not harmful and shameful, but that it is actually beneficial for most people.
2. I was one of the few psychologists in the 1940s and 1950s who told my clients and members of the public that mutually consenting premarital sex for adults, when engaged in with proper precautions for sexually transmitted diseases and pregnancy, are not necessarily bad or immoral and can enhance one's sexual life and life in general.
3. I vigorously opposed the idea that unconventional sex behavior is perverse or deviational, and proposed that sexual "abnormality" is usually a myth.
4. I was a pioneering supporter of feminism, and in particular showed women how they could be assertive and not aggressive.
5. I was one of the few psychologists who strongly advocated gay liberation in the early 1950s and was made an honorary member of the Mattachine Society.
6. Along with Kinsey, and against Freud and his orthodox followers, I disputed the sacredness of the so-called vaginal orgasm in women and showed both sexes how women could achieve satisfactory noncoital orgasm and still be very healthy and "normal".
7. I originated the idea of establishing the Society for the Scientific Study of Sexuality in 1950, but at first failed to enlist enough support for it. Persisting, and with the aid of Hans Lehfeldt, Robert Sherwin, Harry Benjamin, and Henry Guze, I actually got it going a few years later. It now flourishes.

I am proud of these sexological advocacies and accomplishments, but I was hardly alone in fighting for them, as I had other solid sexologists with me—such as Harry Benjamin, G. Lombard Kelly, and Alfred Kinsey. All of us, and many other researchers and clinicians, are steadily making the field of sexology a highly vital and respectable area of science. Let us continue our healthy efforts!

PART II

Rational Self-Help

Introduction to Part II

The following ten articles cover Ellis's thinking on a wide range of individual problems. His approach to self-help comes out of his own clinical experience with individuals and groups in Rational Emotive Behavior Therapy. While there are many different ways that people can change their own irrational beliefs, it may be instructive for readers to have a brief outline of how current REBT works with an REBT therapist or counselor. In general, this is a summary of the process you'd go through if you did REBT under the guidance of a professional psychotherapist.

1. Focus on one specific upsetting emotion at a time. For example, if you are both angry at your boss and anxious about your job, choose one of these to work on first.

2. Separate your practical problems from your emotional disturbances *about* the practical problems. REBT can help you fix, or deal more effectively with, your practical problems, but it first helps you with your emotional problems *about* your practical ones.

3. Once you've chosen a single emotional problem to work on, very carefully begin to sort out your negative emotions about it. Usually, they will be a mixture of healthy negative emotions about the problem (which are self-helping and appropriate, even though they may be unpleasant) and unhealthy, unhelpful emotions. For example, if you lose a good job because of a mistake you made, you might simultaneously feel two kinds of emotions about the loss. You might feel healthily disappointed and regretful over the job loss and your mistake. Even though these certainly aren't pleasurable feelings, they'd still motivate you to look for another job and improve your work efforts. You might also feel depressed, however. REBT would consider this an unhealthy negative emotion, because it usually hinders you from achieving your goals.

4. Assess A—your adversity, or "activating event," more precisely. What particular aspect of losing your job leads you to feel depressed? Is it the possibility of not being able to find another good job, or the fact that you were responsible for making such a bad mistake?

5. Once you've precisely identified the A (activating event) and the C (unhealthy emotional consequence), you can check whether you have any "secondary disturbances" about your C. For example, are you guilty about being so depressed? If so, it often helps to attack these "secondary consequences" first.

6. Once you've chosen a specific C to work on, it's time to identify the irrational beliefs (IBs), with which *you* largely create your own C. After any unpleasant activating event, normally people believe both RBs (rational beliefs) and IBs when they evaluate it. The RBs are usually preferences or desires. For example, "I really wish I hadn't gotten fired. I really sabotaged myself by screwing up. It will be much harder to get what I want out of life with a lesser job." These kinds of preferences would normally lead to healthy, self-helping negative emotions, which don't feel pleasant but which appropriately motivate you to improve your situation.

   On the other hand, humans also create IBs from their own RBs by turning these rational preferences into demands. Therefore, look for your own *musts, shoulds,* and *demands.* "It's horrible that I lost that great job (*as I shouldn't have!*), and I absolutely should have never behaved so badly. I'll never be able to survive without that great job (which I must *have!*)."

7. At point D, Dispute your IB's over and over again until you convince yourself that they really are false, illogical, and self-defeating, and you succeed in replacing them with appropriate RBs. Whenever you succeed in changing one of your "musts" back into a "want," you'll feel a palpable shift in your emotions. For example, you'll feel your self-paralyzing feeling of depression viscerally change into one of self-motivating disappointment. When this happens, quickly make a note of how you made the change so you'll be able to do it again.

8. Once you have one of your IBs on the ropes, *don't let up.* Ordinarily, you'll tend to relapse and slide back periodically. Accept that this is an unfortunate part of human nature and work against "putting yourself down" for having this human weakness, or "awfulizing" about it. Use a broad arsenal of cognitive,

emotive, and behavioral strategies to attack your irrational evaluations and develop a new more effective philosophy about the A.

9. Try to generalize your effective new rational philosophy (E), to other adversities in your life.

Readers will quickly discover that this definitely isn't a one-shot cure, but rather a life-long discipline, like physical exercise and healthy nutrition. But it is a skill that you get better at with time and practice. If you can finally succeed in gaining relief from one spell of emotional turmoil or paralysis by using REBT on yourself, you'll begin to "feel the groove" and make the connection, in your own mind, between your beliefs and your emotions. The process then becomes easier to repeat as other problems come up.

—SHAWN BLAU

10

Rational Psychotherapy

This is the first major paper on Rational Emotive Behavior Therapy, presented at the Annual Convention of the American Psychological Association in Chicago, on August 31, 1956. I had already given briefer versions to psychological meetings in New York in 1955 and had finished writing *How to Live With a "Neurotic"* in the same year. I had also written two articles on REBT for the *Journal of Clinical Psychology* and published them in 1957, but this paper, because of publication delay, was not published in the *Journal of General Psychology* until early in 1958.

Shortly thereafter, REBT really got going among psychologists. I received many worldwide requests for reprints of this paper, and it was cited widely in the literature. Famous therapists like Rudolf Dreikurs and Hans Eysenck endorsed it. Many practitioners urged me to give talks and workshops and to lend them recordings of REBT sessions—which I did. The American Academy of Psychotherapists featured it as one of the main forms of psychotherapies. In 1959, the Institute for Rational Living—later to be called the Albert Ellis Institute for Rational Emotive Behavior Therapy—was incorporated as a nonprofit corporation to promote its messages to the profession and the public. REBT was well on its way!

This paper is pioneering and innovative in several ways. It clearly states, for one of the first times, that thinking, feeling, and behaving are not disparate but are closely related and integrated; it views them holistically, and interrelatedly. It emphasizes, at a time when therapists were mainly obsessed with feelings, the vast importance of cognition in the creation and treatment of psychological disturbance. It specifically describes twelve common irrational beliefs involved in emotional and behavioral upsets and how they can be alleviated with rational beliefs. It shows how psychoanalytic explanations superficially focus on secondary "causes" of disturbances and miss most of the primary philosophic causes. It indicates how important irrational beliefs are in creating disturbances about disturbances. It stresses the acquired and innate tendency of people to insist, necessitize, and "musturbate," and thereby create much of their emotional upsets. It clearly takes the constructivist position that people have the ability to look at their own disturbed thinking, feeling, and behaving, and to proactively change them. It states that disturbed people can make a profound philosophical change, and not merely alleviate their presenting symptoms but also prevent their acquiring new symptoms. It emphasizes cognitive methods of therapy, but also includes eclectic emotive and behavioral techniques, and makes REBT truly integrative. It anticipates a postmodern approach to psychotherapy by showing that disturbance is largely accompanied by absolutistic, dogmatic, rigid, necessitizing goals and attitudes, and that emotional health involves flexibility, seeking alternatives, and unperfectionistic wishing rather than demanding. It stresses the importance of treating each disturbed person individually in accordance with his or her leanings and proclivities.

REBT has grown and developed over the last forty-two years and has added many theories and practices to those described in this paper. But it was obviously ahead of its time when I gave this first major presentation on it in 1956, and in some respects it still is!

The central theme of this paper is that psychotherapists can help their clients to live the most self-fulfilling, creative, and emotionally satisfying lives by teaching them to organize and discipline their thinking. Does this mean that *all* human emotion and creativity can or should be controlled by reason and intellect? Not exactly.

The human being may be said to possess four basic processes—perception, movement, thinking, and emotion—all of which are interrelated. Thus, thinking, aside from consisting of bioelectric changes in the brain cells, and in addition to comprising remembering, learning, problem-solving, and similar psychological processes, is sensory, motor, and emotional. Then, instead of saying, "Jones thinks about this puzzle," we can more accurately say, "Jones perceives-moves-feels-*thinks* about this puzzle." Because, however, Jones's activity in relation to the puzzle may be *largely* focused upon solving it, and only *incidentally* on seeing, manipulating, and emoting about it, we may perhaps justifiably emphasize only his thinking.

Like thinking and the sensori-motor processes, we can define emotion as an exceptionally complex state of human reaction which is integrally related to all the other perception and response processes. It is not *one* thing, but a combination and holistic integration of several seemingly diverse, yet actually closely related, phenomena.

Normally, emotion arises from direct stimulation of the cells in the hypothalamus and autonomic nervous system (e.g., by electrical or chemical stimulation) or from indirect excitation via sensori-motor, cognitive, and other cognitive processes. Therefore, it may theoretically be controlled in four major ways. If you are highly excitable and wish to calm down, you can: take electroshock or drug treatments; use soothing baths or relaxation techniques; seek someone you love and quiet down for his or her sake; reason yourself into a state of healthy feeling by showing yourself how silly it is for you to remain under- or overemotional.

Although biophysical, sensori-motor, and emotive techniques are legitimate methods of controlling emotional disturbances, they will not be considered here. Cognitive techniques will be emphasized. Rational psychotherapy is based on the assumption that thought and emotion are not two entirely different processes but significantly overlap in many respects, and therefore disordered emotions can often (though not always) be ameliorated by changing one's thinking.

In other words, a large part of what we call emotion is nothing more or less than a certain kind of thinking—biased, prejudiced, or strongly evaluative. What we usually label as thinking is a relatively calm and dispassionate appraisal (or organized perception) of a given situation, an objective comparison of many of the elements in the situation, and a coming to some conclusion as a result of this comparing or discriminating process. Thus, a thinking person may observe a piece of bread, see that one part of it is moldy, remember that eating this kind of mold previously made him ill, and cut off the moldy part and eat only the nonmoldy section of the bread.

A highly emotional individual, on the other hand, may observe the same piece of bread and remember her previous experience with the moldy part so violently that she will quickly throw away the whole piece of bread and therefore go hungry. Because the thinking person is relatively calm, she uses the maximum information available to her—namely, that moldy bread is bad, but nonmoldy bread is good. Because the emotional person is relatively excited, she may use only part of the available information—namely, that moldy bread is completely bad.

It is hypothesized, then, that thinking and emoting are closely interrelated and at times differ mainly in that thinking is a more tranquil, less somatically involved (or at least perceived), and a less activity-directed mode of discrimination than is emotion. It is also hypothesized that among adult humans raised in a social culture, thinking and emoting are so closely interrelated that they usually accompany each other, act in a circular cause-and-effect relationship, and in certain respects are essentially the same thing, so that one's thinking becomes one's emotion and emoting becomes one's thought. It is finally hypothesized that since humans are uniquely sign-, symbol-, and language-creating animals, both thinking and emoting often take the form of self-talk or internalized sentences, and that, for all practical purposes, the ideas that human beings keep telling themselves *are* or *become* their thoughts and emotions.

This is not to say that emotion can under no circumstances exist without thought. It probably can, but then it tends to exist momentarily, and isn't to be sustained. For instance, an individual steps on your toe, and you spontaneously, immediately become angry. Or you hear a piece of music and you instantly begin to feel warm and excited. Or you learn that a close friend has died and quickly feel sadness. Under these circumstances, you experience emotion without doing any concomitant thinking. Probably, however, you do, with split-second rapidity, start thinking, "This person who stepped on my toe is an idiot!" or, "This music is wonderful!" or, "Oh, how awful it is that my friend died!"

In any event, assuming that you don't have any conscious thought accompanying your emotion at the very beginning, it appears to be difficult to *sustain* an emotional outburst without bolstering it by repeated ideas. For unless you keep telling yourself something on the order of, "This person who stepped on my toe is an idiot!" or, "How could he do a horrible thing like that to me!" the pain of having your toe stepped on will soon die, and your immediate reaction will die with the pain. Of course, you can keep getting your toe stepped on, and the continuing pain may sustain your anger. But assuming that your physical sensation stops, your emotional feeling, in order to last, normally has to be bolstered by some kind of thinking.

We say "normally" because it is theoretically possible for your emotional circuits, once they have been made to reverberate by some physical or psychological stimulus, to keep reverberating under their own power. It is also theoretically possible for drugs or electrical impulses to keep acting directly on your brain and automatic nervous system, and thereby keep you emotionally aroused. Usually, however, these types of continued direct stimulation of the emotion-producing centers are limited largely to unusual conditions.

It would appear, then, that positive human emotions, such as feelings of love or elation, are often associated with or result from thoughts, or internalized sentences, stated in some form or variation of the phrase, "This is good!" and that negative human emotions, such as anger or depression, are frequently associated with or result from thoughts or sentences that are stated in some form or variation of the phrase, "This is bad!" Without adults employing such thoughts and sentences on some conscious or unconscious level, much of their emoting would simply not exist.

If the hypothesis that sustained human emotion often results from or is directly associated with human thinking and self-verbalization is true, then important corollaries about the origin and perpetuation of states of emotional disturbance, or neurosis, may be drawn. For neurosis would appear to be disordered, over- or underintensified, uncontrollable emotion, and this would seem to be the result of illogical, unrealistic, irrational, inflexible, and childish thinking.

That neurotic or emotionally disturbed behavior is illogical and irrational would seem to be almost definitional, for if we define it otherwise, and label as neurotic *all* incompetent and ineffectual behavior, we will be including actions of truly stupid and incompetent individuals, for example, those who are mentally deficient or brain injured. Therefore, the concept of neurosis only becomes meaningful, when we assume that disturbed people are *not* deficient or impaired, but theoretically capable of behaving in a more mature, controlled, and flexible manner than they actually behave. If, however, neurotics are essentially individuals who act significantly below their own potential level of behaving, or who defeat their own ends though theoretically capable of achieving them, it would appear that they behave in an illogical, irrational, unrealistic way. Neurosis, in other words, consists of stupid behavior by a nonstupid person.

Assuming that emotionally disturbed individuals act in irrational and illogical ways, the questions that are therapeutically relevant are: How do they originally get to be illogical? How do they keep perpetuating their irrational thinking? How can they be helped to be less illogical and neurotic?

Unfortunately, most of the good thinking that has been done in regard to therapy during the past sixty years, especially by Sigmund Freud and his chief followers, has concerned itself with the first of these questions rather than the second and third. The assumption has often been made that if psychotherapists discover and effectively communicate to their clients the main reasons why the clients originally became disturbed, they will thereby also discover how their neuroses are being perpetuated and how they can be helped to overcome them. This is a dubious proposition.

Knowing exactly how people originally learned to behave illogically by no means tells us how they *maintain* their illogical behavior, or what they can do to change it. This is particularly true because people are often afflicted with secondary as well as primary neuroses, and the two may differ significantly. Thus, a man may originally become disturbed because he discovers that he has strong death wishes involving his father and (quite illogically) thinks he should be blamed and punished for having them. Consequently, he may develop some neurotic symptom, such as a phobia against dogs, because dogs remind him of his father, who is an ardent hunter.

Later on, this individual may grow to love or be indifferent to his father, or his father may act better and be no more of a problem to him. His fear of dogs, however, may remain: not because, as some theorists would insist, they still remind him of his old death wishes, but because he now hates himself for having the original neurotic symptom. He may also think that he behaves so stupidly and illogically in relation to dogs that every time he thinks of them his self-hatred so severely upsets him that he cannot reason clearly and combat his illogical fear.

In terms of self-verbalization, this neurotic individual is first saying to himself: "I hate my father—and this is awful!" But he ends up by saying: "I have an irrational fear of dogs—and this is awful!" Even though both sets of self-verbalizations reveal neurotic behavior and his secondary neurosis may be as bad as or worse than his primary one, the two can hardly be said to be the same. Consequently, helping this individual gain insight into the origins of his primary neurosis will not necessarily help him understand and overcome his perpetuating, or secondary, neurotic reactions.

If the hypotheses so far stated have some validity, the psychotherapist's main goals can be those of demonstrating to clients that their self-verbalizations have been and still are the prime source of their emotional disturbances. Clients need to be shown that their internalized beliefs are illogical and unrealistic at certain critical points and that they have the ability to control their emotions by creating more rational and less self-defeating beliefs.

Effective therapists can help to unmask their clients' past and especially, present illogical thinking or self-defeating verbalizations by: bringing these to their attention or consciousness; showing clients how they are causing and maintaining their disturbance and unhappiness; demonstrating exactly what the illogical links in their internalized beliefs are; and teaching them how to rethink and reverbalize these beliefs in a more logical self-helping way. Moreover, before the end of the therapeutic relationship, the therapist cannot only deal concretely with clients' specific illogical thinking, but can also demonstrate what, in general, are the main irrational ideas that human beings are prone to follow and what more rational philosophies of living can be substituted for them. Otherwise, the client who is released from one specific set of illogical notions may well wind up falling victim to another set.

In other words, it is hypothesized that human beings tend to fall victim to several major fallacious ideas; they tend to keep reindoctrinating themselves over and over again with these ideas in an unthinking, autosuggestive manner; and consequently they keep actualizing them in overt behavior. Some of these irrational ideas are, as the Freudians have pointed out, instilled by people's parents during childhood and are tenaciously clung to because of their attachment to the parents and because the ideas were ingrained before later and more rational modes of thinking were given a chance to gain a foothold. However, many of them, as the Freudians have not always been careful to note, are also instilled by the mass media in our culture. And many of the irrational "musts" that children add to the standards their parents teach them are creatively invented by the children themselves.

What are some of the major illogical ideas or philosophies which, when originally held and later perpetuated by men and women in our civilization, frequently lead to self-defeat and neurosis? I will list a few:

1. The idea that it is a dire necessity for you to be loved or approved by significant others instead of concentrating on your own self-respect, winning approval for practical purposes (such as job advancement), and loving rather than being loved.

2. The idea that certain acts are wrong, wicked, or villainous, and that people who perform such acts must be damned and punished—instead of the idea that certain acts are inappropriate or antisocial, and that people who perform such acts had better be restrained, but not damned.

3. The idea that it is terrible, horrible, and catastrophic when things are not the way they "must" be—instead of the idea that it is too bad when things are not the way you would *like* them to be, and that you should certainly try to change or control conditions so that they become more satisfactory, but if changing or controlling uncomfortable situations is impossible, you had better accept their existence and stop telling yourself how awful they are.

4. The idea that unpleasant conditions must not exist and that when they do, they directly cause human disturbance—instead of the idea that much human unhappiness is caused or sustained by the view you take of things rather than the things themselves.

5. The idea that if something is or may be dangerous or fearsome, you must be terribly anxious about it—instead of the idea that if something is or may be dangerous or fearsome, you can frankly face it and try to render it nondangerous, and when that is impossible, think of other things and stop telling yourself it absolutely *must* not exist.

6. The idea that hassles *must* not exist, and that it is easier to avoid than to face life difficulties and self-responsibilities—instead of the idea that in the long run the so-called easy way is almost invariably much harder, and that it is best to solve difficult problems by facing them squarely.

7. The idea that you need something or someone stronger or greater than yourself on which to rely—instead of the idea that it is usually far better to stand on your own feet and gain faith in yourself and your ability to meet the difficult circumstances of living.

8. The idea that you should be thoroughly competent, adequate, intelligent, and achieving in all possible respects—instead of the idea that you had better *do* rather than always need to do *well*, and that you can accept yourself as a quite imperfect creature who has general human limitations and specific fallibilities.

9. The idea that because something once strongly affected your life it should affect it indefinitely—instead of the idea that you can learn from your past experiences but not be overly attached to or prejudiced by them.

10. The idea that others *must* not act the way they do and that you have to change them to act as you would like them to—instead of the idea that other people's deficiencies are largely *their* problems and that demanding that they change is unlikely to help them do so.

11. The idea that human happiness can be achieved by inertia and inaction—instead of the idea that humans tend to be happiest when they are actively and vitally absorbed in creative pursuits, or when they are devoting themselves to people or projects outside themselves.

12. The idea that you have virtually no control over your emotions and that you cannot help feeling certain things—instead of the idea that you have enormous control over your emotions if you choose to work at controlling them.

Once you believe the kind of nonsense included in illogical ideas, you will tend to become inhibited, hostile, defensive, guilty, anxious, ineffective, inert, uncontrolled, or depressed. If, on the other hand, you become thoroughly released from all fundamental kinds of illogical thinking, you would find it exceptionally difficult to become too emotionally upset, or at least to sustain your disturbance for very long.

Does this mean that all the other so-called basic causes of neurosis, such as the Oedipus complex or severe maternal rejection in childhood, are invalid, and that the Freudian and other psychodynamic thinkers have been barking up the wrong tree? Not at all. It only means that these psychodynamic thinkers have been emphasizing secondary causes or results of emotional disturbances rather than truly prime causes.

Let us take, for example, an individual who, when he is young, acquires a full-blown Oedipus complex, that is to say, he lusts after his mother, hates his father, is guilty about his sex desires for his mother, and is afraid that his father is going to castrate him. When he is a child, this person will presumably be disturbed. But if he develops none of the basic illogical and unrealistic ideas we have been discussing, it will be very difficult for him to remain disturbed. For, as an adult, this individual will not be too concerned if his parents or others do not approve all his actions, since he will be more interested in his *own* self-respect than in *their* approval. He will not believe that his lust for his mother is wicked or villainous, but will accept it as a normal part of being a limited human whose sexual desires may easily be indiscriminate. He will realize that the actual danger of his father castrating him is exceptionally slight. He will not feel that because he was once afraid of his Oedipal feelings he should remain so forever. If he still feels it would be improper for him to have sexual relations with his mother, instead of castigating himself for even thinking of such relations, he will merely resolve not to carry his desires into practice and will stick to his resolve. If, by chance, he weakens and actually has incestuous relations, he will again refuse to denigrate himself mercilessly for being weak, but will keep showing himself how self-defeating his behavior is and will actively work at changing it. Under these circumstances, if this individual has a truly logical and realistic approach to life in general, and to the problem of Oedipal feelings in particular, how can he possibly remain disturbed about his Oedipal attachment?

By way of further illustration, take the case of a man who, as a child, is continually criticized by his parents, consequently feels himself loathsome and inadequate, refuses to tackle difficult tasks for fear of failing, and therefore comes to hate himself more. Such a person will be seriously disturbed. But would it be possible for him to sustain his disturbance if he began to think in a truly logical manner about himself and his behavior? Not according to REBT. For, if this man does use a consistent rational approach to his own behavior, he will stop caring too much about what others think of him and will start caring about what he thinks of himself. Consequently, he will stop avoiding difficult tasks and, instead of punishing himself for being incompetent when he makes a mistake, will say to himself: "Now this is not the right way to do things; let me stop and figure out a better way." Or: "There's no doubt that I made a mistake this time; now let me see how I can benefit from it."

If he is thinking straight, this man will not blame his defeats on external events, but will realize that he himself is largely causing them by his illogical or impractical behavior. He will not believe that it is easier to avoid facing difficult things, but will realize that the so-called easy way is usually the harder and more idiotic one. He will not think that he needs something greater or stronger than himself to help him, but will independently buckle down to difficult tasks himself. He will not feel that because he once defeated himself by avoiding doing things the hard way that he must always do so.

With this kind of logical thinking, how could an originally disturbed person possibly maintain and continually revivify her neurosis? Not easily! Similarly, the spoiled brat, the worrywart, the egomaniac, the frightened stay-at-home—all of these disturbed individuals would have the devil of a time indefinitely prolonging their disturbances if they did not continue to believe utter nonsense, namely, the kinds of basic irrational postulates previously listed.

Neurosis, then, usually seems to originate in and be perpetuated by some fundamentally unsound, irrational ideas. People come to believe in some unrealistic, impossible, often perfectionistic goals—especially, that they should always be approved of by everyone, should do everything perfectly well, and should never be frustrated in any of their desires—and then, in spite of contradictory evidence, they refuse to give up their original illogical beliefs.

Some neurotic philosophies, such as the idea that people should be taken care of, are not entirely inappropriate to their childhood state but are quite inappropriate to adulthood. Many of their irrational ideas are specifically taught by their parents and culture, and most of them also seem to be held by the great majority of adults in our society—who theoretically should have been weaned from them as they chronologically matured but never were. Let us not forget that the neurotics we are considering are often statistically normal, or that ours is a generally neuroticizing culture, in which most people are more or less emotionally disturbed because they are raised to believe arrant nonsense that often leads them to become ineffective, self-defeating, and disturbed. Nonetheless, it is not absolutely necessary that humans believe the irrational notions which most of them seem to believe today, and the task of psychotherapy is to wean them from their negative ideas and change their unrealistic and illogical ideas, and to change their self-sabotaging attitudes.

This is the task that rational therapists accept. REBT clinicians believe that most therapeutic techniques show the client that they are unrealistic and illogical and how they originally became so. However, therapists often fail to show how clients presently think crookedly and what they can do to change by building rational philosophies of living and applying them to the practical problems of everyday life. Where most therapists directly or indirectly show the clients that they are behaving irrationally, the rational therapist goes beyond this point to dispute the clients' general and specific irrational ideas and tries to induce them to adopt more rational ones in their place.

REBT makes a concerted attack on the disturbed individual's irrational positions in two main ways. First, the therapist serves as a frank counterpropagandist who directly contradicts and denies the self-defeating propaganda and superstitions clients have originally learned and are now self-propagandistically perpetuating. Even more importantly, the REBT therapist teaches clients how to do their own scientific disputing of their irrational beliefs. Second, the therapist encourages and persuades clients to partake of some kind of activity that itself will act as a forceful counterpropaganda agent against the nonsense they believe. Both of these main therapeutic activities are consciously performed with one goal in mind: that of finally getting clients to internalize a rational philosophy of living just as they originally learned and internalized the illogical musts and superstitions of their early years.

It is the therapist's function not merely to show them that they have these ideas or thinking processes, but to persuade them to change and substitute more rational thought processes for them. If, because clients are exceptionally disturbed when they first come to therapy and need to be approached in a supportive manner, and sometimes be encouraged to vent their feeling in free association, abreaction, role-playing, or other expressive techniques, that may be all to the good. But the therapist understands that these relationship-building and expressive-emotive techniques rarely get to the core of clients' illogical thinking and induce them to think in a more rational manner.

Occasionally clients may come to see, through relationship and emotive-expressive methods, that they are acting self-defeatingly and may resolve to change. More often than not, however, their irrational thinking will be so ingrained from constant self-repetitions, and will be so inculcated in motor pathways (or habit patterns) by the time they come for therapy, that simply showing them, even by direct interpretation, that they are irrational will not greatly help. They will often say to the therapist, "All right, now I understand that I have castration fears and that they are unrealistic. But I still feel afraid of my father."

The therapist, therefore, had better keep disputing the beliefs that underlie clients' fears. She can show clients that they are horrified not of their father, but of being blamed, disapproved of, unloved, imperfect, or a failure. And such extreme fears are thoroughly irrational because: being disapproved is not half so terrible as we think it is; no one can be thoroughly blameless or perfect; people who worry about being blamed or disapproved of are essentially putting themselves at the mercy of the opinion of others, over whom they have no real control; being blamed or disapproved of has nothing essentially to do with our opinion of ourselves.

If the therapist merely tackles a man's sexual fears and shows how ridiculous they are, what is to prevent this individual's showing up a year or two later with some other irrational fear—such as the fear of public speaking? But if the therapist tackles the client's basic irrational thinking, which underlies many kinds of fear he may have, he is unlikely to turn up with a new neurotic symptom some months or years hence. For once an individual truly surrenders ideas of perfectionism, the horror of failing at something, the dire need to be approved of by others, the notion that the world owes him a living, and so on, what else is there for him to be irrationally disturbed about? Not much!

The practitioner of REBT, then, is a frank teacher who believes wholeheartedly in a most rigorous application of the rules of logic, straight thinking, and scientific method to everyday life, and who ruthlessly uncovers vestiges of irrational thinking in clients' experience and energetically urges them into more rational channels. In so doing, REBT does not ignore or eradicate the clients' emotions. On the contrary, it considers them most seriously and helps change them, when they are disordered and self-defeating, through the same means by which they commonly arise in the first place, that is, by thinking and acting. By exerting consistent interpretive and philosophic encouragement of clients to change their thinking, experiences, and actions, the REBT therapist gives a specific impetus to their movement toward mental health.

Can therapy be effectively done, then, with *all* clients mainly through logical analysis and reconstruction? Alas, no. For one thing, many clients are not bright enough to follow a rigorously rational analysis. For another thing, some individuals are so emotionally disturbed by the time they come for help that they are, at least temporarily, in no position to comprehend and follow sensible procedures. Still other clients are too old and inflexible; too young and impressionable; too philosophically prejudiced against logic and reason; too organically or biophysically deficient to accept, at least at the start of therapy, rational analysis.

In consequence, the therapist who employs only logical reconstruction in his therapeutic armamentarium is not likely to get too far with many of those who seek his help. Therefore, it is vitally important that any therapist who has a rational approach to the problem of helping clients overcome their neuroses also be eclectic in his use of supplementary, less direct, and sometimes less rational techniques.

Admitting that REBT is not effective with all types of clients, and that it is most helpful when used in conjunction with other widely employed therapeutic techniques, I would like to conclude with two challenging hypotheses: first, that psychotherapy that includes a high dosage of rational analysis and reconstruction will prove to be more effective with more types of clients than any of the nonrational or semirational therapies now being widely employed; and second, that a considerable amount of REBT will prove to be virtually the only type of treatment that helps to undermine the basic disturbances (as distinguished from the superficial symptoms) of many clients, and particularly of many with whom other types of therapy have already been shown to be ineffective.

11

Psychotherapy and the Value of a Human Being

I began to read the writings of Robert S. Hartman in 1960 and found that he was a unique philosopher of human value. A professor of philosophy as well as a business consultant, he had some of the best arguments in favor of unconditional self-acceptance, and I used some of them in REBT, along with an existential outlook, which I had originally got from Paul Tillich. I was friendly with Hartman, and he visited me a few times for discussions in New York. He mainly taught and worked in Mexico.

In 1970, John William Davis, who was editing a volume in honor of Hartman and his axiological studies, invited me to contribute to the book, and I willingly agreed. In my paper, I review some of Hartman's main points on rating humans, and then come up with my own reasons for achieving unconditional self-acceptance. But I add the REBT notion of people's not rating their self or being at all, but only—yes, only—rating their thoughts, feelings, and behaviors on the basis of their chosen goals and purposes. Hartman was enthusiastic about my essay and said that, as a professor of philosophy, he would credit it as my dissertation and award me a Ph.D. in philosophy. Because philosophy had been my hobby since the age of sixteen, I was delighted to have his endorsement.

From 1970 on I have used the material in this chapter to show hundreds of my clients, and thousands of readers of my writings, the second, and I think more elegant, of the two main solutions to unconditional self-acceptance: accept yourself as good, worthy, or deserving of life and enjoyment just because you are human, alive, and a unique person; and don't evaluate, rate, or measure your self or personhood at all, but only your individual thoughts, feelings, and behaviors on the basis of your chosen goals and purposes. When I convince people of the first of these ratings I am quite pleased. When I convince them of the second solution to the problem of human worth, I am much more pleased.

Almost all modern authorities in psychotherapy believe that people's estimation of their own value, or worth, is exceptionally important, and that if they seriously denigrate themselves or have a poor self-image they will impair their normal functioning and make themselves disturbed. Consequently, it is usually held that one of the main functions of psychotherapy is to enhance the individual's self-respect (or "ego-strength," "self-confidence," "self-esteem," "feelings of personal worth," or "sense of identity") so that he may thereby solve the problem of self-evaluation.

When people do not value themselves very highly, innumerable problems result. They frequently will focus so intensely on what a rotten person they are that they will distract themselves from problem-solving and will become increasingly inefficient. They may falsely conclude that rotten people such as they can do virtually nothing right, and may stop trying to succeed at the things they want to accomplish. They may look at their proven advantages with a jaundiced eye and tend to conclude that they are a phony and that people just haven't as yet seen through them. Or they may become so intent on proving their value that they will be inclined to grovel for others' favor and approval and will give up their own desires for what they think (rightly or wrongly) others want them to do. They may tend to annihilate themselves, either literally or figuratively, as they desperately try to please. They may favor noncommitment and avoidance, and essentially become "nonalive." They may sabotage many or most of their potentialities for creative living. They may become obsessed with comparing themselves to others and their achievements, and tend to be status-seeking rather than joy-exploring. They may frequently be anxious, panicked, and terrified. They may tend to be short-range hedonists and lack self-discipline. They may often become defensive and thus act in a superior, grandiose way. They may assume an unusually rough or "masculine" manner as a form of compensation. They may become quite hostile toward others. They may become exceptionally depressed. They may withdraw from reality and retreat into fantasy. They may become exceptionally guilty. They may present a great false front to the world. They may sabotage a number of special talents which they possess. They may easily become conscious of lack of self-approval, berate themselves for having little or no confidence, and thereby reduce their self-image even more than they have previously done. They may become afflicted with numerous psychosomatic reactions, which then encourage them to defame themselves even more.

This list is hardly exhaustive, since almost the entire psycho-therapeutic literature of the last seventy-five years is more or less concerned with the harm an individual may do to herself and how badly she may maim or destroy her relations with others when she condemns herself, makes herself feel guilty or ashamed about her acts or inactions, and otherwise lowers her self-image. This same literature illustrates the corollary proposition, namely, that when a human somehow manages to accept, respect, and approve of herself, in most instances her behavior changes markedly for the better: her efficiency considerably improves, her anxiety, guilt, depression, and rage lessen, and she becomes less emotionally disturbed.

An obvious question presents itself: If people's perception of their own worth so importantly affects their thoughts, emotions, and actions, how is it possible to help them consistently to appraise themselves so that, no matter what kind of performances they achieve and no matter how popular or unpopular they are, they almost invariably accept or respect themselves? Oddly enough, modern psychotherapy has not often posed this question—at least not in the form just stated. Instead, it has fairly consistently asked another, almost antithetical one: Since people's self-acceptance seems to depend on their succeeding or achieving reasonably well in their society and on having good relations with others, how can they be helped to accomplish these goals and thereby achieve self-esteem?

At first blush, self-acceptance and self-esteem may seem to be very similar, but actually, when they are clearly defined they are quite different. Self-esteem, as it is fairly consistently used by Nathaniel Branden, Ayn Rand, and other devotees of Rand's objectivist philosophy, means that the individual values himself because he has behaved intelligently, correctly, or competently. When taken to its logical extreme, it "is the consequence, expression, and reward of a mind *fully* committed to reason" (italics mine), and "an *unbreached rationality*—that is, an unbreached determination to use one's mind to the fullest extent of one's ability, and a refusal *ever* to evade one's knowledge or act against it—is the *only* valid criterion of virtue and the *only* possible basis of authentic self-esteem" (italics mine).

Self-acceptance, on the other hand, means that the individual fully and unconditionally accepts herself whether or not she behaves intelligently, correctly, or competently and whether or not other people approve, respect, or love her. While only well-behaving (not to mention perfectly behaving) individuals can merit and feel self-esteem, virtually all humans are capable of feeling self-acceptance. And since the number of consistently well-behaving individuals in this world usually appears to be exceptionally small and the number of exceptionally fallible and often ill-behaving persons appears to be legion, the consistent achievement of self-esteem by most of us would seem to be remote, while the steady feeling of self-acceptance would seem to be quite attainable.

Those psychotherapists, therefore, who think and practice in terms of their clients' achieving a high measure of self-esteem or of highly conditional, positive self-regard are clearly misguided. Their aim instead should be to help these clients attain self-acceptance or unconditional positive regard. But the very term *unconditional positive regard*, which was originally coined by Carl Rogers, tends to have misleading overtones, since, in our culture, we usually regard someone positively because of a good thing he has done, for some beauty or strength of character he possesses, or for some talent or particular achievement. Rogers, however, really seems to mean that the individual can be accepted, and can accept himself, without reference to regard or achievement, or that, as I have noted elsewhere, he can accept himself just because he is he, because he is alive, because he exists.

It is mainly philosophers, and existentialist philosophers in particular, who have honestly and determinedly tackled the problem of human value and who have tried to determine what the individual can do to see herself as a worthwhile being even when she is not behaving in a notably competent, successful, or supposedly deserving way. Among these philosophers, Robert S. Hartman has led the field. No one has given more time and thought to the general problem of value than he, and no one, to my knowledge, has come up with a better explication of a human being's worth to himself.

As Hartman himself notes, however, the basic argument in favor of the theory that man has intrinsic value and cannot possibly be worthless is essentially tautological and definitional. There is really no empirical evidence to affirm or confute it, and it looks very much as though there never will be any. True, this theory that humans have intrinsic value has a strong pragmatic appeal, for if the opposite point is made, and it is held that people are bad or unworthy of their own or others' respect, dire consequences will ensue. They had therefore bloody well accept their "goodness" rather than their "badness" if they are to survive long and happily.

I am hardly opposed to this pragmatic argument, as I doubt any effective psychotherapist would be. The trouble, however, is with the inelegance of the philosophic premise that goes with it. Granted that people's thinking of themselves as bad or worthless is usually pernicious and that their thinking of themselves as good or worthwhile is more beneficial, I see no reason why these two hypotheses exhaust the possibilities of useful choices. Instead, I believe that there is a third choice that is much more philosophically elegant, less definitional, and more likely to conform to social reality. That is the seldom-posited assumption that value is a meaningless term when applied to a person's being, that it is invalid to call him either "good" or "bad," and that if educators and psychotherapists can teach people to give up all self-rating concepts and to have no self-images whatever, they may help the human dilemma considerably and enable men and women to be much less emotionally disturbed than they now tend to be.

Must people be self-evaluators? Yes and no. On the yes side, they clearly seem to be the kind of animals who are not merely reared but are also born with strong self-evaluating tendencies. Nowhere in the world, to my knowledge, do people simply accept that they are alive, go about the business of discovering how they can enjoy themselves more and discomfort themselves less, and live their fourscore or so years of existence in a reasonably unselfconscious, nondamning, and nondeifying manner. Instead, they invariably seem to identify and rate their *selves* as well as their *performances*, to be highly ego-involved about accomplishing this and avoiding that deed, and to believe that they will end up in some kind of heaven or hell if they do the "right" thing and eschew the "wrong."

Take, for example, the extremely permissive, hedonistic-oriented people of Polynesia, and especially of Tahiti. The Polynesians, as Bengt Danielsson reports, are still pleasure-seeking and careless, outspoken in sexual matters, premaritally free, have erotic dances, delight in sexual games, practice free love without legal weddings, and are fairly free extramaritally; and in the not-too-distant past they also practiced polygymy and wife-lending, danced in the nude, engaged in sexual intercourse in public, had pleasure houses for young people, permitted periodic sexual liberty, and encouraged deflowering ceremonies.

At the same time, the Polynesians have many taboos, the violation of which makes them feel utterly ashamed and self-hating. For instance, they seriously adhere to circumcision rites when the male reaches puberty; they have separate eating and sleeping houses; and they cling to a rigid division of work between the sexes. In the past, they have practiced sexual privileges based on birth and rank, obligatory marriage of widows, ritual continence, the forbidding of women to concern themselves with religious matters, and the isolation of females during periods of menstruation. Religiously and politically they have been very strict.

To a considerable degree, general discipline in Polynesia has been and still is based on exceptionally ego-raising and ego-debasing rules. I cite these facts to show that even among one of the most sexually permissive and easygoing groups of which we have knowledge, rules and rites of "proper" conduct are the norm rather than the exception, and humans become so ego-involved in following the rules and ashamed to break them that they literally hurt or kill themselves and easily permit themselves to be severely punished or sacrificed when they flout these publicly approved regulations. If there ever was a culture in which practically all the members did not similarly denigrate themselves and bring severe emotional or physical penalties on their own heads for engaging in "wrong" or "bad" behavior, I am not familiar with it.

The reason, I believe, for this practically universal tendency of people to put themselves down is their biological predisposition to be what we call self-conscious. Certainly many of the lower animals (especially the mammals and primates) seem to be somewhat aware of themselves, in that they "know" or "learn" that one kind of behavior (e.g., going where food is likely to be) is more rewarding or reinforcing than another kind of behavior (e.g., randomly exploring their environment). But these lower animals act much more instinctively than humans do; they "think" about their actions much less; they rarely, if ever, appear to think about their thinking; and it is probably impossible for them to think about thinking about their thinking. They are little conscious of their "selves," and are not particularly aware that "they" are responsible for their own "good" or "bad" acts and that, consequently, they are "good" or "bad" individuals. In other words, they are only to a limited degree ego-involved in their performances.

Humans, in contrast, not only have a strong "self-awareness" or "ego," but also have an exceptionally strong, and I again think innate, tendency to tie it up with their deeds. Because they are thin-skinned and highly vulnerable animals (as compared, say, to the rhinoceros, which can be quite careless about its behavior and is not likely to suffer ill effects) and because they rely so heavily on cognition rather than instinct for survival, it is greatly to their advantage to observe and appraise their actions to see whether they are satisfaction- or pain-producing and to keep modifying them in one direction or another. Unfortunately, however, just as they protectively rate their performances in relation to their own survival and happiness, they also dysfunctionally tend to rate their selves, and thereby almost inevitably do themselves in.

Let me graphically illustrate this human tendency with a typical case of Rational Emotive Behavior Therapy, a system of therapy based on the hypothesis that people largely become emotionally disturbed by foolishly giving report cards to their selves as well as to their deeds. Richard came to see me because he was terribly depressed about his work and because he frequently became enraged at his wife and acted cruelly toward her when she had minor lapses of decorum. In a session or two of psychotherapy, I first showed him how and why he was making himself depressed. At point A, *adversity,* he was not doing well at his work and his boss was consistently bringing his poor performance to his attention. At point C—emotional *consequence*—he was becoming depressed. Quite wrongly, he concluded that the action at point A created his disturbed emotional reaction, or consequence, at point C: "Because I am working inefficiently and because my boss is displeased and may fire me, I am depressed." But if A really caused C, I quickly show him, magic or voodoo would exist: for how can an external event (his inefficiency or his boss's disapproval) cause him to think or to feel anything?

Obviously, Richard did something about these outside actions to make himself suffer the consequence of depression. Probably he first observed these actions (noticed that his performance was inefficient and that his boss was disapproving) and then reflected on them (thought about their possible effects and how he disliked them). So, he appraised the possible results in a highly negative way, for if he did not notice his poor work or if he appraised it as good (because it would enable him to get fired from a job he really did not want), he would hardly feel depressed. In fact, he might feel elated!

It was almost certain, therefore, that Richard was telling himself something at point B (his *belief system*) to produce his depressed reactions at point C. Most probably, he was first telling himself a *rational belief* (RB): "I see that I am working inefficiently and that my boss may fire me, and if he did, that would be unfortunate. I certainly wouldn't like being fired." This belief is rational because, in all probability, it would be unfortunate if he were fired. He would then be without income, have to look for another job, possibly have to put up with a displeased wife, and perhaps have to take a worse or lower-paying position. There are several good, empirically ascertainable reasons why it would not be pleasant if he were fired. Therefore, his RB hypothesis that it would be unfortunate for him to keep working inefficiently was both sane and accurate.

If Richard held rigorously to his RB conclusion, he would most probably never feel depressed. Instead, he would feel the healthy consequences (C) of displeasure, disappointment, sorrow, regret, annoyance, or frustration. These are all negative emotions, but are far from the feeling of depression. In order to make himself feel the unhealthy consequence (C) of depression, he would almost certainly have to add to his rational belief a self-defeating, self-denigrating irrational belief (IB): "If I keep working inefficiently and am fired, that would be awful. I couldn't stand my boss disapproving of me and firing me. Not only would that action show that my work is poor, but it would also conclusively prove that I am pretty worthless; that I can never do well at a job like this; and that I deserve to be poor, unloved, and otherwise punished for being such an incompetent!"

Richard's irrational belief is self-defeating for several reasons. First, it is definitional and unverifiable. However unfortunate his working inefficiently and his being fired may be, it is only "awful," "terrible," or "catastrophic" because he thinks it is. Actually, it is still only unfortunate or inconvenient. Second, it is an overgeneralization. Because he doesn't like being fired hardly means that he can't stand it. Because his work is inefficient does not prove that he is not a good human being. Because he now works poorly is not evidence that he will always do so. Third, it is a non sequitur. If he really were a worthless individual who could never succeed at any job, why should he deserve to be unloved and punished? Being thus handicapped, he might well be said to deserve an unusual degree of love and help from the rest of us less-handicapped humans. What just person or deity would ever condemn him for having been born and reared to be deficient? Fourth, it almost invariably leads to dreadful and even more unfortunate results than those that Richard may naturally derive from his inefficient work behavior. For if he thinks it awful to be disapproved of and cannot stand being dismissed, he will probably make himself so anxious that his job efficiency will deteriorate rather than improve, and he will stand even less chance of keeping his job. Moreover, if his boss lets him go and he concludes that he is worthless, on future jobs he will tend to act as if he were unable to perform, and may bring about his self-fulfilling prophecy and be dismissed again.

As a Rational Emotive Behavior therapist, I showed Richard what his rational and irrational beliefs were. I tried to help him discriminate his sensible RB from his foolish IB hypotheses; I indicated how he could keep his RB appraisals of his performances and feel healthy consequences (sorrow, regret, displeasure, increased effort to work more efficiently) and minimize his IB appraisals and their unhealthy consequences (feelings of panic, depression, increased inefficiency, etc.).

I also helped change Richard's feelings of rage against his wife. I showed him that when her actions at point A were inconsiderate, impolite, or unjust, he was probably first signaling himself the rational belief, "I don't like her behavior; I wish she would change it; what a nuisance!" At point C, he was consequently experiencing healthy consequences—that is, emotions of dissatisfaction, disappointment, frustration, and annoyance. At point IB, he had the irrational belief, "Because she is acting badly, I can't stand it. She is a horrible person. I'll never be able to forgive her for acting like that. She deserves to suffer for the awful way she is treating me!" Consequently, at point C, he felt the unhealthy consequences of rage and self-pity. I induced him to retain his sensible RB hypotheses and to surrender his condemnatory IB hypotheses, and thereby to feel displeasure but not rage. He then had a better chance of helping his wife change her unpleasing behavior.

My main point here is that the actions that occur in Richard (or anyone's) life at point A do not fully cause or make him feel depressed or enraged at point C. Rather, his thoughts, appraisals, and evaluations—his beliefs at point B—partly create these feelings. To a large degree he has a choice at point A about what he will feel at point C regarding the actions or agents in his life—as long as he thinks about his thinking, challenges some of his IB conceptions and conclusions, and returns to his empirically based RB hypotheses. Being born and raised a human, however, he naturally tends to make a magical jump from RB to IB conclusions, and, much more often than not, he confuses his total personality with his performances, and automatically evaluates and rates the former along with the latter. Consequently, he frequently ends up by damning himself and other people (that is, denigrating his and their intrinsic value). He thereby gets into all kinds of needless difficulties, or emotional problems, with himself and with others.

Again, I ask: Must humans self-evaluate? Again I answer: Yes, to some degree they must, as it is biologically and sociologically impossible for them not to do so. In terms of self-preservation, if they did not constantly evaluate their performances they would soon be dead. Before they can safely drive a car, climb a mountain, or cultivate a certain kind of food, they had better know how competent they are likely to be in these respects, else they will maim or kill themselves. So, to survive, they really have to assess their deeds and potentials.

Self-appraisal, moreover, has distinct advantages as well as disadvantages. If you (unempirically and unscientifically) rate your self, your being, as "good," "great," or "noble" when you succeed in love, work well on your job, or paint a fine canvas, you will tend, at least for awhile, to be much happier than if you merely rate your performance in a similar manner. If you (unrealistically) appraise your girlfriend or your wife as being a "glorious," "marvelous," or "goddesslike" person when you (more accurately) really mean that she has some highly desirable and pleasing traits, you will also tend to feel ecstatic about your relations with her.

But is it really worth it? Do you absolutely have to rate yourself as a person and evaluate others as people? After spending over half a century busily engaged as a psychotherapist, writer, teacher, and lecturer, my answer to both these questions is no. You have an inborn, as well as a socially acquired tendency, to be a self- and an other-appraiser, but by very hardheaded thinking, along with active work and practice, you can persistently fight against and minimize this tendency. If you do, you will in all probability be considerably healthier and happier. Instead of strongly evaluating yourself and other people's selves, you can rigorously stick to rating only performances. Instead of damning or deifying anyone or anything, you can accept social reality and be truly demonless and godless. Instead of inventing demands and needs, you can remain with desires and preferences. If you do so, I hypothesize that you will not achieve utopia (which itself is changeless, absolutistic, and unrealistic), but you most probably will achieve more spontaneity, creativity, and satisfaction than you have ever previously experienced. Some of the main reasons for my espousing your taking a nonevaluative attitude toward yourself (while still evaluating many of your traits and performances) are as follows:

Both positive and negative self-evaluation are inefficient and often seriously interfere with problem-solving. If you elevate or defame yourself because of your performances, you will tend to be self-centered rather than problem-centered, and these performances will, consequently, tend to suffer. In addition, self-evaluation is usually ruminative and absorbs enormous amounts of time and energy. It may help you cultivate your "soul" but hardly your garden!

Self-rating works well only when you have many talents and few flaws, but few of us are in that class. It also tends to demand universal competence. But, again, can you measure up to such a demand?

Self-appraisal almost inevitably leads to one-upmanship and one-downmanship. If you rate yourself as being "good," you will usually rate others as being "bad" or "less good." If you rate yourself as being "bad," others will be seen as "less bad" or "good." It follows that you practically force yourself to compete with others in "goodness" or "badness" and constantly feel envious, jealous, or superior. Persistent individual, group, and international conflicts easily stem from this kind of thinking and feeling, and love, cooperation, and other forms of fellow-feeling are minimized. To see yourself as having a better or worse trait than another person may be beneficial (since you may use your knowledge of another's superior trait to help achieve that trait yourself). But to see yourself as being a better or worse *person* than another is likely to cause trouble for both of you.

Self-evaluation enhances self-consciousness and therefore tends to shut you up within yourself, to narrow your range of interests and enjoyments. "It should be our endeavor," said Bertrand Russell, "to aim at avoiding self-centered passions and at acquiring those affections and those interests which will prevent our thoughts from dwelling perpetually upon ourselves. It is not the nature of most men to be happy in a prison, and the passions which shut us up in ourselves constitute one of the worst kinds of prisons. Among such passions some of the commonest are fear, envy, the sense of sin, self-pity, and self-admiration."

Blaming or praising the whole individual for a few of his acts is an unscientific overgeneralization. "I have called the process of converting a child mentally into something else, whether it be a monster or a mere nonentity, *pathogenic metamorphosis,*" Jules Henry, a well-known psychologist, declared. "Mrs. Portman called [her son] Pete 'a human garbage pail'; she said to him, 'you smell, you stink'; she kept the garbage bag and refuse newspapers on his high chair when he was not in it; she called him Mr. Magoo, and never used his right name. Thus he was a stinking monster, a nonentity, a buffoon." But Henry failed to point out that had Mrs. Portman called her son, Pete, "an angel" and said to him, "you smell heavenly," she would have equally converted him, by the process of pathogenic metamorphosis, into something he was not—namely, a godlike being. Peter is a human person who sometimes smells bad (or heavenly); he is not a bad-smelling (or heavenly smelling) person.

When human selves are lauded or condemned there is a strong implication that people should be rewarded or punished for being "good" or "bad." But, as noted above, if there were "bad" people, they would already be so handicapped by their "rottenness" that it would be thoroughly unfair to punish them further for being "rotten." And if there were "good" people, they would already be so favored by their "goodness" that it would be superfluous or unjust to reward them for it. Human justice, therefore, is very badly served by self-evaluations.

To rate a person high because of his good traits is often tantamount to deifying him; conversely, to rate him low because of his bad traits is tantamount to demonizing him. But since there seems to be no way of validating or disproving the existence of gods and devils, and since you can well live without this redundant hypothesis, it merely clutters your thinking and acting, and probably does much more harm than good. Concepts of god and the devil, moreover, obviously vary enormously from person to person and from group to group; they add nothing to human knowledge, and they usually serve as obstructions to precise intrapersonal and interpersonal communication.

Bigotry and lack of respect for individuals in their own right are consequences of self- and other-evaluation. For if you accept A because he is white, Episcopalian, and well educated and reject B because he is black, a Baptist, and a high school dropout, you are clearly not respecting B as a human being, and, of course, are intolerantly disrespecting millions of people like him. Bigotry is arbitrary, unjust, and conflict-creating; it is ineffective for social living. As George Axtelle has noted, "Men are profoundly social creatures. They can realize their own ends more fully only as they respect one another as ends in themselves. Mutual respect is an essential condition of effectiveness both individually and socially. Its opposites—hatred, contempt, segregation, and exploitation—frustrate the realization of values for all concerned, and hence they are profoundly destructive of all effectiveness." Once you damn an individual, including yourself, for having or lacking any trait whatever, you become authoritarian or fascistic, for fascism is the very essence of people-evaluation.

By evaluating an individual, even if only in a complimentary way, one is often trying to change him or trying to control or manipulate him, and the kind of change envisioned may or may not be good for him. "Often," Richard Farson notes, "the change which praise asks one to make is not necessarily beneficial to the person being praised but will redound to the convenience, pleasure or profit of the praiser." Evaluation may induce the individual to feel obligated to his evaluator; and to the degree that he lets himself feel compelled or obligated to change himself, he may be much less of the self that he would really like to be. Positive or negative evaluation of a person, therefore, may well encourage him to be less of a self or of a self-directed individual than he would enjoy being.

Evaluation of the individual tends to bolster the Establishment and block social change, for when you give yourself a report card you not only become accustomed to telling yourself, "My deeds are wrong, and I think I'd better work at improving them in the future," but also, "I am wrong, I am a 'no-goodnik' for performing these poor deeds." Since "wrong" acts are largely measured by social standards, and since most societies are run by a limited number of "upper level" people who have a strong, vested interest in keeping standards the way they are, self-evaluation usually encourages the individual to go along with social rules, no matter how arbitrary or foolish they are, and especially to woo the approval of the powers-that-be. Conformity, which is one of the worst products of self-rating, generally means conformity to the time-honored and sometimes unfair rules of the Establishment.

Self-appraisal and the measuring of others tends to sabotage empathic listening. Close and authentic relationships between two people, as Farson points out, are often achieved through intensive listening: "This does not merely mean to wait for a person to finish talking, but to try to see how the world looks to this person and to communicate this understanding to him. This empathic, nonevaluative listening responds to the person's feelings as well as to his words, that is, to the total meaning of what he is trying to say. It implies no evaluation, no judgment, no agreement (or disagreement). It simply conveys an understanding of what the person is feeling and attempting to communicate, and his feelings and ideas are accepted as being valid for him, if not for the listener." When, however, you evaluate a person (and yourself) as you listen to the other person, you are usually prejudicedly blocked from fully understanding her, seeing her as she exists, and uncompetitively understanding and getting close to her.

Person-rating tends to denigrate human wants, desires, and preferences and to replace them with demands, compulsions, or needs. If you do not measure your selfhood, you tend to spend your days asking yourself, "Now what would I really like to do, in my relatively brief span of existence, to gain maximum satisfaction and minimum pain?" If you do measure your selfhood, you tend to keep asking, "What do I have to do to prove that I am a worthwhile person?" As Richard Robertiello, a well-known psychiatrist, has observed, "People are constantly negating their right to take something just purely because they want it, to enjoy something simply because they enjoy it. They can hardly ever let themselves take anything for pure pleasure without justifying it on the basis of having earned it or suffered enough to be entitled to it or rationalizing that, though they enjoy it, it is really an altruistic act that they are doing for someone else's good.... It seems as if the greatest crime is to do something simply because we enjoy it and without any thought of doing good for anyone else or of serving an absolute need in us that is essential for our continued survival." Such is the folly born of self-deservingness!

Placing a value on a human being tends to sabotage free will. You have little enough self-direction in the normal course of events, since even your most "voluntary" activities are significantly influenced by your heredity and environment, and when you think that one of your thoughts, feelings, or actions is really "yours," you ignore some of its most important biosocial causes. As soon as you label yourself as "good" or "bad," as a "genius" or an "idiot," you so seriously stereotype yourself that you will almost certainly bias and influence much of your subsequent behavior. For how can a "bad" person or an "idiot" determine, even to a small degree, what your future actions will be, and how can you work hard at achieving your goals? Moreover, how can a "good" person do nongood acts, or a "genius" turn out mediocre works along with outstanding ones? What asinine, creativity-downing restrictions you almost automatically place on yourself when you think in terms of these general designations of your selfhood!

To give yourself or any human an accurate global rating is probably impossible for several reasons:

1. The traits by which you are to be rated are very likely to change from year to year, even from moment to moment. You are not a thing or an object, but a process. How can an ever-changing process be precisely measured and rated?
2. The characteristics by which you are to be evaluated have no absolute scale by which they can be judged. Traits which are highly honored in one social group are roundly condemned in another. A murderer may be seen as a horrible criminal by a judge but as a marvelous soldier by a general. A person's qualities (such as the ability to compose music) may be deemed fine in one century and mediocre in a later age.
3. To rate yourself globally, special weight would have to be given to each kind of positive and negative action that you performed. Thus, if you did a friend a small favor and also worked very hard to save a hundred people from drowning, your latter act would normally be given a much higher rating than your former one; and if you told a lie to your wife and also battered a child, your second deed would be considered much more heinous than your first. But who is to give an exact weight to your various deeds so that it could finally be determined how globally "good" or "bad" you are? It might be convenient if there existed on earth some kind of St. Peter, who would have a record of every single one of your deeds (and your thoughts, for that matter) and who could quickly assess you as a potential angel or as hell-bound. But what is the likelihood of such a St. Peter (even in the form of a marvelous computer) ever existing?
4. What kind of mathematics could we employ to arrive at a single, total rating of a human being's worth? Suppose you do a thousand good acts and then fiendishly torture someone to death. To arrive at a general evaluation of your being, shall we add up all your good acts arithmetically and compare this sum to the

weighted sum of your bad acts? Shall we instead use some geometric means of assessing your "goodness" and "badness"? What system can we employ to accurately measure your "value"? Is there, really, any valid kind of mathematical evaluation by which you can be rated?

5. Since it is quite impossible for you or anyone else to discover all your characteristics and to use them in arriving at a single universal rating, no matter how many of your traits are known, in the final analysis the whole of you is being evaluated by some of your parts. But is it ever really legitimate to rate your whole by some of your parts? Even one unknown, and hence unevaluated, part might significantly change and, hence invalidate your final rating. Suppose, for example, you score a 91 percent general rating (that is, are considered to have 91 percent of "goodness"). If you unconsciously hated your brother most of your life and actually brought about his early demise, but if you consciously only remember loving your brother and presumably helping him to live happily, you will rate yourself (and anyone but an all-knowing St. Peter will rate you) considerably higher than if you consciously admitted your hatred for him and your causing him needless harm. Your "real" rating, therefore, will be considerably lower than 91 percent; but how will this "real" rating ever be known?

6. If you are given a very low global rating by yourself and others—say, you wind up with a 13 percent general report card on yourself—it presumably means that you were born a worthless individual; that you never possibly could become worthwhile; and that you deserve to be punished (and ultimately roasted in some kind of hell) for being hopelessly worthless. None of these hypotheses can be proved or disproved, and they tend (as stated above) to bring about much more harm than good.

7. Measuring yourself is really a form of circular thinking. If you are "good" because you have "good" traits, your "goodness," in both instances, is based on some kind of value system that is definitional; for who, except some kind of deity, can accurately measure "good" traits? Once your traits are defined as being "good," and your global "goodness" is deduced from your specific "goodnesses," the concept of your being globally "good" will almost inevitably prejudice one's view of your specific traits— which will then seem "more good" than they really may be. And once your traits are defined as being "bad," the concept of your

being globally "bad" will almost inevitably prejudice one's view of your specific traits—which will then seem "more bad" than they really may be. If your "good" traits are seen as being "more good" than they really are, people will keep seeing you as being "good," when you may not actually be. Globally rating yourself, in other words, includes making an estimation of your specific "good" traits, and rating your specific traits as "good" includes making an estimation of your global "goodness." In all probability, both of these estimates will turn out to be "true," whatever the facts of your specific and general "goodness" actually are, for "goodness" itself can never accurately be determined, since the entire edifice of "goodness" is based, as I have said, on concepts that are largely definitional.

8. Perhaps the only sensible way of making a global rating of yourself is on the basis of your aliveness, that is, assuming that you are intrinsically good just because you are human and alive (and that you will be nongood or nonexistent when you are dead). Similarly, if we want to accept religious assumptions, we can hypothesize that you are good because you are human and because Jehovah, Jesus, or some other deity in whom you believe accepts, loves, or gives grace to all humans. This is an empty assumption, because we know (as well as we know anything) that you believe this assumed-deity exists, while we have no way of proving the existence (or nonexistence) of the deity. Nonetheless, such an assumption will work, in that it will refer back to the more basic assumption that you are globally "good" just because you are human and alive. The trouble with this basic concept of general human "goodness" is that it obviously puts *all* humans in the same boat—makes them all equally "good" and leaves no room whatever for any of them to be "bad." Consequently, it is a global rating that is not really a rating, and it is entirely definitional and rather meaningless.

9. The concept of giving any human a general or global evaluation may be an artifact of the inaccurate way in which almost all humans think and communicate with themselves and each other. Alfred Korzybski, the founder of general semantics, and two other well-known general semanticists, S. I. Hayakawa and D. David Bourland, Jr., have pointed out for a good many years that just as pencil one is not the same thing as pencil two, so individual one is hardly the same as individual two. Consequently, generaliz-

ing about pencils and about individuals is never entirely accurate. For several decades Bourland has especially campaigned against using any form of the verb *to be* when we speak about or categorize the behavior of a person. Thus, it is one thing for us to note that "Jones has (or possesses) some outstanding mathematical qualities" and another to say that "Jones is an outstanding mathematician." The former sentence is much more precise and probably "truer" than the latter. Moreover, the latter sentence implies a global rating of Jones that is hardly warranted by the facts, if these can be substantiated, of Jones's possessing some mathematical qualities. If Korzybski and his followers are correct, then global terms and ratings of humans are easily made (indeed, it is most difficult for us not to make them), but would better be fought against and transformed into more specific evaluations of their performances, talents, and traits. Such generalized grades exist, since we obviously keep employing them, but it would be much better if we minimized them.

10. All your traits are different—as apples and pears are different. Just as we cannot legitimately add and divide apples and pears and thereby get a single, accurate global rating of an entire basket of fruit, so we cannot truly add and divide different human traits and thereby obtain a single, meaningful global rating of you, a human individual.

What conclusions can be drawn from the foregoing observations and deductions about psychotherapy and human value? First, that self-reference and self-evaluation are a normal and natural part of people. It seems to be much easier for you to rate your self, your being, as well as your performances, than it is for you only to assess the latter and not the former.

When you do appraise yourself globally, you almost invariably get into trouble. When you term yourself "bad," "inferior," or "inadequate," you tend to feel anxious, guilty, and depressed, to act below your potential level of efficiency, and to falsely confirm your low estimation of yourself. When you term yourself "good," "superior," or "adequate," you tend to feel forever unsure of maintaining your "goodness," to spend considerable time and energy "proving" how worthwhile you are, but still sabotage your relations with yourself and others.

Ideally, it would seem wise for you to train yourself, by thinking rigorously about and working against some of your strongest inborn and environmentally bolstered tendencies, to refuse to evaluate yourself at all. You preferably should continue, as accurately as you can, to assess your traits, talents, and performances so that you can thereby lead a longer, pain-avoiding, and satisfaction-filled life. But you should also accept rather than rate your so-called self and strive for the enjoyment rather than the justification of your existence. According to Freud, people attain mental health when they follow the rule "Where id was, there shall ego be." By ego, however, Freud, did not mean person's self-evaluating tendencies but his self-directing ones. According to my own views and the principles of Rational Emotive Behavior Therapy, you attain maximum understanding of yourself and others, and minimum anxiety and hostility, when you follow the rule "Where ego was, there shall the person be." By ego, of course, I mean your self-rating and self-justifying tendencies.

You are too complex to be measured or given a report card. You are an individual living with others in a world with which you interact. You may be legitimately "valued," in the sense of accepting and abiding by the empirically determinable facts that: you exist; you can suffer satisfaction and pain while you exist; it is usually within your power to continue to exist and to experience more satisfaction than pain; and it is therefore highly probable that you "deserve" to (and had better) go on existing and enjoying. Or, more succinctly stated, you have value because you decide to remain alive and to value your existence. Observations and conclusions other than those based on these minimal assumptions may well be foolishly egocentric and fictional, and in the final analysis human—all too human, but still essentially inhumane.

12

Techniques for Disputing Irrational Beliefs (DIBS)

I originated this technique for disputing irrational beliefs in the early 1970s as one of the homework exercises of REBT. Clients are shown how to directly and vigorously dispute their IBs realistically, logically, and pragmatically, and this exercise gives them illustrative ways of doing so. Once they or anyone using REBT learns how to question and challenge his or her IBs, and to do so forcefully and consistently, DIBS outlines some of the main methods they can use to do this kind of disputing. Thousands of people have used it effectively over the years; and together with other REBT cognitive, emotive-evocative, and behavioral methods, it has often helped them considerably. Try it and see for yourself!

If you want to increase your rationality and reduce your self-defeating irrational beliefs, you can spend at least ten minutes every day asking yourself the following questions and carefully thinking through (not merely parroting!) the healthy answers. Write down each question and your answers to it on a piece of paper, or else record the questions and your answers on a tape recorder.

1. What self-defeating irrational belief do I want to dispute and surrender?

Illustrative answer: I absolutely must receive love from someone whom I really care for.

2. Can I rationally support this belief?
    Illustrative answer: No.

3. What evidence exists of the falseness of this belief?
    Illustrative answer: Many indications exist that the belief that I must receive love from someone for whom I really care for is false:

    a. No law of the universe exists that says that someone I care for *must* love me (although it would be nice if that person did!).

    b. If I do not receive love from one particular person, I can still get it from others and find happiness that way.

    c. If no one I care for ever cares for me, which is very unlikely, I can still find enjoyment in friendships, work, books, and other things.

    d. If someone I deeply care for rejects me, that will be most unfortunate, but I will hardly die!

    e. Even though I have not had much luck in winning great love in the past, that hardly proves that I *must* gain it now.

    f. No evidence exists for *any* absolute "must." Consequently, no proof exists that I *must* always have anything, including love.

    g. Many people exist in the world who never get the kind of love they crave and still lead happy lives.

    h. At times during my life I know that I have remained unloved and happy, so most probably I can feel happy again under unloving conditions.

    i. If I get rejected by someone whom I truly care for, that may mean that I possess some poor, unlovable traits, but it hardly means that I am a rotten, worthless, totally unlovable individual.

    j. Even if I had such poor traits that no one could ever love me, I would still not have to put myself down as a lowly, bad individual.

4. Does any evidence exist of the truth of this belief?
    Illustrative answer: No, not really. Considerable evidence exists that if I love someone dearly and never am loved in return that I will then find myself disadvantaged, inconvenienced, frustrated, and deprived. Therefore, I certainly would prefer not to get rejected, but no amount of inconvenience amounts to a *horror*. I can still *stand* frustration and loneliness. They hardly make the world awful. Nor does rejection make me an ass. Clearly, then, no

evidence exists that I *must* receive love from someone whom I really care for.

5. What are the worst things that could actually happen to me if I don't get what I think I must (or do get what I think I must not get)?

   Illustrative Answer: If I don't get the love I think I must receive:

   a. I would be deprived of various possible pleasures and conveniences.

   b. I would feel inconvenienced by having to keep looking for love elsewhere.

   c. I might *never* gain the love I want, and thereby indefinitely continue to feel deprived and disadvantaged.

   d. Other people might put me down and consider me worthless for being rejected—and that would be annoying and unpleasant.

   e. I might settle for pleasures other than, and worse than, those I could receive in a good love relationship, and I would find that distinctly undesirable.

   f. I might remain alone much of the time, which again would be unpleasant.

   g. Various other kinds of misfortunes and deprivations might occur in my life, none of which I need to define as awful, terrible, or unbearable. They are not totally bad and they *should* exist when they do exist.

6. What good things could I make happen if I don't get what I think I must (or do get what I think I must *not* get)?

   a. If the person I truly care for does not return my love, I could devote more time and energy to winning someone else's love—and probably find someone better for me.

   b. I could devote myself to other enjoyable pursuits that have little to do with loving or relating, such as work or artistic endeavors.

   c. I could find it challenging and enjoyable to teach myself to live happily without love.

   d. I could work at achieving a philosophy of fully accepting myself even when I do not get the love I crave.

You can take any one of your major irrational beliefs—your shoulds, oughts, or musts—and spend at least ten minutes every day, often for a period of several weeks, actively disputing it. To help yourself devote this amount of time to the DIBS method of rational disputing, you may use operant conditioning or the self-management methods originated by B. F. Skinner, David Premack, Marvin Goldfried, and other psychologists. Select some enjoyable activity that you tend to do every day—such as reading, eating, television viewing, exercising, or socializing with friends. Use this activity as a reinforcer or reward by *only* allowing yourself to engage in it *after* you have practiced disputing irrational beliefs for at least ten minutes that day. Otherwise, no reward!

In addition, you may penalize yourself every single day you do *not* use DIBS for at least ten minutes. How? By making yourself perform some activity you find distinctly unpleasant—such as eating something you find repulsive, contributing to a cause you hate, getting up a half-hour earlier in the morning, or spending an hour conversing with someone who bores you. You can also arrange with some person or group to monitor you and help you actually carry out the penalties and lack of rewards you set for yourself. You may, of course, steadily use DIBS without any self-reinforcement, since it eventually becomes reinforcing in its own right. But you may find it more effective if you use it along with rewards and penalties you give yourself immediately after you practice or avoid practicing this rational-emotive method.

Summary of Questions to Ask Yourself in DIBS

1. What self-defeating irrational belief do I want to dispute and surrender?
2. Can I rationally support this belief?
3. What evidence exists of the falseness of this belief?
4. Does any evidence exist for the truth of this belief?
5. What are the worst things that could actually happen to me if I don't get what I think I must (or do get what I think I must *not* get)?
6. What good things could I make happen if I don't get what I think I must (or do get what I think I must *not* get)?

Disputing (D) your dysfunctional or irrational beliefs (IBs) is one of the most effective REBT techniques, but it is still often ineffective, because you can easily and very strongly hold on to an IB (such as, "I *absolutely must* be loved by so-and-so, and it's *awful* and I am an inadequate person when he (or she) does not love me!"). When you question and challenge this IB, you often can come up with an effective new philosophy (E) that is accurate but weak: "I guess that there is no reason why so-and-so *must* love me, because there are other people who will love me when so-and-so does not. I can therefore be reasonably happy without his (or her) love." *Almost* believing this effective new philosophy, or by believing it only lightly, you can still easily and forcefully believe, "Even though it is not awful and terrible when so-and-so does not love me, it really is! No matter what, I still *need* his (or her) affections!"

Weak, or even moderately strong, disputing will therefore often not work very well to help you truly disbelieve some of your powerful and long-held IBs, while vigorous, persistent disputing is more likely to work.

One way to do highly powerful, vigorous disputing is to use a tape recorder and to state one of your strong irrational beliefs into it, such as, "If I fail this job interview I am about to have, that will prove that I'll never get a good job and that I might as well apply only for low-level positions!"

Figure out several disputes to this IB and present them strongly on this same tape. For example: "Even if I do poorly on this interview, that will only show that I failed *this* time, but will never show that I'll always fail and can never do well in other interviews. Maybe they'll still hire me for the job. But if they don't, they don't. Tough! I can learn by my mistakes, do better in other interviews, and probably get the kind of job that I want."

Listen to your disputing on tape. Let other people, including your therapist or members of your therapy group, listen to it. Do it over in a more forceful and vigorous manner and let them listen to it again, to see if you are disputing more forcefully, until they agree that you are getting better at doing it. Keep listening to it until you see that you are able to convince yourself and others that you are becoming more powerful and more convincing.

13

Rational Emotive Imagery

As this chapter notes, Rational Emotive Imagery was created by Maxie C. Maultsby Jr. in 1971 after he had come to New York to study REBT with me for a month in 1968. I saw right away that it was a very useful emotive method of therapy because it stressed people's first getting in touch with their disturbed feelings, then emphasizing and imploding these feelings, and then changing them to healthy negative feelings. Although REBT has often been accused of ignoring feelings, and especially deep feelings, it has actually emphasized them since its beginnings, in 1955. In the 1960s, in addition to the cognitive techniques for which it is famous, it especially used many emotional and experiential methods, including my shame-attacking exercises. One of the best of the emotive techniques that is designed for REBT is Maultsby's Rational Emotive Imagery. It can be presented in a brief period of time, used for only a few minutes a day, and given as a behavioral homework assignment. I have used it successfully with thousands of clients and have presented it to hundreds of others in my life demonstrations at workshops and talks, which I frequently give throughout the world. I particularly use it with the volunteers with whom I give REBT public demonstrations at my regular Friday night workshops at the Albert Ellis Institute in New York. In this way they and the audience learn how to quickly change their unhealthy negative feelings to healthy negative feelings and thereby tackle some of their most disturbed emotions.

I found Maultsby's version of Rational Emotive Imagery to be quite useful, but also found that it overlapped too much with REBT disputing because Maultsby usually had clients who did the imagery go back to their rational coping statements, which they had previously figured out with him, and use them to change their unhealthy negative feelings when they thought about an unfortunate activating event or adversity. I therefore began to use Rational Emotive Imagery in a more emotive-evocative and less disputational way.

In Maultsby's version, you imagine an unfortunate activating event (A) happening in your life and let yourself spontaneously feel very anxious or depressed at point C, a harmful consequence of A. Then you look at your rational beliefs (RBs) about A (e.g., "I don't *like* my failing this task, but I can *stand it* and it doesn't make me a complete failure") and you strongly say them to yourself, replacing your disturbance-creating irrational beliefs. In doing this, you change your unhealthy feelings (C1) to more healthy feelings (C2) of disappointment, regret, or frustration.

To use the REBT version of Rational Emotive Imagery, proceed as follows:

Imagine one of the worst things that might happen to you—such as failing at an important project, getting rejected by people you really want to like you, or being in very poor health. Vividly imagine this unfortunate activating event or adversity (A) occurring and bringing a string of problems into your life.

Let yourself deeply feel the kind of unhealthy, self-defeating feelings that you often experience when the unfortunate activating event you are imagining actually occurs. Thus, let yourself strongly feel very anxious, depressed, enraged, self-hating, or self-pitying, at point C, your emotional consequence. Get in touch with this dysfunctional, happiness-destroying feeling (C1) and *really* feel it. Don't prescribe the unhealthy feeling by telling yourself something like, "Now that I am imagining myself being treated badly, I should make myself feel very enraged," because you may actually spontaneously feel panicked or depressed instead of enraged. So, as you imagine this bad activating event happening, let yourself spontaneously feel whatever you feel and not what you think you are *supposed* to feel at point C1.

Once you feel unhealthfully upset (at C1) as you imagine this Adversity (A), hold this feeling for a minute or two—again, *really feel it*—then work on your dysfunctional feeling until you truly change it to a healthy or self-helping negative feeling (C2). Which one? Well, you can actually prescribe a healthy negative feeling (C2) that will take the place of your unhealthy one (C1). Thus, if you are enraged (C1) at the image or visualization of people treating you unfairly (A), you can prescribe changing your rage to a healthy emotion of feeling very displeased with and sorry about their acts, instead of enraged at and damning them for these acts (C2). If you feel panicked (C1) about your imagining you are doing poorly at a job interview (A), you can change your panic to a feeling of real disappointment at how you are doing instead of horror at *you* for doing so badly (C2). You can also prescribe other healthy or self-helping negative feelings when you vividly imagine adversities. Thus, you can prescribe sorrow, regret, concern, frustration, and sadness (C2) instead of dysfunctional feelings of depression, terror, worthlessness, and fury (C1).

When you work at changing your feelings from self-defeating to potentially helpful negative emotions, be sure that you do not do so by changing the activating event or adversity (A) that you are vividly imagining. Thus, when you are visualizing people treating you very unfairly and letting yourself feel unhealthily enraged and homicidal (C1)—unhealthy because you will obsess yourself with feelings of rage and probably make yourself unable to deal with this adversity adequately—you could instead make yourself feel only distinctly displeased with these people's behavior and *not* enraged at them (C2) by imagining that they are not really treating you so unfairly or imagining that they have special "good" reasons for treating you in an unfair way. This, however, is incorrect use of REI. In doing Rational Emotive Imagery, make yourself keep the exact adverse image (A) that you make yourself enraged about and then work at changing your feeling to a healthy one.

Don't use distraction techniques, such as relaxation, biofeedback, or meditation methods merely to change your unhealthy, negative feelings to healthy ones. Thus, when you visualize people really treating you unfairly (A) and you make yourself feel enraged about this (C1), you could relax or meditate and thereby temporarily rid yourself of your rage. But by doing so you would not be changing your underlying beliefs (Bs) or philosophy about people's unfairness—such as, "They *absolutely must not* treat me in this unfair way! I *can't stand* their acting the way they *must* not! They are *horrible people* for acting this way and deserve to be damned and punished forever!" (IBs).

By using cognitive distraction techniques like relaxation or meditation, you will shunt aside your people-hating philosophy (IB), but you will not really reduce it. Almost inevitably, you will return to it the next time people treat you unfairly and will again become enraged at them. So if you want to relax at first and then go back to changing this underlying hatred-creating philosophy, fine. But don't just stop with distraction methods. Go on to real Rational Emotive Imagery.

To do this, really work at changing your spontaneous disturbed negative feeling (C1) to a prescribed healthy Negative feeling (C2)— such as sorrow, disappointment, regret, frustration, irritation, or displeasure. How? By telling yourself—*strongly* and *repetitively*—a sensible rational belief (RB) or coping statement. For example: "Yes, they really did treat me shabbily and unfairly, which I wish they hadn't done. But there's no reason why they must treat me fairly, however preferable that would be. Alas, that's just not their way—and may never be! Too bad! Tough! But I can hate their *behavior* without completely damning *them*. And if I refuse to upset myself unduly about their unfairness, perhaps I can show them, without deep anger, why I think they are unfair and perhaps get them to change. But if I can't, I can't. I'll just try to stay away from people like that and give them little chance to keep treating me unfairly."

If you do Rational Emotive Imagery correctly, you'll usually find it takes you only a few minutes to change your unhealthy, self-sabotaging negative feelings (C1) to healthy, self-helping ones (C2). Don't give up! Persist! Remember that you created your own destructive feelings of panic, depression, rage, self-hatred, and self-pity (C1). Yes, you—with your irrational beliefs. Therefore, you can always replace them with healthy negative feelings (C2) that will help you deal with unfortunate activating events (As) and then either change them or live a reasonably happy life in spite of them. So persist until you really feel the healthy negative feelings you are prescribing for yourself as a substitute for your self-damaging feelings.

Once you have made yourself feel less disturbed about the unfortunate activating events that have happened to you, or that you have brought upon yourself, you can use Rational Emotive Imagery as well to work on your secondary feeling of disturbance. Thus, if you feel guilty and self-downing (C1) about your rage at someone (A), you can first vividly imagine yourself continuing to create fury and temper tantrums, feeling spontaneously self-hating (if that's how you really feel) about this visualization, and can hate yourself for a short while. Then change your self-talk and philosophy (B) so that you feel only the healthy negative feelings (C2) that you prescribe for yourself about your self-defeating rage; for example, make yourself feel only sorry and disappointed (C2), not self-downing (C1), as you vividly imagine continuing to feel enraged.

At any given moment, you can fairly easily use REI to create healthy, instead of unhealthy, negative feelings about unfortunate activating events in your life. But to use it effectively, you usually have to repeat it many times, such as thirty days in a row, for each unhealthy negative feeling you are trying to change. So if you really work for a number of days at strongly imagining people treating you unfairly (point A) and if you forcefully work on changing your destructive feelings of rage (at point C1, consequence) to the healthy feelings of disappointment and regret (C2, your new consequence), you will usually find that when you thereafter imagine A, or when it actually occurs in your life, you will much more easily and automatically begin to feel the new healthy emotion (that is, C2, a new consequence) rather than the former, unhealthy one (C1).

Rational Emotive Imagery, if done repetitively, thus becomes a useful REBT tool to train yourself more thoroughly to feel healthy emotions, instead of unhealthy, negative ones when bad activating events enter your life. By consistently using REI, you can change both your thinking and feeling habits and make yourself not only less disturbed, but eventually less disturb*able*.

Give yourself the homework assignment to do REI at least once a day for several weeks to overcome a specific dysfunctional feeling. If you find yourself carrying out this assignment regularly, you can reinforce yourself with pleasures you really enjoy—such as reading, listening to music, jogging, or eating your favorite meal. If you fail to do regular REI, you can penalize (but never damn!) yourself with something you find unpleasant—such as cleaning, ironing, talking to boring people, or making a contribution to a cause you loathe. If you force yourself to do REI regularly, however—even when you find it unpleasant—you will soon find the new emotional consequences you keep achieving through its use quite rewarding.

14

REBT Diminishes Much of the Human Ego

This essay was written as a more popular and readable version of my article, "Psychotherapy and the Value of a Human," which is also included in this reader. It was given as a paper at the American Psychological Association Convention in Chicago, in September 1975. It is somewhat repetitious in that it covers much the same material as does the previous essay. The points that it makes, however, are a most important part of REBT and therefore bear repetition.

Its main thesis, that your ego or self exists but that you had better not give it any global rating, is difficult for people to understand and use, since they have both an innate and acquired tendency to rate their whole personhood. Therefore, your reading of more than one version of this major REBT may be particularly useful.

Since I first postulated the value of evaluating your thoughts, feelings, and behaviors but not your totality or being, several other writers—such as David Burns, Windy Dryden, Paul Hauck, and Arnold Lazarus—have endorsed it, and I hope this kind of support heartily continues!

Much of what we can call the human ego is vague and indeterminate and, when conceived of and given a global rating, interferes with survival and happiness. Certain aspects of "ego" seem to be vital and lead to beneficial results: people do exist, or have aliveness, for a number of years, and they also have self-consciousness, or awareness of their existence. In this sense, they have uniqueness, ongoingness, and ego. On the other hand, what people call their "self," or "totality," or "personality" has a vague, almost indefinable quality. People may well have "good" or "bad" traits—characteristics that help or hinder them in their goals of survival or happiness—but they really have no self that "is" good or bad.

To increase their health and happiness, Rational Emotive Behavior Therapy recommends that people attempt to resist the tendency to rate their self or essence and try to stick with only rating their deeds, traits, and performances. In some ways they can also evaluate the effectiveness of how they think, feel, and do. Once they choose their goals and purposes, they can rate their efficacy and efficiency in achieving them. And, as a number of experiments by the famous psychologist, Albert Bandura, and his students have shown, their belief in their efficacy will often help make them more productive and achieving. But when people give a global, overall rating of their self or ego, they almost always create self-defeating, neurotic thoughts, feelings, and behaviors.

The vast majority of systems of psychotherapy seem intent on—indeed, almost obsessed with—upholding, bolstering, and strengthening people's self-esteem. These include such diverse systems as psychoanalysis, object relations, gestalt therapy, and even some of the main cognitive-behavioral therapies. Very few systems of personality change (Zen Buddhism is one of them) take an opposing stand and try to help humans diminish or surrender some aspects of their egos, but these systems tend to have little popularity in the United States and to engender much dispute.

Carl Rogers ostensibly tried to help people achieve "unconditional positive regard" so they can see themselves as "good persons" in spite of their lack of achievement. Actually, though, he induced them to regard themselves as "okay" through their having a good relationship with a psychotherapist. But that, unfortunately, makes their self-acceptance depend on their therapist's acting uncritically toward them. If so, that is still highly conditional acceptance, instead of the unconditional self-acceptance that REBT teaches.

REBT constitutes one of the very few modern therapeutic schools that has taken something of a stand against ego-rating, and continues to take an even stronger stand in this direction as it grows in its theory and application. This paper outlines the up-to-date REBT positions on ego-rating and explains why REBT helps people diminish their ego-rating propensities.

Legitimate Aspects of the Human Ego

REBT first tries to define the various aspects of the human ego and to endorse its legitimate aspects. It assumes that an individual's main goals or purposes include remaining alive and healthy and enjoying himself or herself—experiencing a good deal of happiness and relatively little pain or dissatisfaction. Of course, we may argue with these goals, and not everyone accepts them as "good." But assuming that a person does value them, then he or she may have a valid ego, self, self-consciousness, or personality which we may conceive of as something along the following lines:

"I exist—have an ongoing aliveness that lasts perhaps eighty or more years and then apparently comes to an end, so that 'I' no longer exist."

"I exist separately, at least in part, from other humans, and can therefore conceive of myself as an individual in my own right."

"I have different traits, at least in many of their details, from other humans, and consequently my 'I-ness' or my 'aliveness' is unique. No other person in the entire world appears to have exactly the same traits as I have nor equals 'me' or constitutes the same entity as 'me'."

"I have the ability to keep existing, if I choose to do so, for a certain number of years—to have an ongoing existence, and to have some degree of consistent traits as I continue to exist. In that sense, I remain 'me' for a long time, even though my traits change in important respects."

"I have awareness or consciousness of my ongoingness, of my existence, of my behaviors and traits, and of various other aspects of my aliveness and experiencing. I can therefore say, 'I have self-consciousness.'"

"I have some power to predict and plan for my future existence or ongoingness, and to change some of my traits and behaviors in accordance with my basic values and goals. My 'rational behavior,' as the educational psychologist, Myles Friedman has pointed out, to a large extent consists of my ability to predict and plan my future."

"Because of my 'self-consciousness' and my ability to predict and plan for my future, I can to a considerable degree change my present and future traits (and hence 'existence'). In other words, I can at least partially control 'myself.'"

"I similarly have the ability to remember, understand, and learn from my past and present experiences, and to use this remembering, understanding, and learning in the service of predicting and changing my future behavior."

"I can choose to discover what I like and dislike and to try to experience more of what I like and less of what I dislike. I can also choose to survive or not to survive."

"I can choose to monitor or observe my thoughts, feelings, and actions to help myself survive and lead a more satisfying or enjoyable existence."

"I can have confidence (believe that a high probability exists) that I can remain alive and make myself reasonably happy and free from pain."

"I can choose to act as a short-range hedonist who mainly goes for the pleasure of the moment and gives little consideration to those of the future, or as a long-range hedonist who considers both the pleasures of the moment and of the future and who strives to achieve a fair degree of both."

"I can choose to see myself as having worth or value for pragmatic reasons—because I will then tend to act in my own interests, go for pleasures rather than pain, survive better, and feel good."

"I can choose to accept myself unconditionally—whether or not I do well or get approved by others. I can thereby refuse to rate 'myself,' my 'totality,' my 'personhood' at all. Instead, I can rate my traits, deeds, acts, and performances for the purposes of surviving and enjoying my life more, and not for the purposes of 'proving myself' or being 'egoistic' or showing that I have a 'better' or 'greater' value than others."

"My 'self' and my 'personality,' while in important ways individualistic and unique to me, are also very much part of my sociality and culture. An unusually large part of 'me' and how 'I' think, feel, and behave is significantly influenced—and even created—by my social learning and my being tested in various groups. I am far from being merely an individual in my own right. My personhood includes socialhood. Moreover, I rarely am a hermit but strongly choose to spend much of my life in family, school, work, neighborhood, community, and other groups. In numerous ways I am 'me' and also a groupie! My individual ways of living, therefore, coalesce with social rules of living. My self is a personal *and* social product—and process! My unconditional self-acceptance had better intrinsically include unconditional other-acceptance. I can—and will!—accept other people, as well as myself, with our virtues and our failings, with our important accomplishments and our nonachievements, just because we are alive and kicking, just because we are human! My survival and happiness is well worth striving for and so is that of the rest of humanity."

These, it seems to me, are some legitimate aspects of ego-rating. Why legitimate? Because they seem to have some reality—that is, have some social facts behind them, and because they appear to help those who subscribe to them to attain their usual basic values of surviving and feeling happy rather than miserable.

Self-Defeating Aspects of the Human Ego (Self-Rating)

At the same time, people subscribe to some illegitimate aspects of the human ego, or of self-rating, such as these:

> "I not only exist as a unique person, but as a *special* person. I am a better individual than other people because of my outstanding traits."
> "I have a superhuman rather than merely a human quality. I can do things that other people cannot possibly do and deserve to be deified for doing these things."
> "If I do not have outstanding, special, or superhuman characteristics, I am subhuman. Whenever I do not perform notably, I deserve to be devil-ified and damned."
> "The universe especially and noticeably cares about me. It has a personal interest in me and wants to see me do remarkably well and to feel happy."
> "I *need* the universe to care especially about me. If it does not, I am a lowly individual, cannot take care of myself, and must feel desperately miserable."
> "Because I exist, I *absolutely* have to succeed in life and *must* obtain love and approval by all the people that I find significant."
> "Because I exist, I *must* survive and continue to have a happy existence."

"Because I exist, I *must* exist forever, and have immortality."

"I equal my traits. If I have significant bad traits, *I* totally rate as bad; and if I have significant good traits, *I* rate as a good person."

"I particularly equal my character traits. If I treat others well and therefore have a 'good' character, I am a good person; and if I treat others badly and therefore have a 'bad' character, I have the essence of a bad person."

"In order to accept and respect myself, I must prove I have real worth—prove it by having competence, outstandingness, and the approval of others."

"To have a happy existence, I *must* have—absolutely *need*—the things I really want."

In other words, the self-rating aspects of ego tend to do you in, to handicap you, to interfere with your satisfactions. They differ enormously from the self-individualizing aspects of the ego. The latter involve how or how well you exist. You remain alive as a distinct, different, unique individual because you have various traits and performances and because you enjoy their fruits. But you have ego in the sense of self-rating because you magically think in terms of upping and downing, deifying or devil-ifying yourself for how or how well you exist. Ironically, you probably think that rating yourself or your ego will help you live as a unique person and enjoy yourself. Well, it usually won't! For the most part it will let you survive, perhaps—but pretty miserably!

Advantages of Egoism, or Self-rating

Doesn't egoism (self-rating or self-esteem) have *any* advantages? It certainly does, and therefore, undoubtedly survives in spite of its disadvantages. What advantages does it have? It tends to motivate you to succeed and to win others' approval. It gives you an interesting, preoccupying game of constantly comparing your deeds and your self to those of other people. It often helps you impress others—which in many instances has a practical value. It may help preserve your life, such as when you strive to make more money, for egoistic reasons, and thus aid your survival by means of this money.

Self-rating serves as a very easy and comfortable position to fall into; humans seem to have a biological tendency to engage in it. It can also give you enormous pleasure when you rate yourself as noble, great, or outstanding. It may motivate you to produce notable works of art, science, or invention. It can enable you to feel superior to others—at times, to even feel godlike.

Egoism obviously has real advantages. To give up self-rating completely would amount to quite a sacrifice. We cannot justifiably say that it brings no gains, produces no social or individual good.

Disadvantages of Egoism or Self-rating

These are some of the more important reasons why rating yourself as either a good or bad person has immense dangers and will frequently handicap you:

To work well, self-rating requires you to have extraordinary ability and talent, or virtual infallibility. For you then can elevate your ego only when you do well, and concomitantly depress it when you do poorly. What chance do you have of steadily or always doing well?

To have, in common parlance, a strong ego or real self-esteem really requires you to be above average or outstanding. Only if you have special talent will you likely accept yourself and rate yourself highly. But, obviously, very few individuals can have unusual, geniuslike ability. And will you personally reach that uncommon level? I doubt it!

Even if you have enormous talents and abilities, to accept or esteem yourself consistently, in an ego-rating way, you have to display them virtually all the time. Any significant lapse and you immediately tend to down yourself, and then you tend to lapse more—a truly vicious circle!

When you insist on gaining self-esteem, you basically do so in order to impress others with your great value or worth as a human. But the need to impress others and to win their approval, and thereby view yourself as a "good" person, leads to an obsession that tends to preempt a large part of your life. You seek status instead of seeking joy, and you seek universal acceptance—which you certainly have virtually no chance of ever getting!

Even when you impress others and supposedly gain worth that way, you tend to realize that you do so partly by acting and falsifying your talents. You consequently look upon yourself as a phony. Ironically, then, first you down yourself for not impressing others, but then you also down yourself for phonily impressing them!

When you rate yourself and succeed at giving yourself a superior rating, you delude yourself into thinking you have superiority over others. You may indeed have some superior traits, but you devoutly feel that you become a truly superior person, or demigod, and that delusion gives you an artificial or false sense of self-esteem.

When you insist on rating yourself as good or bad, you tend to focus on your defects, liabilities, and failings, for you feel certain that they make you into an R.P., or rotten person. By focusing on these defects you accentuate them, often making them worse; you interfere with changing them, and acquire a generalized negative view of yourself that frequently ends up in arrant self-deprecation.

When you rate your self, instead of only evaluating the effectiveness of your thoughts, feelings, and actions, you have the philosophy that you *must* prove yourself as good, and since there always exists a good chance that you will not, you tend to remain underlyingly or overtly anxious practically all the time. In addition, you may continually verge on depression, despair, and feelings of intense shame, guilt, and worthlessness.

When you preoccupyingly rate yourself, even if you succeed in earning a good rating, you do so at the expense of becoming obsessed with success and achievement. But this kind of concentration on success deflects you from doing what you really desire to do and from the goal of trying to be happy: some of the most successful people actually remain quite miserable.

By the same token, in mightily striving for outstandingness, success, and superiority, you rarely stop to ask yourself, "What do I really want—and want for myself?" So you fail to find what you really enjoy in life.

Ostensibly, your focusing on achieving greatness and superiority over others and thereby winning a high self-rating serves to help you do better in life. It actually helps you focus on your so-called worth or value rather than on your competency and happiness. Consequently, you fail to achieve many things that you otherwise could. Because you *have* to prove your utter competence, you often tend to make yourself less competent—and sometimes withdraw from competition.

Although self-rating occasionally may help you pursue creative activities, it frequently has the opposite result. For example, you may become so hung up on success and superiority that you uncreatively and obsessively-compulsively go for those goals rather than the pursuit of art, music, science, invention, or other pursuits.

When you rate yourself you tend to become self-centered rather than problem-centered. Therefore, you do not try to solve many of the practical and important problems in life but largely focus on your own navel and the pseudoproblem of *proving* yourself instead of *finding* yourself.

Self-rating generally helps you feel abnormally self-conscious. Self-consciousness, or the knowledge that you have an ongoing quality and can enjoy or not enjoy yourself, can have great advantages. But extreme self-consciousness, or continually spying on yourself and rating yourself on how well you do, takes this good trait to an obnoxious extreme and may seriously interfere with your happiness.

Self-rating encourages a great amount of prejudice. It consists of an overgeneralization: "Because one or more of my traits seems inadequate, I am a totally inadequate person." This means, in effect, that you feel prejudiced against yourself for some of your behavior. In doing this, you tend also to feel prejudiced against others for their poor behavior—or for what you consider their inferior traits. You can thus make yourself feel bigoted against blacks, Jews, Catholics, Italians, and various other groups that include some people you do not like.

Self-rating leads to necessitizing and compulsiveness. When you believe, "I must down myself when I have a crummy trait or set of performances," you usually also believe that "I absolutely *have to* have good traits or performances," and you feel compelled to act in certain "good" ways—even when you have little chance of consistently doing so.

For reasons such as those just outlined, we may make the following conclusions. First, you do seem to exist, or have aliveness, for a number of years, and you also appear to have consciousness, or awareness of your existence. In this sense, you have a human uniqueness, ongoingness, or, if you will, ego. Second, but what you normally call your "self," or your "totality," or your "personality" has a vague, almost indefinable quality, and you cannot legitimately give it a global rating or report card. You may *have* good and bad traits or characteristics that help you or hinder you in your goals of survival and happiness, and that enable you to live responsibly or irresponsibly with others, but you or your self really "aren't" good or bad. Third, when you give yourself a global rating, or have ego in the usual sense of the term, you may help yourself in various ways. On the whole, however, you tend to do much more harm than good and preoccupy yourself with rather foolish, sidetracking goals. Much of what we call emotional disturbance or neurotic symptoms directly or indirectly results from globally rating yourself and other humans. Fourth, you'd therefore better resist the tendency to rate your self, your essence, or your totality and had better stick with only rating your deeds, traits, acts, characteristics, and performances.

In other words, you had better reduce much of what we normally call your human ego and retain those parts of it that can help you experiment with life, choose what you tentatively think you want to do or avoid, and enjoy what you discover is "good" for you and the social group in which you choose to live.

More positively, the two main solutions to the problem of self-rating consist of an elegant and an inelegant answer. The inelegant solution involves your making an arbitrary but practical definition or statement about yourself: "I accept myself as good or evaluate myself as good because I exist." This proposition, though absolute and arguable, will tend to provide you with feelings of self-acceptance or self-confidence and has many advantages and few disadvantages. It will almost always work, and will preclude your having feelings of self-denigration or worthlessness as long as you hold it.

More elegantly, you can accept this proposition: "I do not have intrinsic worth or worthlessness, but merely aliveness. I'd better rate my traits and acts but not my totality or self. I fully accept myself in the sense that I know I have aliveness, and I choose to survive and live as happily as possible, and with minimum needless pain. I only require this knowledge and this choice and no other kind of self-rating."

In other words, you can decide to rate or measure only your *acts* and *performances*—your thoughts, feelings, and behaviors—by viewing them as "good" when they aid your goals and values and as "bad" when they sabotage your individual and social desires and preferences. But you can simultaneously decide not to rate your self, essence, or totality at all. Yes—*at all!*

Rational Emotive Behavior Therapy recommends this second, more elegant solution, because it appears more honest, more practical, and leads to fewer philosophical difficulties than the inelegant one. But if you absolutely insist on a self rating, we recommend that you rate yourself as "good" merely because you are alive. That kind of egoism will get you into very little trouble!

15

How to Maintain and Enhance Your Rational Emotive Behavior Gains

This article was originally written as "Maintenance and Generalization in Rational-Emotive Therapy" for the *Cognitive Behaviorist* in
1984. I quickly saw that it could be made into a useful handout for
clients and self-helpers, and revised it for that purpose. It is given to all
our clients at our psychological clinic at the Albert Ellis Institute in
New York, and many of them report that it is quite helpful. It is also
one of the most popular pamphlets in our catalog.

This essay briefly reviews the main techniques for maintaining
your REBT improvement, shows you how to deal with backsliding,
and how to generalize from working on one emotional problem to
working on other problems. It makes the point, emphasized early in
REBT, and later expounded in *Reason and Emotion in Psychotherapy,
Revised and Updated,* and the third edition of *A Guide to Rational
Living,* that if you persistently and strongly use REBT you can make
yourself not only less disturbed, but less disturbable.

If you work at using the principles and practices of Rational Emotive
Behavior Therapy, you will be able to change your self-defeating

thoughts, feelings, and behaviors and to feel much better than when you started therapy. Good! But at times you will also fall back—sometimes far back. No one is perfect, and practically all people take one step backward to every two or three steps forward. Why? Because that is the nature of humans: to improve, to stop improving at times, and sometimes to backslide.

How can you slow down your tendency to fall back? How can you maintain and enhance your therapy goals? Here are some methods that we have tested at the Albert Ellis Institute's clinic in New York and that many of our clients have found effective.

How to Maintain Your Improvement

When you improve and then fall back to old feelings of anxiety, depression, or self-downing, try to remind yourself and pinpoint exactly what thoughts, feelings, and behaviors you once changed to bring about your improvement. If you again feel depressed, think back to how you previously used REBT to make yourself undepressed. For example, you may remember that:

1. You stopped telling yourself that you were worthless and that you could never succeed in getting what you wanted.
2. You did well in a job or love affair and proved to yourself that you did have some ability and that you were lovable.
3. You forced yourself to go on interviews instead of avoiding them and thereby helped yourself overcome your anxiety about them.

Remind yourself of past thoughts, feelings, and behaviors that you have helped yourself by changing.

Keep thinking, thinking, and thinking rational beliefs (RBs) or coping statements, such as: "It's great to succeed, but I can fully accept myself as a person and have enjoyable experiences even when I fail!" Don't merely parrot these statements, but go over them carefully many times and think them through until you really begin to believe and feel that they are accurate.

Keep seeking, discovering, disputing, and challenging irrational beliefs (IBs) with which you are once again upsetting yourself. Take each important irrational belief—such as, "I have to succeed in order to be a worthwhile person!"—and keep asking yourself: "Why is this true?"

"Where is the evidence that my worth to myself, and my enjoyment of living, utterly depends on my succeeding at something?" "How does failing at an important task make me totally unacceptable as a human?"

Keep forcefully and persistently disputing your irrational beliefs whenever you see that you are letting them creep back in again. And even when you don't actively hold them, realize that they may arise once more, bring them to your consciousness, and preventively—but vigorously!—dispute them.

Keep risking and doing things that you irrationally fear—such as riding in elevators, job hunting, or creative writing. Once you have partly overcome one of your irrational fears, keep acting against it on a regular basis. If you feel uncomfortable in forcing yourself to do things that you are unrealistically afraid of doing, don't allow yourself to avoid doing them—or else you'll preserve your discomfort forever! Practice making yourself as *un*comfortable as you can be, in order to eradicate your irrational fears and to become unanxious and comfortable later.

Try to clearly see the real difference between *healthy* negative feelings—such as those of sorrow, regret, and frustration, when you do not get some of the important things you want—and *unhealthy* negative feelings, such as depression, anxiety, self-hatred, and self-pity.

Whenever you feel *over*concerned (panicked) or *unduly* miserable (depressed) acknowledge that you are having a statistically normal but a psychologically unhealthy feeling and that you are mainly bringing it on yourself with some dogmatic should, ought, or must.

Realize that you are capable of changing your unhealthy (or "musturbatory") feelings back into healthy (or preferential) ones. Take your depressed feelings and work on them until you only feel sorry and regretful. Take your anxious feelings and work on them until you only feel concerned and apprehensive. Use rational emotive imagery to vividly imagine unpleasant activating events even before they happen; let yourself feel unhealthily upset (anxious, depressed, enraged, or self-downing) as you imagine them; then work on your feelings to change them to healthy negative emotions (concern, sorrow, annoyance, or regret) as you keep imagining some of the worst things happening. Don't give up until you actually do change your feelings.

Avoid self-defeating procrastination. Do unpleasant tasks fast—today! If you still procrastinate, reward yourself with certain things that you enjoy, for example, eating, vacationing, reading, or socializing—only *after* you have performed the tasks that you easily avoid. If this won't work, give yourself a severe penalty—such as talking to a boring person for two hours or performing an unpleasant task—every time you procrastinate.

Show yourself that it is an absorbing challenge and something of an adventure to maintain your emotional health and to keep yourself reasonably happy no matter what kind of misfortunes assail you. Make the uprooting of your misery one of the most important things in your life—something you are utterly determined to steadily work at achieving. Fully acknowledge that you almost always have some choice about how to think, feel, and behave; then throw yourself actively into making that choice for yourself.

Remember—and use—the three main insights of REBT that were first outlined in *Reason and Emotion in Psychotherapy* in 1962. First, you largely *choose* to disturb yourself about the unpleasant events of your life, although you may be encouraged to do so by external happenings and by social learning. You mainly feel the way you think. When obnoxious and frustrating things happen to you at point A (activating events or adversities), you consciously or unconsciously select rational beliefs (RBs) that lead you to feel sad and regretful, and you also select irrational beliefs (IBs) that lead you to feel anxious, depressed, and self-hating.

Second, no matter how or when you acquired your irrational beliefs and your self-sabotaging habits, you now, in the present, *choose* to maintain them—and that is why you are disturbed. Your past history and your present life conditions importantly *affect* you; but they don't *disturb* you. Your present philosophy is the main contributor to your current disturbance.

Third, there is no magical way for you to change your personality or your strong tendencies to needlessly upset yourself. Basic personality change requires persistent work and practice to enable you to alter your irrational beliefs, unhealthy feelings, and self-destructive behaviors.

Steadily and unfrantically look for personal pleasures and enjoyments—such as reading, entertainment, sports, hobbies, art, science, and other absorbing interests. Make your major life goal the achievement of not only emotional health but also real enjoyment. Try to become involved in a long-term purpose, goal, or interest in which you can remain truly absorbed. A good happy life will give you something to live for, distract you from many serious woes, and encourage you to preserve and to improve your mental health.

Try to keep in touch with several other people who know

something about REBT and who can help review it with you. Tell them about problems that you have difficulty coping with and let them know how you are using REBT to overcome these problems. See if they agree with your solutions and can suggest additional and better kinds of REBT disputing that you can use to work against your irrational beliefs.

Practice using REBT with some of your friends, relatives, and associates who are willing to let you try to help them with it. The more often you use it with others and are able to see what their IBs are and to try to talk them out of their self-defeating ideas, the more you will be able to understand the main principles of REBT and use them with yourself. When you see other people acting irrationally and in a disturbed manner, try to figure out—with or without talking to them about it—what their main irrational beliefs are and how these could be actively and vigorously disputed.

When you are in REBT individual or group therapy, try to tape-record many of your sessions and listen to these carefully between sessions, so that some of the ideas that you learned in therapy sink in. After therapy has ended, from time to time play these tape-recordings back to yourself to remind you how to deal with some of your old problems or new ones that may arise.

Keep reading rational writings and listening to REBT audio- and videocassettes. Included in the instruction sheet you were given when you started therapy at the Albert Ellis Institute is a list of some of the main books and cassettes giving the principles and practices of REBT. Read and listen to several of these and keep going back to them from time to time.

How to Deal With Backsliding

Accept your backsliding as normal—as something that happens to almost all people who at first improve emotionally and then fall back. See it as part of your human fallibility. Don't make yourself feel ashamed when some of your old symptoms return, and don't think that you have to handle them entirely by yourself and that it is weak for you to seek some additional sessions of therapy or to talk to your friends about your renewed problems.

When you backslide, look at your self-defeating behavior as bad and unfortunate, but refuse to put yourself down for engaging in this behavior. Use the highly important REBT principle of refraining from rating your self or your being and of measuring only your acts, deeds, and traits. You are always a person who acts well or badly—and never a "good" or "bad" person. No matter how badly you fall back and bring on your old disturbances again, work at fully accepting yourself with this unfortunate or weak behavior, and then try—and keep trying—to change your behavior.

Go back to the ABCs of REBT and clearly see what you did to fall back to your old symptoms. At A (Activating Events or Adversity), you usually experienced some failure or rejection. At RB (Rational Belief) you probably told yourself that you didn't like failing and didn't want to be rejected. If you only stayed with these rational beliefs, you would merely feel sorry, regretful, disappointed, or frustrated. But if you felt disturbed, you probably then went on to some irrational beliefs (IBs), such as: "I *must* not fail! It's *horrible* when I do!" "I *have to* be accepted, because if I'm not that makes me an unlovable worthless person!" If you reverted to these IBs, you probably felt, at C (emotional Consequence) once again depressed and self-downing.

Thus, you can ask yourself, "Why *must* I not fail? Is it really horrible if I do?" You can answer: "There is no reason why I *must* not fail, though I can think of several reasons why it would be highly undesirable. It's not horrible if I do fail—only distinctly inconvenient."

You can also dispute your other irrational beliefs by asking yourself, "Where is it written that I *have* to be accepted? How do I become an unlovable, worthless person if I am rejected?" You can answer: "I never *have to be* accepted, though I would very much *prefer* to be. If I am rejected, that makes me, alas, a person who is rejected this time by this individual under these conditions, but it hardly makes me an unlovable, worthless person who will always be rejected by anyone for whom I really care."

Keep looking for, finding, and actively and vigorously disputing your irrational beliefs to which you have once again relapsed and that are now contributing to your feeling anxious or depressed. Keep doing this, over and over, until you build intellectual and emotional muscle (just as you would build physical muscle by learning how to exercise and then by continuing to exercise).

Don't fool yourself into believing that if you merely change your language you will always change your thinking. If you neurotically tell yourself, "I *must* succeed and be approved," and change this statement to "I *prefer* to succeed and be approved," you may still really be convinced that "I really *have to* do well to be loved." Before you stop your disputing and before you are satisfied with your answers to it, keep on doing it until you are *really* convinced of your rational answers and until your feelings of disturbance truly disappear. Then do the same thing many, many times, until your new E (Effective Philosophy) becomes hardened and habitual—which it almost always will if you keep working at it and thinking it through.

Convincing yourself lightly or "intellectually" of your new effective philosophy or rational beliefs won't help very much or persist very long. Do so very strongly and vigorously, and do so many times. Thus, you can powerfully convince yourself, until you *really* feel it: "I do not *need* what I *want!* I never *have* to succeed, no matter how great I *wish* to do so!" "I *can* stand being rejected by someone I care for. It *won't* kill me—and I still can lead a happy life!" "No human is damnable and worthless, including and especially *me!*"

How to Generalize From Working on One Emotional Problem to Working on Other Problems

Show yourself that your present emotional problem and the ways in which you bring it on are not unique and that most emotional and behavioral difficulties are largely created by irrational beliefs (IBs). Whatever your IBs are, you can overcome them by strongly and persistently disputing and acting against them.

Recognize that you tend to have three major kinds of irrational beliefs that lead you to disturb yourself, and that the emotional and behavioral problems you want to relieve fall into one, two, or all three of these categories:

1. "I *must* do well and *have to* be approved of by people whom I find important." This leads you to feel anxious, depressed, and self-hating, and to avoid doing things at which you may fail or relationships that may not turn out well.
2. "Other people *must* treat me fairly and nicely!" This contributes to your feeling angry, furious, violent, and overrebellious.
3. "The conditions under which I live *must* be comfortable and free from major hassles!" This tends to produce feelings of low frustration tolerance and self-pity, and sometimes anger and depression.

Recognize that when you employ any one of these three absolutistic musts—or any of the innumerable variations on them—you derive other irrational conclusions from them, such as:

1. "Because I am not doing as well as I *must*, I am an incompetent worthless individual!" (Self-downing)
2. "Since I am not being approved by people whom I find important, as I *have to* be, it's *awful* and *terrible!*" (Awfulizing)
3. "Because others are not treating me as fairly and as nicely as they *absolutely should* they are utterly rotten people and deserve to be damned!" (Damnation)
4. "Since the conditions under which I live are not that comfortable, and since my life has several major hassles, as it *must* not have, I can't stand it! My existence is a horror!" (Can't-stand-it-it-is)
5. "Because I have failed and been rejected as I absolutely *ought not* have been, I'll *always* fail and *never* get accepted, as I *must* be! My life will be hopeless and joyless forever!" (Overgeneralizing)

Work at seeing that these irrational beliefs are part of your general repertoire of thoughts and feelings and that you bring them to many different kinds of situations. Realize that in most cases in which you feel seriously upset and act in a self-defeating manner, you are consciously or unconsciously sneaking in one or more of these IBs. Consequently, if you reduce them in one area and are still emotionally disturbed about something else, you can use the same REBT principles to discover your IBs in the new area and minimize them there.

Repeatedly show yourself that you normally won't disturb yourself and remain disturbed if you abandon your absolute *shoulds, oughts,* and *musts* and consistently replace them with flexible and unrigid (though still strong) *desires* and *preferences.*

Continue to acknowledge that you can change your irrational beliefs by rigorously (not rigidly!) using realistic and healthy thinking. You can show yourself that your irrational beliefs are only hypotheses, not facts. You can logically, realistically, and pragmatically dispute them in many ways, such as these:

1. You can show yourself that your IBs are self-defeating, that they interfere with your goals and happiness, for if you firmly convince yourself that you *must* succeed at important tasks and *have to* be approved by all the significant people in your life, you will fail at times—and thereby inevitably make yourself anxious and depressed instead of sorry and frustrated.
2. Your irrational beliefs do not conform to social reality—and especially do not conform to the facts of human fallibility. If you always *had* to succeed, if the universe commanded that you *must*

do so, obviously you always *would* succeed! But of course you often don't. If you invariably *had* to be approved of by others, you could never be disapproved of. But obviously you frequently are. Clearly, the universe is not arranged so that you will always get what you demand, so although your desires are often realistic, your godlike commands definitely are not!

3. Your irrational beliefs are illogical, inconsistent, or contradictory. No matter how much you *want* to succeed and to be approved of, it never follows that therefore you *must* do well in these (or any other) respects. No matter how desirable justice or politeness is, it never *has to* exist. Although REBT disputing is not infallible or sacred, it efficiently helps you discover which of your beliefs are irrational and self-defeating and how to use realistic, pragmatic, and logical thinking to minimize them. If you keep using flexible thinking, you will avoid dogma and set up assumptions about yourself, other people, and world conditions so that you always keep them open to change.

Try to set up some main goals and purposes in life—goals you would like very much to reach but that you never tell yourself you absolutely must attain. Keep checking to see how you are progressing with these goals, and at times revise them. Keep yourself oriented toward the goals that you select and that are not harmful to you or others. Instead of making yourself extremely self-interested or socially-interested, a balanced absorption in both these kinds of goals will often work best for you and the community in which you live.

If you get bogged down and begin to lead a life that seems too miserable or dull, review the points made here and work at using them. If you fall back or fail to go forward at the pace you prefer, don't hesitate to return to therapy for some booster sessions or to join one of the Institute's regular therapy groups.

16

A Dictionary of Rational Emotive Feelings and Behaviors

Ted Crawford has been in touch with me for over thirty-five years, ever since he contacted me about the first edition of *Reason and Emotion in Psychotherapy*. Though he lives in California, we have been close friends all this time, and I visit him about once a year when I am giving talks and workshops on the West Coast. He works in the field of communication and is one of the best developers and teachers of how people can relate to each other in this country. He has adapted REBT to the communication process, and I am writing a book with him on how people can improve their relationships. It includes some highly original points by Ted on communication guidelines.

The concept of Rational (self-helping) Beliefs (RBs) and irrational (self-defeating) Beliefs (IBs) seems simple enough after you use REBT for awhile. But Ted wanted to make them even clearer and more useful, so he suggested that we publish a dictionary of rational feelings, thoughts, and behaviors. I agreed, and we soon came up with this article. It doesn't pretend to be exhaustive or even complete, but we think it gives a good idea of what rational and irrational beliefs lead to healthy and unhealthy feelings and emotions.

17

Achieving Self-Actualization

A chieving emotional health and self-actualization are goals that overlap but are not quite the same. As REBT shows, when you are anxious, depressed, enraged, and self-hating, you strive for certain healthy goals, such as unconditional self-acceptance, unconditional other-acceptance, and high frustration tolerance. But even if you achieve these aims and are hardly ever miserable, you still may be far from happy or self-actualizing. So REBT usually helps you, first, to be less disturbed, and second, to discover what you really enjoy in life. It then helps you to get more of that and to discover what you really dislike, and helps you to get less of that. Seems simple, but it has, as this paper points out, its complications. Other authorities on self-actualization—including Abe Maslow, Carl Rogers, S. I. Hayakawa, and Ted Crawford—have given imperfect answers to solving this problem. So here is the imperfect REBT answer!

Critique of Self-Actualization Theories

The self-actualization theories of Abraham Maslow, Carl Rogers, and other authorities have been seriously questioned by a number of critics. I shall now consider some of their major objections to see how Rational Emotive Behavior Therapy theory and practice deals with them.

Is self-actualization too individualistic, self-seeking, and indulgent? Maslow's concept of self-actualization has often been attacked for these reasons. This is partly true, but the REBT theory includes both self-interest *and* social interest. Because humans choose to live with others, their morality, emotional health, and self-actualization had better always include their being quite concerned about the present and future welfare of others *and* their entire social group. Their very survival—especially in a nuclear age—seems to require a great deal of social interest.

M. Daniels questions whether deciding to pick self-actualizing goals defeats people's spontaneous ways of living in a more fully-functioning manner. No, says REBT, not if people adopt an and/also and not merely an either/or approach. One of the main goals of actualizing can be to seek *more* spontaneous ways of living, and one main by-product of spontaneously (and risk-takingly) trying new pursuits is to discover new enjoyments and then to make re-achieving them a future *goal*. Experimentation partly *is* goal-seeking, and goal-seeking partly *is* spontaneously experimenting with new endeavors. They can both be spontaneous and planned. I once planned to unspontaneously force myself to speak in public in order to overcome my public speaking phobia, and as I did so, I began to spontaneously enjoy what I was doing. As a teenager, I spontaneously had my first orgasm without realizing that I was about to bring it on, and thereafter I plotted and schemed to bring on more and more of them!

Do people have an essential "real self" which they can discover and actualize? Maslow, Karen Horney, and to some extent Carl Rogers hold that people have an underlying biological or transpersonal "real" or "true" self that they can discover and actualize. But, as Daniels points out, their biological real self is somewhat restrictive, and REBT holds that it is quite different for all individuals and that, with experimentation and hard work, it can even be significantly changed. Thus, people with strong biological tendencies to be weak-willed, undisciplined, or irrational can learn and work hard to overcome their unfulfilling handicaps.

REBT holds that several human aspirations and goals—such as sex, love, gustatory, and meaning-oriented desires—are at least partly (and individualistically) motivated but that they are also strongly socially and environmentally influenced; and, they can also be distinctly—and consciously—self-developed and modified. REBT is highly skeptical that humans have any "true" transpersonal, transcendental, or mystical selves, though they are certainly often born and reared with strong propensities to think or experience that they do. REBT acknowledges that a belief in religion, God, mysticism, pollyannaism, and irrationality may help people at times. But it also points out that such beliefs often do much more harm than good and block a more fully functioning life.

Daniels rightly observes that the biological "real" self of Horney, Maslow, and Rogers is supposed to be "truer" and "better" than a socially acquired conforming self, but that this idea "leads to the denial of constructive social involvement, to existential isolation and individualism." REBT upholds both individualism *and* social involvement— *not* either/or. It says that because people *choose* to live in a social group (family, community, nation) and not to be asocial hermits, they need to learn to care for themselves *and* for others, and preserve—and help actualize—themselves *as well as* their sociality. They can choose—or not choose—to put themselves first in some respects, but preferably should put others—particularly some selected other—a close second.

Maslow held that self-actualizing people are biologically and personally motivated (have a "real" self), and, somewhat contradictorily, held that they are also motivated by nonpersonal, objective, and universal "values of being". He also saw self-transcendence as altruistic and socially interested, and devoted to mystical pathways that transcend human consciousness and have a nonbodily, "spiritual" aspect. REBT holds that people can be biologically-inclined to be self-interested *and also* biologically and sociologically inclined to be altruistic and socially involved. So it unites or integrates Maslow's and Rogers's individualistic and socialized goals.

REBT, however, sees no evidence that humans ever truly transcend their humanity and develop a transpersonal, transcendental, or superhuman "self" that achieves "higher, miraculous states of consciousness." They frequently aspire to such mystical states, and devoutly believe that they experience them. But they are probably self-deluded and do not really achieve Absolute Truth, godliness, or completely nonhuman consciousness. So, however much human mystics experience Nirvana, selflessness, unity with the Universe, or similar "transpersonal" states, it is unlikely (though not impossible) that they really have superhuman powers and very unlikely that their special state of altered consciousness is "better" than the usual state of consciousness. In some ways it appears to be a deficient, pollyannaish, unauthentic state!

A. McIntyre partly concurs with L. Geller that moral consensus and agreed-upon self-actualization are based on conflicting premises that are mainly emotive and include assertions of personal preference or imply some more arbitrary ideal that should be achieved but is never really agreed upon. Again, this seems to be true, but mainly means that no single "ideal" set of characteristics will suffice for all people at all times, but that they can still select "ideal" (or "nonideal") traits and then experiment (which is almost the REBT essence of health and actualization) to determine whether they are suitable.

McIntyre says that because self-actualization involves a goal, as we search for progress in achieving it we discover more about it and change it. Daniels agrees that "a theory of self-actualization…can therefore only be particularly accurate; it is forever vague and incomplete."[1] REBT adds that not only the theory but also the *practice* of self-fulfillment is almost by necessity experimental, changing, and incomplete.

Geller holds that it is meaningless to speak of general self-actualization, because it is highly multidimensional and involves the pursuit of excellence or enjoyment in whatever ways each individual chooses to desire and emphasize. This argument has much truth to it, since both "healthy" and "enjoyable," not to mention "maximally enjoyable" pursuits, differ from culture to culture and from individual to individual in each culture. "*Self*-actualizing," in fact, implies to some degree being chosen and actualized by each individual self. However, because almost all humans have many similar biological tendencies (e.g., to like to perform well and be approved of by others) and because most cultures abet many of these tendencies (though, of course, in different ways), the REBT hypothesis is that much of the time most contemporary people will lead both a "healthier" and "more enjoyable" life if they achieve several of the "self-actualizing" characteristics listed in this chapter.

Does self-actualization mean "peak experiences" and "altered states of consciousness"? Maslow sometimes implied that maximum self-actualization is achieved by what he called "peak experiences," though at other times he said that they "can come at any time in life to any person."[2] Other writers have identified self-actualization with "altered states of consciousness." Both "peak experiences" and "altered states of consciousness," however, have several different meanings, and none seem to be intrinsically involved with self-actualization, as I shall now indicate.

Both Maslow and S. R. Wilson identify "peak experiences" and "altered states of consciousness" with the "real self" and its somatic-experiential element. They hold that people can learn to minimize their rational, symbolic interactional, or judging selves and become aware of somatic states and feelings that they otherwise ignore, and thereby achieve "peak" or "altered" experiences and become more self-actualizing. I (and REBT) hold that this is partly true, but that most humans only occasionally achieve this "unconscious" state; that they usually achieve it by consciously, philosophically striving for, interpreting, and defining it; that they almost always achieve it very briefly and keep flitting back to regular evaluative consciousness; and that "peak experiences" are both cognitive and somatic-experiential, as Maslow also said. Seymour Epstein, a well-known psychologist, has a view of the experiential part of our personality as being both cognitive and emotional that is illuminating in this respect.

Some authorities, such as the Zen Buddhists, identify "peak experiences" and "altered states of consciousness" with nonego, allegedly nonjudgmental, pure contemplative states (which, paradoxically, are judged to be "better" than ordinary states of consciousness). Such states probably can be—again, occasionally and briefly—achieved. REBT partly goes along with this view, since it encourages people to never judge nor measure their selves, essence, totality, or being, for that will lead them to overgeneralize and self-defeatingly deify or devil-ify themselves. But REBT favors people still rating their deeds, acts, and performances as "good" or "bad" for certain chosen values and goals, and I think that humans would not survive if they did none of this kind of rating.

Moreover, even if people could often achieve pure egolessness, zero judging, and a Zen state of no-mind, and even if that state helped them (at least temporarily) give up feelings of depression, panic, and damnation, they would then throw away the baby with the bath water, probably achieve little or no pleasure, and therefore be dubiously self-actualized. They could *define* egolessness (and its concomitant, desirelessness) as self-actualization. But in any usual sense of the word, would it really be that?

Psychologist Sid Wilson identifies people's "real," "somatic" self and "altered states of consciousness" with what Mihali Csikszentmihalyi calls flow experiences—that is, activities in which people become so intensely or flowingly involved that they derive unusual fun or joy because, as Wilson puts it, their "self-sustaining, self-protective thought processes that characterize ordinary consciousness are minimized."[3] This "flow experience" is similar to what REBT calls a "vital absorbing interest" and indeed often adds to people's enjoyment.

However, as Wilson notes, most flow activities include rational thought and also include people's evaluating their performances but only minimally evaluating their selves or personhoods. I would call them a somewhat different but hardly an altered state of consciousness. Flow activities are definitely encouraged in REBT, but REBT also encourages and teaches people how to nondamn and nondeify their selves in innumerable nonflow, as well as in flow, activities. Flow may well lead to reduced self-judgment, but conscious, philosophic use of REBT will lead to even less self-judgment. What is more, flow is almost always temporary, and flowing individuals then return to self-evaluation—unless they use REBT or some other highly conscious thinking to permanently minimize it.

Maslow, Charles Tart (a transcendental psychologist), and others identify "peak experiences" and "altered states of consciousness" with mystical, transcendental experiences. This may well be an illegitimate connection, as it can easily be argued whether transcendental experience really exists. Thus, I can *believe* and *feel* that I am God, the Center of the Universe, the Devil, an Eternal Force, or what I will. But *am* I truly what I say and feel I am? Or am I deluded? Even if we call mystical, transcendental experiences "real" (and in one sense we may because my belief that I am God or the Center of the Universe itself is some kind of experience), is it good, is it enjoyable, is it self-actualizing for me to have this mystical feeling? Only if I (and my fellow mystical-minded individuals) think it is, for I could feel terrified by my believing myself to be the Devil—or God! And I could be delighted to be my all-too-human self who has no transcendental experiences. So mystical "altered states of consciousness," or "peak experiences," can be anti- instead of self-actualizing.

Rational Emotive Behavior Therapy, like most other therapies, has a dual goal: first, to help people overcome their emotional blocks and disturbances; and second, to help them become more fully functioning, self-actualizing, and happier than they otherwise would be. I have elsewhere outlined the REBT goals of nondisturbance, so let me now describe some of the goals that presumably would be desirable for a more fully functioning or self-actualizing person.

I take my main outlook in this respect from my friend Ted Crawford, who has been working on a theory of the fully functioning person and finds that most people are split or fragmented and think, feel, and act in terms of either/or rather than and/also. They need to go beyond the acceptance of an integrated wholeness that helps them accept and cope with meaning that has logic and consistency but that also acknowledges ambiguity, paradox, inconsistent "truths," and other troublesome cognitions that seem to block individuals from becoming fully functioning. To achieve this integrated wholeness, they can choose to accept the principles and practice of and/also many, many times "until the skills and attitudes that enable one to successfully go beyond 'and/also' are a stable habit."[4]

Actively Choosing Self-Actualization

I have worked with Ted Crawford for a number of years on his theory of self-actualization and its linkage with Rational Emotive Behavior Therapy, so let me now state his latest, succinct version and then expand on it. To make a stable habit full functioning, Ted states that one had better "consciously choose the goal or purpose of becoming fully functioning."[5]

Yes, REBT holds that people are born as well as reared with strong tendencies both to defeat themselves, and to ignore their capacity to function more fully *and* to change their self-destructive thoughts, feelings, and behaviors to achieve fuller functioning. To a large degree, they *choose* emotional-behavioral disturbance (or health) and *choose* restricted (or fuller) functioning. Therefore, to more fully actualize themselves, they had better *choose* to work at achieving more growth, development, and happiness.

More specifically, to make themselves more fully functioning, people need to ask themselves, "What do I really like and dislike?" "How can I experiment and discover what I truly prefer and prefer not to feel and do?" "Which of my likes (e.g., smoking) and dislikes (e.g., exercising) will probably be self-harming as well as enjoyable?" "What am I likely to prefer and abhor in the future?" "What do I do to enhance my preferences and decrease my dislikes?" "How can I align my opinions more closely to the data of my experiences?"

By discovering the answers to relevant questions like these, and then by *acting on* this information, most people can push themselves toward greater self-actualization.

Ted Crawford advises that people who want to achieve greater self-actualization had better "dispute or otherwise let go of shoulds and musts." This is a cardinal theory and practice of REBT. More specifically, REBT holds that people usually make themselves needlessly anxious, depressed, self-hating, and self-pityingly and needlessly dysfunctional when they take their healthy preferences for achievement, approval, and comfort and change them into dogmatic, extreme musts, demands, and commands on themselves, others, and the environment. In so doing, they almost always sabotage their self-fulfilling urges and potentials. Therefore, as Crawford advises, they had better dispute or otherwise let go of their shoulds and musts.

How? By using a number of REBT cognitive, emotive, and behavioral methods. Thus, they can cognitively question and challenge their own absolutist demands and commands, reframe them, convince themselves of rational coping statements, read and listen to REBT materials, talk others out of *their* musts, use problem-solving methods, and otherwise acquire a basic philosophy of tolerance, self-acceptance, and long-range hedonism. Emotively, people can surrender their self-sabotaging musts by using strong coping statements, rational emotive imagery, shame-attacking exercises, role-playing, and other REBT dramatic evocative techniques. Behaviorally, nonactualizing people can act against and dispel their musts by making themselves use the REBT (and other cognitive-behavioral) methods of in vivo desensitization, forceful homework assignments, reinforcement and penalizing procedures, and skill-training techniques.

As Crawford points out, self-actualizing solutions can be better achieved if people "join the problem without the requirement of a solution or the promise of a solution. The requirement that a solution should and must be available blocks the development toward self-actualization."[6] When people join a self-actualizing problem in an and/also way, they flexibly observe, guess, invent a theory, revise their guesses, and grow an emergent "solution" or new possibilities.

More concretely, people don't absolutely have to find a solution to the problem of actualizing themselves. If they tell themselves, "I *must* actualize myself! I *must* not fail to achieve perfect self-actualization!" that is akin to saying, "I *must not* think of a pink elephant!" Then they most probably *will* think of a pink elephant—and will block their actualizing themselves. The thought that it is necessary to achieve actualization will interfere with their asking and answering the kinds of questions mentioned above that will lead to their individually discovering what it is, how to achieve it, and how to work at achieving it.

Crawford notes that people who want to actualize themselves had better "explore the problem as a system without blaming anyone for the status quo or for resisting the 'solution' one has, and thereby redesign the system. When there is a problem, all participants contribute to the situation (or system) that creates the problem—even when they are innocent of wrongdoing. They are responsible for what they do but not blameworthy or damnable as *persons*."[7] In more concrete REBT terms this means:

Don't blame *anyone*, including yourself, for *anything*. Acknowledge that you (and others) may behave ineffectually and thereby defeat yourself and others about many important goals and values. But only negatively rate or assess what you and they *do*, and actively refrain from measuring your *self*—or their *selves*—for poor performances. Work at unconditionally accepting your self, your *you*ness, your humanity, *whether or not* you perform well or are approved of by others.

At the same time, measure or rate what your problem in actualizing yourself is; how well you are working at "solving" it; how good your "solutions" probably are; and how you can keep working to improve them. But don't evaluate, nor especially damn, yourself (or other people) for the poor "solutions" you or they devise. You (and others) may act badly about your (and their) self-actualization, and you may use your "bad" solutions to work for "better" ones—but not if you denigrate yourself and them for both of your responsibility for low-level self-actualization.

Because you refrain from condemning *people*, your self-actualizing plans and accomplishments will very likely remain perpetually open-ended and revisable—which is one of the main characteristics (one might almost say requisites) of a more fully-functioning person. According to REBT, rational people consider and utilize alternate, nonrigid paths to happiness, and are therefore open to endless *re*actualization.

Ted Crawford notes that fully-functioning individuals "meet the challenge of a situation as soon as feasible in contrast to procrastination. Procrastination delays, usually significantly, the development of such a stable habit."[8] More specifically, REBT adds to his anti-procrastination stance:

You additionally sabotage your emotional health and maximum fulfillment, after doing so by damning yourself and others, by indulging in low frustration tolerance (LFT). When you keep believing that life is too hard, that it *must not* be that hard, and that you can't stand the hassles and efforts required to enjoy it, you add discomfort, anxiety, and depression to ego disturbance, and thereby increase your frustrations and annoyances.

Procrastination and low frustration tolerance not only make you dysfunctional and miserable, but also enormously block your ability to learn and use REBT and other effective therapies. Catch-22: whining about life's unniceties creates LFT and then LFT augments whining and sabotages self-actualizing change!

Characteristics of Self-Actualizing Persons

The REBT view of self-actualization overlaps with views from other schools of thought, such as those of Carl Rogers and Abraham Maslow, which at times differ significantly from REBT. But the REBT view also mirrors the ideas of Alfred Korzybski, the founder, and S.I. Hayakawa, the promulgator, of general semantics, a school of thought that it is close to and which has significantly influenced REBT. As Hayakawa points out, some of the characteristics of the more fully-functioning individual that are endorsed by Maslow, Rogers, and general semantics, and with which REBT agrees, are these:

Nonconformity and individuality. Fully-functioning persons (FFPs) are not "fully adjusted" to nor outrightly rebellious against the social group. "The semantically well-oriented person is primarily concerned with the territory and not with the map, with the social reality rather than the social façade."[9] REBT has always endorsed sensible nonconformity and individuality in sex, love, marital, vocational, recreational, and other aspects of life. It has, from its start, also been a highly unconventional form of psychotherapy and has only recently been accepted as a leader in the more conventional cognitive-behavioral movement.

Self-awareness. FFPs are aware of their own feelings, do not try to repress them, often act upon them, and even when they do not act upon them are able to admit them to awareness. In REBT terms, they *acknowledge* their negative feelings (e.g., anxiety and rage) but do not necessarily *act out* on them. They often make efforts to *change* their feelings when they are unhealthy and self-defeating. They "know themselves" but also know how little they know about themselves.

Acceptance of ambiguity and uncertainty. FFPs accept ambiguity, uncertainty, the unknown, approximateness, and some amount of disorder. "Emotionally mature individuals accept the fact that, as far as has yet been discovered, we live in a world of probability and chance, where there are not, nor probably ever will be, absolute necessities nor complete certainties. Living in such a world is not only tolerable but, in terms of adventure, learning, and striving, can even be very exciting and pleasurable."[10]

Tolerance. FFPs are extensional—responding to similarities *and differences,* rather than intensional—tending to ignore differences among things that have some name. They do not see all trees as green, all education as good, nor all modern art as silly. The REBT version: "Emotionally sound people are intellectually flexible, tend to be open to change at all times and are prone to take an unbigoted (or, at least, less bigoted) view of the infinitely varied people, ideas, and things in the world around them."[11]

Acceptance of human animality. FFPs accept their and others' physical and "animal" nature, and rarely disgust themselves about body products, odors, or functions. In REBT terms, they may not like various sensations and feelings but refrain from "awfulizing" about them.

Commitment and intrinsic enjoyment. FFPs tend to enjoy work and sports as ends or pleasures in themselves and not merely as means toward ends (e.g., working for money or playing sports to achieve good health). As REBT puts it, commitment to people, things, and ideas, mainly because people *want to* be absorbed and committed, is one of the main aspects of emotional health and happiness. Robert Harper and I have particularly endorsed people's throwing themselves into a long-term vital and absorbing interest in order to achieve maximum fulfillment and happiness.

Creativity and originality. Maslow, Rogers, and Hayakawa, as well as many other authorities, show that fully-functioning personalities are usually innovative, creative, and original about artistic as well as commonplace problems. In REBT terms, they tend to be self-directed rather than other-directed, original rather than conformist, flexible rather than rigid, and "seem to lead better lives when they have at least one major creative interest."[12]

Social interest and ethical trust. S. I. Hayakawa, endorsing Alfred Korzybski, Abraham Maslow, and Carl Rogers, holds that FFPs are deeply ethical, trustworthy, constructive, and socialized. REBT, following Alfred Adler, puts the same point of view this way: "Emotionally and mentally healthy people tend to be considerate and fair to others; to engage in collaborative and cooperative endeavors; at times to be somewhat altruistic; and to distinctly enjoy some measure of interpersonal and group relationships.[11]

Enlightened self-interest. Healthy and enjoying people are true to themselves as well as to others, often put themselves first, usually put a few selected others a close second, and the rest of the world not too far behind. Their self-interest is mainly directed toward *enjoying*, and not to *proving*, themselves.

Self-direction. FFPs, while interdependent and supporting, and at times asking support from others, largely plan and plot their own destiny (albeit within a social context) and do not overwhelmingly *need* outside support for their effectiveness and well-being.

Flexibility and scientific outlook. Science not only uses empiricism and logic, but as Karl Popper, Bertrand Russell, Ludwig Wittgenstein, and other philosophers of science have shown, it is intrinsically open-minded and flexible. As REBT emphasizes, people largely neuroticize themselves with rigid, imperative musts and shoulds, and, conversely, are significantly less neurotic and self-actualizing when they scientifically dispute their dogmatic, unconditional musts and change them to preferences and alternative-seeking desires.

Unconditional self-acceptance. Carl Rogers and Paul Tillich emphasized unconditional self-acceptance, and from the start REBT has held that humans will rarely be undisturbed and self-fulfilling unless they rate *only* their deeds and performances and *not* their global "selves." Instead, they can choose to accept "themselves" *whether or not* they perform well, are approved by significant others, or have deficits and handicaps. Many other psychotherapies, for example, that of Nathaniel Branden, encourage people to strive for self-esteem or self-efficacy, accepting themselves *because* they perform well and predict that they will continue to do so. But REBT tries to help them not rate their selves, their totality, at all, but rate only their behaviors, or, less elegantly, rate themselves as "good" or "worthy" just because they exist, because they *choose* to do so. Using REBT, self-actualizing people can reframe their "failures" as feedback rather than as self-damnation. This feedback provides important information about what does not work, and therefore calls for a change in approach to a situation rather than giving up on it.

Risk-taking and experimenting. Self-actualization without risk-taking and experimenting is almost unthinkable. People had better experiment with many tasks, preferences, and projects in order to discover what they really want and don't want, and to keep risking new defeats and failures in order to achieve better enjoyments.

Long-range hedonism. As REBT has noted since its inception in

1955, short-range hedonism—"Eat, drink, and be merry, for tomorrow you may die!"—has its distinct limitations, for tomorrow you will probably be alive with a hangover! Therefore, maximum self-actualization can largely be achieved by aiming for intensive and extensive pleasures today *and* tomorrow, and where the former (as in many addictions) sabotage the latter, immediate gratification had often better be avoided and long-range hedonism sought out and abetted.

Work and practice. As noted above, the three major insights of REBT are: (1), take responsibility for disturbing yourself and do not cop out by blaming others; (2), face the fact that your early disturbances do not automatically *make* you disturbed today; (3), understand that no magical forces will change you, but only your own strong and persistent work and practice—yes, *work and practice.* Similarly with self-actualization: Only by working at planning, plotting, scheming, and steadily acting at it are you likely to become a fully-functioning person.

Conclusion

The REBT view of human nondisturbance and self-actualization agrees with other therapeutic outlooks in many respects. Thus, a study of 610 clinical psychologists showed that all five major groups—psychoanalytic, behavioral, humanist-existential, eclectic, and cognitive—reported substantial agreement on the importance of self-system development, self-examination, and exploratory activities in personal change.[14]

The self-actualizing characteristics that REBT emphasizes perhaps more than many other leading psychotherapies are flexibility and a scientific outlook, self-acceptance instead of self-esteem, and long-range hedonism. In regard to achieving, and not merely endorsing, a more fully functioning personality, it advocates the points that Ted Crawford and I outlined at the beginning of this paper:

1. Actively choosing self-actualization
2. Disputing absolutist shoulds and musts that block its achievement
3. Preferring, but not requiring, the solving of self-actualizing problems
4. Tolerance of oneself and others

5. Overcoming procrastination and low frustration tolerance
6. Framing the problem as a systemic problem to be redesigned
7. Moving from either/ors toward and/alsos—including ambiguity, paradox, inconsistency, and confusion and then working toward an integrated wholeness

In this manner, Rational Emotive Behavior Therapy not only strongly endorses a self-actualizing, action-oriented philosophy, but also actively encourages some important ways in which it may be achieved. Above all, it stresses that the views outlined in this paper are its *current* formulations that had better be experimentally tried, and, when and if falsified, be quickly revised or abandoned.

18

Using Rational Emotive Behavior Therapy Techniques to Cope With Disability

I wrote this paper in 1995 for presentation at the Annual Convention of the American Psychological Association in New York. I was happy to give this talk, in my eighty-second year, for a large audience, and to discuss how I personally coped with my disabilities.

Aging and disability and how to handle them are of course becoming increasingly important topics for many of us. As noted in this chapter, Michael Abrams and I dealt with them at length in our book *How to Cope With a Fatal Illness*. More recently, Emmett Velten and I have written a book, *Optimal Aging*. I take the optimistic view that we all have to age and many of us have to suffer with disabilities, but we largely determine how severely we have to suffer from these problems.

I have had multiple disabilities for many years and have always used Rational Emotive Behavior Therapy to help me cope with them. That is one of the saving graces of having a serious disability—if you really accept it and stop whining about it, you can turn some of its lemons into quite tasty lemonade.

I started doing this with my first major disability soon after I became a practicing psychologist in 1943, at the age of thirty. At age nineteen I began having trouble reading and was fitted for glasses, which worked well enough for sight purposes but left me with easily tired eyes. After I read or even looked steadily at people for no more than twenty minutes, my eyes began to feel quite fatigued, and often, as if they had sand in them. Why? Probably because of my prediabetic condition of renal glycosuria.

Anyway, from nineteen years old onward I was clearly handicapped by my chronically tired eyes and could find no steady release from it. Today, over a half-century later, it is still with me, sometimes a little better, sometimes a little worse, but generally unrelieved. So I stoically accepted my tired eyes and still live with them. And what an annoyance it is! I rarely read, especially scientific material, for more than twenty minutes at a time—and I almost always keep my eyes closed when I am not reading, working, or otherwise so active that it would be unwise for me to shut them.

My main sight limitation is during my work as a therapist. For many years, I have seen more clients than almost any other therapist in the world. For at our clinic at the Albert Ellis Institute for Rational Emotive Behavior Therapy in New York, I usually see individual and group clients from 9:30 A.M. to 11:00 P.M.—with a couple of half-hour breaks for meals, and mostly for half-hour sessions with my individual clients. So during each week I may easily see over eighty individual and forty more group clients.

Do I get tired during these long days of working? Strangely enough, I rarely do. I was fortunate enough to pick high-energy parents and other ancestors. My parents were both exceptionally active, on-the-go people until my mother died of a stroke at the age of ninety-three and my father died, also of a stroke, at the age of eighty.

Anyway, for more than a half century I have conducted many more sessions with my eyes almost completely shut than I have with them open. This includes thousands of sessions I have done on the phone without ever seeing my clients. In doing so, I have experienced some real limitations but also several useful advantages. Advantages? Yes, such as these:

With my eyes shut, I can focus unusually well on what my clients are telling me and can listen carefully to their tones of voice, speech hesitations, and speed-ups, and other aspects of their verbal communication.

With my eyes closed, I can focus better on what my clients are telling themselves to make themselves disturbed: on their basic irrational meanings and philosophies that are crucial to most of their symptoms.

When I am not looking at my clients I am quite relaxed and can easily avoid bothering myself about how well I am doing. I avoid rating myself and producing ego problems about what a great therapist and noble person I am—or am not!

My closed eyes and relaxed attitude seem to help a number of my clients relax during the sessions, to open up to concentrating on and revealing their worst problems.

Some of my clients recognize my personal disabilities. They see that I refuse to whine about my adversities, that I work my ass off in spite of them, and that I have the courage to accept what I cannot change. They therefore often use me as a healthy model and realize that they, too, can happily work and live in spite of their misfortunes.

I am not recommending that all therapists, including those who have no ocular problems, should make a habit of shutting their eyes during their individual therapy sessions. But some might experiment to see what advantages closing their eyes may have.

Despite the fact that I could read only for about twenty minutes at a time, I started graduate school in clinical psychology in 1942, when I was twenty-eight, finished with honors, and have now been at the same delightful stand for well over a half century—still with my eyes often shut and my ears wide open. I am handicapped and partially disabled, yes—but never whining and screaming about my disabilities, and always forging on in spite of them.

In my late sixties my hearing began to deteriorate, and in my mid-seventies I got two hearing aids. Even when in good working order they have their distinct limitations and have to be adjusted for various conditions, and even for the loudness and pitch of the voices of the people I am listening to. So I use them regularly, especially with my clients, but I am still forced to ask people to repeat themselves or to make themselves clearer.

So I put up with all these limitations and use Rational Emotive Behavior Therapy to convince myself that they are not awful, horrible, and terrible, but only a pain in the ass. Once in a while I get overly irritated about my hearing problem—which my audiologist, incidentally, tells me will definitely get a little worse as each year goes by. But usually I live very well with my poor auditory reception and even manage to fulfill my large number of public lecture and workshop commitments every year, in the course of which I have some trouble in hearing questions and comments from my audiences but still manage to get by.

At the age of forty, I was diagnosed as having full-blown diabetes, so that has added to my disabilities. Diabetes, of course, does not cause much direct pain and anguish, but it clearly does lead to severe restrictions. I was quickly put on insulin injections twice a day and on a seriously restricted diet. I, who used to take four spoons of sugar in my coffee in my prediabetic days, plus half cream, was suddenly deprived of both. Moreover, when I stuck with my insulin injections and dietary restrictions, I at first kept my blood sugar regularly low but actually lost ten pounds off my already all-too-thin body. After my first year of insulin taking, I became a near-skeleton!

I soon figured out that by eating twelve small meals a day, literally around the clock, I could keep my blood sugar low, ward off insulin shock reactions, and maintain a healthy weight. So for over forty years I have been doing this and managing to survive pretty well. But what a bother! I am continually, day and night, making myself peanut butter sandwiches, pricking my fingers for blood samples, using my blood metering machines, carefully watching my diet, exercising regularly, and doing many other things that insulin-dependent diabetics have to do to keep their bodies and minds in good order.

When I fail to follow this annoying regimen, which I rarely do, I naturally suffer. Over the many years that I have been diabetic, I have ended up with a number of hypoglycemic reactions, including being carried off three times in an ambulance to hospital emergency wards. In spite of my keeping my blood sugar and blood pressure healthfully low over these many years, I have suffered from various sequelae of diabetes and have to keep regularly checking with my physicians to make sure that they do not get worse or that new complications do not develop. So, although I manage to keep my health rather good, I have several physicians whom I regularly see, including a diabetologist, an internist, an ear, nose, and throat specialist, a urologist, an orthopedist, and a dermatologist. Who knows what will be next? Oh, yes: Because diabetes affects the mouth and the feet, my visits to the dentist and podiatrist every year are a hell of a lot more often than I enjoy making them. But whether I like it or not, I go.

Finally, as a result of my advancing age, perhaps my diabetic condition, and who knows what else, I have suffered for the last few years from a bladder that is easily filled and slow to empty. So I run to the toilet more than I used to do, which I do not particularly mind. But I do mind the fact that it often takes me much longer to urinate than it did in my youth and early adulthood. That is really annoying!

Why? Because for as long as I can remember I have been something of a time watcher. I figured out when I was still in my teens and was writing away like a demon, even though I had a full schedule of courses and other events at college, that the most important thing in my life, and perhaps in almost everyone else's life, is time. Money, of course, has its distinct value; so does love. But if you lose money or get rejected in your sex-love affairs, you always have other chances to make up for your losses, as long as you are alive and energetic. If you are poor, you can focus on getting a better income; if you are unloved and unmated, you can theoretically get a new partner up until your dying day. Not so with time. Once you lose a few seconds, hours, or years, there is no manner in which you can get them back. You cannot retrieve them. *Tempus fugit*— and time lost, wasted, or ignored is distinctly irretrievable.

Ever since my teens, then, I have made myself allergic to procrastination and to hundreds of other ways of wasting time and letting it idly and unthinkingly go by. I assume that my days on earth are numbered and that I will not live a second more than I actually do live. So, unless I am really sick or otherwise out of commission, I do my best to make the most of my sixteen daily hours, and I frequently manage to accomplish this by doing two or more things at a time. For example, I very frequently listen to music while reading and have an interesting conversation with people while preparing a meal or eating.

This is all to the good, and I am delighted to be able to do two things at once, to stop my procrastinating and my occasional daydreaming and, instead, do something that I would much rather get done in the limited time that I have to be active each day and the all too few years I will have in my entire lifetime. Consequently, when I was afflicted by the problem of slow urination in my late seventies, I distinctly regretted the five to ten minutes of extra time it began to take me to go to the toilet several times each day and night. What a waste! What could I effectively do about saving this time?

Well, I soon worked out that problem. Instead of standing up to urinate as I had normally done for all my earlier life, I began to do so sitting down, making sure I had some interesting reading for the several minutes that it took me to finish. But then I soon figured out that I could do other kinds of things as well to use this time.

For example, when I am alone in the apartment I share with my mate, Janet Wolfe, I usually take a few minutes to heat up my regular hot meal in our microwave oven. While it is cooking, I often prepare my next hot meal and put it in a microwave dish in the refrigerator, so that when I come up from my office to our apartment again, I can pop it in the oven. Therefore I am usually cooking and preparing two meals at a time. As the old saying goes, two meals for the price of one!

Once the microwave oven rings its bell and tells me that my meal is finished, I take it out of the oven, and instead of putting it on our kitchen table to eat, I take it into the bathroom and put in on a shelf by the side of the toilet, together with my eating utensils. Then, while I spend the next five or ten minutes urinating, I simultaneously eat my meal out of the microwave dish and thereby accomplish my eating and urinating at the same time. Now some of you may find this is inelegant or even boorish. My main goal is to get two important things—eating and urinating—done promptly, to polish them off as it were, and then to get back to the rest of my interesting life. As you may well imagine, I am delighted with this arrangement and am highly pleased with having efficiently worked it out!

Sometimes I actually arrange to do tasks while I am also doing therapy. My clients, for example, know that I am diabetic and that I have to eat regularly, especially when my blood sugar is low. So, with their permission, I usually eat my peanut butter and sugarless jelly sandwiches while I am conducting my individual and group sessions, and everyone seems to be comfortable with it.

However, I still have to spend a considerable amount of time taking care of my physical needs and dealing with my diabetes and other disabilities. I hate doing this, but I accept the fact that I have little other choice. So I use REBT to overcome any tendencies toward low frustration tolerance that I may still have. Whenever I feel that I am getting impatient or angry, I tell myself about my various limitations, "Too damned bad! I really do not like taking all this time and effort to deal with my impairments and wish to hell that I didn't have to do so. But, alas, I do. It is hard doing so many things to keep myself in a relatively healthy condition, but it is much harder, and in the long run much more painful and deadly, if I do not keep doing this. There is no reason whatsoever why I absolutely must have it easier than I do. Yes, it is unfair for me to be more afflicted than many other people are, but, damn it, I should be just as afflicted as I am! Unfairness *should* exist in the world—to me, and to whomever else it does exist—because it exists! Too bad that it does—but it does!"

So, using my REBT training, I work on my low frustration tolerance and accept what I cannot change. Of course, barring a medical miracle, I cannot change any of my major disabilities, but I can live with them, and I do. I can even reduce them to some extent, but I still cannot get rid of them. Tough! But it is not awful.

REBT posits that there are two main instigators of human neurosis: first, low frustration tolerance (I *absolutely must* have what I want when I want it and must never, never be deprived of anything that I really, really desire); second, self-denigration (when I do not perform well and win others' approval, as at all times I *should, ought,* and *must,* I am an inadequate person, a retard, a no-goodnik!).

In addition to suffering from the first of these disturbances, many disabled people in our culture suffer even more seriously from the second. People with serious disabilities often have more performance limitations in many areas (at school, work, and sports) than those who have no disabilities. To make matters worse, they are frequently criticized, scorned, and put down by others for having their deficiencies. From early childhood to old age, they may be ridiculed and reviled, and shown that they really are not as capable or as "good" as others are. So they not only suffer from decreased competence in various areas but also from much less approval than more proficient members of our society often receive. For both these reasons—because they notice their own ineptness and because many of their relatives and associates ignore or condemn them for it—they falsely tend to conclude, "My deficiencies make me a deficient, inadequate individual."

I largely taught myself to forgo this kind of self-deprecation long before I developed most of my present disabilities. From my early interest in philosophy during my teens, I saw that I did not have to rate myself as a person when I rated my efficacy and my lovability. I began to teach myself, before I reached my mid-twenties, that I could give up most of my feelings of shame and unconditionally accept myself as a human even when I did poorly, especially at sports. As I grew older, I increasingly worked at accepting myself unconditionally. While I use my REBT-oriented high frustration tolerance to stop myself from whining about disabilities, and rarely inwardly or outwardly complain about this, I also use my self-accepting philosophy to refrain from ever putting myself down about these handicaps. In REBT, one of the most important things we do is to teach most of our clients to rate or evaluate only their thoughts, feelings, and actions and not rate their self, essence, or being. So for many years I have followed this principle and fully acknowledged that many of my behaviors are unfortunate, bad, and inadequate because they do not fulfill my goals and desires. But of course, I strongly philosophize that I am not a bad or inadequate person for having these flaws and failings.

I must admit that I really hate growing old. Because, in addition to my diabetes, easily tired eyes, and poor hearing, old age definitely increases my list of disabilities. Every year that goes by I creak more in my joints, have extra physical pains to deal with, slow down in my pace, and otherwise am able to do somewhat less than previously. So old age is hardly a blessing!

However, as I approach the age of eighty-five, I am damned glad to be alive and to be quite active, productive, and enjoying. My brother and sister, who were a few years younger than I, both died almost a decade ago, and just about all my close relatives are also fairly long gone. A great many of my psychological friends and associates, most of whom were younger than I, unfortunately have died, too. I grieve for some of them, especially for my brother Paul, who was my best friend. But I also remind myself that it is great that I am still very much alive, as is my beloved mate Janet, after more than thirty years of our living together. So, I really am very lucky!

Do my own physical disabilities actually add to my therapeutic effectiveness? I would say, yes—definitely. In fact, they do in several ways, including the following. With my regular clients, most of whom have only minor disabilities or none at all, I often use myself as a model and show them that, in spite of my eighty-five years and my physical problems, I fully accept myself with these impediments and give myself the same unconditional self-acceptance that I try to help these clients achieve. I also often show them, directly and indirectly, that I rarely whine about my physical defects but have taught myself to have high frustration tolerance (HFT) about them. This kind of modeling helps teach many of my clients that they, too, can face real adversities and achieve USA and HFT.

I particularly work at teaching my disabled clients to have unconditional self-acceptance by fully acknowledging that their deficiencies are unfortunate, bad, and sometimes very noxious, but that they are never, except by their own self-sabotaging definition, shameful, disgraceful, or contemptible. Yes, other people may often view them as horrid, hateful people because our culture and many other cultures often encourage such unfair prejudice. But I show my clients that they never have to agree with this kind of bigotry and can actively fight against it in their own lives as well as help other people with disabilities to be fully self-accepting.

I often get this point across to my own clients by using self-disclosure and other kinds of modeling. Thus, I saw Michael, a forty-five-year-old man with brittle diabetes. He had great trouble maintaining a healthy blood sugar level, as his own diabetic brother and sister were able to do. He incessantly put himself down for his inability to work steadily, maintain a firm erection, participate in sports, and achieve a good relationship with an attractive woman who would mate with him in spite of his severe disabilities.

When I revealed to Michael several of my own physical defects and limitations, such as those previously mentioned, and when I showed him how I felt sad and disappointed about them but stubbornly refused to feel at all ashamed or embarrassed for having them he strongly worked at full self-acceptance, stopped denigrating himself for his inefficacies, shamelessly informed prospective partners about his disabilities, and was able to mate with a woman who cared for him deeply in spite of them.

In this case, I also used REBT skill training. It shows people with physical problems how to stop needlessly upsetting themselves about their drawbacks. But it also teaches them various social, professional, and other skills to help them minimize and compensate for their hindrances. In Michael's case, in addition to teaching him unconditional self-acceptance, I showed him how to socialize more effectively; how to satisfy female partners without having perfect erections; and how to participate in some sports, such as swimming, despite his physical limitations. So although still disabled, he was able to feel better and perform better as a result of his REBT sessions. This is the two-sided, or duplex, kind of therapy that I try to arrange with many of my clients with disabilities.

Partly as a result of my own physical restrictions, I am also able to help clients with their low frustration tolerance (LFT) whether or not they have disabilities. As I noted earlier, people with physical restrictions and pains usually are more frustrated than those without such impediments. Consequently, they may well develop a high degree of LFT. Consider Denise, for example. A psychologist, she became insulin dependent at the age of thirty and felt horrified about her newly acquired restrictions. According to her physicians, she now had to take two injections of insulin and several blood tests every day, give up most of her favorite fat-loaded and salt-saturated foods, spend a half hour a day exercising, and take several other health-related precautions. She viewed all of these chores and limitations as "revolting and horrible," and became phobic about regularly carrying them out. She especially kept up her life-long gourmet diet and gained twenty extra pounds within a year of becoming diabetic. Her doctors' and her husband's severe criticism helped her feel guilty, but it hardly stopped her in her foolish self-indulgence.

I first worked with Denise on her LFT and did my best to convince her, as REBT practitioners often do, that she did not need the eating and other pleasures that she wanted. It was indeed hard for her to impose the restrictions her physical condition now required, but it was much harder, I pointed out, if she did not follow them. Her increased limitations were indeed unfortunate, but they were hardly revolting and horrible; I insisted that she could stand them, though never necessarily like them.

At first I had little success in helping Denise raise her LFT because, as a bright psychologist, she irrationally but quite cleverly parried my rational arguments. However, using my own case as an example, I was able to show her how, at my older age and with disabilities greater than hers, I had little choice but to give up my former indulgences or die. So, rather than die, I gave up putting four spoons of sugar and half cream in my coffee, threw away my salt shaker, stopped frying my vegetables in sugar and butter, surrendered my allergy to exercise, and started tapping my fingers seven or eight times a day for blood tests. When Denise heard how I forced my frustration tolerance up as my pancreatic secretion of insulin went down, and how for over forty years I have thereby staved off the serious complications of diabetes that probably would have followed from my previous habits, and from her present ones, she worked on her own LFT and considerably reduced it.

Simultaneously, I also helped Denise with her secondary symptoms of neurosis. As a bright person and as a psychologist who often helped her clients with their self-sabotaging thoughts, feelings, and behaviors, she knew how destructive her own indulgences were, and she self-lambasted and made herself feel very ashamed of them, thereby creating a symptom about a symptom: self-downing about her LFT. So I used general REBT with her to help her give herself unconditional self-acceptance in spite of her indulging in her LFT. I also specifically showed her how, when I personally slip back to my predisability ways and fail to continue my antidiabetic exercise and other prophylactic routines, I only castigate my behavior and not my self or personhood. I therefore see myself as a goodnik who can change my no-goodnik actions, and this attitude helps me correct those actions. By forcefully showing this to Denise, and using myself and my handling of my disabilities as notable examples, I was able to help her give up her secondary symptom, self-deprecation, and go back to working more effectively to decrease her primary symptom—low frustration tolerance.

In this article, I have mainly tried to show how I have personally coped with some of my major disabilities for over sixty years. But let me say that I have found it relatively easy to do so because, first, I seem to be a natural born survivor and coper, which many disabled (and nondisabled) people are not. This may well be my innate predisposition, but also may have been aided by my having to cope with nephritis from my fifth to my eighth year and my consequent training of myself to live with physical adversity. Second, as noted earlier, I derived an epicurean and stoic philosophy from reading and reasoning about many philosophers' and writers' views from my sixteenth year onward. Third, I originated REBT in January 1955 and have spent over forty years, the great majority of my professional life, teaching it to clients, therapists, and members of the public.

For these and other reasons, I fairly easily and naturally use REBT methods in my own life and am not the kind of difficult customer (DC) that I often find my clients to be. With them, and especially with DCs who have disabilities and who keep complaining about them and not working too hard to overcome and cope with them, I often use a number of cognitive, emotive, and behavioral techniques for which REBT is famous and which I have described in my book, *How to Cope With a Fatal Illness*, and in many of my other writings.

Several other writers have also applied REBT and cognitive behavior therapy (CBT) to people with disabilities, including Rochelle Balter, Warren Johnson, Rose Oliver, Fran Bock, and J. Sweetland. Louis Calabro has written a particularly helpful article showing how the antiawfulizing philosophy of REBT can be used with individuals suffering from severe disabilities, such as those following a stroke, and Gerald Gandy has published an unusual book, *Mental Health Rehabilitation: Disputing Irrational Beliefs*.

The aforementioned writings include a great many cognitive, emotive, and behavioral therapy techniques that are particularly useful with people who have disabilities. Because, as REBT theorizes, human thinking, feeling, and acting significantly interact with each other, and because emotional disturbance affects one's body as well as one's physical condition affects one's kind and degree of disturbance, people who are upset about their disabilities often require a multifaceted therapy to deal with their upset state. REBT, like Arnold Lazarus's multimodal therapy, provides this kind of approach and therefore is often helpful to people with disability-related problems.

Let me briefly describe a few of the cognitive REBT methods that I frequently use with my clients who have disabilities and who are quite anxious, depressed, and self-pitying about having these handicaps. I bring out and help them dispute their irrational beliefs (IBs). Thus, I show these clients that there is no reason why they must not be disabled, although that would be distinctly desirable. No matter how ineffectual some of their behaviors are, they are never inadequate persons for having a disability. They can always accept themselves while acknowledging and deploring some of their physical and mental deficiencies. When other people treat them unkindly and unfairly because of their disabilities, they can deplore this unfairness but not damn their detractors. When the conditions under which they live are unfortunate and unfair, they can acknowledge this unfairness while not unduly focusing on and indulging in self-pity and horror about it.

Preferably, I try to show my disabled clients how to make a profound philosophical change, and thereby not only minimize their anxiety, depression, rage, and self-pity for being disadvantaged, but become considerably less disturbed by future adversities. I try to teach them that they have the ability to consistently and strongly convince themselves that nothing is absolutely awful, that no human is worthless, and that they can practically always find some real enjoyment in living. I also try to help them accept the challenge of being productive, self-actualizing, and happy in spite of the unusual handicaps with which they may unfortunately be innately endowed or may have acquired during their lifetimes. I also point out the desirability of their creating for themselves a vital absorbing interest, that is, a long-range devotion to some cause, project, or other interest that will give them a real meaning and purpose in life, distract them from their disability, and give them ongoing value and pleasure.

To aid these goals of REBT, I use a number of other cognitive methods as well as many emotive and behavioral methods with my disabled clients. I have described them in many articles and books, so I shall not repeat them here. Details can be found in *How to Cope With a Fatal Illness.*

Do I use myself and my own ways of coping with my handicaps to help my clients cope with theirs? I often do. I first show them that I can unconditionally accept them with their disabilities even when they have partly caused these handicaps themselves. I accept them with their self-imposed emphysema from smoking or their one hundred extra pounds of fat from indulging in ice cream and candy. I show them how I bear up quite well with my various physical difficulties and still manage to be energetic and relatively healthy. I reveal some of the time-saving, self-management, and other discipline methods I frequently use in my own life. I indicate that I have not only devised some sensible philosophies for people with disabilities, but that I actually apply them in my own work and play, and I show them how. I have survived my handicaps for many years and damned well intend to keep doing so for perhaps a good number of years to come.

I might never have been that interested in rational or sensible ways of coping with emotional problems had I not had to cope with a number of fairly serious physical problems from the age of five onward. But rather than plague myself about my physical restrictions, I devoted myself to the philosophy of remaining happy in spite of my disabilities, and out of this philosophy I ultimately originated REBT, in January 1955. As I was developing REBT, I used some of its main principles on myself, and I have often used them with other people with disabilities. When I and these others have worked to acquire an antiawfulizing, unconditional, self-accepting philosophy, we have often been able to lead considerably happier and more productive lives than many other handicapped individuals. This hardly proves that REBT is a panacea for all physical and mental ills. It is not. But it is a form of psychotherapy and self-therapy especially designed for people who suffer from uncommon adversities. It points out to clients in general, and to physically disadvantaged ones in particular, that however much they dislike the harsh realities of their lives, they can manage to make themselves feel the healthy negative emotions of sorrow, regret, frustration, and grief while stubbornly refusing to create and dwell on the unhealthy emotions of panic, depression, despair, rage, self-pity, and personal worthlessness. To help in this respect, it uses a number of cognitive, emotive-evocative, and behavioral methods. Its results with disabled individuals has not yet been well researched with controlled studies. Having used it successfully on myself and with many other individuals, however, I am strongly prejudiced in its favor. But controlled investigations of its effectiveness are an important next step.

PART III

Rational Living in an Irrational Society

Introduction to Part III

R unning throughout everything Ellis has written in his long career is his abiding interest in how very imperfect human beings can make the best of their lives in what is a very imperfect, uncaring society. In fact, the title of one of his most popular books is *How to Stubbornly Refuse to Make Yourself Miserable About Anything—Yes, Anything!*

Ellis's main goal has always been to enable individuals to maximize their happiness and minimize their unhappiness in this very difficult, definitely nonutopian world. Ellis's overall strategy has three parts. The first step is for you to accept your own imperfection (that you are "a fallible, fucked-up human," as Ellis would say), and to work on unconditional self-acceptance regardless of your successes or failures. The second step is to stop "awfulizing" about the obnoxious conditions which admittedly abound in the world. Our human tendency to experience "discomfort disturbance" only makes the very real hassles all of us encounter that much harder to cope with. The third step is to go after your own individual goals with as much energy and efficiency as possible.

Combining these three goals with REBT's theory of individual personality yields the following strategies, among others:

1. Choosing to exercise nonhostile *assertion*, instead of resorting to hostile *aggression*.
2. Choosing to try to stop other people from behaving badly, by penalizing their bad *behaviors* without blamefully damning *them*.
3. Accepting that *you* are ultimately responsible for your own feelings, and that other people normally don't *cause* your emotional pain.
4. Refusing to globally rate other people, just as you *choose* not to globally rate yourself. That is, focus on rating people's individual actions and traits rather than their total selves or essences. Ellis has often said, just to be deliberately provocative, that "even Hitler wasn't a bad person, just a person who did many bad acts."

5. Refusing to feel ashamed or guilty (that is, "self-downing") even when other people belittle you and blame you.
6. Seeking cooperation with other people to achieve your mutual goals as efficiently as possible.
7. Accepting that rage almost never helps you, and even though it sometimes *feels* good temporarily, in the long run it's almost always self-defeating.

For many years, Ellis has kept a large file of newspaper clippings of true stories about people who have used this "tough shit" approach to overcome truly great adversities—such as physical incapacitation, fatal illness, profound loss, and imprisonment.

Rational Sensitivity

Ellis has always been interested in business. He originally got his bachelor's degree in business administration, started several businesses in his twenties, and put himself through graduate school by working in an executive position at a gift and novelty wholesaler in New York City. He has always had an interest in improving business efficiency, and early on he put his mind to applying REBT to the workplace.

Perhaps his major book in this area, *Executive Leadership: A Rational Approach*, advises executives to develop what he termed "rational sensitivity" in order to enhance their leadership skills and become more decisive. The chapter "Rational Effectiveness Training" in this reader covers much of this same ground. Basically, "rational sensitivity" in business means becoming more sensitized to and aware of your own and other people's inefficiencies, but becoming less vulnerable to emotional turmoil when you or other people do poorly.

Ellis maintains that many management guides give great advice about solving practical problems in business, but they fail to address the emotional problems that business executives often have *about* their practical problems. Thus, Ellis shows business people how to overcome their own all-too-human tendencies to procrastinate, be indecisive, let their concentration wander, become overly hostile, and supervise subordinates inefficiently.

In addition to problems of the workplace, in Part III Ellis weighs in on such major social concerns as education, religion, addiction, and efficiency in psychological treatment, among many others. In each area,

Ellis hews to his central tenet—that human reason is a great ally in making the happiest lot for ourselves in this often imperfect, uncaring world.

Autobiography of Self-Therapy

In many ways, the final chapter is my favorite of the whole book. First, because of its unflinching honesty, in which Ellis reviews his attempts to overcome his own weaknesses, "warts and all." Second, it gives a unique inside view into how a major theoretician's intellectual development is so closely intertwined with his own personal development in life. And finally, Ellis's own life is instructive as a model for how people can apply REBT to themselves to maximize their own happiness in the face of their own all-too-human weaknesses and the world's inevitable adversities.

—Shawn Blau

19

Rational-Effectiveness Training: A New Method of Facilitating Management and Labor Relations

Rational Effectiveness Training (RET) first began in 1967, when Professor Milton Blum, a college friend of mine to whom I had been sending my papers on REBT since 1957, clearly saw that it was easily adaptable to business and industry, and wrote the first version of this paper with me. We published it in *Psychological Reports,* and soon after I began to do workshops on Rational Effectiveness Training with Dr. Leonard Haber, a Miami psychologist who was into consulting activity.

Our workshops were quite successful and turned many business people on to RET. Milt Blum and I were set to write a book on the subject, *Executive Leadership,* but he objected to my down-to-earth language, so we agreed that I would write the book myself, and I published it in 1972. Perhaps Milt was right, and American business was not ready for the "tough shit!" approach that I espoused in this volume.

Anyway, at first RET didn't directly take off. Indirectly, however, it influenced many business writers, from Peter Drucker to Stephen Covey. To this day the American Management Association and many similar organizations and businesses sponsor scores of workshops and courses which essentially apply REBT and Cognitive Behavior Therapy (CBT) to business and management. More and more organizational training is becoming REBT and CBT, because, I say in my own prejudiced manner, this is the way to go if people are to best cope with their own disturbances and also to function better in the workplace. Rational Effectiveness Training, when used with or without credit, actually seems to work!

Rational Effectiveness Training can help people function more effectively in the workplace by actively teaching them certain basic principles of interpersonal relations that promote better self-under-standing as well as increase insight into others. It is applicable to all levels of management in business and industry, as well as to those individuals who work in the area of "people contact," including managers, labor officials, sales representatives, teachers, clergy, and officers in the armed forces. It also is applicable to employees, supervisees, and others who have bosses or managers over them.

Like any other educational experience, RET can be learned by a variety of techniques. It can be taught by individual instruction, reading materials, audio-visual methods, and programmed instruction, but it is especially well adapted to group workshops and can, via this means, be learned and applied in a surprisingly short period of time. In fact, the characteristics of RET and its objective of promoting better interpersonal relations is best put into practice in group situations where learning becomes both the vehicle and the exercise at the same time.

RET is not sensitivity training, group psychoanalysis, or a conventional management training course. Then what is it? What kind of specific ideas and experiences does it have to offer business, industrial, and professional people or employees? Trainees are helped to achieve the following kinds of goals through RET sessions.

Rational Effectiveness Training Goals

Achieving more through eliminating fear of failure. RET shows people how to accept themselves fully and never condemn themselves as persons even when they are not thoroughly adequate and achieving. It helps them minimize unrealistic, impossible demands on themselves and enables them to be much more risk-taking as well as decisive. RET changes people's self-perception by encouraging them to no longer define themselves as worthless persons when they make mistakes or fail at certain projects.

Becoming tolerant and less hostile toward superiors, associates, or subordinates. RET demonstrates that childish grandiosity and placing unreasonable demands on others can cause violent outbursts of temper or hostility, the end products of which create ulcer-encouraging angers and affect bottom-line profits in the organization by diverting energy and time from important tasks. It shows executives and workers how to be truly more tolerant of the fallibility of others and how to stop denigrating them, while helpfully correcting their errors—even when they are quite wrong and annoying.

Gaining unqualified self-acceptance and self-respect. RET reveals that irrational, impossible needs for the approval of others, which people convince themselves they *must* have, can destroy their own independence and self-acceptance. It teaches members of the training group precisely how they can be less dependent on other people and more capable of living fully *whether or not* everyone around adores them. After all, to be loved by all is practically impossible to achieve! In a study conducted at a major corporation, the need for approval was determined to be one of the major causes for failure of the performance appraisal process. Managers often rated employees with excessively high scores to avoid their disapproval.

Achieving minimal anxiety and insecurity. RET shows people how they needlessly make themselves anxious by failing to discriminate between real physical dangers and those that they create and exaggerate in their own heads. It promotes more realistic ways of looking at business and life situations by putting them into a more proper time perspective.

Gaining maximum self-determination. RET teaches people that most severe misery is not caused by outside people and events: rather, it is the view they take of adversities that creates needless misery. By learning to correct their own distorted view of themselves and the world, they can direct their own destiny more effectively. By changing their rigid musts and demands to flexible preferences, they can feel strongly but appropriately and work to get more of what they want in life.

Achieving high frustration tolerance. RET clearly informs the training session members that what they "tell" themselves creates self-defeating impatience and low frustration tolerance. It helps them question their belief that things are really that terrible when they are not the way people would like them to be. It helps them to accept the inevitable annoyances of life and to cope with things when they are not exactly the way they want them to be. After all, things are not the way we would like them to be very often; the big question is how to minimize our impatience and rage even when we are frustrated.

Acquiring vitally absorbing interests. RET demonstrates that once people give up their inordinate dependency based on how others approve of them, and once they fully accept that they can truly regulate their own emotional fate, they can then acquire some vital absorbing interests. As a result, newer vocational and avocational directions help them become more creative individuals. RET helps them see that inertia and apathy are unrewarding ways of life, and that they can literally create a significant meaning for their existence, and thereby enjoy themselves more fully while striving to appropriately achieve within their capacities.

Problem Areas Dealt With

What kinds of specific problems are usually handled in Rational Effectiveness Training groups? Almost every possible kind of business, professional, social, personal, and even familial problem is brought up and handled in RET. Mainly, however, questions relating directly or indirectly to the best vocational functioning of the individual are given the most detailed analysis. These issues may be raised spontaneously by members of the training group in accordance with their own desires, or significant problems that are of general importance may be raised by the training leader.

Techniques Employed

RET employs several different kinds of specialized techniques of group discussion and instruction. Most of these are utilized in certain forms of classroom procedures, but they have often been ignored in modern encounter or training groups, which often avoid active-directive methods. RET is a unique mode of group interchange which integrates the educational with the participant-observer approach. Some of the main types of techniques that it uses are the following:

Directiveness. The training leader usually knows what some of the main goals of the various sessions probably will be and firmly directs the discussion into productive channels related to these objectives. Trainers actively prevent the group from wandering too far afield. In order to achieve the session's objectives, they may introduce new topics or call a halt to ongoing discussions when they become rambling or overly prolonged. To ensure that all members participate (and that some group members do not talk too much or others too little), the group leaders generally guide the proceedings. In doing so, they keep group members from stewing in their own juices, rambling, or becoming bogged down.

Activity. The group leaders actively participate in the discussion, especially at critical points, as well as see to it that the other members truly participate. Leaders may initiate questions, start role-playing sessions, induce individuals to interact with each other, or even play the devil's advocate. An important role for the leader is to see that the group members keep on their toes and stay with the discussion.

Structuring. The training leaders see to it that the group is focused on some specific topic, and that all the members devote their attention to that topic rather than engaging in little side remarks or tête-à-têtes of their own. They prevent the discussion from getting continually sidetracked and try to press for some kind of closure on one theme before another is cavalierly put in its place. They encourage an organized, unrambling, and relevant discussion, keep in mind the time limitations of each session, and try to help the group to avoid abstract philosophizing and to remain with practical, helpful points and issues.

Authoritativeness. RET leaders are authoritative without being authoritarian. They are experts in the field of human relations, management, and psychology, and, as a result, at times do not hesitate to briefly answer direct questions from group members or present relevant factual information to them. They do not give lectures or make long speeches, but do a great deal of active teaching that they fully integrate within the group discussion.

Individual Centered. Although the RET group frequently reaches a consensus of opinion on certain issues, its main object is to present information and solutions that will be most useful to individual members. A typical group meeting most often has individuals taking turns in presenting their problems to the group. Most of the time a single individual talks with the rest of the group about one or more of his or her own specific problems.

Homework assignments. In the course of the training sessions, individuals are not only shown exactly what they can do to help themselves with their work problems but are frequently given specific homework assignments and encouraged to undergo the practice required to solve their problems. During subsequent training sessions they are followed up to see whether they actually carried out these assignments, how well they did them, and what they learned in the process.

Supplementary reading. Before, during, and after the training sessions, the group members are given relevant reading material that outlines some of the main principles of rational training to help them learn and work with these principles. Lectures, tape recordings, audiovisual aids, and other types of supplementary educational materials are also employed as aids to the training sessions.

Closure. An effort is made by the training leader to see that some kind of closure for each individual takes place as a result of the training sessions. Leaders try to see that important points are not left hanging in the air, that individuals who may become upset are effectively calmed down, and that the participants will do something about applying the principles and methods they have learned to their lives in general and their work in particular.

The procedures used in RET are not eclectic. Rather, they are part of an integrated system of Rational Emotive Behavior Therapy, a personality theory and therapy method backed by considerable clinical work and a sizable body of outcome studies.[1]

RET specializes in its applications to business and industrial problems. Klarreich, DiGiuseppe, and DiMattia, in a study of over six hundred employees in a major corporation, found that RET, when used in an employee assistance setting, yielded a cost/benefit ratio of $2.74 saved for every $1 spent. RET has also been applied to management training, sales training, human resources development, and risk-taking and leadership development.[2] Leaders trained to conduct rational effectiveness sessions specifically strive for the kinds of results obtained in the above-presented session. Because they are trained in the basic principles of Rational Emotive Behavior Therapy, the leaders also are often able to handle and help particularly disturbed individuals who may be present in the training group.

In accordance with the basic principles of RET, the training participants are shown that it is not the events or stimuli they experience at point A that make them anxious, guilty, depressed, apathetic, angry, or otherwise disturbed at point C. Rather, it is the irrational ideas with which they easily seem to reindoctrinate themselves at point B that mainly create their disordered emotions and dysfunctional behavior at point C.

As the group members learn the A-B-Cs of RET during the training sessions, and as they are given down-to-earth experiences and practice in applying these principles of rational thinking, they often make amazing progress in a relatively short period of time. What is perhaps even more important, they begin to become habituated to a practical method of thinking about themselves and others that continues to be of inestimable value for the rest of their lives. Rational Effectiveness Training offers them not only unusually deep insights into human relationships and effective solutions to many of their present problems, but a healthier outlook on life and work that may well prove to be the most significant knowledge they have ever discovered.

20

The Objectivist View of Self-Esteem

In 1967 I wrote a book, *Is Objectivism a Religion?*, after I had a spirited debate with Nathaniel Branden on Rational Emotive Behavior Therapy versus objectivist psychology. Branden refused to let us distribute the tape recording of the debate, largely because his mentor and lover, Ayn Rand, made something of an ass of herself by screaming out from the audience during the debate that I was not allowed to criticize her as a writer in the course of it. According to her, I was only to talk about Branden and not about her—even though the debate was entitled "Rational Emotive Psychotherapy versus Objectivist Psychology." At this time Branden devoutly upheld objectivist psychology and, along with Ms. Rand, was its main spokesperson.

While my book was going through the process, Rand and Branden vindictively split and wrote manifestos calling each other vile names—and substantiated much of the material I included in the debate and in this book. As both Nathaniel Branden and his wife, Barbara, later wrote in biographies of Ayn Rand, Rand couldn't accept Branden's affair with his new woman friend, Patricia, though for years Rand had accepted his marriage to Barbara. Hell hath no fury like a woman scorned, and although a leading atheist, Rand condemned Branden to purgatory, hell, and then some!

My book was partially intended to disrupt the Branden-Rand empire, but the two leaders abolished it without too much help from me. The main point I made in the book went over solidly with readers, and many of them to this day still congratulate me on it. That point was that religion itself is not misleading and harmful; it is the rigid, dogmatic, absolutist way in which secular religion, such as Ayn Rand's objectivism, vies with theistic, church-held religion to be narrow and prejudiced. Both forms of extremism, moreover, tend to base human worth or value on firm adherence to the following of absolutistic rules of conduct. They make self-acceptance highly conditional instead of, as REBT does, unconditional. In this crucial sense they devalue human existence. This is what Ayn Rand and Nathaniel Branden did. This is what the chapter "The Objectivist View of Self-Esteem" is about.

Most psychological and psychotherapeutic systems are unclear about the problem of self-esteem, worth, or self-confidence because they lump several things together under the one concept of self-concept or self-respect. Let us therefore seek a little clarification in this regard.

The individual's "self" is difficult to define because it has at least two aspects, which may overlap but are hardly the same. First, his "self" is his entire organism: everything he perceives, thinks, feels, and does. Second are his feelings about himself, his self-image, self-concept, or self-regard. It is this second notion of the self that we largely talk about when we use terms like ego or self-esteem.

When the individual has a good self-image or a worthy concept of herself, she usually possesses one, two, or three different kinds of confidence. The first of these is work-confidence. This means that she accepts herself because she thinks she is sufficiently capable, because she knows how to handle herself in the world, and because she thinks she has a sane attitude toward life. The second is love-confidence. This means that the individual respects herself because she knows that others approve her and that she has a good chance of winning and keeping more approval.

Usually, if a person has work-confidence and love-confidence, we say that he also has self-confidence. But this is not quite true. For self-confidence (or self-esteem, self-acceptance, or self-respect), when it truly exists, means that the individual fully accepts himself *whether or not* he thinks he is highly capable and whether or not others approve of him.

Objectivism, like most current philosophies about the individual and her self, seems to have little conception of true self-confidence or self-esteem, or of what Carl Rogers has called unconditional positive regard. Instead, it insists that the individual's acceptance of herself must be contingent on several other things, and therefore must be highly conditional. Here are some ways in which objectivist psychology posits a limited, false, and sometimes pernicious concept of self-esteem.

According to objectivism, "self-esteem...is the conviction that one is *competent* to live and *worthy* of living....If a person were to think himself 'stupid' or 'insane,' he would necessarily regard this as a devastating reflection of his ability to deal with reality."[1] This is statistically true. Most humans *do* think of themselves as pretty worthless if they are not competent to take care of themselves, stupid, or insane.

The fact remains, however, that it is quite possible for a person to acknowledge that she is not able to take care of herself adequately and that she is more stupid or psychotic than others, and still accept herself as a worthy person. As long as she accepts the idea that just because she is human, just because she is alive, she deserves to continue to exist and to be happy, she can unqualifiedly accept herself in spite of her unquestioned ignorance.

Going still further, objectivist psychology holds that when a child or an adult "surrenders the expectation of achieving efficacy, he surrenders the possibility of achieving full self-esteem....If he regards cognitive efficacy as an absolute, not to be surrendered or relinquished, he thereby activates a process of growth and development which continually raises his mind's power."[2] Here the empirical observation that it is *desirable* for a person to think and work efficiently is irrationally raised to the absolutistic notion that it is utterly necessary for him to be efficacious, and that the more ineffective he is the less he can value himself as a human being. Obviously, if this is to be the standard of self-acceptance, only an exceptionally small number of humans can meet it, including, I would guess, a small number of dyed-in-the-wool objectivists! The rest of us poor mortals will be left with pretty low self-esteem.

Even Ayn Rand, according to Barbara Branden in her biographical essay on the founder of objectivism, often became depressed when minor interruptions prevented her from working. Depression, almost invariably, is a reflection of an individual's low estimation of herself, because the depressed individual feels that: "Things are going badly in my life"; and "I am too weak and inadequate to handle these things or make them better, and therefore I am a pretty bad person."

When the individual insists that, *because* she works hard, accomplishes something, is good at winning the love of others, or achieves anything else, she is a worthy individual, she tends to make herself depressed when one or more of those clauses on which her self-esteem depends are no longer true. If she follows the objectivist credo and places her self-worth on the balance scales of achievement, she tends to remain underlyingly anxious and depressed even when her life is a fine model of productivity. For she will always have moments—or years!—when this productivity may subside.

"A man's moral worth," the objectivist position states, "is not to be judged by the content of his emotions; it is to be judged by the degree of his rationality; only the latter is directly in his volitional control."[3] And again, from the same source: "If he proceeds to defy his reason and his conscious judgment and to follow his emotions blindly, acting on them while knowing they are wrong, he will have good grounds to condemn himself."

According to this dictum, only an individual who chooses to be highly rational is a good person, and anyone who knows that he is irrational or neurotic and who does not immediately correct his false judgments and his disordered emotions should justifiably condemn himself.

This, as I point out in *Reason and Emotion in Psychotherapy* and *A Guide to Rational Living*, puts the disturbed person into an impossible bind. She becomes neurotic in the first place largely because she condemns herself for her errors and her inappropriate behavior (instead of more sanely acknowledging these errors and calmly accepting herself with them and working to minimize them). Then, when she acts neurotically, she condemns herself for having her symptoms, and concludes that such a worthless person can never change for the better. It is bad enough that people afflicted with poor judgment and neurosis tend to think this way, without the objectivists stoutly encouraging them to continue this self-defeating, viciously circular kind of thinking.

Objectivist psychology believes that "whether the values by which he judges himself are conscious or subconscious, rational or irrational, consistent or contradictory, life-serving or life-negating—every human being judges himself by *some* standard; and to the extent that he fails to satisfy that standard, his sense of personal worth, his self-respect, suffers accordingly."[4] Here again objectivism confuses the individual with his performances, and insists that because the latter have to be rated and judged—which they probably to some extent have to be in order for the individual to survive—the self, or the person as a whole, has to be rated, evaluated, or judged.

Rational Emotive Behavior Therapy, in conjunction with certain existentialist and humanist philosophies, maintains that although humans have a strong tendency to rate or judge themselves, they do not *have to* do so, and they are irrational when they do. Their self or total personality is a rather meaningless abstraction or overgeneralization, and even if it can be precisely defined, there seems to be no mathematically precise method of evaluating it—of giving it a single global rating.

In the last analysis, it is invariably rated by some kind of fairly arbitrary definition: thus, the individual claims that she, or her self, is good because she performs well, because she is popular with others, because some god she invented loves her, or simply because she exists. If she must rate herself, then we'd be sensible to pick some safe standard— such as the belief that she is good because she exists, rather than some anxiety-provoking standard such as the belief that she is good because she performs well.

There is no necessary reason why the individual *has* to evaluate himself at all. He could simply accept the fact that he exists and let it go at that. Thus, he could say, "I exist. Because I exist, I prefer to stay alive, and while I am alive, I prefer to be happy. If performing well or inducing others to approve of me will bring me practical rewards and make me happier, then I shall try to be efficient and popular. But if I am neither efficient nor popular, there is a high probability that I can still find *some* way of remaining alive and being happy, so I shall look for that way. As long as I can somehow remain alive and derive some amount of joy from living, I shall consider life worthwhile. If this no longer becomes true and I think that I shall never find any happiness in life, I may then consider my life valueless and may kill myself.

"No matter how much or how little I consider living valuable, however, I do not have to rate myself in terms of any standard—since doing so is invariably arbitrary and will very likely get me into unnecessary difficulties. In particular, it will tend to make me so anxious that I shall not live up to the arbitrary standard I have set. So why need I rate myself at all?"

A human can, in other words, fully accept her existence and the desirability of finding happiness and freedom from anxiety without giving herself any rating whatever. She will still have to rate her performances—since if she doesn't, for example, acknowledge the fact that she is a poor automobile driver, may end up killing herself.

But he doesn't have to rate, evaluate, or esteem his *self*. He merely has to accept himself—or, more accurately, accept the fact that he is alive and that there is a good likelihood that he can find *some* kind of enjoyment if he remains alive. This kind of unqualified self-acceptance is a far cry from the usual kind of self-rating which virtually all humans do, which almost invariably leads to conscious or underlying anxiety, and which objectivists think is inevitable.

"Man," states Branden, "needs self-respect because he has to achieve values and in order to act he has to value the beneficiary of his values—namely, himself."[5] This may be largely true; but self-respect, or what I call self-acceptance, or the individual's considering himself worthy or living and of enjoying himself, is by no means the same thing as self-esteem, pride, or self-approval. The former relates only to the individual's "aliveness" and his potentiality for happiness, while the latter relates to his proving himself worthy of being alive and happy—and to doing this by performing well and by showing his superiority over others.

In other words, self-confidence means valuing yourself under virtually all conditions; self-esteem means valuing yourself only when you behave unusually well—and especially when you put down others. In this connection, it is interesting to note that if you think you *must* have self-esteem—meaning, that you must perform well in order to accept yourself—you will usually be so anxious about your not being competent that you will incessantly focus on *how*, instead of *what*, you are doing, and consequently will perform badly and have little confidence in yourself.

Anyone who *must* have something or *must* do well will tend to be anxious about the possibility of not doing as well as he supposedly *mus*. The idea of *must* is itself anxiety-producing, even when—and perhaps especially when—it is applied to the idea, "I *must* have self-esteem." Objectivism, with its continual emphasis on shoulds, oughts, and musts, therefore leaves the true believer in this kind of philosophy with practically no chance of attaining full, secure self-acceptance.

According to objectivist thinking, "constant growth is...a *psychological* need of man. It is a condition of his mental well-being. His mental well-being requires that he possess a firm sense of control over reality, of control over his existence—the conviction that he is *competent* to live. And this requires, not omniscience or omnipotence, but the knowledge that one's *methods* of dealing with reality—the *principles* by which one functions—are right....Self-esteem, the basic conviction that one is competent to live, can be maintained only so long as one is engaged in a process of growth, only so long as one is committed to the task of increasing one's efficacy."[6]

Here the objectivists outdo themselves! Not only, they contend, must a person be highly competent in order to deserve the right to live and be happy; she must also be engaged in a process of continuous growth, and must become ever increasingly competent. Note, again, that they do not say that constant growth and increased competence are *desirable* or *preferable* traits. No, they contend that self-esteem can be maintained *only* if you possess these traits.

Objectivists seem to completely ignore the fact that perhaps one-quarter of the people in the world today are too little intelligent and too uneducated to be exceptionally competent or to foster their own continuous growth. They also ignore the fact that perhaps another one-quarter of the populace—including those who have severe personality disorders and psychoses—are sufficiently bright and educated to think intelligently in many areas of their lives but are still so disturbed that they are lucky if they can hold their heads above water, economically and socially, most of their lives, let alone behave on a high level of competence to begin with and then continue to grow to still higher levels of efficacy.

By adherents of Ayn Rand and Nathaniel Branden, it may be objected that they are merely describing ideal conditions for human functioning in statements such as that quoted above. But reread Branden's statement, and ask yourself if it sounds as though he is talking about an ideal.

An indication of how even the objectivists themselves do not live up to their notions of self-esteem is given by Ayn Rand, who tells us that "during a question period at Nathaniel Branden Institute, a student asked: 'Can you tell me how to read the newspapers without getting depressed?' Mr. Branden replied: 'When you find the answer, please let us know.'" According to this anecdote, even the chief spokespersons for objectivism are not able to ward off feelings of depression—which means, to my way of thinking, that they do not respect themselves enough to accept the frustrations of reality and hence to keep themselves undepressed.

The idea that an individual is able to accept himself only because he possesses "a firm sense of control over reality" and is competent to live, to know that the principles by which he functions are absolutely right, and to keep constantly growing is a highly demanding philosophy. If you fail in any of these respects you, by definition, doom yourself to feelings of worthlessness. It is tantamount to the proposition, "I accept myself because objectivism is right and I am a good objectivist." This is similar to dogmatic religionists, who invent the "right" god and the "right" religion and who then convince themselves that they are worthwhile people because they are loved by this god and this religion.

A much more elegant approach to self-acceptance is found in the REBT view, which says, "I accept myself and consider myself worthy of life and enjoyments simply because I exist, because I am alive." Both the devout religious and the objectivist views are inelegant solutions because they require additional and unnecessary assumptions about god and objectivism. The religious view boils down to the proposition that "Since I am I, since I am alive, and since I am able to invent and define the attributes of a god, I can therefore invent a god to whom I am acceptable, and thereby indirectly accept myself." And the objectivist view boils down to the proposition that "Since I am I, since I am alive, and since I am able to invent a system of self-acceptance based on the proposition that I must be an ever-growing competent person (not to mention a classical capitalist!), I can thereby indirectly accept myself."

Both dogmatic religous and the objectivist conceptions of self-worth are true only by definition—because the human individual decides to make them true for himself. And they both stem from the basic assumption that since I am alive and since I, just by dint of being alive, deserve to be happy, I can invent definitions of my own worth which will help me accept myself and be happy. They both, however, go needlessly beyond the original assumption and gratuitously and inelegantly add other assumptions, which, ironically, may then interfere with self-acceptance and enjoyment.

For if I invent a god who, by accepting me, enables me to accept myself, I allow the possibility that he will not accept me under certain conditions—and I thereby limit my self-acceptance. And if I invent an objectivist-type god (the absolute necessity that I be competent and ever-growing), I again allow for the possibility that I will not be that competent, and I again greatly limit my self-acceptance. To dream up gratuitous requisites for self-acceptance is philosophically inelegant and pragmatically dangerous. Moreover, because humans easily make themselves anxious, to demand this gratuitous essential for self-acceptance is downright irrational.

Rational Emotive Behavior therapy (and other humanist principles) prefer to stick with the simplest, most elegant, and least philosophically assailable assumption regarding human worth: I exist; I appear to have a good possibility of being happy if I continue to exist; therefore I deserve to exist (or think it would be better to preserve my existence) and to live happily.

The fact that objectivists have a highly perfectionistic and unrealistic conception of human worth is shown by their inevitable—I might almost say compulsive—tendency to start with a fairly reasonable definition of self-acceptance and then quickly bolix it up with grandiose ideals. Thus Branden's statement that "self-esteem is the conviction that one is able to live and worthy of living," which is sensible enough, since by any reasonable and workable conception of self-worth the individual *is* worthy of living just because he is able to live. But Branden immediately continues: "which means: that one's mind is competent to think and one's person is worthy of happiness."[7] This implies that stupid individuals and those who can but do not think well are not worthy of happiness, even though they may somehow manage to achieve some degree of it.

To make matters worse, Branden continues: "Self-esteem…is the consequence, expression, and reward of a mind fully committed to reason. Commitment to reason is commitment to the maintenance of a full intellectual focus, to the constant expansion of one's understanding and knowledge, to the principle that one's actions must be consistent with one's convictions, that one must never attempt to fake reality, or place any consideration above reality, that one must never permit oneself contradictions."

Here objectivist psychology surpasses itself in its inordinate demands on humans. Where it usually fails to make clear that certain goals of human behavior are *desirable* but not *necessary,* in this instance it posits goals that are not even desirable: commitment to the maintenance of a full intellectual focus, to the constant expansion of one's understanding and knowledge, and to *never* permitting oneself contradictions. If an individual were truly as devoted to these goals as the objectivists urge him to be, he would be compulsively rational—and therefore inhuman and irrational!

In his statement, Branden is saying that not only are these goals desirable but that their achievement is absolutely necessary if the individual is to like herself. So here he is taking traits of highly questionable desirability and insisting that they *must* be achieved for purposes of self-worth. He pyramids one irrational premise on top of another, once again showing that objectivism is not entirely a rational philosophical or psychological system.

The objectivist theory of human worth is internally inconsistent and contradictory. Thus, we are told that the individual is sufficient unto himself, that his main goal in life is to be himself and not to worry about what others think of him, that he should selfishly pursue his own interests, and that "no one who values human life would preach that man has no right to exist for his own sake."[8] But then, in direct contradiction to these views, the objectivists preach that people have no right to exist for their own sake *unless* they work hard, think straight, maintain steady growth and development, and otherwise fulfill the tenets of the Calvinist-objectivist credo. If they construe existing for their own sake as being dependent on others, being lazy, or making a living as, say, a gambler, then they presumably have no right to this kind of self-determination and do not deserve to live, even if they can manage to survive and (perversely enough!) be happy with their antiobjectivist philosophy.

Again: The objectivists contend that you can rid yourself of feelings of anxiety and worthlessness by choosing self-accepting values. But if you happen to choose—as I, for one, do—the value system that is least likely to cause you to feel emotionally insecure (namely, the existentialist-humanist value system that postulates that you can fully accept yourself no matter what you do and no matter how badly you perform), objectivist psychology tells you that you are deliberately choosing (according to its biased standards) to think unclearly and be less competent than you could be, and that therefore you *should* be anxious and self-hating.

Still again, objectivism states that when you are insecure, you *volitionally* choose the kind of false thinking that creates your insecurity. But it also states that to think crookedly *volitionally* is criminal, that you *deserve* to hate yourself when you make this choice, and that you cannot possibly have self-esteem unless you have "an intransigent determination to think and act on [your] rational judgment."[9] This means that if you feel worthless and you accept the objectivist postulate that you made yourself feel this way and should not have done so, you will quite probably make yourself feel worthless for feeling worthless or make yourself anxious about being anxious, and will thereby make yourself still more emotionally disturbed. This is why, if objectivist views are strictly followed in the course of psychotherapy, they will tend to help the majority of patients feel more worthless and hopeless (if that is possible) than when they first come to see an objectivist therapist.

Like O. Hobart Mowrer and other religiously oriented psychotherapists, the objectivists fail to distinguish properly between responsibility and sin. A man who makes a mistake is usually responsible for his actions (because he has caused them) and therefore can be held accountable for his errors. But a man who is a sinner is generally held to be: responsible for his actions; condemnable as a person for performing them; and deserving of punishment (either on earth or in hell) for committing them. Mowrer insists that a wrongdoer *is* a sinner, and that he had therefore better admit his sinning, atone for it, and make absolutely certain that he never commits a sin again. If he keeps volitionally sinning he is a rotter and deserves punishment—and he especially deserves to feel guilty or to lose his self-esteem.

Objectivist psychology takes essentially the same view: that a wrongdoer who *volitionally* chooses not to think straight and produce competently is not worthy of his own (or others') respect, is a rotter, and deserves punishment—and he especially deserves to feel guilty or to lose his self-esteem.

In contradistinction to the views of Mowrer and objectivism, there is the humanist-existentialist view (as epitomized in the theory and practice of REBT) which holds that an individual can be wrong, mistaken, and irresponsible, and can even choose to be a wrongdoer, but that nonetheless he may accept himself, not be condemned as a person by himself or others, and not deserve to be punished for his irresponsibilities. It would be much better if he stopped behaving irresponsibly, because in all probability he will harm himself and be penalized socially if he remains the way he is. But there is no inexorable law of the universe which says that he should, ought, or must be responsible, or that he is worthless even if he never is responsible.

REBT accepts (and tries to help) the so-called sinner while acknowledging and pointing out the error of his so-called sin. It objectively concerns itself with his performance but refuses to castigate him personally for performing badly. Like Mowrerism, objectivism unobjectively condemns the "sinner" and his "sin"—and thereby provides little hope of helping him become less "sinning" and more self-accepting. By confusing irresponsibility with sin and failing to see that human performances may well be reprehensible (but that humans *themselves* really cannot be), objectivism further obfuscates the important problem of human worth.

What the objectivists are truly intent on upholding is not the individual's sense of self-acceptance, but his feeling of pride. Pride is a tricky term, because it has several different meanings: (a) an overhigh opinion of oneself and exaggerated self-esteem; (b) a sense of one's own dignity or worth, self-respect; (c) delight or satisfaction in one's achievements, possessions, children, etc.; (d) a feeling of superiority over others, one-upmanship. Although the second and third meanings of the term are well within the realm of realism and mental health, the first and fourth meanings are not. Most people who say that their sense of pride means a sense of self-respect and delight in their own achievements are hiding the fact that they really feel superior to others, and that that is why they accept themselves or experience self-esteem.

Another way of stating this is to say that it is healthy for an individual to feel pride in the sense of her telling herself, "I acted competently today or I sanely disciplined myself—and it is good that I did so (because such behavior has real advantages)." But it is not so healthy for her to feel pride in the sense of her telling herself, "I acted competently today or I sanely disciplined myself—and I am good because I did so" or "I acted competently today and therefore I am a better person than you are."

When a person feels pride in himself (rather than in his activity or character) for performing well he must also, if he is at all logical, denigrate himself (rather than negatively assess his activity) when he performs badly. If, in relation to his central being, he accepts the virtue of pride, he also has to accept the hell of worthlessness, and he remains irrationally caught up in theology (as epitomized by the Judeo-Christian tradition). If he really wants to feel consistently worthwhile or accept himself unqualifiedly as a person, he had better surrender the concepts of self-pride *and* self-deprecation.

Objectivism apotheosizes pride and, as far as I can tell, teaches that in order to be proud a man must: perform his volitional acts quite well; be proud of *himself* for his fine performances; and feel superior to others who choose to perform less well. Thus, Ayn Rand tells us that "when you learn that pride is the sum of all virtues, you will learn to live like a man."[10] And again: "The virtue of pride can best be described by the term: 'moral ambitiousness.' It means that one must earn the right to hold oneself at one's own highest value by achieving one's own moral perfection—which one achieves by never accepting any code of irrational virtues impossible to practice and by never failing to practice the virtues one knows to be rational—by never accepting an unearned guilt and never earning any, or, if one *has* earned it, never leaving it uncorrected—by never resigning oneself passively to any flaws in one's character—by never placing any concern, wish, fear, or mood of the moment above the reality of one's own self-esteem."[11] In this last passage, note that Miss Rand's perfectionism is so blatant that even she takes note of it, and uses the term "moral perfection" to describe the state that the individual must achieve if he is to feel pride in himself.

Nathaniel Branden backs up his mentor's views on pride with these statements: "Of the various pleasures that man can offer himself, the greatest is pride." And: "Self-esteem pertains to a man's conviction of his fundamental efficacy and worth. Pride pertains to the pleasure a man takes in himself on the basis of and in response to *specific* achievements or actions. Self-esteem is confidence in one's capacity to achieve values. Pride is the consequence of having achieved some particular value(s). Self-esteem is 'I can.' Pride is 'I have.' A man can take pride in his actions in reality, i.e., in his existential achievements, and in the qualities he has achieved in his own character. The deepest pride a man can experience is that which results from his achievement of self-esteem: since self-esteem is a value that has to be earned, the man who does so feels proud of his attainment."[12]

Note here that Branden deifies the pleasure to be obtained from feelings of pride; strongly links pride to specific achievements; indicates that self-esteem is possible only to the individual who knows that he *can* achieve and that therefore he *will* feel pride; and shows that the achievement of self-esteem itself is something about which the individual should feel inordinately proud. In this respect, the objectivist system is certainly consistent.

The trouble is that, in the first and last analysis, it still insists that a person can only fully accept herself if she produces mighty accomplishments, and that she'd damned well better be proud of herself for such accomplishments or else she won't experience the greatest of life's pleasures. This may be a great philosophy for promoting human productivity, but it has dubious advantages even in that respect. For if a person thinks that she *must* achieve high-level production in order to accept herself, she frequently becomes so terrified of nonachievement or lesser achievement that she hardly produces at all. Moreover, even if the objectivist creed encourages productivity, it hardly abets self-acceptance. On the contrary, it will usually lead to varying degrees of self-hatred. As the old saying goes, pride goeth before a fall!

The objectivist position on self-esteem is taken to its ultimate absurdity in this statement of Nathaniel Branden: "An unbreached rationality—that is, an unbreached determination to use one's mind to the fullest extent of one's ability, and a refusal ever to evade one's knowledge or act against it—is the only valid criterion of virtue and the only possible basis of authentic self-esteem."[13] Even assuming that a human *has* unusual rationality and great determination to use his mind fully, how the devil is he going to assure himself that his rationality and determination are unbreached? By working very hard at making them so? By becoming an objectivist? By berating himself for his breaches? Hardly! For all this, he will still inevitably be fallible, error prone.

What, then, is this poor mistake-making human to do? Obviously, according to objectivist notions, she must suffer. She can absolutely never, as Branden states, acquire authentic self-esteem. So she is left with a choice of false self-esteem, little self-esteem, or no self-esteem whatever. Grim!

A person has one possible way out. He can forget about objectivism and take himself into the humanist fold. He can then teach himself—as the followers of Rational Emotive Behavior Therapy are taught and as they teach themselves—to accept himself unqualifiedly, with his myriads of mistakes, and with or without great achievements, just because he is alive, just because he exists. Then, with this groundwork laid for feeling truly emotionally secure, he can go on (if he wishes) to strive for whatever he would like to achieve in life, and then, probably, he will have a much better chance of internal and external attainment.

21

The Case Against Religiosity

I first wrote "The Case Against Religion: A Psychotherapist's View" for Lyle Stuart's the *Independent* in 1962, and took quite a dim view of the mental health of religionists. Over the years I saw that I was unduly negative in this respect and thoroughly revised my essay in 1983 to show that religion itself is not necessarily inimical to emotional health, but that devout religiosity, or dogmatic and rigid adherence to religious ideas, frequently is. In my revised "Case Against Religiosity," I think I made the unique point that secular religiosity, as shown in extreme nationalism (such as nazism and fascism) and in rigid communism (such as Stalinism and Maoism), is in many ways the same as theistic religiosity, and that both credos tend to impair emotional functioning. I still largely believe this, as the present chapter shows.

Since 1983, however, I have seen that there are many kinds of religion, including kinds of devout religiosity. Thus, two of my religious colleagues, Stevan Nielson, a Mormon priest and psychologist, and Brad Johnson, a professor of clinical psychology at a Protestant university, are able to use REBT very well with some devout Christians, because many of its core philosophies are included in Christian teachings. The Christian philosophy of accepting the sinner but not the sin is essentially the same as the REBT philosophies of unconditional self-acceptance (USA) and unconditional other acceptance.

As Kenneth Pergament, Lee A. Kirkpatrick, and Richard Gorsach, psychologists who have studied religious people, have pointed out, those religionists who embrace "the-sinners-in-the-hands-of-a-merciful-God" model are quite different from—and enjoy better possible mental health outcomes than those—religionists who believe in an "angry God" model. Perhaps this is because they are less dogmatic and devout than those who believe in the angry God model. So my points in the following chapter may be accurate.

As I am noting in a book on REBT and religion, which I am writing with Steve Nielsen and Brad Johnson, religious and non-religious beliefs themselves may not help people to be emotionally "healthy" as may the *kinds* of religious and nonreligious beliefs they hold. Considerably more research needs to be done to throw light on this question.

Before I attempt to write about the advantages and disadvantages of devout religion (or religiosity), let me try to clearly define these terms. Traditionally, the term religion has meant some kind of belief in the supernatural. Thus, *Webster's New World Dictionary* defines religion as: "(1) belief in a divine or superhuman power or powers to be obeyed and worshipped as the creator(s) and ruler(s) of the universe; (2) expression of this belief in conduct and ritual." However, in recent years religion has also come to be defined in broader terms than this; so that the same dictionary continues: "(3) Any specific system of belief, worship, conduct, etc., often involving a code of ethics and a philosophy: as, the Christian religion, the Buddhist religion, etc. Loosely, any system of beliefs, practices, ethical values, etc. resembling, suggestive of, or likened to such a system: as, humanism is his religion."

This article discusses two particular forms of devout religion or religiosity. The first of these is a devout or orthodox belief in some kind of supernatural religion, such as Judaism, Christianity, or Moham-medanism—or pious adherence to the kind of religion mentioned in Webster's first two definitions. The second form of religiosity discussed here is a devout or rigid belief in some kind of secular religion (such as Libertarianism, Marxism, or Freudianism)—that is, a dogmatic, absolutistic conviction that some political, economic, social, or philosophic view is sacrosanct, provides ultimate answers to virtually all important questions, and is to be piously subscribed to and followed by everyone who wishes to lead a good life.

Webster's third definition of religion is outside the scope of this article. It is used to denote a mild system of beliefs, practices, or ethical values that are not connected with any assumed higher power, and I do not think that this kind of "religion" leads to any specific individual or social harm. So a vague, general, or moderate set of "religious" beliefs will not be scrutinized, but only a devout and pious brand of religiosity. Stated a little differently, my attempt is to relate absolutist religiosity, rather than mild religion, to mental and emotional health.

Although no group of authorities fully agree on a definition of the term *mental health*, it seems to include several traits and behaviors that are frequently endorsed by leading theorists and therapists. I have outlined the desirability of these "healthy" traits in several of my writings on Rational Emotive Behavior Therapy, and they have also been generally endorsed by many other therapists, including Sigmund Freud, Carl Jung, Alfred Adler, Karen Horney, Erich Fromm, Rudolf Dreikurs, Fritz Perls, Abraham Maslow, Marie Jahoda, Carl Rogers, and Rollo May. These include such traits as self-interest, self-direction, social interest, tolerance, acceptance of ambiguity, acceptance of reality, commitment, risk-taking, self-acceptance, rationality, and scientific thinking. Not all mentally healthy individuals possess the highest degree of these traits at all times, but when people seriously lack them or when they have extreme opposing behaviors, we often consider them to be at least somewhat emotionally disturbed.

Assuming that the above criteria for mental health and a few other related criteria are reasonably correct, how are they sabotaged by a system of devout religious beliefs or religiosity? And how are they abetted by adherence to the principles of unbelief, skepticism, and atheism? Let us now consider these questions.

Self-Interest

Emotionally healthy people are primarily true to themselves and do not masochistically subjugate themselves to or unduly sacrifice themselves for others. Realizing that if they do not primarily take care of themselves no one else will, they tend to put themselves first, a few selected others a close second, and the rest of the world not too far behind.

Rather than be primarily self-interested, devout deity-oriented religionists put their hypothesized god(s) first and themselves second—or last! They are so overconcerned about whether their god loves them, and whether they are doing the right thing to continue in this god's good graces, that they sacrifice some of their most cherished and enjoyable interest to supposedly appease this god. If, moreover, they are a member of any orthodox church or organization they feel forced to choose their god's precepts first, those of their church or organization second, and their own views and preferences third.

Masochistic self-sacrifice is an integral part of many major organized religions, as shown, for example, in the ritualistic self-deprivation that Jews, Christians, and Muslims must continually bear if they are to keep their faith. Orthodox religions deliberately instill guilt (self-damnation) in their adherents and then give them guilt-soothing rituals to temporarily allay this kind of self-damning feeling.

Instead of bowing to supernatural gods, pious secular religionists create semidivine dictators (for example, Stalin and Hitler) and absolutistic entities (for example, the Third Reich), and masochistically demean themselves before these "noble" powers—again to the detriment of their own self-interest.

Self-direction

Mentally healthy people largely assume responsibility for their own lives, enjoy the independence of mainly working out their own problems, and, while at times wanting or preferring the help of others, do not think that they absolutely *must* have such support for their effectiveness and well-being.

Devout religionists (both secular and divine) are almost necessarily dependent and other-directed rather than self-sufficient. To be true to orthodoxies, they first must immolate themselves to their god or godlike hero; then to the religious hierarchy that runs their church or organization; and finally to all the other members of their religious sect, who are watching them closely to see if they defect an iota from the conduct that their god and their churchly leadership define as proper.

Therefore, if devout religiosity is often masochism, it is even more often dependency, for it is well nigh impossible for humans to be true believers and also strong and independent. Devout religiosity and self-sufficiency are contradictory terms.

Social interest

Emotionally and mentally healthy people are normally gregarious and decide to try to live happily in a social group. Because they want to live successfully with others, and usually to relate intimately to a few of these selected others, they work at feeling and displaying a considerable degree of social interest and interpersonal competence. While they still are primarily interested in their personal survival and enjoyment, they also tend to be considerate and fair to others; to avoid needlessly harming these others; to engage in collaborative and cooperative endeavors; at times to be somewhat altruistic; and to distinctly enjoy some measure of interpersonal and group relationships.

Devout, deity-inspired religionists tend to sacrifice human love for godly love and to withdraw into monastic and holy affairs at the expense of intimate interpersonal relationships. They frequently are deficient in social competence. They spend immense amounts of time, effort, and money on establishing and maintaining churchly establishments rather than on social welfare. They foment religious fights, feuds, wars, and terrorism in the course of which orthodox believers literally batter and kill rather than cooperatively help each other. They encourage charity that is highly parochial and linked to god's glory more than to the alleviation of human suffering. Their altruism is highly alloyed with egotistically proving to God how great and glorious they can be as human benefactors.

Devout secular religionists are often much more interested in the propagation of absolutistic creeds (for example, Maoism) than they are in intimately relating to and in collaboratively helping humans. Like the god-inspired religionists, their charity is exceptionally parochial and is often given only to members of their own religious group while discriminating against members of groups with opposing credos.

Tolerance

Emotionally healthy people tend to give other humans the right to be wrong—as Dr. Robert A. Harper and I urged in the original edition of *A Guide to Rational Living*, which we authored in 1961. While disliking or abhorring others' *behavior*, they refuse to condemn *them* as total *persons* for performing poor behavior. They fully accept the fact that all humans seem to be remarkably fallible; they refrain from unrealistically demanding and commanding that any of them be perfect; and they desist from damning people in toto when they err.

Tolerance is anathema to devout, divinity-centered religionists, since they believe that their particular god is absolutely right and that all opposing deities and humans are positively and utterly false and wrong. According to orthodox religious *shalts* and *shalt nots*, you become not only a wrongdoer but an arrant sinner when you commit ethical and religious misdeeds, and, as a sinner, you become worthless, undeserving of any human happiness, and deserving of being forever damned on earth (excommunicated) and perhaps eternally roasted in hell.

The pious secular religionist, without invoking god or hell, believes that the rules and regulations of his or her group or community are completely right and that, at the very least, social ostracism, political banishment, and perhaps torture and death should be the lot of any strong dissenter. By setting up absolute standards of godly or proper conduct, devout religiosity makes you intolerant of yourself and others when you or they slightly dishonor these standards. Born of this kind of piety-inspired intolerance of self and others come some of the most serious emotional disorders—such as extreme anxiety, depression, self-hatred, and rage.

Acceptance of Ambiguity and Uncertainty

Emotionally mature individuals accept the fact that, as far as has yet been discovered, we live in a world of probability and chance, where there are not, nor probably ever will be, absolute necessities or complete certainties. Living in such a world is not only tolerable but, in terms of adventure, learning, and striving, can even be very exciting and pleasurable.

If one of the requisites for emotional health is acceptance of ambiguity and uncertainty, then divinity-oriented religiosity is the unhealthiest state imaginable because its prime reason for being is to enable the religionist to believe in god-commanded certainty. Just because life is so uncertain and ambiguous, and because millions of people think that they cannot bear its vicissitudes, they invent absolutist gods, and thereby pretend that there is some final, invariant answer to human problems. Patently, these people are fooling themselves. Instead of healthfully admitting that they do not need certainty but can live comfortably in this often disorderly world, they stubbornly protect their neurotic beliefs by insisting that there must be the kind of certainty that they wrongly believe they need.

This is like a young boy's believing that he must have a kindly father in order to survive, and then, when his father is unkind or perhaps has died, the boy dreams up a father (who may be a neighbor, a movie star, or a pure figment of his imagination) and insists that this dream father actually exists.

Devout secular religionists invent the "certainty" of unequivocally knowing that their special political, economic, social, or other creed is indubitably true and cannot be falsified. Like the superhuman-oriented religionists, they also pigheadedly refuse to accept ambiguity and uncertainty—and thereby render and keep themselves neurotically defensive and immature.

Flexibility

Emotionally sound people are intellectually flexible, tend to be open to change at all times, and are prone to take an unbigoted (or at least less bigoted) view of the infinitely varied people, ideas, and things in the world around them. They can be firm and passionate in their thoughts and feelings, and they comfortably look at new evidence and often revise their notions of "reality" to conform with this evidence.

The trait of flexibility, which is so important to effective emotional functioning, is frequently blocked and sabotaged by profound religiosity. For the person who dogmatically believes in god and who sustains this belief with a strong faith unfounded on fact—which a pious religionist of course does—clearly is not open to many aspects of change, and instead sees things narrowly and bigotedly.

If, for example, a man's church scriptures tell him that he shalt not covet his neighbor's wife—let alone have actual adulterous relations with her—he cannot ask himself, "Why should I not lust after this woman, as long as I don't intend to do anything about my desire for her? What is really wrong about that?" But because his god and his church have spoken, there is no appeal from this arbitrary authority. He has brought himself to unconditionally accept it.

Any time, in fact, that people unempirically establish a god or a set of religious postulates that supposedly have a superhuman origin, they can no longer use empirical evidence to question the dictates of this god or those postulates, since they are, by definition, beyond scientific checking. Rigid secular religionists, too, cannot change the rules that their pious creeds establish. Thus, devout Nazis cannot accept any goodness of Jews or Gypsies, even when it can be incontrovertibly shown that such individuals performed good acts.

The best that devout religionists can do, if they want to change any of the rules that stem from their doctrines, is change their religion itself. Otherwise they are stuck with its absolutist axioms, as well as their logical corollaries, that the religionists themselves have initially accepted on faith. Again we may note that, just as devout religion is masochism, other-directedness, intolerance, and refusal to accept uncertainty, it also seems to be synonymous with mental and emotional inflexibility.

Scientific Thinking

Emotionally stable people are reasonably objective, rational, and scientific. They not only construct reasonable and empirically substantiated theories relating to what goes on in the surrounding world (and with their fellow creatures who inhabit this world) but they also, if they follow the teachings of REBT, are able to apply the rules of logic and of the scientific method to their own lives and to their interpersonal relationships.

In regard to scientific thinking, it practically goes without saying that this kind of cerebration is antithetical to religiosity. A host of philosophers of science, including Bertrand Russell, Ludwig Wittgenstein, Hans Reichenbach, Herbert Feigl, Karl Popper, W. W. Bartley, and Michael Mahoney, have pointed out the main requisites of the scientific method: scientific theories must be stated in such a manner that they are at least partly confirmable by some form of human experience, by some empirical referent; and scientific theories are those that can in some way be falsified.

Deity-oriented religionists contend that the superhuman entities that they posit cannot be seen, heard, smelled, tasted, felt, or otherwise humanly experienced, and that their gods and their principles are therefore beyond the realm of science. Pious deists and theists believe that the gods or spirits they construct are transcendent, which means, in theology or religion, that they are separate or beyond experience; that they exist apart from the material universe; that, no matter what science says, they are indubitably true and real.

To devoutly believe in any of the usual religions, therefore, is to be unscientific, and we could well contend that the more devout one is, the less scientific one tends to be. Although a pious religionist need not be entirely unscientific (or, for that matter, neither need be a raving maniac), it is difficult to see how such a person could be consistently scientific.

While people may be both scientific and vaguely or generally religious (as, for example, many liberal Protestants and reformed Jews tend to be), it is doubtful whether they may simultaneously be thoroughly devout and reasonably in touch with social reality. Devout secular religionists (such as fanatic believers in phrenology or reincarnation) are not necessarily driven to believe in superhuman and supernatural concepts. But they almost inevitably favor absolutist convictions about certain other issues, and absolutism and dogma are the antithesis of science. Just about all absolutists, secular and godly, tend to flout some of the basic postulates of the scientific method.

Commitment

As I have noted on several occasions in my writing on Rational Emotive Behavior Therapy (REBT), emotionally healthy and happy people are usually absorbed in something outside of themselves, whether this be people, things, or ideas. They seem to lead better lives when they have at least one major creative interest, as well as some outstanding human involvement, which they make very important to themselves and around which they structure a good part of their lives.

In regard to the trait of commitment, devoutly religious people may have some advantages. If they are truly religious, and therefore seriously committed to their god, church, or creed, they acquire a major interest in life. Pious religious commitment, however, frequently has its serious disadvantages, because it tends to be obsessive-compulsive and may well interfere with other kinds of healthy commitments—such as deep involvements in sex-love relationships, scientific pursuits, and even artistic endeavors. Moreover, religious commitment is an absorption that is often motivated by guilt or hostility, and that may consequently serve as a frenzied covering-up mechanism that masks, but that does not really eliminate, these underlying disturbed feelings. Moreover, pious god-inspired commitment is frequently the kind that is based on falsehoods and illusions and that therefore easily can be shattered, thus plunging the previously committed individual into the depths of disillusionment and despair.

In other words, not all forms of commitment are equally healthy or beneficial. The grand inquisitors of the medieval Catholic church were utterly dedicated to their "holy" work, and Hitler and many of his associates were fanatically committed to their Nazi doctrines. But this hardly proves that they were emotionally stable humans. In fact, a good case can be made for the proposition that although involved or passionate commitment to some cause or ideal is normally healthy and happiness-producing, devout, pious, or fanatic commitment to the same kind of cause or ideal is potentially pernicious and frequently (though not always) does much more harm than good. Both deity-oriented and secular manifestations of piousness may have distinct advantages for committed individuals—but let us not forget their enormous disadvantages!

Risk-Taking

Emotionally sound people are able to take risks. They ask themselves what they would really like to do in life, and then try to do it, even though they have to risk defeat or failure. They are reasonably adventurous (though not foolhardy); are willing to try almost anything once, if only to see how they like it; and look forward to different or unusual breaks in their usual routines.

In regard to risk-taking, I think it is fairly obvious that pious theists are determined to avoid adventure and refuse to take many of life's normal risks. They strongly believe in rigid and unvalidatable assumptions precisely because they are often afraid to follow their own preferences and aims. They demand a guarantee that they will be safe and secure, come what may, and because the real world does not provide them with any such guarantee, they invent some god or other higher power that will presumably give it to them. Their invention of this deity, and their piously subjugating themselves to it, confirms their view that the world is too risky; it gives them a further excuse for sticking to the straight and narrow (and often joyless) paths of existence.

Devout nontheistic religionists mainly substitute dogmatic belief in some philosophy or cause for a fanatical belief in god, and they use this sacredized cause to protect themselves against adventure and risk-taking. Thus, pious nutritionists will under no conditions risk eating white bread or sugar, even when it might temporarily do them some good. And devout adherents of cognitive therapy (including devout REBTers) may not tolerate the idea that *any* feeling can be free of thought and will insist that *all* dysfunctional behaviors (such as headaches and feelings of depression) *must* be of purely ideological origin.

Fearing failure and rejection, and falsely defining their own worth as humans in terms of achievement and approval, devout religionists sacrifice time, energy, and material goods and pleasures to the worship of their assumed gods or godlike philosophies, so that they can at least be sure that their god loves and supports them or that an inherent Rightness is on their side. All devout religions seem to be distinctly inhibiting—which means, in effect, that piously religious individuals sell their soul, surrender their own basic urges and pleasures, in order to feel comfortable with the heavenly helper or the indubitably correct creed that they have invented or adopted. One of the major ingredients of religiosity, then, is needless, self-defeating inhibition.

Self-acceptance

People who are emotionally healthy are usually glad to be alive and to accept themselves as "deserving" of continued life and happiness just because they exist and because they have some present or future potential to enjoy themselves. In accordance with the principles of REBT, they fully or unconditionally accept themselves (or give themselves what Carl Rogers called unconditional positive regard). They try to perform competently in their affairs and win the approval and love of others; but they do so for enjoyment and not for ego gratification or self-deification. They consequently try to rate only their acts, deeds, and traits in the light of the goals, values, and purposes they choose (such as the goals of graduating from school or of having an enjoyable sex-love relationship), and they rigorously try to avoid rating their self, being, essence, or totality.

Healthy people, in other words, unconditionally accept themselves because they *choose* to do so, regardless of how much approval they receive from others. They distinctly *prefer* to act competently and to win others' favor, and they accordingly assess and criticize their own behaviors when they fail in these respects. But they don't hold that they absolutely *must* do well or be loved, and they therefore don't conclude that they, in toto, are good people when they succeed and are rotten individuals when they fail.

In regard to self-acceptance, it seems clear that devout religionists cannot accept themselves just because they are alive and because they have some power to enjoy life. Rather, orthodox theists make their self-acceptance contingent on their being accepted by the god, church, clergy, and other members of the religious denomination in which they believe. If all these extrinsic persons and things accept them, then and then only are they able to accept themselves, which means that these religionists define themselves only through the reflected appraisals of god and other humans. For such individuals, fanatical religion almost necessarily winds up with lack of unconditional self-acceptance and, instead, with a considerable degree of self-abasement and self-negation—as, of course, virtually all the saints and mystics have found.

What about theistic religions like Christianity, that presumably give grace to all people who accept their tenets and thereby allow all humans to accept themselves unconditionally? As far as I know, there are no theistic creeds that actually do this. The best of them—like Science of Mind—state that God (or Jesus) is all-loving and that s/he therefore always gives everyone grace or unconditional acceptance. But these theistic religions still require their adherents to believe: that a god (or son of god) must exist; that s/he personally gives you unconditional acceptance or grace; and that consequently you must believe in this religion and in its god to receive this "unconditional" grace. Unless you accept these three conditions of grace, you will presumably never be fully self-accepting. And these conditions, of course, make your accepting of yourself conditional rather than unconditional. Nonreligious philosophies, such as REBT, teach that you can always choose to accept yourself just *because* you decide to do so, and require no conditions or redundant beliefs in god or religion to help you do this choosing.

Ironically, in fact, when you do decide to adopt a religious view and choose to accept yourself conditionally (because you believe in a grace-giving god or son of god), *you* choose to believe in this religion, and *you* consequently create the grace-giver who "makes" you self-acceptable. In the final analysis, all religious-inspired forms of self-acceptance therefore depend on *your* belief system, and they are consequently actually self-inspired. Even when a religion supposedly "gives" you grace, you really choose it yourself, and the religious trappings in which you frame your self-acceptance consist of a redundant hypothesis (that god exists and that s/he gives you grace) that is basically unprovable and unfalsifiable, and that really adds nothing to your own decision to be self-accepting.

Although liberal religionists, like the followers of Science of Mind, may be largely self-accepting, devout religionists have much more trouble in gaining any measure of unconditional self-acceptance. This goes for devout secular as well as pious theistic believers. For the former cannot unconditionally accept themselves because they invariably seem to make self-acceptance (or, worse yet, ego inflation or self-esteem) depend on their rigid adherence to the tenets of their particular creed. Thus, fanatical Nazis see themselves (and others) as good people only if they are good Nazis, and if they perform non-Nazi or anti-Nazi acts (for instance, espouse internationalism or help Jews or Gypsies), they damn themselves as rotten individuals who presumably deserve to suffer and die. Ku Klux Klanners, along with downing blacks, Jews, Catholics, and others, excoriate themselves as worthless when they fail to live up to ideal KKK standards. Pious secular religionists, like fanatical theists, seem incapable of unconditionally accepting themselves (or others), since one of the essences of devoutness or fanaticism is to thoroughly damn and attempt to censor and punish all those who even mildly disagree with the fanatic's view.

A special way in which devout religiosity sabotages unconditional self-acceptance is its strong tendency to encourage ego aggrandizing, or grandiosity. It is clearly self-defeating to tell yourself, "I am a good person because I have good character," or "I can esteem myself because I am highly competent." For if you give yourself this kind of ego bolstering you make yourself highly liable to self-downing as soon as it can be shown that your character is not so good or that you are beginning, in some important way, to act incompetently.

You will do even worse if you make such self-statements as, "I am a great or noble person because I do outstandingly well at work or at art," or "Because I subscribe to this particular fine philosophy or cause I am better than you are and am indeed a superior individual!" For this kind of holier-than-thou self-rating, or arrant grandiosity, assumes that you and other people can be truly superior and godlike—and that you and they are thoroughly ordinary and worthless when they are not looking down from some kind of heavenly perch.

Devout religiosity particularly foments ego bolstering and grandiosity. Where mild religionists think of themselves as good people because they are members in good standing of their own religious group, pious ones frequently think of themselves as utterly noble and great because of their religious convictions. Thus, pious Christians, Jews, Fascists, and Communists tend to deify themselves for their beliefs and allegiances, and probably devout atheists also tend to feel somewhat godlike and holy! Grandiosity is one of the most common of disturbed feelings, and it often compensates for underlying feelings of slobhood. In fact, as Camilla Anderson, a notably sane psychiatrist, has shown, few of us would ever wind up feeling like jerks if we did not start off with the grandiose assumptions that we must—yes, *must*—be noble and great.

Anyway, devout religionists are frequently attracted to and bound to their piety largely because it presumably offers them holier-than-thouness and one-upsmanship over nonreligionists. And through its appeal to such disturbed individuals, devout religious creeds encourage some of the craziest kinds of thoughts, emotions, and behaviors, and encourage severe manifestations of neurosis, borderline personality states, and sometimes even psychosis.

Acceptance of Social Reality

Emotionally healthy people, it almost goes without saying, accept WIGO (what is going on) in the world. This means several important things: (1) they have a reasonably good perception of social reality and do not see things that do not exist and do not refuse to see things that do; (2) they find various aspects of life, in accordance with their own goals and inclination, "good" and certain aspects "bad"—but they accept both these aspects, without exaggerating the "good" ones and without denying or whining about the "bad" ones; (3) they do their best to work at changing those aspects of life they view as "bad," to accept those they cannot change, and to acknowledge the difference between the two.

Devout theistic religionists frequently refuse to accept social reality in all three of the ways just listed. They are frequently sure that they see things—gods, angels, devils, and absolute laws of the universe—for which there is no confirmatory empirical data and that in all probability do not actually exist. And they refuse to see some obvious things that almost certainly do exist, such as the ubiquity of human fallibility and the overwhelming unlikelihood that any humans will ever be perfect. They often whine and scream—and even have their gods whine and scream (as Jehovah presumably did when he turned Lot's wife into a pillar of salt for looking back at Sodom and Gomorrah) when they see something "bad." They especially indulge in childish whining and in temper tantrums when other religionists or nonbelievers refuse to see the virtues of the devout theists' favored religious dogmas. Instead of working hard to change grim facts, they often pray to their god(s) and potently sit on their rumps waiting for their prayers to be answered. When certain obnoxious things are unchangeable—such as the propensity of humans to become ill and die—they refuse to accept these things and often invent utopian heavens where humans presumably live forever in perfect bliss without suffering any kinds of affliction. Obviously, therefore, devout theists often ignore, deny, and hallucinate about things, and—as the long history of religion shows—the more devout they are, the more delusionary and hallucinatory they seem to be.

Devout nontheistic religionists, such as orthodox and closed-minded capitalists, Communists, and rationalists, rarely seem to deny social reality as much as do devout theists. But because they dogmatically and absolutistically follow narrow creeds, they frequently look at the world and the people in it with heavily pollyannaish and/or overly pessimistic glasses, and thereby significantly distort life by seeing it in enormously wishful-thinking ways.

If we summarize what we have been saying, the conclusion seems inescapable that devout religiosity is, on almost every conceivable count, opposed to the normal goals of mental health. Instead, it encourages masochism, other-directedness, social withdrawal, intolerance, refusal to accept ambiguity and uncertainty, unscientific thinking, lack of self-acceptance, and reluctance to acknowledge and deal adequately with social reality. In the one area where devout religion has some advantage—that of encouraging commitment to a cause or project in which people may become vitally absorbed—it even tends to sabotage this advantage in two important ways: First, it encourages its adherents to commit themselves to its tenets for the wrong reasons—that is, to cover up instead of to face and rid themselves of their personal insecurities; second, it encourages a fanatic, obsessive-compulsive kind of commitment that may be a form of emotional disturbance in its own right.

This is not to deny that for some people, some of the time, religious notions, even when they are devoutly and rigidly held, have some benefits. Of course they do. Devout adherence to a theistic or secular form of religion can at times motivate people to help others who are needy, give up unhealthy addictions, follow valuable disciplines such as dieting or exercising, go for psychotherapy, strive for world peace, follow long-range instead of short-range hedonism, and work for many other kinds of valuable goals. Historical and biographical data abound to show this good side of religiosity. But I would still contend that on the whole religious piety and dogma do more harm than good, and the beneficent behaviors that they sometimes abet would most likely be more frequent and profound without their influence.

As a good case in point, let us take the issue of interpersonal and political war and peace. Unquestionably, many devout religionists, such as St. Francis and St. Theresa, have led notably unangry and loving existences themselves, and many others, including several of the popes, have helped in the creation of human peace. So pious religion and surcease from human aggression hardly are completely incompatible. The fact remains, however, that fanaticism of any kind, especially religious fanaticism, has clearly produced and in all probability will continue to produce enormous amounts of bickering, fighting, violence, bloodshed, homicide, feuds, wars, and genocide. For all its peace-inviting potential, arrant (not to mention arrogant) religiosity has led to immense individual and social harm by fomenting an incredible amount of antihuman and antihumane aggression. It can therefore be concluded that anger-attacking and peace-loving religious views that are held undevoutly and unrigidly, as well as similar views that are held by nonreligionists and antireligionists, probably serve humankind far better than religious-inspired peace efforts.

Religion, then, is not all bad, and even devout religiosity has some saving graces. But on the whole and in the main, the legacy and the future of dogmatic religion seem to be indicative of considerably more human harm than good.

If religiosity is so inimical to mental health and happiness, what are the chances of unbelief, skepticism, and thoroughgoing atheism helping humans in this important aspect of their lives? I would say excellent. My own view—based on almost fifty years of research and clinical work in the field of psychology and psychotherapy, but still admittedly prejudiced by my personal predilections and feelings—is that if people were thoroughly unbelieving of any dogmas, if they were highly skeptical of all hypotheses and theories that they formulated, if they believed in no kinds of gods, devils, or other supernatural beings, and if they subscribed to no forms of absolutistic thinking, they would be minimally emotionally disturbed and maximally healthy. Stated a little differently: If you, I, and everyone else in the world were thoroughly scientific, and if we consistently used the scientific method in our own lives and in our relationships with others, we would rarely upset ourselves about anything—and I mean *anything*!

If you dispute your irrational, dogmatic, devout musts, and keep disputing them, the theory and practice of REBT says that you will rarely feel emotionally disturbed and will seldom foolishly act against your own interests, and when you do, you will quickly be able to see what you are doing to needlessly upset yourself and will be able to unupset yourself.

But let me repeat so that there will be little misunderstanding about this: REBT does *not* show you how to be completely calm, serene, detached, unfeeling, passive, or resigned. As its name implies, it is a rational-*emotive* type of therapy, and it assumes that you, like practically all humans, strongly desire to remain alive and be happy. Therefore, in many ways, it helps you feel *more* than you normally would—pleasure, joy, elation, and occasional ecstasy when things are going the way you want them to go, and to sometimes strongly feel sorrow, regret, frustration, and annoyance when you are not getting what you would really want out of life.

The disputing that you do when you use REBT is synonymous

with the scientific method of challenging, or disputing unrealistic or illogical hypotheses, and it is the same kind of skepticism and unbelief that you would use if you were desirous of uprooting your (or anyone else's) devout religiosity. REBT, therefore, is equivalent to the flexible scientific method and is one of the most powerful foes of religious piety, fanaticism, and dogma.

To sum up what I have been saying in this essay: Vague, general, or mild "religion" seems to consist of people's having some serious philosophy of life, and especially an outlook about important questions like those of ethics, death, and immorality, and the origin, development, and outcome of the universe. It is sometimes (and sometimes not) connected with a belief in superhuman sources and powers. This kind of religion seems a natural part of the human condition and does not seem to be intrinsically connected to mental health, since it has not been shown that vague religionists—whether they be theists, pantheists, or humanists—are emotionally healthier or unhealthier than nonreligionists. In fact, if we talk only about vague or moderate forms of "religion," it is not clear that any thoroughgoing "nonreligionists" even exist!

Devout or pious religionists, or devotees of religiosity, seem to be distinctly different from mild religionists in that they hold to their beliefs in a distinctly dogmatic, orthodox, absolute, rigid, closed manner. Many of them are devoutly or piously theistic—e.g., orthodox Jews, Catholics, Protestants, Muslims, or mystics—and therefore worship divine or superhuman power(s). But many of them are devout secular religionists—e.g., fanatical Communists, Nazis, liberationists, or right-wing or left-wing terrorists—who are nontheistic. Devout theistic and devout secular religionists differ in some important ways, but in regard to their fanaticism and absolutism they are remarkably similar.

It is my contention that both piestic theists and secular religionists—like virtually all people imbued with intense religiosity and fanaticism—tend to be emotionally disturbed. For they strongly and rigidly believe in the same kinds of profound irrationalities, absolute musts, and unconditional necessities in which disturbed people powerfully believe. When, moreover, they employ the logico-empirical methods of science, and when they fully accept social reality (while often distinctly disliking and actively trying to change it), they are able to surrender their devoutness and to become significantly less disturbed. Indeed, I hypothesize that the more scientific, open-minded, and straight-thinking about themselves, others, and the world people are, the less neurotically they will think, feel, and behave. This is my major hypothesis about the relationship between absolutistic religious belief (religiosity) and mental health. The clinical and experimental evidence that I have found, in support of this hypothesis (as well as the evidence falsifying the hypothesis that devout religiosity is significantly correlated with and probably causes good mental health) seems to be impressive. But much more investigation needs to be done, because it is up to me and others to empirically bolster or disconfirm these hypotheses.

22

Rational Emotive Behavior Therapy and Its Application to Emotional Education

When I created REBT in 1955, I could see that it followed an educational rather than a medical model of psychotherapy. It held that people both learned and taught themselves to be neurotic and that they often could be taught, in a few sessions, what irrational beliefs they were acquiring and inventing, and shown how to change these to rational beliefs. Moreover, they could do so, in public settings and with psychoeducational materials, such as books and pamphlets.

Although I saw mainly adolescents and adults for therapy, a group of educational and school psychologists were attracted to REBT in the 1960s, including Morley Glicken and Clay Lafferty, and used it in school settings. And in 1966 Milton Blum, a professor of organizational management at the City College of New York, collaborated with me to introduce it to business and labor relations. In both school and business settings it went over very well, so in 1971 the Albert Ellis Institute established the Living School, a private grade school for middle-class and economically deprived children, and for five years trained regular elementary school teachers to use REBT in the classroom. This paper, which was given at the Seventeenth International Association of Applied Psychology at Liege, Belgium, on July 26, 1971, described how REBT was taught, mainly in classroom situations, to two classes of young children at the Living School.

This pioneering program was a great success—except financially.

The tuition for the school was deliberately kept low, and many scholarships were given to children from poor and minority families. As a result, the institute lost close to $100,000, which it could ill afford to lose, over the five years that the school was in existence, and consequently it had to be closed in 1975. Nonetheless, it succeeded in showing that the main elements of REBT could be taught—and successfully used—by classroom teachers to children from six to twelve years of age.

Many controlled experiments have since been done teaching REBT to children in the classroom, and most of them show that this can be successfully done. Michael Bernard, William Knaus, Jerry Wilde, Ann Vernon, and other psychologists have written books on how it can be used in emotional education. These are listed in the latest catalogue of the Albert Ellis Institute. Many school training programs, such as the famous Pumsey series, use REBT and other cognitive-behavioral methods to help school children with their personal problems.

In addition, REBT and similar cognitive-behavioral programs are now widely used in business, industry, and organizational settings, and much of the training that is done for employees and managers in these areas adopts the REBT educational model. As a result of this activity, I have said for many years that the future of REBT lies more in public education than in psychotherapy. It has now been shown that children, adolescents, and adults can be taught how to use REBT principles and methods to alleviate emotional problems and even prevent them. This may be more important than the usefulness of REBT in psychotherapy. Its psychoeducational applications are almost endless.

Rational Emotive Behavior Therapy is a form of psychotherapy which I originated in the 1950s, after practicing classical psychoanalysis, psychoanalytically-oriented psychotherapy, and various other methods. Although I did as well with these techniques as any of the other practitioners in the field, I began to see with greater clarity that they all were largely ineffective. For no matter how much insight I was able to help my clients achieve, how emotionally they abreacted, and how they were utterly sure that they now understood themselves deeply and were no longer going to continue their maladaptive behavior, they largely kept making New Years' resolutions to change rather than significantly modifying their actions and actually giving up their phobias, obsessions, compulsions, shirking, psychosomatic reactions, depressions, hostilities, and other complaints. Not that they didn't usually improve to some degree; they did. But I could see, and they usually could see too, that their improvements were moderate rather than profound, and that they still had a long way to go, after the completion of "successful" therapy, to overcome their basic self-defeating patterns.

Consequently, I kept trying new techniques and finally realized that unless they included a great deal of activity, both on my part and that of the client, they were not likely to be very effective. For the average client is terribly anxious about doing some act poorly—such as failing in his social, sexual, academic, or vocational affairs—and to quell his anxiety he inhibits himself and stays away from the "dangers" that he has largely created by *defining* these activities as perilous. No matter how much he tries to convince himself that it is not really too risky or too "awful" to fail, he underlyingly continues to believe that it *is* horrible until he has actually forced himself to do the so-called dangerous act many, many times. Thus, no matter how often he tells himself that seeing black cats is not unlucky, he will still tend to superstitiously believe that it is until and unless he forces himself to approach black cats and pats a sufficient number of them on the head.

As I learned this therapeutic fact, I gave up more and more of my psychoanalytic passivity, began to actively disabuse my clients of the irrational beliefs, values, and philosophies that caused their emotionally disordered behavior, and gave them concrete activity-oriented homework assignments that would help them contradict in practice what I was helping them disbelieve in theory. The better this new therapeutic method worked, the more I thought about why it was working and constructed Rational Emotive Behavior Therapy to back up my procedures.

Although I designed and have kept modifying REBT procedures mainly for the treatment of individuals with emotional disturbances, and although there is now a good deal of experimental and clinical evidence that it works quite well in those areas, it has also been found that its theory and practice are so simple and direct that they can be used with "normal" populations. Thus, it has been used effectively with organizational executives, and it has been found valuable when used with children in regular classroom situations.

How, exactly, can rational-emotive psychology be employed in regular schooling? To answer this question, the Albert Ellis Institute ran a private school for children, the Living School, for five years. The purpose of the school was to teach children the regular elements of academic education, but at the same time to provide them preventively with emotional education. And by emotional education we do not merely mean encouraging the children to enjoy themselves, make freer choices of what they do in school, or express themselves affectively. These are all worthy goals, but at most they are merely aids to, rather than the essence of, what we conceive of as emotional training.

In REBT we do not merely see children as a product of their early environment, nor do we believe that they are naturally fully healthy, self-actualizing, creative creatures and that their parents and their society unduly restrict, constrict, and warp them so that they soon become disturbed. Instead, we think that children's emotional constriction or overimpulsiveness result from their innate as well as their acquired tendencies to think crookedly, be grandiosely demanding, and refuse to accept a hassle-filled life.

In other words, children naturally acquire several basic irrational ideas with which they tend to sabotage their lives forever. They religiously, devoutly believe that they absolutely *need* and utterly *must have* others' approval; that they've *got to* achieve outstandingly and thereby prove how worthwhile they are; that people who act unjustly or inconsiderately to them are rotten persons who should be severely condemned and punished for their villainy; that it is awful and catastrophic when things are not the way they would like them to be; that obnoxious situations and events *make them* feel anxious, depressed, or angry; that if they endlessly worry about something they can control whether or not it happens; that it is easier for them to avoid than to face certain difficulties and responsibilities of life; and that they absolutely need a well-ordered, certain, picture-perfect universe. These are the same kinds of crazy ideas that most human adults more or less tend to believe, but children often believe them more rigidly and profoundly.

The main reason for the Living School's existence was to teach its pupils that these typical irrational beliefs do not hold water, will usually lead to poor results, can be radically changed, and would better be surrendered and surrendered and surrendered, until the child only weakly holds them. This teaching was done almost exclusively by the regular school teacher and not by psychologists, counselors, or other special personnel. The teachers were trained—along with the psychotherapists we train at the institute—to understand and use Rational

Emotive Behavior Therapy methods, and then they employed them with the children. Here are some of the ways in which the REBT philosophy was taught:

Regular lessons in rational thinking were given. The children were shown how to distinguish rational ideas, such as "I would like to do well in school because it has certain specific advantages," from irrational ones such as, "I *must* do well in school because otherwise I am a worthless individual." Discussions of emotional behavior, and how one produces healthy and unhealthy reactions in oneself, were frequently held.

Emotional problems that arose during classroom situations were often dealt with immediately and were used for purposes of general emotional education. If Jane was shy about reciting, she might be shown that her shyness really consists of extreme anxiety about what others would think of her if she did not recite perfectly well, and she was shown how to challenge and dispute the notion that she *had to* do well in this or any other respect. If Jane did not soon see what her real problem was and how to handle it, other children in the class were asked what they thought she was doing to upset and constrict herself, and what she could do instead of this.

In situations outside the classroom, as, for example, when the children were in the playground or on a trip to a museum, destructive and disruptive behavior was called to their attention and alternative, more constructive ways of behaving were considered and suggested.

Stories, fables, plays, and other forms of literature were employed to put across rational philosophies of living. Stories, such as the conventional fairy tales, were frequently read and discussed to show the children that the main point of such stories might well be an entirely irrational belief, such as the belief that Cinderella completely *needs* the love of her stepmother and stepsisters, a fairy godmother, and a fairy prince before she can accept her existence as being potentially enjoyable and worthwhile, and that this belief can be observed, disputed, and rejected.

Audiovisual aids, such as filmstrips, films, recordings, and video tapings, were employed to help the children understand and utilize some of the REBT principles of effective living.

Group counseling was regularly held, with the teacher (at first under psychotherapeutic supervision and later on her own) talking to six or eight of the children about their personal problems, including their home problems, and showing them (just as regular REBT therapists show their group counseling adolescents and adult clients) how to handle these problems.

Individual sessions were often held between the teacher and a child who was temporarily upset about something, to get at the basic sources of his upset, and to show him exactly what he was doing to make himself disturbed and what he could do to undisturb himself.

Behavior therapy principles and methods were employed, so that the children were rewarded or reinforced for some of their effective and constructive conduct and penalized for some of their ineffectual behavior. However, at the same time that the children were penalized if they acted disruptively or antisocially, a strong attempt was made to help them distinguish between penalty and punishment—to show them that *they* were never damnable or rotten, even though some of their *deeds* and *performances* were wrong and not allowable.

Instead of trying to create an atmosphere of schools without failure, as William Glasser and certain other affective educators try to do, the teachers in the Living School sometimes deliberately went to the other extreme and pretended that the children had failed at some task or test when they actually had not done badly at it. Their reactions to this "failure" were then elicited and analyzed in an attempt to show them that although it is good (for practical purposes) to succeed and unfortunate to fail, they could always unconditionally accept themselves and strive for an enjoyable life *whether or not* they failed at academic or other tasks.

Various means of encouraging the children to express themselves openly and authentically and to reveal their real feelings about themselves and others were employed. Through games, plays, role-playing, sports, art, writing, and other means, they were stimulated to show what they really thought and felt. But just as REBT group and encounter therapy does not merely emphasize authentic self-expression, but also tries to show the group member that some of his feelings (such as assertion) are healthy while others (such as rage) are unhealthy, so did the teachers try to help the children acknowledge and understand the feelings they expressed, and considered constructing alternative emotions when they were over- or underreacting to life's stimuli. REBT teaching makes use of encounter methods with adults, particularly in the marathon weekends of rational encounter which I and my associates give in many parts of the country every year; it also used these methods of affective encountering and release with the children in the Living School. But it always placed them within a cognitive-behavioral framework and did not see them as sacrosanct in their own right.

As noted above, REBT is one of the main psychotherapies that has pioneered in the giving of explicit, activity-oriented homework assignments to adolescent and adult clients. Similarly, the teachers in the Living School used rational-emotive methods when working with the children's problems while they were in the classroom and also gave them emotionally educating homework. Thus, if Robbie was shy and withdrawn in his relations with his peers, he was assigned the task of trying to make one new friend or acquaintance a week, and if Susan fought incessantly with her sister over which TV program they were going to watch, she was assigned to try going along with her sister's choices for a few weeks, while convincing herself that it was not awful, horrible, and catastrophic to be deprived of the programs she most wanted to see.

In sum, in many important ways REBT methodology was applied to emotional education. What emerged at the Living School was a full-fledged meaning of this term. For REBT is intrinsically didactic, pedagogic, instructional, *and* educative, more concretely and more fully, perhaps, than any other widely used form of psychotherapy. Not every therapeutic orientation is easily adaptable to teaching. Freud's psychoanalysis has largely failed in this respect, while Adler's individual psychology has succeeded much better. I think that we shall eventually show that REBT psychology is as beautifully designed for the educative process as the process is already largely designed for it. For schooling, essentially, is a concerted, long-range attempt to help the child grow up in many ways and assume adult roles and responsibilities that will presumably be creative, productive, and enjoyable. REBT schooling, as we experimentally practiced it at the Living School, was a concerted, long-range attempt to help the child grow up emotionally and become a reasonably independent-thinking, self-actualizing, minimally disturbed person.

By person I mean a human person, for REBT is one of the most humanistic psychologies in contemporary use. It doesn't deal with anything that smacks of the superhuman or the subhuman. It believes that people can fully accept themselves as enormously fallible, incredibly *human* beings who have no magical powers, and who reside in an immense but still material and unmystical universe that doesn't really give a special damn about them and most probably never will. It holds that there is no absolute truth, and that although reasoning and the logico-empirical method of checking social reality have their distinct limits (because they, too, originate with and are employed by eminently fallible humans), they are the best means we have of understanding ourselves and the world and should be fairly rigorously applied in the understanding of life processes.

Consequently, rational-emotive-behavioral education teaches children to fully accept themselves as humans, give up all pretensions of reaching heaven or finding the Holy Grail, stop denigrating the value of themselves or any other person, accept their mortality, and become unabashed long-range hedonists: individuals who heartily strive to have a ball in the here-and-now *and* in their future lives without giving too much heed to what others dogmatically think that they should, ought, or must do. This humanistic way of life was explicitly taught—and I mean *taught*—in the Living School.

23

Humanism and Psychotherapy: A Revolutionary Approach

O ne of the most disillusioning and disheartening experiences that I had, about which I could have easily depressed myself without the use of REBT, was the formation of the Association for Humanistic Psychology (AHP) in the early 1960s and its quickly being dominated by mystical crackpots. While it promulgated some of the same philosophies as the American Humanistic Association (AHA), a very sensible group, it also favored some exceptionally antiscientific and potentially harmful ideas, as this paper shows.

Along with Paul Kurtz, Frederick Edwards, and other leading secular humanists, I have fought these mystical and antiscientific humanists of the AHP for many years, but to little avail, for they still seem to run the organization, and I finally resigned from it. I was awarded the Humanist of the Year Award by the AHA in 1971 and gave this paper as my acceptance speech at its annual convention in Chicago. It attempts to show how almost all psychotherapy is humanistic but how Rational Emotive Behavior Therapy and Cognitive Behavior Therapy (CBT), which are often accused of being mechanical and antihumanistic, actually follow and implement the "real" humanistic outlook. Would that the mystical-minded members of the AHP could see this!

In speaking about humanism and psychotherapy, it is desirable first to define humanistic psychology. That is not easy! At the very first annual meeting of the Association for Humanistic Psychology some years ago, a subgroup of the assembled members came up with at least twenty different concepts of what they thought humanism was as applied to psychology. As you might well guess, these concepts radically differed in several significant respects. Moreover, as Charlotte Buhler pointed out in her presidential address to the First International Invitational Conference on Humanistic Psychology, there are certain allegedly humanistic concepts which do not fit together because they contradict each other, and between which one has to choose. Thus, she indicated, one cannot simultaneously believe in the humanistic end goal of homeostasis and the end goal of a fulfilling self-realization.

To make matters still more complex, the term *humanism* itself has at least two major meanings which overlap but are not necessarily the same. Psychologically, it seems to mean the study of the person, of the individual as a whole (as opposed to the study of his discrete traits and performances), with the aim of helping him live a happier, more self-actualizing, and more creative existence. Ethically, it seems to mean the establishment of a set of rules for people to live by, characterized by an emphasis on human interests rather than the interests of some assumed natural order or god. The first of these meanings is emphasized by organizations such as the Association for Humanistic Psychology, and the second by groups such as the American Humanist Association.

As I am a member in good standing of both these organizations, and since I believe that their goals are in many ways mutually collaborative, I would like to present a definition of humanistic psychotherapy that includes both these concepts. In so doing, I believe that the meaning of humanism which I am about to postulate also keeps humanistic psychology squarely within the scientific framework and discourages it from wandering into anti-intellectual, unscientific, magical, and religious pathways, where it is highly wont to wander these days and where I think it doesn't belong. For it seems to me that the essence of humanism, in both psychological and ethical areas, is that people are fully acknowledged to be human—that is, limited and fallible—and that in no way are they superhuman or subhuman. One of their highly human, and utterly fallible, traits is that they have the ability to fantasize about and strongly believe in all kinds of nonhuman entities and powers: such as devils, demons, and hells on the one hand, and angels, gods, and heavens on the other. As far as we know, there are no subhumans or superhumans, and it highly unlikely there will ever be.

When Abraham Maslow originated the so-called "third force" in psychology and added humanism to behaviorism and psychoanalysis, he had no intention of becoming unscientific. But many of his followers have rushed pell-mell into astrology, magic, ESP, transpersonal psychology, fortune-telling, and all kinds of nonscientific and antiscientific realms in their frantic need to "push back the boundaries of the human mind." In the process, they have practically thrown "humanistic psychology" back into the dark ages and have dogmatically espoused all kinds of unfalsifiable claptrap.

Ethical humanism, however, is closely allied to the scientific method. For its fundamental postulate is that until someone definitely proves otherwise, there is probably nothing godlike or superhuman, and that for a human to substantiate any hypothesis, it must be backed by some observable and duplicatable data. Any hypothesis that cannot be in some way falsified is deemed to be a theological, supernatural, or magical hypothesis, and is not considered in psychological science, though it may have some value to humans.

Humanistic psychology, by this rule, becomes the study of the whole individual, by means that are distinctly human, for the purpose of helping her live a happier, more self-actualizing, and more creative existence. It completely accepts people with their human limitations; it particularly focuses upon and employs their experiences and values; it emphasizes their ability to create and direct their own destinies; and it views them as holistic, goal-directed individuals who are important in their own right just because they are alive, and who (together with their fellow humans) have the right to continue to exist and enjoy and fulfill themselves. This concept of humanistic psychology, which includes both an ethical and a scientific orientation, has been espoused, at least implicitly and often explicitly, by many leading psychological theorists and practitioners, such as Charlotte Buhler, Wilhelm Dilthey, Viktor Frankl, Kurt Goldstein, Karen Horney, Abraham Maslow, Rollo May, Carl Rogers, and Ludvig von Bertalanffy.

Humanistic psychotherapy is an important offshoot of humanistic psychology, but it has often gone off in its own idiosyncratic realms, and in recent years has been particularly preoccupied, with experiential, nonverbal, and physical approaches to personality change. It has assumed that people have become too intellectualized, technologized, and unemotional, hence alienated and dehumanized, and it has therefore proposed itself as a corrective experiential force to make up for the lapses of classic behaviorism and orthodox psychoanalysis. In this respect, it has made notable contributions to psychotherapy and the actualizing of human potential.

However, humans do not live by emotional (and by highly emotionalized) bread alone. They are remarkably complex, cognitive-emotive-behaving creatures. Of their main traits, their ability to think on a high level—and especially their ability to think about their thinking—is probably their one unique and most "human" quality. Therefore, if humans are to work effectively against their strong individual and social tendencies to "dehumanize" themselves, they need to learn to vigorously employ some of the highest-level thinking and metathinking of which they are innately capable but which they easily neglect and avoid.

The cognitive-behavioral therapies are in the vanguard of those methods that can be effectively used to preventatively and psychotherapeutically help man's "humanization." Because I am the founder and leader of one of the best-known cognitive schools—namely, Rational Emotive Behavior Therapy—let me briefly describe this system and try to show why it, like similar cognitive schools, is one of the most revolutionary humanistic psychotherapies ever practiced.

Unlike the orthodox psychoanalytic and the classical behavioristic psychologies, REBT places humans squarely in the center of the universe and of their own emotional fate, and it gives them almost full responsibility for choosing to make or not make themselves seriously disturbed. Although it weights biological and early environmental factors quite importantly in the chain of events that lead to human disorganization and disorder, it holds that, nonetheless, individuals can, and usually do, significantly intervene between their environmental input and their emotionalized output, and therefore have an enormous amount of potential control over what they feel and do. Moreover, when they unwittingly and foolishly make themselves disturbed by devoutly believing in irrational and dysfunctional assumptions about themselves and others, they can almost always make themselves undisturbed again—and often within a relatively short time—by utilizing REBT procedures.

REBT employs the A-B-C-D-E method of revealing and disputing irrational, self-defeating beliefs (which are detailed in other chapters of this reader). In addition, it employs a large variety of evocative-emotive and behavioral-motorial methods of helping troubled individuals change their basic irrational values and philosophies and acquire more sensible, joy-producing, and pain-minimizing ideas. Because it is exceptionally persuasive, educational, and active-directive, and because it straightforwardly challenges many of the sacred myths and superstitions that are so prevalent among humans (and even among psychologists and other scientists), REBT is often viewed as being antihumanistic, especially when it contends that people do not absolutely *need* love or success and that they have considerable ability to think about and change their self-defeating emotions. REBT has been criticized by some as being overintellectualized, mechanistic, and manipulative.

These accusations are not only mistaken, they miss an important point, namely, that efficient therapies that stress the potentialities of cognitive control over dysfunctional emotional processes are in many respects the most humanistic means of personality change yet developed. They are usually person-centered, creatively-oriented, and relevant to the maximum actualization of human potential. Although experientially-oriented psychologists, such as Abraham Maslow, Fritz Perls, and Carl Rogers are outstanding humanists, so too are cognitive-oriented therapists such as Aaron T. Beck, Eric Berne, Charlotte Buhler, George Kelly, and Arnold A. Lazarus.

The cognitive therapies in general, and Rational Emotive Behavior Therapy in particular, are among the most humanistic of psychological treatment procedures for a number of reasons:

Cognitive therapies deal mainly with beliefs, attitudes, and values rather than with stimuli and responses, as many other therapies do. Psychoanalysis, for example, heavily emphasizes the activating events of an individual's life, especially the stimuli that impinged upon him during his early childhood. Classical behavior therapy is mainly preoccupied with his responses or symptoms. Experiential and encounter therapies are also focused on his responses or experiences. But REBT quickly zeros in on and primarily stays with his most uniquely human behaviors, namely, his cognitions and his beliefs. It recognizes, as Magda Arnold and Rudolph Arnheim have shown, that his perceptions, on the one hand, and his emotions, on the other hand, are both significantly influenced and even caused by his concepts and constructs, and that while lower animals may be importantly conditioned and deconditioned by externally-applied reinforcement and extinction, humans seem to be the only creatures who can literally recondition or retrain themselves by changing their basic ideas. REBT specifically deals with humans as humans and not merely as representatives of the animal kingdom.

Cognitive therapies squarely put people in the center of the universe and give them a somewhat wider range of choice, or existential freedom, than many other therapies do. REBT holds that people's behavior, although to some degree determined and limited by their biological nature and history, is considerably less determined than the orthodox Freudians or behaviorists seem to think it is. It shows people how they can extend their choices of action and significantly change their personalities by understanding precisely how they needlessly constrict themselves, uprooting and modifying their rigidicizing philosophies of life, and actively working against their self-defeating habituations until they break through their gratuitously restricting shell.

Cognitive therapies do not merely accept humans the way they are, nor utilize their biosocial tendencies to be highly suggestible, prejudiced, and conforming to their social reality. They also enhance the possibility of people's transcending some of their biological and social limitations and making themselves into a radically changed and different (though not superhuman) person. REBT, in particular, teaches people to be less conditionable and suggestible, to think largely for themselves no matter what the majority of their fellows thinks and feels, and to minimize their dire need for approval and success that often force them into constructive conformity. Instead of relying only on ordinary kinds of reinforcement to effect personality change, it also emphasizes the reinforcement of independent and creative thinking as an integral part of the human "hedonic calculus."

Cognitive-behavior therapies are deeply philosophic and reeducative, emphasizing the more elegant types of personality-restructuring solutions, as opposed to symptom-removal types of solutions to human problems. Psychoanalysis, experiential, and behavior therapy may all help a troubled individual to forego a specific phobia, such as her fear of failing at love or work. But she will rarely arrive at the point where she is not overly concerned with *any* form of failure unless the therapist engages in a depth-centered philosophic discourse about the general issues of failure, anxiety, and human worth. REBT is one of the few psychotherapies in which the client can be elegantly shown that self-acceptance is a purely tautological and definitional concept, and may always be had for the asking by a person whose definitions are in good order; that humans do not have to rate themselves at all, although they are generally better off if they accurately rate their traits and deeds; and that virtually all human disturbance is the result of absolutistic thinking (or believing in shoulds, oughts, and musts) and can therefore be directly minimized by helping the individual think and feel preferentially rather than "musturbatorily." Then not only can the person who is troubled gain insight into her fundamental difficulties in the course of relatively few sessions, she can also be taught a method of dealing with her problems that can serve her for the remainder of her life.

The perceptual-cognitive-philosophic approach to therapy helps provide the individual with a neater, saner balance between his individualistic, self-seeking tendencies and his being a helpful and cooperative member of his social group than does virtually any other kind of treatment approach. Some methods of therapy, such as experiential or psychodynamic methods, may encourage him to indulge himself and somewhat antisocially hate others. Other methods, such as relationship therapy, may encourage him to be overly concerned with others' approval and sacrifice himself for his social group. REBT attempts to provide well-rounded discussions of questions such as individualism versus conformity, enabling him to arrive at a sensible mean between two unreasonable extremes. Most major problems of living involve the individual's taking a two-sided, tolerant, and somewhat compromising attitude toward himself, others, and the world. This kind of attitude is much more likely to be arrived at through intelligent, fact-centered psychophilosophical discussion with a well-trained and wise therapist than through immersion in more monolithic types of therapy.

The cognitive-behavioral therapies make maximum use of a humanistic-scientific methodology that is based on relevance and pleasure-seeking, but that is also closely tied to scientific thinking. REBT starts frankly with a human value system, namely, the assumption that pleasure, joy, creativity, and freedom are good or efficient for human living and that pain, joylessness, uncreativeness, and bondage are bad or inefficient. It also assumes that what we call emotional disturbance is largely self-created and can therefore be self-dispelled. However, because it relies on induction from empirical evidence, logic, and the flexible seeking of alternatives, it ties its human-centered, hedonistic goals to the best available methods of achieving them. Instead of being anti-intellectual and antitechnological, as so many systems of psychotherapy and of philosophy are today, it tries to use modern science and technology for clear-cut humanistic purposes. For example, REBT shows the individual that she is *not* alienated by technology and science, but that she alienates *herself* by irrationally sacredizing these human tools, and that she can unalienate, or get in touch with herself, and use such instruments to her own human advantage.

The cognitive-emotive therapies help the individual strike a sensible balance between short-range and long-range hedonism. Virtually all psychotherapies are essentially hedonistic, in that they encourage the individual to minimize needless pain (for example, anxiety and depression) and to maximize pleasure (for example, love and creative work). Many therapies, however—especially experiential and encounter-type methods—stress the short-range goals of here-and-now enjoyment. REBT, being philosophic and nonextremist, emphasizes both the releasing pleasures of the here-and-now *and* the longer-range goals of future gain through present-day discipline. It holds that humans have the capacity to be contemporary *and* future-oriented hedonists; to actively work for personal and social changes *and* be relatively patient; to enjoy a wide range of healthy negative feelings (including, at times, deep sadness or regret) *and* control and change their unhealthy negative emotions (such as depression and rage).

The cognitive-behavior therapies employ a wide variety of educational and reeducational methods. REBT teaches individuals how to understand themselves and others, how to react differently, and how to change their basic personality patterns through the therapist's giving the client full empathic acceptance, a nonjudgmental environment, and practice in individual and group relating. It dramatically pushes him into risk-taking and adventurous activities, both inside and outside the therapy sessions. It forces her to express herself in more authentic, less defensive ways. It employs behavioral desensitizing and operant conditioning procedures. Along with these highly emotive and behavioral methods, it also didactically and directly teaches the client the facts of life and the intricate pathways of his own self-defeatingness and childish demandingness through explanations, stories, persuasive arguments, scientific data, bibliotherapy procedures, audiovisual aids, philosophic discussions, and a host of other educational procedures. For many individuals, this wide range of interventions proves more efficient than the one-sidedly dramatic or the one-sidedly behavioral approaches used in many other therapies. Humans, obviously, do not live by intellect alone, but they rarely live very well without it. REBT integrates the rational-cognitive elements with many of the other time-tested, less didactic methods of psychotherapy.

The cognitive behavioral therapies are unusually effective for pain reduction and are therefore exceptionally humanistic. All psychotherapies are designed to help reduce unnecessary emotional and physical suffering. But many of the most popular methods—especially classical psychoanalysis—take a minimum of two years and a maximum of five or more before the client is appreciably helped to become less anguished. REBT—because it stresses an active-directive, concentrated, multifaceted attack on the individual's basic irrational thought and behavior—is frequently able to help her significantly in a matter of days or weeks. Moreover, as has been shown in clinical research studies of REBT and other forms of cognitive therapy, these methods are often able to achieve better results with problem-afflicted individuals than are less cognitive-oriented forms of therapy.[1]

The cognitive-emotive therapies tend to be unusually accepting of human fallibility and to encourage maximum understanding of and tolerance for human frailty. Many psychotherapies wittingly or unwittingly encourage the individual to judge and condemn himself or others. Thus, psychoanalysis teaches him that his parents are to blame for his emotional problems, and implies that they are therefore reprehensible. Experiential, cathartic, and encounter therapies often show him that he is right in hating others and that he'd better openly vent his spleen on them. In many instances, they also encourage him to feel deeply hurt by others' rejections, and thereby to be self-damning.

In summation, REBT is one of the few kinds of therapy that specifically and vigorously opposes all types of blaming, including the individual's negatively judging himself, others, or the universe. It persistently shows the ashamed, hostile, and self-pitying individual that *no one* is to be blamed or damned for anything; that he can always unconditionally accept himself and others, no matter what his or their deficiencies are; and that no matter how rough or unfair the world is, it is a waste of time and energy for him to whine about it and rant against it. In other words, it shows the person with problems how he can humanistically refuse ever to loathe himself, other fallible people, or the world at large, and how he can realistically accept humans as humans (instead of as superhumans or subhumans) and desist from deifying and devil-ifying himself or any of his fellows. In this particular sense, in its complete acceptance of people as being incredibly human and never anything but fallible and ungodlike, REBT is surely the epitome of humanistic psychology and psychotherapy.

In view of human complexity, I can see no perfect solution to individual and world problems. "Solving" these problems now often seems to create the need for newer, often quite different, "solutions" later. So is our task hopeless? Not quite, for as George Kelly, an outstanding modern humanist, has said, people are easily irrational and self-destructive, but they are also marvelously constructive, creative, experimental, and scientific. I view the process of helping them to be more constructive and less hostile to themselves and others as one of the most important humanistic goals. An attitude that is absolutist, open-minded, scientific, nondogmatic, and flexible seems to provide one possible answer. Let us experimentally—and humanistically—try it.

24

The Biological Basis of Human Irrationality

I became interested in human irrationality when I was only twenty years old and not yet thinking of becoming a psychologist. When I was in my early twenties I began writing a thousand-page (single-spaced) manuscript, *A History of the Dark Ages: The Twentieth Century,* to show how stupid and crazy we humans still are, when, unlike the earlier dark ages, we have the knowledge to correct our ways. My manuscript was praised by several editors, but never published. I now have collected thousands of items on human irrationality to add to it, but it would take, perhaps, ten volumes to print them. At present, I just am too busy to get around to writing them up.

The brief summary of irrationality in this paper was written for a presentation at the American Psychological Association Annual Convention, in September 1975, and almost never got published. It was rejected by several leading journals, and I was almost about to give up on it when Guy Manaster almost begged me for a paper for the *Journal of Individual Psychology,* which was then having a hard time getting suitable articles to fill its pages because it favored strictly Adlerian articles. I sent him this article and, maybe out of desperation, he published it. It was immediately widely criticized, and is still one of my least accepted publications.

Why? Because social scientists, although faced by immense evidence of the biological factors in human irrationality and disturbance, are still are often hardcore environmentalists. They acknowledge the great influence of nurture but seem to conclude that if nature also has much to say about human functioning, we are hopelessly stuck in foolish ways and cannot possibly change them. False! We can change them constructively, in many philosophical, educational, and physical ways, if we acknowledge how difficult it is to do so and use the famous REBT slogan, PYA—push your ass!

Since this paper was written in 1975 two things have happened. One, the irrationalities and insanities that I have outlined in it have almost all continued or increased. Two, immense biological, neurological, and physiological evidence has been published that shows that these human tendencies are both learned and innate, and that great human effort is required to reduce and correct them. First let us admit this—and then get on with our psychoeducational tasks!

Before stating any hypothesis about the basis of human irrationality, let us define *biological basis* and *irrationality*. *Biological basis* means a characteristic that partly arises from the organism's natural, easy predisposition to behave in certain stipulated ways. It is an innate tendency. This does not mean that this characteristic or trait has a purely instinctive basis, that it cannot undergo major change, nor that the organism would perish or at least live in abject misery without it. It simply means that because of its genetic and/or congenital nature, an individual easily develops this trait and has a difficult time modifying or eliminating it.

Irrationality means any thought, emotion, or behavior that leads to self-defeating or self-destructive consequences that significantly interfere with the survival and happiness of the organism. More specifically, irrational behavior usually has several aspects. People believe, often devoutly, that it is realistic and will get them what they want when they are in some important respects unrealistic. People who adhere to it significantly denigrate or refuse to accept themselves. It interferes with their getting along satisfactorily with members of their primary social group, and seriously blocks their achieving the kind of interpersonal relations that they would like to achieve. It hinders their working gainfully and joyfully at some kind of productive labor. Lastly, it interferes with their own best interests in other important respects.

Humans ubiquitously and constantly act irrationally in many important respects, and just about all of them do so during their whole lives, though some considerably more than others. Therefore, there is some reason to believe that they do so naturally and easily, often against the teachings of their families and culture, and their own conscious wish and determination. Although modifiable to a considerable extent, their irrational tendencies seem partly ineradicable and intrinsically go with their biological (as well as sociological) nature.

This hypothesis goes back to the statements of some of the earliest historians and philosophers and has received adequate documentation over the years by a host of authorities.[1] Parker has noted that "most people are self-destructive; they behave in ways that are obviously against their best interest." Nonetheless, whenever I address an audience of psychologists or psychotherapists and point out this fairly obvious conclusion and state or imply that it arises out of the biological tendency of humans to behave irrationally, a great many died-in-the-wool environmentalists almost always rise with horror, foam at the mouth, and call me a traitor to objective, scientific thinking.

Since the amount of supporting evidence assumes overwhelming proportions and would literally take many volumes to summarize properly, what follows is a brief summary of some of the main reasons behind the thesis that human irrationality roots itself in basic human nature. This summary is confined to outlining the multiplicity of major irrationalities and giving some of the logical and psychological reasons why it seems almost certain that they have biological origins.

First are listed some of the outstanding irrationalities among the thousands I have collected over the years. The following manifestations of human behavior certainly do not appear completely irrational, for they also have (as what behavior has not?) some distinct advantages. Some people, such as those Eric Hoffer calls true believers, will even hold that many of them bring about much more good than harm. Almost any reasonably objective observer of human affairs, however, will probably tend to agree that these manifestations include a large amount of foolishness, unreality, and danger to our survival or happiness.

1. Custom and Conformity Irrationalities
   Outdated and rigid customs
   Ever-changing, expensive fashions
   Fads and popular crazes
   Hazings of schools, fraternal organizations, etc.
   Circumcision conventions and rituals

Rigid laws of etiquette and manners
Blue laws
Strong disposition to obey authority, even when it makes unreasonable demands

2. Ego-Related Irrationalities

Tendency to deify oneself
Dire need to have superiority over others
Tendency to give oneself a global, total, all-inclusive rating
Tendency to desperately seek status
Tendency to prove oneself rather than enjoy oneself
Tendency to believe that one's value as a human depends on one's competency at an important performance
Tendency to value oneself or devalue oneself in regard to the performances of one's family
Tendency to value or devalue oneself in regard to the performances or status of one's school, neighborhood group, community, state, or country
Tendency to denigrate or devil-ify oneself

3. Prejudice-Related Irrationalities

Strong prejudice
Dogma
Racial prejudice
Sexual prejudice
Political prejudice
Social and class prejudice
Religious prejudice
Appearance prejudice

4. Common Kinds of Illogical Thinking

Overgeneralization
Magnification and exaggeration
Use of non sequiturs
Strong belief in antiempirical statements
Strong belief in absolutes
Gullibility and oversuggestibility
Strong belief in contradictory statements
Strong belief in Utopianism
Strong adherence to unreality
Strong belief in unprovable statements
Shortsightedness
Overcautiousness

Giving up one extreme statement and going to the other extreme

Strong belief in shoulds, oughts, and musts

The dire need for certainty

Wishful thinking

Lack of self-perspective

Deep conviction that because one believes something strongly it must have objective reality and truth

5. Experiential and Feeling Irrationalities

Strong conviction that because one experiences something deeply and "feels" its truth, it must in fact be correct

Strong conviction that the more intensely one experiences something the more factual reality and truth it has

Strong conviction that because one authentically and honestly feels something it must exist in the external world

Strong conviction that all authentic and deeply experienced feelings represent healthy feelings

Strong conviction that when a powerful thought or feeling exists (for example, a mystical feeling that one understands everything in the universe) one has a deeper, more important, and factually truer idea than if one has a fact-based thought or perception

6. Habit-Making Irrationalities

The acquiring of nonproductive and self-defeating habits easily and unconsciously

The automatic retention and persistence of nonproductive and self-defeating habits in spite of one's conscious awareness of their irrationality

Failure to follow up on conscious determination and resolution to break a self-defeating habit

Inventing rationalizations and excuses for not giving up a self-defeating habit

Backsliding into self-defeating habits after one has temporarily overcome them

7. Addictions to Self-Defeating Behaviors

Addiction to overeating

Addiction to smoking

Addiction to alcohol

Addiction to drugs

Addiction to tranquilizers and other medicines

Addiction to work at the expense of greater enjoyments
Addiction to approval and love

8. Neurotic Symptoms and Severe Personality Disorders
Overweening and disruptive anxiety
Depression and despair
Hostility and rage
Extreme feelings of self-downing and hurt
Extreme feelings of self-pity
Childish grandiosity
Refusal to accept undesirable realities
Paranoid thinking
Delusions
Hallucinations
Psychopathy
Mania
Extreme withdrawal or catatonia

9. Religious Irrationalities
Devout faith unfounded in fact
Slavish adherence to religious dogma
Deep conviction that a supernatural force must exist
Deep conviction that a supernatural force or entity has special, personal interest in oneself
Deep conviction in Heaven and Hell
Religious bigotry
Persecution of other religious groups
Wars between religious groups
Scrupulous adherence to religious rules, rites, and taboos
Religious antisexuality and extreme puritanism
Religious conviction that all pleasure equates with sin
Complete conviction that some deity will specifically heed one's prayers
Absolute conviction that one has a spirit or soul entirely divorced from one's material body
Absolute conviction that one's soul will live forever
Absolute conviction that no kind of superhuman force can possibly exist

10. Population Irrationalities
Population explosion in many parts of the world
Lack of education in contraceptive methods
Families having more children than they can afford to support

Restrictions on birth control and abortion for those who want them

Some nations deliberately fomenting a population explosion

11. Health Irrationalities

Fear of air pollution

Noise pollution

Harmful and misleading drug advertising and promotion

Poor health education

Harmful food additives

Uncontrolled medical costs and resultant poor health facilities

Unnecessary surgical procedures

Avoidance of physicians and dentists by people requiring diagnostic and medical procedures

Neglect of medical research

12. Acceptance of Unreality

Widespread acceptance and following of silly myths

Widespread acceptance and following of extreme romanticism

Widespread acceptance and following of foolish, inhumane fairy tales

Widespread acceptance and following of unrealistic movies and radio and TV dramas and serials

Widespread Pollyannaism

Widespread Utopianism

13. Political Irrationalities

Wars

Undeclared wars and cold wars

Civil wars

Political corruption and graft

Foolish election procedures

Political riots

Terrorism

Political persecution and torture

Extreme patriotism

Extreme nationalism

Constant international bickering

Sabotaging of attempts at world collaboration and cooperation

14. Economic Irrationalities

Ecological waste and pollution

Poor use and development of natural resources

Economic boycotts and wars

Needless employer-employee bickering and strikes
Extreme profiteering
Business bribery, corruption, and theft
Extreme economic status-seeking
Union bribery, corruption, and graft
Misleading and false advertising
Needless restrictions on business and labor
Inefficiency in business and industry
Addiction to foolish economic customs
Inequitable and ineffectual taxes
Gambling abuses
Foolish consumerism (e.g., expensive funerals, dog funerals, weddings, alcohol consumerism, etc.)
Production of shoddy materials
Lack of intelligent consumer information and control
Inefficiently run welfare systems
Inefficiently run government agencies

15. Avoidance Irrationalities
     Procrastination
     Complete avoidance of important things, inertia
     Refusal to face important realities
     Oversleeping and avoidance of sufficient sleep
     Refusal to get sufficient exercise
     Lack of thought and preparation for the future
     Needless suicide

16. Dependency Irrationalities
     Need for approval and love of others
     Need for authority figures to run one's life
     Need for superhuman gods and devils
     Need for parents when one has matured chronologically
     Need for a helper, guru, or therapist
     Need for a hero
     Need for magical solutions to problems

17. Hostility Irrationalities
     Condemning people totally because some of their acts appear undesirable or unfair
     Demanding that people absolutely must do what one would like them to do and damning them when they don't
     Setting up perfectionistic standards and insisting that people have to follow them

Commanding that justice and fairness must exist in the universe and making oneself quite incensed when they do not

Insisting that hassles and difficulties must not exist and that life is absolutely awful when they do

Disliking unfortunate conditions and not merely working to overcome or remove them, but overrebelliously hating the entire system that produced them and the people involved in this system

Remembering past injustices and vindictively feuding against the perpetrators of these injustices forever

Remembering past injustices in gory detail and obsessing about them and their perpetrators forever

18. Excitement-Seeking Irrationalities

Continuing to gamble compulsively in spite of serious losses

Leading a carousing, playboy or playgirl type of life at the expense of other, more solid enjoyments

Engaging in dangerous sports or pastimes, such as mountain climbing, hunting, or skiing under hazardous conditions

Deliberately having sex without taking contraceptives or precautions for venereal disease

Engaging in college hazing or other pranks of a hazardous nature

Turning in false fire alarms

Dangerous forms of dueling

Engaging in stealing or homicide for excitement

Engaging in serious forms of brawling, fighting, rioting, or warring for excitement

Engaging in cruel sports, such as clubbing baby seals or cock-fighting for excitement

19. Magic-Related Irrationalities

Devout belief in magic, sorcery, witchcraft, etc.

Devout belief in astrology

Devout belief in phrenology

Devout belief in mediums and ghosts

Devout belief in talking animals

Devout belief in extrasensory perception

Devout belief in demons and exorcism

Devout belief in the power of prayer

Devout belief in superhuman entities and gods

Devout belief in damnation and salvation

Devout belief that the universe really cares for humans

Devout belief that some force in the universe spies on humans and regulates their lives on the principle of deservingness and nondeservingness

Devout belief in the unity and union of all things in the world

Devout belief in immortality

20. Immorality Irrationalities

Engaging in immoral and criminal acts opposed to one's own strong moral code

Engaging in immoral or criminal acts for which one has a good chance of getting apprehended and severely penalized

Engaging in immoral and criminal acts when one would have a good chance of gaining more with less effort at noncriminal pursuits

Firmly believing that virtually no chance exists of one's getting caught at immoral and criminal acts when a good chance actually exists

Strong belief that because a good chance exists that one can get away with a single criminal act, a good chance also exists that one can get away with repeated acts of that nature

Stubborn refusal to amend one's immoral ways even though one suffers severe penalties for engaging in them

Engaging in criminal, assaultive, or homicidal acts without any real sense of behaving irresponsibly or immorally

21. Irrationalities Related to Low Frustration Tolerance or Short-Range Hedonism

Strong insistence on going mainly or only for the pleasures of the moment instead of those of the present and future

Obsession with immediate gratifications, whatever the costs

Whining and strongly pitying oneself when one finds it necessary to surrender short-range pleasures for other gains

Ignoring the dangers inherent in going for immediate pleasures

Striving for ease and comfort rather than for greater satisfactions that require some temporary discomfort

Refusing to work against a harmful addiction because of the immediate discomfort of giving it up

Refusing to continue with a beneficial or satisfying program of activity because one views its onerous aspects as too hard and devoutly believes that they should not exist

Chomping at the bit impatiently when one has to wait for or work for a satisfying condition to occur

Procrastinating about doing activities that one knows would turn out beneficially and that one has promised oneself to do

Significantly consuming a scarce commodity that one knows one will very much want in the future

22. Defensive Irrationalities

Rationalizing about one's poor behavior instead of trying to honestly admit it and correct it

Denying that one has behaved poorly or stupidly when one clearly has

Avoiding facing some of one's serious problems and sweeping them under the rug

Unconsciously repressing some of one's "shameful" acts because one will savagely condemn oneself if one consciously admits them

Projecting one's poor behavior onto others and contending that they did it in order to deny responsibility for it

Using the sour grapes mechanism, and claiming that you really do not want something you want when you find it too difficult to face not getting it

Identifying with outstanding individuals and unrealistically believing that you have the same kinds of abilities or talents that they have

Confusing people who affected you seriously in your past life with those whom you have interests in today and assuming that the present individuals will act the same way as the past ones did

Expressing reverse feelings (such as love) for someone for whom you really have the opposite feelings (such as hate)

23. Attribution Irrationalities

Attributing to people feelings for you that they really do not have

Attributing certain motives for people's behavior when they do not actually have those motives

Attributing to people a special interest in you when they have no such interest

Attributing certain characteristics or ideas to people because they are a member of a group whose constituents frequently have such characteristics or ideas

24. Memory-Related Irrationalities

Forgetting painful experiences soon after they end, and not using them to avoid future pain

Embellishing the facts about people's behavior and inventing exaggerations and rumors about them

Focusing mainly or only on the immediate advantages or disadvantages of things and shortsightedly ignoring what will probably happen in connection with them in the future

Repressing one's memory of important events so as not to feel responsibility or shame about their occurring

Remembering and obsessing about some things too well and thereby interfering with effective thought and behavior in other respects

25. Demandingness-Related Irrationalities

Demanding that one must do well at certain goals in order to accept oneself as a human

Demanding that one must win the approval or love of significant others

Demanding that one must do perfectly well at practically everything and/or win the perfect approval of practically everyone

Demanding that everyone must treat one perfectly fairly, justly, considerately, and lovingly

Demanding that the conditions of life must remain easy and that one must get practically everything one wants quickly, without any undue effort

Demanding that one must have almost perfect enjoyment or ecstasy at all times

26. Sex-Related Irrationalities

The belief that sex acts have intrinsic dirtiness, badness, or wickedness

The belief that sex acts are absolutely bad or immoral unless they go with love, marriage, or other nonsexual relationships

The belief that orgasm has a sacred quality and that sex without it has no real joy or legitimacy

The belief that intercourse has a sacred quality and that sex without it has no real joy or legitimacy

The belief that one must have sexual competence and that one's worth as a person depends on it

The belief that good sex always must include simultaneous orgasm

The belief that masturbation and petting to orgasm have a shameful quality, and that only intercourse is legitimate

The belief that men can legitimately and morally have more sex or less restricted sex than can women

The belief that sex competence should occur spontaneously and easily, without any particular kind of knowledge or practice

The belief that women have little natural interest in sex, remain naturally passive, and have inferior sexual abilities and capacities

The belief that two people who love each other can have little or no sexual interest in other individuals

27. Science-Related Irrationalities

The belief that science provides a panacea for the solution of all human problems

The belief that the scientific method constitutes the only method of advancing human knowledge

The belief that all technological inventions and advances are good for humans

The belief that because the logico-empirical method of science does not give perfect solutions to all problems and has its limitations, it has little or no usefulness

The belief that because indeterminacy exists in scientific observation, the logico-empirical method is entirely useless

The belief that because science has found evidence and explanations for hypotheses that originally existed only in the human imagination (e.g., the theory of relativity), it has to and undoubtedly will find evidence and explanations for other imagined hypotheses (such as the existence of a soul or of God)

The belief that because a scientist gets recognized as an authority in one area (e.g., Einstein as a physicist), he or she must have authoritative views in other areas (e.g., politics)

The strong tendency of highly competent, exceptionally well-trained scientists to act in a highly prejudiced, foolish manner in some important aspects of their scientific endeavors, and to behave even more foolishly in their personal lives

The strong tendency of applied social scientists—such as clinical psychologists, psychiatrists, social workers, counselors, and clergymen—to behave self-defeatingly and unscientifically in their personal and professional lives.

The foregoing list of human irrationalities, which in no way pretends to exhaust the field, includes almost 250 major happiness-sabotaging tendencies. Admittedly, some of these overlap, so the list includes repetitions. At the same time, it consists of only a bare outline. Under each of its headings we can easily subsume a large number of other irrationalities. Under the first heading, "Custom and Conformity Irrationalities," for example, we could easily include hundreds of idiocies related to courtship, marriage, and wedding customs, many of them historical but many still extant.

Psychotherapy represents one of the most tragic examples in this respect. It is mentioned briefly, under the heading "Science-Related Irrationalities," as "the strong tendency of applied social scientists—such as clinical psychologists, psychiatrists, social workers, counselors, and clergymen—to behave self-defeatingly and unscientifically in their personal and professional lives." This hardly tells the tale! For psychotherapy supposedly consists of a field of scientific inquiry and application whose practitioners remain strongly devoted to helping their clients eliminate or minimize their irrational, self-destructive thoughts, feelings, and behaviors. Actually, the opposite largely appears to hold true. For most therapists engage in ubiquitous antiscientific activities that help their clients maintain or even intensify their unreasonableness.

There are more than a few major irrationalities of psychotherapeutic "helpers." For example, instead of taking a comprehensive, multimodal, cognitive-emotive-behavioral approach to treatment, many of them fetishistically and obsessively-compulsively overemphasize some monolithic approach, such as awareness, insight, emotional release, understanding of the past, experiencing, rationality, or physical release. They sometimes have their own dire needs for their clients' approval and frequently tie these clients to them in an extended dependency relationship. They frequently abjure scientific, empirically-based analysis for far-fetched conjectures that they rarely relate to factual data. They sometimes dogmatically assume that their own system or technique of therapy, and it alone, helps people, and have a closed mind to other systems or techniques. They often ignore the biological bases of human behavior and assume that special situational reasons for all disturbances must exist, and, worse yet, that if one finds these special reasons the disturbances will almost automatically disappear. They frequently turn more and more to magic, faith healing, astrology, tarot cards, and other unscientific means of "transpersonal" psychotherapy.

This list is not exhaustive, and could easily be doubled or tripled. To repeat the main point: virtually all the main headings and subheadings in the above list of major human irrationalities have a score or more further subdivisions, and for each subdivision a fairly massive amount of observational and experimental confirmatory evidence exists.

Granted that all the foregoing major human irrationalities exist—and many more like them!—can one maintain the thesis that they have, in all probability biological roots and stem from the fundamental nature of humans? Yes, on several important, convincing grounds, which follow.

All the major human irrationalities seem to exist, in one form or another, in virtually all humans. (Not equally, of course!) Some of us, on the whole, behave much less irrationally than others, but go find *any* individual who does not fairly frequently subscribe to *all* of these major irrationalities. For example, using only the first nine headings that apply to personal self-sabotaging, do you know of a single man or woman who has not often slavishly conformed to some asinine social custom, not given himself or herself global, total ratings, not held strong prejudices, not resorted to several kinds of illogical thinking, not fooled himself or herself into believing that strong feelings represented something about objective reality, not acquired and persisted in self-defeating habits, not had any pernicious addictions, remained perfectly free of all neurotic symptoms, and never subscribed to religious dogmas? Is there a single such case?

Just about all the major irrationalities that now exist have held rampant sway in virtually all social and cultural groups that have been investigated historically and anthropologically. Although rules, laws, mores, and standards vary widely from group to group, gullibility, absolutism, dogmas, religiosity, and demandingness *about* these standards remain surprisingly similar. Thus, your parents and your culture advise or educate you to wear one kind of clothes in the

Western civilized world and another in the South Sea Islands. But where they tend to inform you, "You had better dress in the right or proper way so that people will accept your behavior and act advantageously toward you," you irrationally escalate this "proper" standard into, "I *must* dress properly, because I absolutely *need* other people's approval. I can't stand their disapproval and the disadvantages that may thereby accrue to me, and if they do not like my behavior that means they do not like *me* and that I rate as a completely rotten person!" Although your parents and your teachers may encourage you to think in this absolutistic, self-downing manner, you have the innate human propensity to gullibly take them seriously, carry on their nonsense for the rest of your life, and invent it yourself if they happen to provide you with relatively little absolutism.

Many of the irrationalities that people profoundly follow go counter to almost all the teachings of their parents, peers, and the mass media. Yet they refuse to give them up! Few parents encourage you to overgeneralize, make unrealistic statements, or uphold contradictory propositions, yet you tend to do this kind of thing continually. Your educational system strongly encourages you to learn, unlearn, and relearn, yet you have great difficulty doing so in many important respects. You encounter strong persuasive efforts of others to get you to forego nonproductive and self-defeating habits, like overeating and smoking. But you largely tend to resist this constant teaching.

You may have parents who raise you to be extremely skeptical or antireligious, yet you can easily adopt some extreme religious orthodoxy in your adult years. You learn about the advisability of regularly visiting your physician and dentist from grade school onward, but does this teaching make you go? Does widespread reading about the facts of life quiet your Pollyannaism or Utopianism, or rid you of undue pessimism? Thousands of well-documented books and films have clearly exposed the inequities of wars, riots, terrorism, and extreme nationalism. Have they really induced you to strongly oppose these forms of political irrationality?

Virtually no one encourages you to procrastinate and avoid facing life's grim realities. Dangerous excitement-seeking rarely gets you the approval of others. Does that stop you from indulging in it? The vast majority of scientists oppose magical, unverifiable, absolutistic, devout thinking. Do you always heed them? You usually know perfectly well what moral and ethical rules you subscribe to, and almost everyone you know encourages you to subscribe to them. But do you? Low frustration tolerance and short-range hedonism rarely prove acceptable to your elders, teachers, clergymen, and favorite writers. Does their disapproval stop you from frequently giving in to immediate gratification at the expense of future gains? Who teaches you to rationalize and reinforces you when you do so? What therapist, friend, or parent goes along with your other kinds of defensiveness? But does their almost universal opposition stop you? Do significant others in your life reward you for demanding perfection of yourself or of them, or for whining and wailing that conditions *must* be the way you want them to be?

Certainly, a good many irrationalities have an important cultural component. But a good many seem minimally taught, and many others are severely discouraged, yet still ubiquitously flourish.

As mentioned before, practically all the irrationalities listed in this chapter hold true not only for ignorant, stupid, and severely disturbed individuals but also for highly intelligent, educated, and relatively undisturbed persons. Ph.D.s in physics and psychology, for example, have racial and other prejudices, indulge in enormous amounts of wishful thinking, believe that if someone believes something strongly—or intensely experiences it—it must have external reality. They fall prey to all kinds of pernicious habits (including addictions like alcoholism), foolishly get themselves into debt, devoutly think that they must have others' approval, and invent rumors about others which they then strongly believe. Unusually bright and well-educated people probably hold fewer or less rigid irrationalities than average members of the populace, but they hardly have a monopoly on rational behavior!

So many humans hold highly irrational beliefs and participate in exceptionally self-defeating behaviors so often that we can only with great difficulty uphold the hypothesis that they entirely learn these ways of reacting. Even if we hypothesize that they mainly learn how to behave so badly, the obvious question arises: Why do they allow themselves to get taken in so easily by the teachings of their culture, and if they do imbibe these during their callow youth, why don't they teach themselves how to give up these inanities later? Almost all of us acquire political, social, and religious values from our parents and institutions during our childhood, but we often give them up later, after we go to college, read some hardheaded books, or befriend people who subscribe to quite different values. Why don't we do this about many of our most idiotic and impractical views, which clearly do not accord with reality and which obviously do us considerable harm?

Let's examine, for instance, the following ideas: (1) "If my sister did me in as a child, all women are dangerous and I'd better not relate to them intimately." (2) "If I lack competency in an area, such as academic performance, I am a totally worthless individual and deserve no happiness." (3) "Because you have treated me unfairly, as you *absolutely must not,* you absolutely have to change your ways and treat me better in the future." (4) "Since I enjoy smoking very much, I can't give it up; and although others are seriously disadvantaged from continuing it, I can most probably get away with smoking without harming myself." (5) "Because blacks are arrested and convicted for more crimes than whites, they all are immoral and I'd better have nothing to do with them." (6) "If biology and heredity factors play an important part in emotional disturbance, we can do nothing to help disturbed people, and their plight is hopeless."

All these irrational statements, and hundreds of similar ones, clearly make little or no sense and wreak immense social and individual harm. Yet we devoutly believe them in millions of cases. Even if we can show that some significant part of these beliefs stems from social learning (as it probably does), why do we strongly imbibe and so persistently hang on to them? Clearly because we have a powerful innate predisposition to do so.

When bright and generally competent people give up many of their irrationalities, they frequently tend to adopt other inanities or go to opposite irrational extremes. Devout religionists often turn into devout atheists. Political left-wing extremists wind up as right-wing extremists. Individuals who procrastinate mightily may later emerge as compulsive workers. People who surrender one irrational phobia frequently turn up with another equally irrational but quite different phobia. Extremism tends to remain as a natural human trait that takes one foolish form or another.

Humans who seem least afflicted by irrational thoughts and behaviors, however, still revert to them, and sometimes seriously so. A man who rarely gets angry at others on occasion becomes so incensed that he almost or actually murders someone. A woman who fearlessly studies difficult subjects and takes complicated examinations may feel that she can't bear rejection in a job interview and may fail to look for a suitable position. A therapist who objectively and dispassionately teaches his clients how to behave more rationally may, if one of them stubbornly resists, act quite irrationally and agitatedly dismiss that person from therapy. In cases like these, unusual environmental conditions often bring out silly behavior by normally sane individuals. But these individuals obviously react to these conditions because they have some basic disposition to act irrationally under unusual kinds of stress, and that basic disposition probably has innate elements.

People highly opposed to various kinds of irrationalities often fall prey to them. Agnostics give in to devout, absolutistic thoughts and feelings. Highly religious individuals act quite immorally. Psychologists who believe that guilt or self-downing are self-defeating make themselves guilty and self-downing.

Knowledge or insight into one's irrational behavior only partially, if at all, helps one change it. You may know full well about the harmfulness of smoking and yet smoke more than ever! You may realize that you hate sex because your parents puritanically taught you to do so, but you may nonetheless keep hating it. You may have clear-cut "intellectual" insight into your overweening egotism but have little "emotional" insight into how to change it. This largely arises from the basic human tendency to have two contradictory beliefs at the same time—an "intellectual" one which you lightly and occasionally hold and an "emotional" one which you vigorously and consistently hold, and which you therefore usually tend to act upon. This tendency to have simultaneous contradictory beliefs again seems part of the human condition.

No matter how hard and how long people work to overcome their irrational thoughts and behaviors, they usually find it exceptionally difficult to overcome or eradicate them, and to some degree they always remain exceptionally fallible in this respect. We could hypothesize that because they overlearn their self-defeating behaviors at an early age, they therefore find it most difficult to recondition themselves. But it seems simpler and more logical to conclude that their fallibility has an inherent source, and that their early conditionability and proneness to accepting training in dysfunctional behavior itself represents a significant part of their innate fallibility. Certainly, they hardly acquired conditionability solely through having someone condition them!

It appears reasonably clear that certain irrational ideas stem from personal, nonlearned (or even antilearned) experiences; that we inventively, though crazily, invent them in a highly creative manner. Suppose, for instance, you fall in love with someone and you intensely feel, "know," and state, "I know I'll love you forever!" You certainly didn't learn that knowledge, since you not only read about Romeo and

Juliet but also read lots of other information, such as divorce statistics, which show that people rarely romantically adore each other forever. You consequently choose your "knowledge" out of several other realms of data you could have chosen to "know." And you most probably do so because romantic love among humans frequently carries with it the intrinsic illusion that "Because my feeling for you has such authenticity and intensity, I *know* it will last forever." You self-centeredly create the false and irrational "knowledge" that goes with your genuine feelings.

There is a natural tendency of humans that seems to "prove" that if they have profound feelings, this "proves" something about the external universe.

If we look closely at some of the most popular irrational forms of thinking, it appears that humans figure them out. They start with a sensible or realistic observation, and end up with a non sequitur type of conclusion. Thus, you start with, "it would be very enjoyable if Jane loved me," and falsely conclude, "Therefore she *has* to love me, and I find it awful if she doesn't." If you begin with the even stronger observation, "It would be exceptionally and uniquely enjoyable if Jane loved me," you have even more of a tendency to conclude, "Therefore she *must!*" But no matter how true the first part of your proposition may be, the second part remains a non sequitur, making no sense whatever.

Similarly, you tend to irrationally conclude, "Because I find order desirable, I *need* certainty." And, "Because I find failure most undesirable: (1) I *must not* fail; (2) I did not cause myself to fail—he *made* me do it; and (3) Maybe I didn't really fail at all." And, "Because it would be very hard for me to give up smoking, I find it too hard, and I can't do it." All these non sequiturs stem from autistic, grandiose thinking—you simply *command* that what you greatly desire must exist and what you find obnoxious must not. This kind of autistic thinking largely appears innate.

Many types of irrational thinking largely consist of arrant overgeneralizations, and as Alfred Korzybski and his followers have shown, overgeneralizations seem a normal (though foolish) part of the human condition. Thus, you again start with a sensible observation: "I failed at that test," and then overgeneralize to, "I will always fail; I have no ability to succeed." Or you start with, "They sometimes treat me unjustly," and then overgeneralize to, "They always treat me unjustly, and I can't stand their continual unfair treatment!" Again, this seems the way that normal humans naturally think. Children, as Jean Piaget has shown, lack good judgment until the age of seven or eight. Adults frequently lack it forever!

Human thinking not only significantly varies in relation to people's intelligence levels, but some forms of thinking stem largely from left-brain or right-brain functioning. Both intelligence and left-brain or right-brain functioning have a significantly hereditary element and do not arise merely out of learned experiences.

Some forms of irrationality, such as low frustration tolerance or the seeking of the specious rewards of immediate rather than long-term gratification, exist in many lower animals as well as in humans. George Ainslie reviews the literature on specious reward and shows how a decline in the effectiveness of rewards occur in both animals and humans as the rewards get delayed from the time of choice.[2] Again, a fairly clear-cut physiological and hereditary element seems obvious here.

There is evidence that people often find it much easier to learn self-defeating than nondefeating behavior. Thus, they very easily overeat but have great trouble sticking to a sensible diet. They can learn to smoke cigarettes, usually from their foolish peers but if other peers or elders try to teach them to give up smoking or to act with more self-discipline in other ways, they resist this teaching to a fare-thee-well! They fairly easily pick up prejudices against blacks, Jews, Catholics, and Orientals, but rarely heed the teachings of tolerance. They quickly condition themselves to feel anxious, depressed, hating, and self-downing, but take an enormous amount of time and effort getting rid of these disturbed feelings. They don't seem exactly doomed to a lifetime of stupid, foolish, asinine behavior—but pretty nearly!

25

Addictive Behaviors and Personality Disorders

This article was written in July 1995 for the *Addiction Newsletter* of the Division of Addictive Behaviors of the American Psychological Association. It briefly summarizes the REBT theory of addiction, especially as it applies to individuals with severe personality disorders. I have written several papers, mostly in the *Journal of Rational-Emotive and Cognitive-Behavior Therapy,* on the treatment of individuals with personality disorders, and show in these papers how they are different from what I call the "nice neurotics." This article, along with some of my other recent writings, shows how individuals with a "double diagnosis"—that is, addiction and personality disorder—can be properly assessed and treated with REBT.

I have been working with various kinds of addicts since 1943—well over half a century! My first major interest and specialization was in sex, love, and relationship therapy, so I saw a good many addicts, both straight and gay, in those areas. But sex and love addicts frequently, as you can well guess, compulsively drink, drug, smoke, overeat, and make themselves over-dependent on other people. So I soon was involved with multiple addictions—what are now called dual diagnoses. Soon after I started doing Rational Emotive Behavior Therapy in the 1950s, I began to suspect that a large percentage of my severely addicted clients were not merely, as I originally thought, "nice neurotics," but that I could more accurately see them and treat them as having severe personality disorders (PDs).

Not all addicts, of course, are this disturbed. As Michael Abrams, Lydia Dengelegi, and I say in our book *The Art and Science of Rational Eating*, "addicts," when they are not bulimic or anorexic, may be no more disturbed than nonaddicts, and many of them have normal biological tendencies to get back to their "set points" when they diet too rigorously. Many smokers and sex "addicts" are gusty and lusty individuals who may at times overdo their strong psychophysical urges but are, at worst, common everyday neurotics.

Some of the worst addicts I have seen are mainly "sick" because the appetitive centers in their brain have, for one reason or another, gone awry—so that they oversatiate themselves with alcohol, sweets, chocolate, or other substances mainly because of their physiological anomalies, and not primarily because of their psychological aberrations. Other addicts, such as some gamblers and potheads, seem to be mainly neurotic and have abysmal low frustration tolerance. Because they like some substance or activity very much, they childishly insist that they *absolutely must* indulge in it, even when they "know" how harmful to themselves and their loved ones this indulgence is. Addiction, then, comes in many shapes and sizes, and has multiple "causes," several of which tend to overlap and interact with each other.

What about the most serious addicts—such as the inevitable drinkers who go back to bingeing in spite of several hospitalizations, smokers who won't stop even when they have emphysema, and the sex offender who keeps molesting children when he is still on parole for his last offense. What drives these "hopeless" addicts to their almost certain destruction? Why are they so resistant to help from friends, relatives, therapists, and improved socio-economic conditions?

I would say, for many reasons:

Many—perhaps the great majority—of these inveterate addicts have one or more severe PDs. I find them to very often be paranoid, schizoid, antisocial, borderline, avoidant, dependent, and/or obsessive-compulsive. When they are not quite diagnosable in these regular PD categories, and would often be deemed to be "neurotic," I often find them to be exceptionally prone to endogenous anxiety, panic, depression, and rage. Endogenous? Yes, I think that they often have an innate, biological tendency to easily overreact and/or underreact to the stresses and strains of everyday living.

Many of these individuals with severe PDs come from households where their close relatives, too, were innately highly disturbable. Therefore, their childhood and later years involved more stresses than the rest of us tend to experience. So the interaction between their innate disturbability *plus* their poor environment contributed significantly to making them even more upsetable than they otherwise would have been. But my long experience with thousands of clients convinces me that people who are biologically eminently disturbable will often think, feel, and act self-defeatingly no matter how favorable their early and later environments.

Practically all humans are both born and reared with strong tendencies to neuroticize themselves according to the A-B-Cs of REBT and cognitive behavior therapy. Unfortunate activating events or adversities (As) occur in their lives, and they then adopt and invent dysfunctional or irrational beliefs (IBs) about these As. Their core IBs, which are both conscious and unconscious (or implicit), are: "I *absolutely must* perform well and be lovable or I am a pretty worthless person"; "Other people *absolutely must* treat me kindly and fairly or they are no damned good"; "Conditions under which I live *absolutely must* be comfortable and not too frustrating or else my existence is intolerable and horrible." When people learn, and invent, these IBs—which at times all of them seem to do—they create neurotic consequences (Cs) which take the form of self-defeating thoughts (e.g., obsessive thoughts), feelings (e.g., panic and depression), and behaviors (e.g., severe inhibitions and compulsions).

Almost all people with severe PDs start off with several main kinds of disturbance: their strong biological tendencies to think, feel, and behave abnormally, especially in complex social relationships; the poor life consequences (Cs) that they therefore create and are inflicted with because of their biological (and social) deficits; and the interactions among their poor adversities (As), dysfunctional beliefs (Bs), and self-defeating consequences (Cs).

If I am correct—as, of course, I may not be—people with severe PDs are usually biologically handicapped at the start, or at least quite early in their lives. They have distinct cognitive deficits or deficiencies (e.g., attention deficit disorder, focusing problems) emotional deficits (e.g., under- or overresponsiveness) and behavioral deficits (e.g., avoidant or compulsive proclivities). Like children who are born mentally deficient or with physical anomalies (e.g., cardiac or respiratory defects), they are distinctly handicapped.

Because of their innate and environmentally exacerbated deficiencies, they have unusual difficulties at *all* the A-B-Cs of human disturbance: At point A (adversity) they have more unfortunate experiences than nonhandicapped children (e.g., disturbed parents and siblings and negative reactions from other children and adults who criticize and/or overprotect them because of their peculiarities). At point B (belief system) they think crookedly about the unusual As (because of their innate cognitive-emotive deficiencies) and therefore end up with what we call severe PDs (e.g., schizoid personality or obsessive-compulsive disorder [OCD]). Thus, they are handicapped, innately *and* environmentally, at A, B, and C!

Like almost all of us humans, individuals with severe PDs are also neurotic or self-defeating. Therefore they take their desires and preferences for success, approval, justice, and comfort and make them into grandiose demands—into absolutistic musts, shoulds, and oughts. As I have hypothesized for forty years, neurosis is practically the human condition because humans are both innate and socially taught "musturbators." Whenever unfortunate adversities occur in their lives, they often *demand* that they *must not* exist, foolishly panic, depress, and enrage themselves about these As, and then (ironically!) are less effectual at improving them. To make matters worse, when they use their grandiose musts (and other cognitive distortions that go with them) to create neurotic consequences, such as panic and depression, they often command, "I *must not* be panicked!" "I *must* be undepressed!" They thereby make themselves panicked about their panic, depressed about their depression, and so forth. As I often humorously—but still seriously—tell my clients and audiences, they are nutty about their nuttiness—and thereby circularly neurotic.

Where does addiction come in? The REBT theory says that when people are "normal neurotics"—and not personality disordered—addiction has several ideological causes at B, people's belief systems. Thus, they have two main forms of low frustration tolerance (LFT): Primary LFT: "I like this harmful substance (alcohol, coke, cigarettes) or this activity (gambling, watching TV) very much and therefore I *absolutely must* have it, no matter what its disadvantages are! I can't stand being deprived! It's awful to stop indulging in it!" and Secondary LFT: "I utterly hate the discomfort and pain from my neurotic feelings (panic, depression) and I *absolutely must not* experience them! I *have to* stop blaming myself for the failures and rejections that go with them! So I *must* indulge in some substance or activity that is immediately gratifying, distracts me from my pain, and temporarily makes me feel good!"

Neurotic addiction, then, stems largely from horrifying oneself about adversities and from awfulizing about one's cognitive-emotional-behavioral disturbances. These neuroses themselves mainly stem from grandiose demands (rather than preferences) that one perform well, be lovable, treated fairly, and live comfortably, and when these demands lead to disturbances—which they usually do—neurotics also have dysfunctional insistence that they *must not* feel disturbed. Addictive substances and activities temporarily allay both primary and secondary neuroses. So many neurotics then demand the distraction and relief from pain that their addictions temporarily produce.

If I am correct, people with severe PDs are more prone to addiction than are "nice neurotics" for the following reasons:

1. They have more adversities and disturbed consequences than the rest of us neurotics.
2. They are therefore more frustrated than non-PDs.
3. Because of their greater and often overwhelming frustrations, many of them develop unusual degrees of LFT.
4. Because of their greater failures and rejections, many of them also develop neurotic self-damnation about their deficits, handicaps, and failings.
5. For biological reasons, some of them may be more prone than neurotics to demand that they must not be frustrated and must perform well. They may be more irrational in this respect than neurotics.
6. For both biological and environmental reasons, persons with PDs often feel so disturbed that they are compulsively driven to alcohol, drugs, food, gambling, or other substances to temporarily allay their disordered thoughts, feelings, and actions.
7. Some of them, for biosocial reasons, are particularly afflicted with obsessive-compulsive disorders and/or have neurological anomalies that interfere with normal appetite and desire-controlling brain centers, and disrupt their ability to stop their compulsive indulgences.

To make matters still worse, if all that I have just said is even partially true, individuals with the dual diagnosis of addiction and PD will tend to: addict themselves more often than neurotics; have more severe addictions (such as to barbiturates and heroin); and be more resistant to giving up their addictions. Their resistance to change would result, again, from several factors, including:

1. Strong biological tendencies to have many thinking, feeling, and behavioral deficits
2. Their long history of being severely disturbed
3. Their history of poor social relationships, including their relationships with helpers and therapists
4. Their innate and acquired tendency to take the easy way out. This interferes with the very hard work that therapy, and especially antiaddiction therapy, almost always requires
5. Their old friendships and partnerships with other addicts
6. Their neurotic damning of themselves for their PDs, for their foolish addictions, and for their other failings and social rejections
7. Their deep-seated feelings of worthlessness and hopelessness that many PDs often have, and that may be an intrinsic, biologically based aspect of their having a severe PD

For reasons such as these, therapists need to recognize the important differences between "nice neurotic" addicts and those with severe PDs, and have at their disposal special techniques of treating the latter.

26

General Semantics and Rational Emotive Behavior Therapy

For the first ten years of REBT, almost all professionals firmly opposed its principles, except a few members of the New York society for General Semantics, such as Rachel Lauer. Through her influence, I was invited to talk to the Society several times and usually got a warm reception from Harry Maynard and the other leading members.

I particularly recall one society meeting in which I was attacked by an audience member for "brainwashing" my clients into thinking rationally. Before I could answer my opponent, Harry vociferously responded for me that, oh no, I was doing the opposite of that. According to the principles of general semantics, said Harry, I was "brainwashing the brainwashing" of my clients, as Alfred Korzybski, the founder of general semantics, had often done when he taught his followers to stop their overgeneralizing and think more sanely.

I liked Harry's statement and saw more clearly, as I had said in my talk, that the teachings of REBT were very similar to those of general semantics. Since that time in the 1960s, I have given several more talks to the New York Society for General Semantics and have seen a number of its members for therapy. Later on, Dr. Robert Moore, of Clearwater, Florida, became one of the leading practitioners of REBT; he wrote a Ph.D. thesis on general semantics and influenced me to write the first psychology books ever written in David Bourland's E-Prime.

As this article shows, REBT and Korzybski's teachings significantly overlap. I was therefore delighted in 1991 to be invited to give the annual Alfred Korzybski Memorial Lecture in New York and to present this paper. I have learned a great deal from general semantics and will continue to incorporate some of its best principles in Rational Emotive Behavior Therapy.

⚹

I never would have originated Rational Emotive Behavior Therapy had I not been strongly influenced by philosophers rather than psycho-therapists. For when I founded REBT in 1955, the field of therapy was almost completely run by clinicians, ranging from psychoanalysts to behaviorists, who firmly, and rather dogmatically, believed that people's early experiences, especially with their parents, made them or conditioned them to become emotionally disturbed.

This theory has some degree of validity, because all humans live in an environment. As Alfred Korzybski put it, a person is "an organism-as-a-whole-in-an-environment."[1] People seem to be born teachable and self-teachable and therefore partly acquire their feelings from their experiences with others and from the objects and things they encounter in their early and later life. Also, because they are more gullible or influenceable when they are young, they may well be more disturbable in their childhood and adolescence than when they are older.

Fortunately, however, as philosophers have shown for many centuries, a crucial aspect of people's disturbance stems from the part they play in their interactions with the environment—from what they think about and tell themselves about the unfortunate events that occur in their lives. As Epictetus, a Greek-Roman stoic, said two thousand years ago, "People are disturbed not by things, but by the views which they take of them." Asian philosophers, such as Confucius and Gautama Buddha, said something similar; Marcus Aurelius echoed Epictetus's view; and many Western philosophers—especially Spinoza, Kant, Dewey, Russell, Heidegger, Sartre, and Popper—all seem to agree that what people feel and do stems largely from the way they actively and creatively construct and reconstruct reality rather than from their passively reacting to it.

When you create absolutist, unconditional demands, you clearly put yourself in emotional jeopardy. For you often make yourself panicked before you try to fulfill your goals because you know that you may not succeed as you *must* at these goals. You severely depress yourself if you actually do fail, and even if you are doing very well at work and if Mary Jones happily returns your love, you keep worrying and worrying whether this fine state of affairs will continue tomorrow and into the future. As, of course, it *must!*

As you can see—and as I think Alfred Korzybski was a pioneer in seeing—thinking realistically about yourself, others, and about the world in which you live leads to both *Science and Sanity,* the title of his seminal book, written in 1933. On the other hand, perceiving and thinking in unrealistic, absolutist, all-or-nothing, either-or, over-generalized terms very likely leads you to what we call emotional disturbance and to doing poorly in both intrapersonal and interpersonal relationships.

Korzybski seems to have had a picture of human functioning similar to that of the A-B-C theory of REBT. Thus, he said that when we "perceive" a happening or event we "silently" or "nonverbally" react with evaluations about it, and our "emotions" and "evaluations" are organismically combined together and interact with our verbalizations, which quickly follow our silent thinking-feeling level. He quoted George Santayana as showing that humans are much better at believing than seeing.

In my first major paper on REBT, at the American Psychological Association Convention in Chicago, in August 1956, I specifically said that people's cognitions, emotions, and behaviors are not pure, but are part of an organismic or holistic interaction. Again, Korzybski seems to have predated me by seeing each human as "an organism-as-a-whole-in-an-environment," as he states, "There is no perception without interpolation and interpretation."[2] Obviously, before REBT was formulated, some of its basic A-B-C theories were included in his writings.

As I noticed after practicing Rational Emotive Behavior Therapy for a short while, and as I think Korzybski would have again agreed, once you demand and command that you absolutely *must* do well and that you always *have to* be approved of by others, and once you thereby make yourself panicked, depressed, enraged, or self-hating, you frequently show what a natural self-misled "musturbator" you are by dogmatically telling yourself, "I *must* not be panicked! I *must not* be depressed!" You then become—or much more accurately stated, *make* yourself—panicked about your panic, depressed about your depression, and self-hating about your self-hatred. You thereby create a secondary neurosis that is often more intense and pervasive than your primary disturbance, and that, in fact, tends to stop you from clearly seeing how you first made yourself upset and what you can do to change your thinking and unupset yourself.

I think that Korzybski would have endorsed REBT's continual crusading against people's absolutistic, dogmatic, overgeneralized shoulds and musts. He noted, "The fact that we do abstract on higher orders becomes a danger if we are not conscious that we are doing so and retain the primitive confusions or identifications of orders of abstractions."[3] He also advocated our increasingly using the term *etc.* because it "facilitates flexibility and gives a greater degree of conditionability in our semantic reactions. This device trains us away from dogmatism, absolutism, etc."[4] Korzybski also formulated the REBT concept of secondary symptoms (such as anxiety about anxiety) by talking about "second-order reactions ('thinking about thinking,' 'doubt of doubt,' 'fear of fear,' etc.)."[5]

Once again, from 1920 to 1951, Korzybski presented some unusual ideas that I seem to have taken from him and other philosophers and have solidly incorporated into REBT along the lines I have stated in the previous several paragraphs. Thus, he endorsed physico-mathematical methods of thinking and said that they link science, "and particularly the exact sciences, with problems of sanity in the sense of adjustment to 'facts' and 'reality.'"[6] He warned that "elementalistic or metaphysical terms are not to be trusted, and that speculations based on them are misleading or dangerous."[7] In my various criticisms of mystical and transpersonal ideas and practices in psychotherapy, I have expanded upon Korzybski's crusading against dangerous kinds of mysticism.

Science and Sanity

The more I think about Korzybski's masterpiece *Science and Sanity*, the more I am enthralled by its revolutionary title. For after practicing REBT for several years and trying to assess its effectiveness by using the scientific method to check its results, and after helping hundreds of disturbed people by scientifically, realistically, and logically disputing—at point D in REBT—their neurosis-producing irrational beliefs, I saw that REBT and the other cognitive-behavior therapies that dispute people's dysfunctional beliefs tend to show that neurosis and antiscience are very similar, and that mental health and science distinctly overlap.

Why is this so? Because science includes four main attributes: First, it is realistic and tries to make its theories consistent with the facts of social "reality." It postulates no absolute "reality," because all "things" and "facts" are viewed phenomenologically, through human perceptions and interpretations. But science tries to check and falsify or partially verify its theories in relation to external "facts."

Second, science uses logic, both Aristotelian and non-Aristotelian, to check its hypotheses, and usually ends up with theories that are not self-contradictory and are not falsified by other views of people and the world. It rules out magic, cavalierly jumping to conclusions, and many illogical nonsequiturs.

Third, and perhaps most important, science is invariably open-minded and nondogmatic. It holds even its best theories tentatively and sees them as always subject to change, and does not claim that they describe the nature of things for all possible conditions and for all times. It is exceptionally flexible and never devout.

Fourth, science is alternative-seeking and keeps looking for new, better theories and interpretations. It is never absolutist and has no final or invariant technique or answer.

REBT holds that neurosis, unlike science, tends to be replete with the kind of thinking, feeling, and behavior that is unrealistic, illogical, dogmatic, devout, and rigid. In this sense, as I think Korzybski strongly implied and as REBT agrees, science and unneurotic sanity tend to be similar.

Why is this so? Why do so many people much of the time think crookedly, misperceive reality, reason illogically, become dogmatic and devout, and stick rigidly to misleading perceptions, overgeneralizations, and conclusions? REBT's answer is that they are innately predisposed to do this. They are strongly inclined by their biological tendencies, their human experiences, *and* their social learning to make themselves self-defeating and socially sabotaging. As Jean Piaget noted, children actively construct their view of the world and their adjustments to it, and REBT and other constructivist therapies say that they keep *re*constructing their thoughts, feelings, and actions all their lives. It is their "nature" to do so, even though this "nature" is changeable.

Moreover, once people adopt and create unrealistic, rigid, non-alternative-seeking ideas, they have a strong biosocial tendency to carry them into dysfunctional action, repeat these actions many times, and to habituate themselves to destructive behaviors. They don't *have to* do this, for they always have *some* degree of choice. But they very frequently are innately inclined to habituate themselves to dysfunctional thoughts, emotions, and actions, and find it difficult, though not impossible, to change them.

Fortunately, however, the very nature of human constructivism includes a strong proactive changing and self-actualizing element. People are not merely born and reared to defeat themselves, for if that were so the human race would soon die out. They are also born and raised with a powerful tendency to choose, remember, think, think about their thinking, change, grow, and develop. What's more, if they choose to do so, they can use their abilities to think and change to largely overcome their propensities to perceive, think, and interpret crookedly.

This is the goal of general semantics: to show people how they can become aware of their misperceptions, overgeneralizing, and poor judgments and how they can reconsider and reconstitute them so that they help themselves to more accurately perceive, accept, and live more comfortably with "reality."

This goal of general semantics is remarkably similar to that of REBT. REBT has faith in disturbed people's ability to reconstruct their adopted and self-constructed distorted views of themselves, others, and the world with which they needlessly disturb themselves. It teaches them how to strongly dispute their absolutist musts, shoulds, and demands; to reduce their overgeneralizing, awfulizing, and I-can't-stand-it-itis, and to evaluate and rate only what they and others think, feel, and do while rigorously refraining from judging others' self, being, essence, or personhood.

REBT has two main goals: First, to help people see and correct their dogmatic, absolutistic attitudes and dysfunctional feelings and behaviors, and to make themselves, as Korzybski called it, subject to greater sanity. Second, as people are making themselves less disturbed and more functional, REBT tries to help them fulfill more of their human potential, actualize themselves, and enjoy themselves more fully (as Epicurus more than Epictetus advocated). Korzybski also strongly urged people to try to achieve more of their human potential. He said, "With a time-binding consciousness, our criteria of values, and so behavior, are based on the study of human potentialities, not on statistical averages on the level of *homo homini lupos* drawn from primitive and/or unsane evaluational reactions which are on record."[8]

In other words, both general semantics and REBT hold that if people think about their thinking and minimize their "natural" tendency to overcategorize, they can significantly, though perhaps never completely, free themselves from some of their thought-language limitations and achieve a more self-fulfilling life.

We can speculate that humans in primitive times had to jump to quick conclusions, make their wishes into "musturbatory" demands, and act overemotionally because they were thin-skinned animals living in a very dangerous world. Perhaps their imprecise perception, their seeing part of the picture as a whole, their rigid ways of approaching life, and their other cognitive weaknesses which Korzybski pointed out and that REBT often details, helped them survive in a grim and hostile world. Thus, by insisting that they *must* perform well and that others *had to* do their bidding, they may have made themselves needlessly anxious and angry thousands of years ago but may have survived better than if they were more reasonable. Perhaps. In any event, they did survive with their innate tendencies to reason better than other organisms *and* to often think sloppily. Now, using general semantics and REBT, they can use more reason and less dogma to survive more freely and more happily

The Is of Predication

Let me continue with the agreements between general semantics and REBT. Korzybski showed that using the *is* of predications leads us to think imprecisely. Thus, statements like, "I *am* good" and "I *am* bad" are inaccurate overgeneralizations, because, more correctly, I am a person who sometimes acts in a good and sometimes in a bad manner. In REBT, we teach our clients not to rate themselves or their being but only what they *do*. All self-ratings seem to be mistaken, because humans are too complex and many-sided ever to be given a global evaluation. Moreover, REBT holds, if you aim to be a good person you are too fallible to achieve that all-good status. And if you say, "I *must* be good," you will fail and then see yourself, quite falsely, as being bad. When you think in terms of dichotomous, good and bad terms, you will tend to demand that you *always* act well, for otherwise you will "become" bad. So even when you are doing well, you will be at great risk and will be quite anxious.

Moreover, when you strive to be a good *person* (rather than a person who tries to do good *things*), you make yourself grandiose, try to be better than other humans, and tend to deify yourself. Then, when you fall back and do stupid things, you see yourself as a bad *person,* and consequently devil-ify yourself. This is the essence of much neurosis! So REBT is perhaps the only therapy that specifically teaches, "*You* are not good and *you* are not bad. You are only *you*, a *person* who acts well and badly."

We can avoid the *is* of predication, as Korzybski points out, by saying, "I see myself as good" or "I see myself as bad," for then we do not claim that our "goodness" or "badness" really exists in the universe, but only that we *choose* to interpret ourselves in a "good" or "bad" manner. Because we are entitled to our personal definitions, we can *decide to* see ourselves as "good" because that will help us function better, rather than *decide to* see ourselves as "bad," for that will help us bring about worse results.

So REBT teaches people that they can arbitrarily define themselves as "good," and that will work much better than if they define themselves as "bad." They can attach their "goodness," for example, to their existence and tell themselves, "I am good because I am human and alive." This is a pretty safe definition of themselves because they then will always be "good" as long as they are human and alive— and will only have to worry about being "bad" after they are dead. Quite safe, you can see!

The trouble with this definition of human worth is that it *is* definitional and cannot be validated or falsified. Thus, you could say, "I am good because I am human and alive" and I can object, "But I think you are bad because you are human and alive." Which of us is correct? Neither of us, because we are both definitional, and definitions are useful but cannot be checked against "facts" or social "reality."

Moreover, both statements—"I *am* good" and "I *am* bad"—are overgeneralizations because, as noted above, all people do both "good" and "bad" deeds, and cannot really be categorized under a single, global heading—as *being* "good" or "bad." So the pragmatic solution to the problem of human "worth" is not a very good one and had better be replaced by the REBT more elegant solution: "I *am* neither good or bad; I am just a *person* who sometimes acts 'well' and sometimes acts 'badly.' So I'd better rate or evaluate what I *do* and not what I *am*." I am pretty sure Korzybski would endorse this more elegant REBT solution to the very important problem of self-rating.

Korzybski's writings on the *is* of predication encouraged me to help REBT clients stop using several kinds of overgeneralizations. For if they say, "I am good," they strongly imply that they have an essence or "soul" of goodness, that they only do "good" things, and therefore deserve to live and enjoy themselves. This is misleading, because they cannot prove that they have any essence (which is a very bad, vague, and mystical word), and if they do have one, they cannot show that it is always at all times "good."

To be much more precise, as Korzybski would put it, I help my clients say, "I am a person who *does* good things (e.g., helps others in trouble) but who also does many 'neutral' and 'bad' things (e.g., harms others). I am never really *entirely* 'good,' 'bad,' nor 'neutral.' Because I am, as a human, much too complex and many-sided to perform only 'good,' 'bad,' or 'neutral' behaviors."

REBT particularly follows Korzybski in this respect, largely because before I even formulated it I read S. I. Hayakawa and other general semantics writers and saw that the *is* of predication is not only a misleading overgeneralization, it also leads people to rate and evaluate their self, being, and totality, rather than to only evaluate what they *do* and what they *don't* do.

Since its very beginnings, in 1955, REBT has taught people not to rate their self or personhood but only their acts, deeds, and performances in relation to their goals and purposes. Thus, if you choose to stay alive and happy, you are acting well or sensibly when you keep your eyes open and avoid cars as you cross the street. But if you choose to commit suicide, you may be acting badly or foolishly when you carefully cross the street.

Let me repeat this important point: Following Korzybski, REBT is one of the very few psychotherapies that tries to help people rate, measure, and evaluate only what they *do* and *don't do,* and not rate their self, totality, or personhood. Let me say that teaching clients and other people merely to rate their acts, feelings, and thoughts and not to give themselves a misleading self-rating is quite difficult. For, as Korzybski implied, humans naturally and easily conclude that "Because I act in a 'good' manner, I am a 'good person,' and that because I act 'badly' I am a 'bad person.'" Obviously, both these views are mistaken and will often produce poor results. Because if you view yourself as a "good person" when you behave well, you will almost immediately see yourself as a rotten person and thereby produce anxiety, depression, and self-hatred when you fall back, as you inevitably will, to behaving "badly" again.

To make matters worse, when you say, "I am a good person when I do good acts," you are not really proving—factually—that your entire self is good because of your good deeds, for there is no exact way of validating or falsifying this proposition. You are merely defining *yourself,* tautologically, in terms of one set of acts, which are good according to your goals and purposes, and you could theoretically define yourself in terms of *any* kinds of acts, "good," "bad," or "neutral." Thus, Hitler could say, "My goal is to kill Jews and Gypsies, and therefore I am a good person when I kill more of them." Would you agree with him? Or someone could say, "The human race is no good and deserves to die out. Therefore, if you do 'good' deeds by helping other humans survive, you are really a bad person!" Would this individual who rates you as "bad" for your supposedly "good" deeds be right or wrong? Who can say?

REBT uses another kind of disputing (D) of people's irrational beliefs (IBs) when they think and say, "Because I do many bad *things,* I am a bad *person.*" I tell such disturbed people, "When you say you are a bad person for doing bad things, you are engaging in what Bertrand Russell called a category error. For the bad things you are doing are in one category and you, the doer of these things, are in a quite different category. You do all kinds of things, good, bad, and indifferent. So if you categorize these things as "good" or "bad," you jump to a different category when you call yourself, the doer, "good" or "bad." You are not what you *do.* So you'd better rate only the *things* you do and not identify them with your *youness,* which is quite a different category."

I got the idea for this kind of disputing from Bertrand Russell, and in recently rereading Korzybski in order to write the present paper, I was pleased to note that he gives Russell due credit for his "epoch-making work in his analysis of subject-predicate relations."[9] Even before I read Korzybski I was significantly influenced by Russell, so I am happy to acknowledge that REBT owes a real debt to both these modern philosophers. Russell, Korzybski, and REBT all join in examining and revealing the limitations of the *is* of predication.

The Is of Identify

Korzybski objected to the *is* of identity, to people saying, "I am a man," "I am a woman," "I am a good (or bad) person." I think he was correct about this, because once again these statements are all gross overgeneralizations. Moreover, as REBT points out, to identify with *any* group or concept implies the loss of oneself, and leads to what Helmuth Kaiser called neurotic fusion. Thus, to identify with your peer group gives you a sense of belonging and security. But, ironically, it also takes away from your own identity, makes you overconforming, and therefore less of an individual in your own right. You are really a person who chooses to be in the group but had better not be a devout follower of the group. When the latter occurs, you are believing something like, "I absolutely *must* be a group adherent, or else I am nothing." That is hardly a good state of mental health!

Identity is a poor word because it has conflicting meanings. I am I, myself, and am not really any other person. So that is fairly clear. But I also call myself a New Yorker, an American, and a man, and as I do so I partly lose my identity as myself, a unique human being. Of course, as a person I am normally a member of a social group, and, as Edward Sampson and others have pointed out, I take some of the main parts of my personality from that group, such as the way I dress, the kind of foods I eat, and the language I speak. So I am never *just* myself, nor had I better even be *just* a group member. For me to say that I am *only* I or *only* a member of a certain class is wrong on both counts.

Korzybski seems to solve this problem by noting that I am neither only myself nor only identified with a group. He would presumably say I am both/and rather than either/or. That is what REBT says, too. I am partly an individual in my own right, but once I choose to be in or to remain in a group that I was put in at birth (e.g., choose to remain an "American"), I am no longer only responsible for and to myself but also to the group I choose to remain a member of.

REBT, like Korzybski, I think, gives *some* degree of human choice (for I can even choose to be a hermit), but it also says that I have *limited* choice, because my biology and my upbringing help make me a social creature; therefore I am never completely a person in my own right. If I accept this "reality" I shall probably get along fairly well both as an individual and a social person. If I reject or deny it, I shall probably get into both personal and social difficulty.

To make things still more confusing, you will practically insure that you will end up making yourself anxious and depressed if you believe, "I am a good person when I do good things" for you will tend to "logically" conclude, "And I am a bad person when I do bad things." You will be very anxious even when you are acting in a "good" manner, for as a fallible human you will know that you can easily act "badly" tomorrow and your acts will then "make" you a "bad" person. When you do behave "badly," you will then tend to view yourself as a rotten individual and make yourself depressed. So unless you are perfect and always perform well, defining your self or your personhood in terms of your "good" and "bad" behaviors is, as Korzybski held, an antifactual overgeneralization. From an REBT standpoint, it just won't work.

Therefore, if you insist on rating your self or your person, globally, REBT advises that you pick a safe or self-helping definition, such as, "I am 'good' or 'okay' just because I exist, just because I am human, just because I choose to view myself this way." This is still a definitional or tautological self-rating that cannot really be validated or falsified. But, pragmatically, it is safe and will get you into little trouble!

Better yet, as noted above, REBT helps people refuse to rate their self, their totality, at all, but merely to evaluate what they *do*. Then when they act "badly" they can tell themselves, "*That* was 'bad' or 'foolish' but I am a person who acted that way. I am not a bad person and therefore I am capable of changing my behavior and of probably acting better next time. If *I* am 'bad' I am hopelessly stuck. But if what I *do* is 'bad' I can usually change."

Absolutist Shoulds and Musts

Korzybski did not clearly differentiate between people's preferences and their demands, as REBT does, nor did he show how when they take their *preferably* shoulds and change them into *absolute, unconditional* shoulds, they make themselves neurotic. But he implied that virtually all absolutist, unconditional thinking encourages us to make ourselves "unsane."

Thus, when speaking against identity, he said, " 'Identity' as a 'principle' is defined as 'absolutely sameness in "all" ("every") respects.' It can never empirically be found in this world of ever-changing processes, nor on silent levels of our nervous systems."[10]

REBT shows that when you believe, "I *preferably should* succeed and win the approval of significant others," you explicitly or tacitly include buts and alternative solutions to your desires, such as: "But if I don't succeed, I can try harder next time." "But if I'm not approved of, too bad, but it's not the end of the world." When your preferably shoulds are not fulfilled, REBT holds, you normally feel *healthily* sorry, disappointed, and frustrated (rather than *un*healthily panicked, depressed, and self-hating).

On the other hand, when you strongly believe, "Because I want to succeed and be approved of by significant others, I *absolutely, under all conditions and at all times must do so*," you create anxiety when you may not do well and severe depression when you do not act well or win others' approval. For with your absolute, under all conditions shoulds and musts, you allow yourself no alternative solutions to your desires, box yourself in, and needlessly make yourself miserable.

Korzybski wasn't as clear as REBT is about this, but he fought vigorously against absolutist, dogmatic, "allness" and "neverness" thinking. Therefore, general semantics obviously opposes self-statements like, "Because I want to succeed at my profession and want to win the approval of significant others, I *absolutely, under all conditions, at all times must* do so." In REBT, we frequently encourage people to change their inaccurate self-defeating language to more precise languages, and therefore show our clients how to change this all-or-nothing sentence to something like, "Because I want to succeed at my profession and win the approval of significant others, I very much *prefer* to do so. But if I don't, I can find other things to succeed at. If I never succeed at any important project, I can still enjoy doing what I can do and can still have a reasonably happy life. As for winning the approval of significant others, I *want* very much to do so, but I never *have* to. If I keep trying, I can practically always find *some* people who will like me as I like them. But if I somehow never do, there are many other aspects of life that I can enjoy, so I'll keep looking until I find them."

Precise Thinking and Language

Alfred Korzybski was a pioneer in linguistics and pointed out that when we think imprecisely our crooked thinking works its way into our language, and then our dysfunctional language leads us into engaging in more imprecise thinking. Ever since I started doing REBT, I found that people habituate themselves to poor language habits that then interfere with their accepting reality, that they largely are responsible for their own dysfunctional language, feelings, and actions, and that therefore they can change them.

Thus, when my clients say, "Joe lied to me and that made me furious," I interrupt, "How could that, or Joe, get into your gut and *make* you furious?" "Oh, I see," they often reply. "Yes, Joe lied to me, and *I* chose to infuriate myself about *his* lying." "Yes," I say. "Isn't that a much more accurate description of what happened and how *you* chose to create your fury?"

So REBT often shows people how to correct their language and their thinking, and to stop sneaking overgeneralizing, labeling, demandingness, and other unscientific verbalizations into their thinking and behaving. It employs a scientific technique called *semantic precision* or *accurate language* to do this, and in this respect is one of the very few therapies that puts Korzybski's theory of language and meaning into therapeutic practice.

Biological Underpinnings of Behavior

Although I was mainly an environmentalist as a young psychologist, when I practiced REBT for a few years I saw that people are born as well as reared to think irrationally and dysfunctionally and to sink their crooked thinking into inappropriate feelings and self-sabotaging behaviors. I believe that Korzybski held similar views, for he consistently shows how practically all people at all times in all parts of the world make profound semantic errors and thereby help upset themselves and others. If our parents and our culture mainly taught us to overgeneralize, label, and commit the cognitive misperceptions and jumping to conclusions that Korzybski talks about, some of us would do so and some of us would not. But all of us, to one degree or another, often seem to be embroiled in these kinds of errors. So although there appears to be some environmentally-inculcated factors in our doing so, we also seem to be innately prone to distorted semantic processes. Thus, Korzybski notes, "Practically all humans, the most primitive not included, have some types of either-or orientation."[11] And, "Our old habits of evaluation, ingrained for centuries if not millenniums, must be reevaluated."[12] And again, "A 'name' involves for a given individual a whole constellation of configuration of labeling, defining, evaluating, etc., unique for each individual, according to his socio-cultural, linguistic environment and his heredity."[13]

REBT and general semantics, then, seem to fully acknowledge the important biological as well as environmental roles in human dysfunctional thinking.

Self-Change and Self-Actualization

While general semantics and REBT seem to agree that people are innately predisposed to create and construct semantic errors, they also agree that people can learn to minimally do so. REBT says that just because humans are active constructivists, rather than passively conditioned to be disturbed by their parents, teachers, and culture, they also have the innate tendency to change themselves and choose to behave less defeatingly. They are thus able to think about their thinking, realistically assess their unrealistic attitudes, dispute their irrational beliefs, and work hard at reconstructing their disordered thoughts, feelings, and behaviors. Moreover, once they keep working at reformulating their disturbed ideas and feelings, they can also creatively work at growing, developing, and bringing about greater degrees of happiness and involvement.

Korzybski and his followers obviously have similar ideas. The Institute of General Semantics and many members of the institute solidly believe that people can be taught the principles of general semantics and be shown how to think and communicate more clearly with themselves and each other and thereby help themselves change. REBT and general semantics are both psychoeducational approaches to helping humans improve their intrapersonal and interpersonal relationships.

The Use of E-Prime

In order to encourage people to give up the *is* of predication and the *is* of identity, Bourland advocated and used E-Prime, the English language without any inclusion of various forms of the verb *to be* or its various tenses. Although writing in E-Prime is difficult and does not completely make a writer and reader avoid all linguistic and semantic errors, it does offer some help. REBT has favored E-Prime more than has any other form of psychotherapy, and I think it is still the only form of therapy that has some of its main books written in E-Prime.

Use of Forceful Persuasion

Korzybski noted that we humans have "to change our habitual methods of thinking, and this is not so easy as it seems."[14] He implied that our overgeneralized, misleading thinking gets into our body-mind system and into our action-habit patterns. REBT has always said that thinking, feeling, and behaving are not disparate, but importantly influence and affect each other. As I noted in my very first paper on REBT, delivered in 1956: "Thinking...is and to some extent has to be sensory, motor, and emotional behavior...Emotion, like thinking and the sensori-motor processes, we may define as an exceptionally complex state of human reaction which is integrally related to all the other perception and response processes. It is not one thing, but a combination and holistic integration of several seemingly diverse, yet actually closely related, phenomena."[15]

Because of its holistic emphasis, REBT has always favored strong and direct cognitive, emotive, and behavioral methods of showing people exactly what they are doing to needlessly disturb themselves and what they can do to active-directively minimize their self-disturbance. In consonance with Korzybski's disavowal of either/or solutions to human problems, REBT does not favor *either* thinking *or* emotive *or* behavioral methods of therapy. It consciously and actively employs all three kinds of therapy, and, following and/also and et cetera facilitations, it has no hesitation in combining psychotherapy with pharmacological treatment, environmental changes, and any other kinds of psychophysical methods that are likely to help various clients.

Realism and Profound Philosophic Change

Korzybski was in many ways a profound realist and empiricist, and noted that the revised structure of language that he advocated "necessitates 'thinking' in terms of 'facts,' or visualizing processes, before making generalizations."[16] He also noted that while Aristotelian either-or language fosters our evaluating "by definition" or "intension," his own "non-Aristotelian or physico-mathematical orientation involves evaluating 'by extension,' taking into consideration the actual 'facts' in the particular situation confronting us."[17]

REBT's original method of helping people to dispute (at point D) their self-defeating ideas, inferences, attributions, and overgeneralizations, showed them how to scientifically challenge these ideas in the light of "reality" or "facts." Thus, if Joan asks Harry to marry her and he refuses to do so, she may foolishly conclude: "I made a mistake in asking him"; "He hates me!"; and "That proves I'm no good, that I am a bad person!" REBT, and the other main cognitive-behavior therapies often confront Joan with the "facts," which tend to show that her inferences about Harry's refusal are invalid overgeneralizations, because: Joan was probably right, not wrong, in asking Harry to marry her, for by doing so she has gained some valuable information about his feelings for her; there is no evidence that Harry hates her, but only evidence that he doesn't want to marry her and live with her (actually, he may deeply love her and still, for various reasons, not want to marry her); his refusal to marry her never proves, of course, that she *is* no good nor *is* a bad person, though it may possibly show that "factually," or in Harry's eyes, she has some undesirable traits.

REBT and Cognitive-Behavior Therapy therefore use "facts" or "reality" to show Joan her dysfunctional beliefs, and they therefore accord with Korzybski's views. But REBT goes further than the other therapies and asks, in Joan's case, "What is the underlying musturbatory overgeneralization that leads an intelligent woman like Joan to make such silly inferences that are obviously unsupported by the 'facts' or 'reality'?"

Seek and ye shall find. Looking for Joan's tacit, implicit, or unconscious musts that she probably believes and from which she largely derives her antifactual inferences, we find that she very likely brings in her proposal to Harry the basic, core philosophy: "Whenever I ask any person I really like, such as Harry, to grant me any important favor, such as marrying me, he *absolutely must under all conditions* accede to my requests, or else: I made a mistake in asking; he or she hates me; and that proves I am no good and that I am a bad person."

In other words, I am contending that if Korzybski were a psychotherapist—which, actually, he partially was—he would surely have disputed Joan's irrational inferences and refuted them "factually" and "empirically." But I suggest he would also look, as REBT does (and as most other cognitive-behavior therapies do not), for the higher-order abstractions that seem to lie behind and to help instigate many of Joan's disturbance-creating inferences.

Korzybski noted that "making us conscious of our unconscious assumptions is essential."[18] He also said that "abstracting by necessity involves evaluating, whether conscious or not, and so the process of abstracting may be considered as a process of evaluating stimuli."[19] Again: "The fact that we do not abstract on higher orders becomes a danger if we are not conscious that we are doing so and retain the primitive confusions of identifications of orders of abstractions."[20]

If I interpret Korzybski correctly, he is saying here that to understand ourselves in depth we need not look only for our conscious inferences about unfortunate events in our lives (such as Joan's conscious inferences about her self when Harry rejects her) but we need also look for our unconscious, tacit assumptions that underlie many of our self-disturbing inferences. This is what REBT does when it looks for core "musturbatory" philosophies behind Joan's (and other people's) antifactual inferences. In this respect, REBT is not only more depth-centered than most other cognitive-behavior therapies, and is not only one of the most constructivist therapies in today's world, but it also—ironically enough!—seems to be considerably more depth-centered than psychoanalysis. Why? Because psychoanalysis is not particularly philosophic, does not explore and look behind people's disturbing assumptions, creates vague, almost undefinable higher-order abstractions of its own (such as ego, id, and superego) and almost entirely ignores the depth-centered semantic problems that Korzybski raised and went a long way toward solving.

A purely Korzybskian analysis of people's cognitive-emotional-behavioral problems, such as Wendell Johnson attempted, will, I wager, do people more good and much less harm than will psychoanalysis. When REBT is employed, incorporating as it does much of Korzybski's work with other important elements of cognitive-behavior therapy, I predict even more depth-centered, philosophically profound therapy will often occur. Compared to this kind of "deep" analysis, psycho-analysis seems to be quite superficial.

Conclusion

As I think can be seen by many of the parallels between REBT and Korzybski's general semantics, the two disciplines overlap in many important respects. This is hardly coincidental, as I was distinctly influenced by several of Korzybski's ideas when formulating and developing REBT. This does not mean that were Alfred Korzybski alive today he would enthusiastically endorse REBT and place it above all the other psychotherapies. In keeping with his own extensional thinking, I would guess that he would agree with *some* of REBT's theory and practice *some* of the time under *some* conditions. As my own life and my practice of REBT continues, I try to take a similar attitude. REBT practice works quite well some of the time under some conditions with some people. It is not, and will never be, a panacea for all of all people's cognitive-emotive-behavioral problems. There is no reason for it to take an either-or position, nor to claim that all people with all disturbances have to be treated with REBT or else they will not improve. Rubbish! As Korzybski would probably have recommended, and as I have previously noted, REBT needs to be integrated with the most useful of other therapies so that it becomes and remains effective with many (but not all) people much (but not all) of the time.

27

Is Psychoanalysis Harmful?

When I wrote this article in 1967, psychoanalysis, particularly of the Freudian kind, was far and away the leading form of psychotherapy in the United States. Other modes of therapy, including REBT and cognitive behavior therapy, had not yet become very popular, and those that were beginning to be practiced more, such as Reichian, Sullivanian, Horneyian, Transactional Analysis, Gestalt, and object relations therapy, included a great deal of psychoanalytic theory and practice. At that time, even early behavior therapy, which was much more active than psychoanalysis, emphasized the early childhood origin of emotional disturbance and largely omitted its constructionist philosophic underpinnings.

Naturally, REBT was anathema to the psychoanalysts of the day, and they savagely reviled it and me for widely promoting it. I was denounced for being "superficial," "intellectual," "authoritarian,"—you name it. Of course, I expected this kind of misinterpretation and vilification of REBT and me personally, and I nicely used REBT methods on myself to work against being hurt and hostile because of this "unfair" criticism. I hardly always succeeded, and sometimes, at public symposia, returned heated attacks of my analytically-biased opponents.

Mainly, however, I presented my antianalytic views (and data) calmly and forcefully and almost always won over good parts of my audience to my side. My refusal to upset myself about the vituperation of the analysts often won out. One time at the University of Nebraska Medical School, the director of the Department of Psychiatry cut off my invited address a full hour before it was to end, with the specious excuse that we were running out of time; I was healthfully sorry and disappointed but not unhealthfully angry or depressed, and induced many of my listeners to join me in another room to discuss my views on REBT. The director of the Department of Psychiatry nearly split a gut.

When a conventional journal, *Psychiatric Opinion*, asked me to write an article on the harmfulness of psychoanalysis, I was happy to do so. I did such a good—though brief—job in this paper that my plans for doing an entire book on REBT and psychoanalysis were postponed. They still are, because of the effectiveness of this article. I received scores of requests for reprints of it, and it has been widely quoted in the psychological literature. So to this day I have felt no need to publish a more complete account of the harm of psychoanalysis. If I live long enough perhaps I shall do so, as I could say a good deal more about it than I say in this paper. Here, however, without apology, are some of the main points I made over thirty years ago about psychoanalytic shortcomings.

Many articles and books have been written which purport to show that psychoanalysis is an ineffective form of psychotherapy. Behavior therapists, existentialists, physical scientists, rational philosophers, Marxists, and many other kinds of thinkers have held that psychoanalytic therapy rests on unverified assumptions and that it is largely a waste of time. Relatively few critics, however, have objectively pointed out some of the actual harm that may occur if an individual enters classical psychoanalysis or even undergoes intensive psychoanalytic psychotherapy.

To give and to document all the main reasons why virtually any form of truly psychoanalytic therapy is frequently injurious to clients would take a sizable book, and someday I may write it. For the present, let me briefly and inadequately outline some ways in which analysis does more harm than good.

Sidetracking

Probably the greatest harm that psychoanalysis does is sidetrack clients from what they need to do to improve and to give them a "good" excuse not to work hard at helping themselves. What disturbed people preferably should do is fairly simple (although it is not at all easy), namely, to understand precisely the self-defeating irrational ideas they firmly believe and vigorously contradict them, both verbally and actively. Thus one of the main senseless notions they usually hold is, "Unless I am remarkably competent and popular, and unless I am superior to others, I am rather worthless as an individual." They can strongly contradict this philosophy by asking themselves, "Why am I no good just because many of my *performances* are poor? Where is the evidence that I cannot accept myself if others do not like me? How is my self-acceptance really dependent on external criteria?" And they can actively work against their self-defeating attitudes by performing, even when they may not do very well; by risking social disapproval when they want to achieve a desired goal; and by experimenting with potentially enjoyable pursuits in spite of the possibilities of failure and rejection.

Psychoanalysis verbally sidetracks health-seeking individuals by encouraging them to concentrate on innumerable irrelevant events and ideas: such as what happened during their early years, how they came to have an Oedipus complex, the pernicious influence of their unloving parents, the meanings of their dreams, how all-important are their relations with the analyst, how much they now unconsciously hate their mates, and so forth. These may all be interesting pieces of information about clients, but they not only do not reveal, they often seriously obscure, their basic irrational philosophies that originally caused, and that still instigate, their dysfunctional feelings and behavior. Being mainly diagnostic and psychodynamic, analysis is practically allergic to philosophy, and therefore often never gets around to the basic ideological assumptions and value systems with which humans largely *create* their symptoms.

To make matters much worse, psychoanalysis is essentially a talky, passive, insight-seeking process which encourages clients mainly to lie on their spine or sit on their behinds in order to get better. Sensible unorthodox analysts frequently supplement this passive procedure by giving advice, directing the clients to do something, helping them change their environment, etc., but they do so against psychoanalytic theory, which stoutly insists that they do otherwise. Meanwhile, the poor analysands, who have probably remained disturbed for most of their lives largely because they will *not* get off their asses and take risk after risk, are firmly encouraged, by the analytic procedure and by the nondirective behavior of the analyst, to continue their avoidant behavior. They now have the excuse that they are "actively" trying to help themselves by being analyzed. But, of course, this is a delusion if anything like classical procedures are being followed, and they consequently tend to become more passive, and possibly even more disturbed, than before.

Dependency

Most clients are over-dependent individuals who are afraid to think and act for themselves and to risk being criticized for making mistakes. Psychoanalysis is usually a process that greatly fosters dependency. The sessions are often several times a week; they continue for a period of years; the analyst frequently forbids the client to make any major changes in his life during treatment; a positive transference between the analyst and analysand is usually encouraged; the clients are constantly brainwashed into accepting analytic interpretations, even when they seem to have a far-fetched relationship to the facts of their lives; and in analytic group therapy, a familylike setting is often deliberately fostered and maintained. While many forms of therapy also abet the patient's being dependent on the therapist, classical analysis is surely one of the worst, and psychoanalytically-oriented psychotherapy one of the second-worst, modes in this respect. On the other hand, several activity-directed forms of therapy, such as assertive therapy, REBT, and structured therapy, urge clients, as soon as feasible, into independent action and teach them how to think clearly for themselves

Emphasis on Feelings

Because it heavily emphasizes free association, dream analysis, and the involvement of the client and therapist in transference and countertransference relations, psychoanalysis inevitably puts a premium on the expression of feelings rather than the undermining of neurotic ideas. A good deal of the improvement in analytic therapy seems to come from clients' feeling better, as a result of catharsis and abreaction, and because they believe that the analyst really understands and likes them. This tendency of clients to *feel* better, however, frequently sabotages their potential to *get* better.

Thus, the analysand who is terribly depressed about his being refused a job and who gets these feelings off his chest in an individual or group session will often come away relieved, and feel that at least his analyst (or the group) heard him out, that someone really cares for him, and that maybe he's not such a worthless slob after all. Unfortunately, in getting himself to "feel good," he forgets to inquire about the self-defeating beliefs he told himself that maintain his depression, namely, "If this employer who interviewed me today doesn't like me, probably *no* employer will, and if I can't get a very good job like this one, that proves that I'm incompetent and that I don't really deserve anything good in life." The expressive, cathartic-abreactive method that is such a common part of analysis doesn't encourage this client to stop and think about his philosophic premises; instead, it enables him to "feel good"—at least momentarily—in spite of the fact that he strongly retains these same premises, and in spite of the fact that he will almost certainly depress himself, because of his holding them, again and again.

In the expression of hostility that psychoanalysis encourages, the situation is even worse. Starting with the assumption that it is bad for the client to feel hostile and to hold in her hostile feelings—which is a fairly sensible assumption since there is evidence to support it—psychoanalysts usually derive from this view another, and rather false, assumption: that the *expression* of hostile feelings will release and cure basic hostility. Nothing of the sort is probably true; in fact, just the opposite frequently happens. The individual who, in analytic sessions, is encouraged to express her hatred for her mother, husband, or boss may well end up becoming still more hostile, acting in an overtly nasty fashion to this other person, engendering return hostility, and then becoming still more irate.

Moreover, expression of hostility is one of the best psychological cop-outs. By convincing herself that other people are awful and that they deserve to be hated, the client can easily ignore her own maladaptive behavior and self-loathing and can nicely avoid doing anything to look into her own heart to change her irrational thinking and her dysfunctional feelings and acts. One of the main functions of an effective therapist is to help the client minimize her hostility (while keeping her dislike of unfortunate events and nasty people, so that she can do something to solve her problems connected with them). Psychoanalysis, because it falsely believes that present hostility stems from past occurrences (rather than largely from the individual's philosophic attitude toward and consequent interpretations about those occurrences), has almost no method of getting at the main sources of hatred and eradicating them. By failing to show the client how to change her anger-creating views and by encouraging her to become more hostile in many instances, it tends to harm probably the majority of analytic clients (or should we say victims?).

Bolsters Conformism

The main reasons why most human beings feel sufficiently disturbed to come for therapy are their misleading beliefs that they *need* the love and approval of others, that they can't possibly be happy at all when they are alone, and that unless they are successful they are no damned good. Because psychoanalysis is essentially nonphilosophic, and because it does not show clients how to distinguish clearly between their *wanting* and their *needing* to be approved of and successful, most analysands wind up, at best, becoming better adapted to the popularity- and achievement-demanding culture in which they live rather than becoming persons in their own right who give themselves permission to think and enjoy themselves in unconforming ways. Psychoanalysis basically teaches the client, "Since your parents were overly critical and therefore made you hate yourself, and since you are able to see that I, your analyst, uncritically accept you in spite of your poor behavior, you can now accept yourself." And also, "Since you have been achieving on a low level because you were afraid to compete with your father or your brother, and I have helped you gain insight into this reason for your doing poorly, you can now compete successfully with practically anyone and make the million dollars you always wanted to make."

What psychoanalysis fails to teach the individual is: "You can always unqualifiedly accept yourself even if I, your analyst, do not particularly like you, because your value to yourself rests on your existence, your being, and not on how much *anyone* approves you." And: "There are several reasons why succeeding at vocational or avocational activities is usually advantageous; but you don't *have* to be outstanding, ultrasuccessful, or noble in order to accept yourself. The main purpose of life is not necessarily achievement, but often enjoyment."

Because analysis is largely concerned with historical events in people's lives rather than their ideological reactions to these events; because it encourages passivity and dependency; because it over-emphasizes the personal relationship between the analyst and analysand—for these and other reasons it often encourages clients to be more successful conformers rather than ever-growing, courageously experimenting, relatively free persons. The analyst himself, rigidly-bound as he often is by the orthodox rules of the therapeutic game he is playing, and self-condemned by following these rules to be a nonassertive, undaring individual himself, tends to set a bad example for the client and to encourage her or him to be a *re*actor rather than an actor in the drama we call life.

Strengthens Irrationality

Clients' basic problems often stem from assuming irrational premises and making illogical deductions from them. If they are to be helped with their basic disturbance, they had better learn to question their assumptions and think more logically and discriminate more clearly about the various things that happen to them and the attitudes they take toward these happenings. In particular, they'd better realize that their *preferences* or *desires* are not truly *needs* or *demands,* and that just because it would be better if something occurred, this is no reason why it absolutely *should, ought to,* or *must* occur.

Instead of helping clients with this kind of cognitive, semantic, and logical analysis, psychoanalysis provides them with many unfalsifiable premises and irrationalities of its own. It usually insists that they must be disturbed because of past events in their lives; that they *need* to be loved and *have to* become angry when thwarted; that they must have years of intensive analysis in order to change significantly; that they must get into and finally work through an intense transference relationship with their analyst, etc. All these assumptions—as is the case with most psychoanalytic hypotheses—are either dubious or misleading, and analysands are given additional irrationalities to cope with over and above the handicapping crooked thinking they bring to therapy. In innumerable instances, they become so obsessed with their analytic nonsense that psychoanalysis becomes their religious creed and their be-all and end-all for existing, and though it may somewhat divert them from the nonsense with which they first came to therapy, it does not really eliminate it but at best covers it up with this new psychoanalytic mode of "positive thinking." Rather than becoming less suggestible and more of a critical thinker through analysis, they frequently become worse in these respects.

Absorbs and Sabotages Health Potentials

When clients come for psychoanalysis, they are usually reasonably young and have considerable potential for achieving mental health, even though they are now disturbed. Psychoanalysis, particularly in its classical modes, is such a long-winded, time-consuming, expensive process that it often takes many of the best years of clients' lives and prevents them from using these years productively. To make matters much worse, in most instances analytic therapy leads to such abysmally poor results that analysands are often highly discouraged, are convinced that practically all the time and money they spent for analysis is wasted, that there is no possibility of their ever changing, and that they'd better avoid all other types of psychotherapy for the rest of their lives and adjust themselves, as best they can, to living with their disturbances. An untold number of ex-analysands have become utterly disillusioned with all psychological treatment because they believe that psychoanalysis *is* psychotherapy, and that if they received such poor results from being analyzed nothing else could possibly work for them. If the facts in this regard were ever known, it is likely to be found that analysis harms more people in this way than in any of the other many ways it is deleterious. The number of people in the United States alone who feel that they cannot afford any more therapy because they fruitlessly spent many thousands of dollars in psychoanalysis is probably considerable.

Wrong Therapeutic Goals

The two main functions of psychotherapy, when it is sanely done, are: to show clients how they can significantly change their disordered thinking, emoting, and behaving; and to help them, once they are no longer severely disturbed, lead a more creative, fulfilling, growing existence. Instead of these two goals, psychoanalysis largely follows a third one: to help people understand or gain insight into themselves, and particularly to understand the *history* of their disturbances.

Humans—in contradistinction to the analytic assumptions—do not usually modify their basic thoughts and behaviors by insight into their past, relating to a therapist, or even understanding their present irrational assumptions and conflicting value systems. They change mainly by work and effort. They consequently had better be helped to *use* their insights, which usually means to concretely understand what they are believing and assuming right now, in the present, and to actively challenge and question these self-defeating beliefs and assumptions until they finally change them. They also had better be helped to act, experiment, accept discomforts, and force themselves to do many things of which they are irrationally afraid so that their *actions* effectively depropagandize them to give up their dysfunctional beliefs.

Psychoanalytic therapy, instead of devoting much time to encouraging and teaching clients to dispute and act against their self-defeating thoughts, feelings, and behaviors, takes them up the garden path into all kinds of irrelevant (though sometimes accurate) insights, which gives them a lovely excuse to cop out from doing the work, practice, effort, and self-deprivation by which alone they are likely to truly change their basic self-sabotaging philosophies of life. Even if it were a good method of psychological *analysis* (which it actually is not), it is an execrable method of *synthesis*. It does not notably help people make themselves whole again, and it particularly does not show them how to live more fulfillingly when they have, to some degree, stopped needlessly upsetting themselves. Because it implicitly and explicitly encourages people to remain pretty much the way they are, though perhaps to get a better understanding of themselves (and often to construct better defenses so that they can live more efficiently *with* their irrational assumptions about themselves and others), it frequently does more harm, by stopping them from really making a concerted attack on their fundamental disturbances. They would usually benefit more if they received a nonanalytic form of psychotherapy or even if they resolutely tried to help themselves by reading, talking to others, and doing some hard thinking.

Summary

Psychoanalysis in general and classical analysis in particular are fundamentally wrong in their assumptions about why human beings become emotionally disturbed and what can and should be done to help them become less anxious and hostile. Consequently, analytic therapy largely wastes considerable time teaching clients often-mistaken theories about themselves and others. Although these theories are frequently highly interesting and diverting, they at best may help the client to *feel* better rather than to *get* better.

The one thing that analysis usually insures is that analysands will *not* understand the philosophic core of their disturbance-creating tendencies, and consequently will *not* work and practice, in both a verbal-theoretical and active-motor way, to change their basic assumptions about themselves and the world, and thereby ameliorate their symptoms and make themselves less disturbable. Although ostensibly an intensive and ultra-depth-centered form of psychotherapy, analysis is actually an exceptionally superficial, palliative form of treatment. Because it deludes clients that they are truly getting better by following its rules, and because it dissuades them from doing the difficult reorganizing of their underlying philosophical assumptions, psychoanalysis usually does more harm than good and is contraindicated in the majority of instances in which it is actually used.

My rather biased opinion is that analysts frequently help people by sneaking nonanalytic or antianalytic forms of treatment into their "psychoanalysis." But the closer they stick to truly psychoanalytic theory and practice, the more harm they tend to do.

28

How I Manage to Be a Rational *Rational Emotive Behavior Therapist*

I was invited to participate in a symposium, "Leaving It at the Office—Preventing and Ameliorating Distress," sponsored by several divisions of the American Psychological Association Annual Convention in New York, on August 14, 1995. I was delighted to appear with a highly respectable panel whose members I knew would be uptight about telling the audience how they really handled their own problems as therapists and as persons. I decided to present myself frankly and honestly and rouse some heated discussion.

Our panel had six speakers, and each of us had only ten minutes in which to present. As I am famous for doing at professional meetings, I used my regular Anglo-Saxon language, said what I really wanted to say, and took the chance that one of the conventional psychological journals would not print my talk because of my outspokenness. Well, I was right about this. Though all the papers of the symposium would normally have been published, the chairman decided not to submit our papers because of my use of four-letter words. So be it. I published it in our own journal, the *Journal of Rational-Emotive and Cognitive-Behavior Therapy,* which of course will publish almost any damned thing I write. However, I would have been more interested in seeing what reaction it would have produced had it been published in a conventional professional publication. I can only imagine!

More seriously, I still stand by this honest appraisal of therapists, including myself, and their problems as professionals and as persons. Many of them are so disturbed to begin with that they are driven into therapy. Then they meet difficult customers as clients and become more disturbed. Then they often become disturbed about their double disturbances. It's circular and endless! If they used REBT on themselves, as I briefly show in this paper, they would presumably stop their disturbances in their tracks.

How the hell do I leave my work at the office and stubbornly refuse to take my clients home with me? By doing the same thing with myself that I advise for the therapists I supervise at the Albert Ellis Institute. As you might slightly suspect, most of them are pretty nutty. No, not because they are therapists, but because they are human.

For many years now I have had the quaint idea that all humans— yes, the whole five billion of them on this planet—are out of their fucking minds. No, not because I extrapolate from my clients, who are admittedly neurotic. I also have closely observed my friends and relatives, who usually pretend to be sensible and sane. But having a number of friends and relatives of your own, of course you know how batty they are. Or haven't you noticed?

Now I have another quaint idea—that I, too, am human, and therefore reasonably screwy. Moreover, having figured out a marvelous theory of human disturbance—which I now call Rational Emotive Behavior Therapy (REBT)—I take the unprejudiced view that it most probably applies to me too. So I apply it.

I assume—as the principles of REBT brilliantly posit—that if and when I am out of my goddamned head, I foolishly make myself dogmatically "musturbate" about my goals and desires instead of merely strongly *preferring* to fulfill them. I do this as a person, as a friend, as a relative—and even as a therapist. Like other people, including the screwballs I therapize and supervise, I often construct and create—not to mention imbibe and adopt from my not-too-rational culture—three neurotic commands and insistences:

1. I (ego) *absolutely must* be an outstanding therapist, *must* help practically all my clients incredibly, and *must* be totally adored by them—and by all my colleagues, relatives, friends, and country-

men and countrywomen as well—for being so outstandingly great! If I don't prodigiously excel, as again I *must*, I am a turd for acting turdily and I'd better go back to being a beachcomber.

2. My clients *must* heed everything I say *completely*, *must* love me dearly, *must always* work their asses off to help themselves improve, and must spread the word of my miracle cures to everyone they meet. If they don't react to my therapy as they utterly *must*, they deserve to stay miserable forever—damn their stubborn hides!

3. The conditions that prevail in therapy, as well as in my general life, *unquestionably must* be totally easy, comfortable, and enjoyable. If they are not and if therapy includes any hassles, troubles, or lack of enormous rewards, it's awful and horrible! I can't stand it! I might as well quit and win ten million dollars in the lottery or marry a rich partner to take care of me!

Being a fallible human and having extraordinarily little power to be a perfect therapist, to induce all my clients to kiss my ass in Macy's window, and to make every single therapy session 110 percent hassle-free, I have for the last forty years used the principles and practice of Rational Emotive Behavior Therapy (REBT) to forcefully dispute my irrational beliefs—such as the "musturbatory" horseshit just described—until I take it out of my head and heart and (hopefully!) stick it up my behind. Why should I insanely keep following it when I try so hard in my office to help my clients become aware of their own irrationalities and work hard to reduce them? What do you think I am—stupid?

Shall I be more specific about how I leave my work at the office? Indeed I shall. Actually, I paradoxically *don't* leave my therapy at the office. I first use it at the office itself—on *me*, I mean, and not just on my poor benighted clients. I then take it with me wherever I go: at home, at social affairs, on my trips to give talks and workshops, and when I write on planes, trains, or wherever else I can wield a pen or rattle away on a typewriter.

At all of these places and in all these situations, I often make myself quite aware of my absolutistic shoulds, oughts, musts, and demands, and actively and forcefully lambaste them with a number of cognitive, emotive, and behavioral methods that I constantly practice by showing my REBT clients how to use them. Employing these active-directive methods on myself, I consistently, though still imperfectly, come up with the following profound core antimusturbatory philosophies:

There is no damned reason why I *absolutely must* be an outstanding therapist, colleague, socialite, or anything else! That would be lovely and perhaps beneficial. But if few or none of my clients, supervisees, and other people approve of me and follow my teachings, that's TFB—too fucking bad! I am determined to always give myself unconditional self-acceptance *whether or not* I perform well and *whether or not* I am loved and approved.

My clients, supervisees, and associates never *have to* listen to me, heed my teachings, or work hard to improve themselves as I would *like* them to. As fallible humans, they have the right to wrongly ignore and frustrate me. It is highly unfortunate, but never awful and unbearable, for them to foolishly resist me. TS: Tough shit! That's the way they behave right now—and that's the way they *should* behave, because, alas, they *do*! In my opinion they often *act* badly, but they are never, never, never bad *people*! They are often talented at resisting my noble efforts to help them, as, again, they right now *should* be!

The conditions that often prevail in therapy don't always *have to* be easy, comfortable, and enjoyable. In fact, they often aren't. Unfortunate! Inconvenient! But not the end of the world. Just a royal pain in the ass! Now how can I do my best to improve them—or unwhiningly accept what I can't change? What's my alternative? More silly whining!

Do I steadily use these REBT core philosophies either in or outside the office? No—inside *and* outside. Still, I, a fallible human, often bother myself while I am doing therapy, and when I am away from it. But not for long! Bullshit is bullshit—whether it be my clients' or my own. So I use the same antihokum with them and with myself. Even if they foolishly refuse to accept it, *I* am not exactly that stupid! Obviously not!

The Evolution of Albert Ellis and Rational Emotive Behavior Therapy

The Evolution of Psychotherapy Conference is held every five years, led by Dr. Jeffrey Zeig of the Milton H. Erickson Foundation. It includes outstanding psychotherapists, such as Victor Frankl, Carl Rogers, and Rollo May. I have always been one of the main participants, and for its third conference in 1995 I presented this paper. For a change, it is largely biographical and shows some of my personal experiences and philosophies that led to the creation of REBT.

In commenting on this paper at the conference, Aaron Tim Beck said: "There is no question that [Ellis] was the pioneer in modern-day psychotherapy. He really cleared the road for the rest of us who followed behind him.... He's absolutely right about the shoulds and the musts....I do want to...personally thank him for what he's done in helping me to develop my own therapeutic techniques." Thank you, Tim Beck, for doing so much research to promote and develop cognitive therapy.

I have picked quite a topic for myself!—"The Evolution of Albert Ellis and Rational Emotive Behavior Therapy." Even if I stick to only the first part of the topic—"The Evolution of Albert Ellis"—I could easily take the whole fifty hours of this conference to partly summarize that glorious and noble process. That, alas, would leave no time for the other main presenters to show how they magnificently evolved—and they may not like that.

Fortunately, as I shall soon show, I don't give too much of a shit about other presenters disliking me. Most of them already do! They hate me telling them that I am, of course!, right and that they are, indubitably!, wrong. In my youth, I would have stupidly bothered myself about that, shown a dire need for their approval, and would have told them that they were great guys or gals and scholars instead of the real turds I thought they were. What, me be honest and impolite? Never!

It took me almost my first two decades to talk myself out of that crap of being ingratiating. I was born and reared to be shy and scared. Throughout my childhood and teens I had a real social phobia. I viewed public speaking as a fate worse than public masturbation. I opened my physically large mouth only among a group of my close friends. I avoided telling jokes for fear of flubbing the punch lines. I said nothing—literally nothing—about my feelings for the pretty young girls that I kept falling madly—in fact, obsessively-compulsively—in love with. As for approaching any of the young women I immoderately lusted after from the age of twelve onward, forget it! I heard and saw nothing but "evil" and "horrible" rejection, so I kept my big trap shut. In spite of my deranged passion for everything in skirts, up to the age of twenty my dating amounted to zero.

As you can imagine, I was highly unenthusiastic about my extreme social inhibitions. I knew I was scared witless, and from my reading and observations of my more popular male friends, I even knew what to do about it—take risks. I didn't. I decided to—but didn't. I almost began to—and froze.

Naturally, I beat myself for all this evasion. I knew what I wanted—and I knew that I was copping out. So I castigated myself for, first, avoiding "dangerous" social situations; second, feeling desperately anxious about them; and third, knowing how to lick my anxiety and stubbornly refusing to go through the pain of overcoming it.

I even put myself down for the efforts I made to overcome my social phobias. I read many articles and books on psychology and philosophy, particularly from the age of sixteen onward. I became interested in the philosophy of human happiness and made myself much less miserable about some of my other problems. How? Mainly by reading Confucius, Gautama Buddha, Epicurus, Epictetus, Marcus

Aurelius, and other ancient philosophers. Also, from studying modern thinkers like Spinoza, Kant, Hume, Emerson, Thoreau, Santayana, Dewey, and Russell.

I gained a lot in these self-help ventures. In my early teens, I was plagued with insomnia and often was able to sleep only a few restless hours a night. But I learned that I was worrying about sleeping itself and was able to stop that kind of worrying and use monotony-focusing techniques. As a result, I soon was sleeping much better.

I began my writing career at the age of twelve and soon had scores of rejection slips for the stories, essays, and comic poems that I kept sending out. But I strongly convinced myself that I was not a rotten writer—nor certainly a rotten person—when I was not getting published.

At the age of sixteen, I thought I was addicted to masturbation and was guilty about that. No, not because of the sex aspect, but because at first I wrongly thought I was overdoing it and was lacking self-control. But I soon saw that I was not a worm for acting wormily. I managed to accept myself as a happy masturbator, and to never put myself down when my penis went up.

Like most young students, I was also a miserable procrastinator. In high school, I never took a textbook home, did my homework in the ten-minute periods between classes, and studied for exams the night before I had to take them. In college, I did the same for my freshman year but then realized how stupid and self-defeating this was. So I taught myself to finish my term papers within a few weeks after the beginning of the term—which amazed all my professors!—and to allow a few weeks before my exams to study for them. Thus I became, or made myself into, an elegant nonprocrastinator.

As you can see—especially if you are peering behind the lenses of your own neurotic self-defeatism—I did very well with several of my own neuroses in my early and late adolescence. Not—as Carl Rogers might have foolishly claimed—because I had a close, trusting, open, congruent relationship with a therapist or anyone else. I didn't. At that time, I had no close relationships with anyone except my younger brother, Paul. Not with my family, or with any of my good number of male acquaintances. Certainly not with any of the women I madly loved and would have given my all to be close to.

My main influences—and they were profound—were philosophers, psychologists, essayists, novelists, dramatists, poets, and other writers, all of whom I voluminously ingested And digested For I was never a true believer. I *thought about* what I read, and critically ripped most of it up. I could fairly easily see that Socrates was something of a sophist. That Plato was often a silly idealist. That Kant courageously threw out God and then cravenly brought him in the back door. That Freud was an arrant overgeneralizer. That Jung was a brilliant but sloppily mystical thinker. That Wilhelm Reich was pretty psychotic. That Carl Rogers was a nice fellow but an FFB—fearful fucking baby. Et cetera!

So I *thought about* what I read, and experimentally used it on myself. Later, I tried it out with many of my clients. I did very well, except, at first, with my social phobia. I could speak one-to-one or in small groups of friends; I had school and political associates. But, aside from my brother Paul—who was younger than I and almost always followed my teachings—no really close friends. And no lovers! Hell— as noted above, I had no damned dates.

So at the age of nineteen, mainly for political reasons, I decided to work at overcoming my terror of public speaking. I was appointed the leader of a radical youth group but never spoke for it in public. So I used my philosophical teachings to strongly convince myself that nothing terrible would happen if I spoke for my group, and that however uncomfortable I would be in the process, I would hardly die of this discomfort. In other words, I started to convince myself of the two main philosophies that I later incorporated in Rational Emotive Behavior Therapy:

Unconditional Self-Acceptance (USA). People, including me, can always decide to accept themselves *un*conditionally—just because they *choose* to do so. You, I, and everyone can resolve and agree to accept ourselves *whether or not* we perform well and *whether or not* other people approve of us or love us. Better yet, according to REBT, we can *decide* to only rate our thoughts, feelings, and actions, in accordance with how they fulfill our chosen goals and purposes—but not to rate or evaluate our self, being, essence, or personhood at all. No, not *at all*.

High Frustration Tolerance. We are born and then raised with tendencies to feel highly frustrated and annoyed about many things that happen to us and about many of our unfulfilled desires. This is fine and healthy, because frustration motivates us to improve our lives. But we often also whine and needlessly upset ourselves when bad things happen to us and good things don't. Therefore, in addition to teaching people unconditional self-acceptance, REBT encourages them to have high—though not too high!—frustration tolerance.

Applying these two philosophies to myself in my late teens, I decided to overcome my public speaking phobia. I read that John B. Watson, the first behaviorist, and his assistant, Mary Cover Jones, did in vivo desensitization with young children. They deconditioned them to their fear of mice or rabbits, which they at first placed ten feet away from the children, by distracting them and gradually moving the animals closer to them. In a short time, most of their subjects were joyfully petting these previously terrifying animals.

"Shit," I said to myself. "If in vivo desensitization is good enough for little children, it's good enough for me. I'll try it with my terror of public speaking. If I fail, I fail. If I die of discomfort, I die! Too damned bad!"

REBT was practically born during the next three months. For after anxiously and painfully giving political talks during that time, I discovered several important things. First, I didn't die. Second, I did reasonably well at my talks, in spite of my great discomfort. Third, my anxiety soon began to wear off. Fourth, I got better and better at speaking. In fact, as my friends and listeners pointed out, I later discovered that peculiarly enough, I had a talent for public speaking that had been totally obscured by my horrified avoidance of risking even a single speech.

This was all somewhat unsuspected. But the real surprise was that within several months I started to greatly enjoy public presentations, was practically never anxious in the course of them, and made them a large part of my life. I made what amounted to a 180-degree turn in this respect and effected what is still fairly rare in psychotherapy—a complete cure.

"Great!" I said to myself. "But what is more important to me than public speaking? What do I *really* want to do that I'm completely avoiding doing? Obviously: approaching the 101 percent of women that I lust after and want to mate with. I'd even like to marry a few of them! What the hell am I going to do about that?"

I soon made plans to right the grievous wrong that I had been inflicting on myself and the women of the world. I lived near the Bronx Botanical Gardens, one of the loveliest places in New York. About 150 days a year I went there to smell the flowers, lie on the grass, read, and silently flirt with innumerable women—flirt, but never, never encounter. Typically, I would sit on a bench on the Bronx River Parkway, a few feet away from a seemingly suitable woman seated on another bench. I'd look at her and often she would look back at me, and

I could sense that some of these women were interested. But no matter how much I told myself that the time was ripe to approach, I soon copped out and walked away, cursing myself for my abysmal cowardice. Of course, I knew, especially after my overcoming my public-speaking panic, that I wouldn't die of rejection. But I still felt much too uncomfortable to try even a single approach.

During the summer of 1933, when I was on vacation from college and about to go back for my final year, I gave myself a historic homework assignment that greatly changed my own life—and in some ways changed the history of psychotherapy. I spoke to myself very strongly. "Look!" I said. "You forced yourself to get over the horror of making public speeches and now you're goddamned good at doing that. You actually enjoy it! So why not do the same with your silly terror of picking up women? No nonsense! Do, don't stew!"

My assignment to myself was simple. I would go to the Bronx Botanical Gardens every day in the month of July when it wasn't raining; would look for women sitting alone on park benches; and, instead of sitting a bench away, as I always anxiously did, would sit on the same goddamned bench with them. I would then give myself one minute—one lousy minute!—to talk to each one of them. No debate, no caviling, no nonsense! If they bit me, they bit me! One lousy minute!

That was a very wise homework assignment, for I was knowingly risking failure and rejection, and I was doing what was most uncomfortable for me to do. Moreover, I was giving myself no time to procrastinate about trying, no time to ruminate and thereby to build up my worrying.

Well, I forthrightly did it. I went to the park every day in August and found 130 women sitting alone on a park bench, all manners, shapes, and sizes. Certainly enough to provide me with reasonable excuses—that they were too young, too old, too short, or too tall to talk to. But I allowed myself no excuse whatsoever—none! I sat next to all of them—the entire 130.

I found that thirty of them immediately waltzed away. They rejected me before I even got going! But, I said to myself strongly, "That's okay. That leaves me a sample of an even hundred—good for research purposes!"

So I continued my research. I spoke to the entire hundred of these women, and within one lousy minute! About the birds, the bees, the flowers, the trees, their knitting, their reading—about anything and everything. Mind you, I had never done this a single time before. But I was determined! On to the fray!

If Fred Skinner, who was at that time a young psychologist at Indiana University, had known about my experiment he would have probably concluded that I would have got extinguished. For out of the hundred women I talked to, I was finally able to make only one date—and she didn't show up! But I found, empirically, that nothing terrible happened. No one took out a butcher knife and cut my balls off. They only do that to men *these* days! No one vomited and ran away. No one called a cop. In fact, I had one hundred pleasant conversations, and began to get quite good at talking to strange women in strange places. So good, in fact, that for my second hundred subjects I became more persuasive, and was able to make three different dates with women. None of whom, fortunately, I married.

Once again, as happened with my public speaking, I was able to make a 180-degree change. For the rest of my life I have been able to talk to women whenever I wish to do so—on planes, trains, elevators, park benches—and you name it. And with one of these pickups I actually did live for awhile!

How does all this relate to my finally creating Rational Emotive Behavior Therapy, using it successfully on myself and with thousands of my clients, and promulgating its principles and practices throughout the world? In several important ways. Let me recount just a few of them.

First of all, I discovered the great value of cognition, philosophy, reasoning, and self-persuasion in changing one's dysfunctional feelings and actions. I had been mildly devoted to the ideas of novelists, dramatists, and poets since the age of twelve, and got some great ideas from writers like Byron, Shelley, Fyodor Dostoyevsky, H. G. Wells, George Bernard Shaw, Upton Sinclair, Theodore Dreiser, Edgar Lee Masters, and others. I had been even more deeply devoted to card-carrying philosophers, such as those mentioned above, since the age of sixteen. I thought about what the philosophers I read had said, tried out some of their suggestions, and never would have forced myself to speak uncomfortably in public and to encounter new women without first changing some of my ideas about absolutely *needing* to succeed and *having* to be approved of without help from these sources. So with the aid of these thinkers, I made the understanding of cognitive processes one of the main elements of my prepsychoanalytic therapy from 1943 to 1947, and after I practiced psychoanalysis and found it to be just about the least efficient form of therapy ever invented, I returned to active-directive therapy in 1953, and emphasized cognition again—and again and again!

I was always skeptical of orthodox psychoanalysis, mainly because I read all the major works of Freud, Jung, and other leading analysts between my sixteenth and twentieth years, and found them interesting but unhelpful. Their sexual ideas helped make me into a sexual liberal, but I could easily see that psychodynamic understanding, in itself, led to little personality change. Later on, when I read Fromm, Horney, Sullivan, and other neo-analysts—almost all of whom were actually neo-Adlerians—I became more attached to psychoanalytic inquiry and planned change. But I still saw that it was not sufficiently philosophical and active-directive. Its deficiencies in these respects encouraged me to originate a form of therapy, REBT, that was as active as I had been with myself while I was overcoming my panic about public speaking and socializing.

My early self-training in cognitive and behavioral therapy fortunately turned me off on Carl Rogers, whose therapy was notably deficient in both areas. Carl—who from my personal contact with him always seemed to be somewhat shy and diffident himself—took from the existentialists, such as Martin Heidigger and Paul Tillich, the same philosophy of unconditional self-acceptance (USA) that I also derived from them. But he unfortunately thought that USA could mainly be conveyed to people by modeling and by giving them, personally, unconditional positive regard. He signally failed to see that it usually has to be actively taught and encouraged, as well as given. After working hard to give USA to myself, I realized how passive Rogers was, and therefore incorporated the energetic teaching of USA into REBT.

I learned from writers, and particularly from novelists and dramatists, the value of unconditional other acceptance (UOA). I practiced this on myself when I was sixteen, and decided that my hostility toward my sister, Janet, wasn't doing me, her, or anyone else any good, and was in fact sabotaging some of my own desires. So, although Janet at that time was a royal pain in the ass to me, our family, and most other people, I decided to forgive her and permit her to use my large collection of popular and semiclassical songs. My brother Paul, who still hated Janet, was startled to see the change in me and never went along with it until many years later. But I saw that I felt immensely better and relieved, stopped obsessing myself with negative thoughts about her, and actually benefited from several nice things that she did for me thereafter. So I kept working at forgiving my enemies, and incorporated unconditional acceptance of others, along with many antihostility techniques, into REBT.

I particularly noted, when I discovered that my anxiety *about* my sleeping was interfering with my sleeping, that I had both primary and secondary symptoms of my neurosis. I may have been aided in this respect by philosophers, some of whom noted the same thing. Thus, Seneca, over two thousand years ago, was perhaps the first to note what Franklin D. Roosevelt's speechwriter later cribbed from him: "We have nothing to fear but fear itself." So I may have been impressed with that. I was especially helped by a book I read on insomnia when I was seventeen, which pointed out that first insomniacs worry about some problem or possible failure, and thereby keep themselves awake. But once they produce their symptom, insomnia, they worry about having this symptom—and then create a secondary symptom that may be worse than the primary one in keeping them from sleeping. So, as noted above, I worked at stopping worrying about my possible failures, as well as at stopping my worrying about losing sleep, and did very well at improving my insomnia.

When I started to do therapy, and especially when I stopped doing psychoanalysis, I saw clearly that a large percentage of my clients had both primary and secondary symptoms—especially anxiety about anxiety and depression about depression—and I incorporated into REBT the techniques of therapists' assuming that this kind of disturbance often exists, pointing it out to clients, and showing these clients how to minimize it.

Perhaps the most distinctive aspect of REBT that is somewhat different from the theories of other cognitive behavior therapies (CBTs), such as those of A. T. Beck, J. S. Beck, Arnold Lazarus, Michael Mahoney, Maxie Maultsby, Donald Meichenbaum, and Victor Raimy, is its assumption that the basic philosophies, schemas, or core irrational beliefs that people usually follow to make themselves neurotic largely involve their adopting and creating absolutist musts. Virtually all the popular CBTs include these musts but do not hold, as does REBT, how basic and underlying they are, and how they lead to most of the other profound irrationalities, such as awfulizing, I-can't-stand-it-itis, and self-denigration, with which people often plague themselves. I saw this fairly clearly when I read Karen Horney's *Neurosis and Human Growth* in 1950, because she emphasized the "tyranny of the shoulds."

Actually, however, I had largely figured out this exceptionally important trigger of emotional disturbance from reading several philosophers, especially Epictetus, and from my personal experience in 1936, when I was twenty-three years of age. At this time I was madly in love with Karyl, the woman who was to become my first wife, and I was getting nowhere with her because of her indecision about how much she loved me in return. On the one hand, she would say her love for me would put Heloise's passion for Abelard to shame. On the other hand, a few days later she would say I was too esthetic for her, show interest in other men, and neglect me considerably. Several talks with her and thirty-page letters to her about her inconsistency got me and her nowhere. She rigidly stuck to her indecisiveness.

One midnight, when I had spent a wonderfully conflicting evening with Karyl and was on my way home to my apartment in the Bronx, I was sorely troubled about our still seesawing relationship and decided to go for a walk by the lake in Bronx Botanical Gardens and reconsider our on-and-off affair. In walking around the deserted lake, I thoughtfully decided that my love for Karyl was stupendous but that it had too much pain attached to it—especially when she continued her stark ambivalence. Maybe, I thought, I should quit the whole affair and find someone who would love me steadily instead of with startling intermittency.

Suddenly I saw the way out of my dilemma—not to mention Karyl's. It was not my strong *desire* for her that gave me so much trouble when it was not thoroughly fulfilled. No, it was my dire *need* for her love. I foolishly believed that she *absolutely had* to return my feelings in kind, and that and only that would solve our problem. Well, that was horseshit! I saw that if I wished, I could keep my powerful desire, urge, and love for Karyl—and I could simultaneously give up my need, demand, and insistence that she feel exactly the same way I did.

That was really an astonishing insight: I could love without needing! Indeed, I now started to see that all those other girls with whom I kept obsessively falling in love with since the age of five, whom I couldn't get out of my mind, and whom I was terribly anxious about their loving me back, were in the same category as Karyl. I foolishly thought that I *needed* them—that I couldn't live happily without them, and *had to* cement a stupendous relationship with them forever—yes, even though I was too damned shy to let any of them know my feelings.

Need, not love, was the issue! That, I saw as I went for my walk in the woods, was my and everyone else's real problem when we were anxious, depressed, and enraged. We needed—or foolishly *thought* we needed—something that we importantly wanted. We asininely insisted that we absolutely *must,* under all conditions and at all times, *must* be loved, *should* get what we wanted, and ought *never* suffer serious frustration. What quaint ideas! How pernicious! How could we possibly be happy—really and persistently happy—when we rigidly held to these unrealistic notions? We couldn't.

So, believe it or not, in that one twenty-minute walk by the lake, I gave up most of my neediness, especially my dire need for Karyl's love. I still desired very much to be with her and would still try to win her love. But I definitely didn't *need* it. Just as soon as I could, I would tell her this, tell her that I had stopped insisting that she *had to* return my strong feelings, and then see what kind of a relationship, if any, we could work out. If, at worst, she wanted to break up, I could accept that. If she wanted to go on with the relationship and still be ambivalent, I could accept that, too. But if so, I would eventually find another woman who would be more constant. Not that I *needed* to, but just that I *wanted* to find one.

I got together with Karyl the very next night, told her how I had propelled myself out of my need for her, and asked her what she wanted to do now. To my surprise, she was very impressed with my newly found nonneediness, wished that she could have it herself whenever she was madly in love, and suggested that we should have an experimental, nonneedy marriage. We would secretly marry—because we didn't yet have the income to live together—maintain an open relationship, and see how it all worked out. As long as we were both nonneedy, maybe it would, but if it didn't, too bad. Neither of us would have to feel hurt, angry, or depressed.

How Karyl and I actually began and later ended our marriage is another story. The main point of this one is that I really did make a startling change in myself during my walk around the lake in Bronx Botanical Gardens. For the rest of my life I have had very strong desires (many of them!) which I have striven to fulfill. But I have rarely thereafter thought that I *absolutely needed* what I wanted, nor *strongly needed* to avoid what I abhorred. And later I put antineediness, antiawfulizing, and antimusturbation solidly into REBT.

I did so in 1955, at the start of Rational Emotive Behavior Therapy. The dozen irrational beliefs that I originally postulated as a main source of human neurosis all include explicit or implicit musts and needs. Later on, when I had used REBT for a few years with hundreds of clients and had done a few research studies on it, I more clearly stated that when people are classically neurotic they seem to have one, two, or three basic or core musts and needs: "I *absolutely must* do well or I am no good!" "You *decidedly must* treat me fairly and considerately or you are a rotten person!" "My life conditions *absolutely have to* be the way I want them to be, or I can't stand it and can't have any real happiness at all!" Many other irrational or self-defeating beliefs exist, as I and other cognitive-behavior therapists have pointed out. But underlying them and basic to them seem to be implicit or explicit musts, shoulds, demands, and commands. Whether I would have ever seen this so clearly without my getting over my own neediness during my walk around the lake in 1936, of course I'll never know. But that walk and the thinking I did in the course of it certainly helped!

Another distinctive aspect of REBT is its notion, which most other psychotherapies still resist accepting, that there are two basic, and somewhat distinct, kinds of negative feelings: healthy ones, such as sorrow, regret, frustration, and annoyance when something goes against your personal interests and tastes, and unhealthy negative feelings, such as depression, despair, rage, panic, and self-hatred when similar unfortunate events occur. In other words, REBT quarrels with Joseph Wolpe's Subjective Units of Discomfort Scale, which puts negative feelings from zero to one hundred, but has only one scale that includes what REBT calls healthy and unhealthy negative emotions. I hold, instead, that when you experience failure, rejection, and discomfort, you can feel mild to strong negative feelings of regret and frustration, or you can add to these healthy negative feelings mild to strong feelings of depression, horror, and panic. Thus, REBT gives you two continua of negative feelings for the price of one!

I partly worked out this distinction for myself when I was in the children's ward of the old Presbyterian Hospital in New York for ten months during my seventh year, suffering from nephritis. My father, who was a businessman who neglected his three young children, rarely came to visit me, and my mother, who had my younger brother and sister to care for, only visited me once a week. Meanwhile other mothers, fathers, and family members visited their children regularly twice a week.

Especially on Sundays, when all the other children in my ward had a number of visitors and I usually had none, at first I was angry, and sometimes depressed, about my great deprivation. But as I saw that this deprivation was definitely going to continue, I worked at making myself feel quite sorrowful and regretful, but rarely seriously upset, about my lack of visitors. This experience seemed to teach me that whenever something went wrong in my life I had the choice of *how* badly I would let myself feel about it; I continued to use this knowledge, and created healthy instead of unhealthy negative feelings when I was deprived. So, in 1955, when I started REBT, I clearly distinguished positive feelings from negative feelings: healthy ones from unhealthy ones. The belief that REBT neglects or downplays people's feelings is quite incorrect. It even encourages them to feel *strongly* displeased, sorry, frustrated, regretful, and annoyed when things go wrong in their lives. That is what I managed to make myself feel when I was a seven-year-old patient in New York's Presbyterian Hospital.

I hadn't really thought about this until I began writing the present paper, but REBT's concept of helping people to make themselves less disturbed and also less disturb*able* also probably originated in my personal antineurosis campaign when I was a youngster. For I started to get this idea when, as I have described, I worked on making myself unneedy, as well as on getting over my terror of public speaking and approaching strange women. In both of these instances, I made a 180-degree turn and went from serious disturbance to just about complete nondisturbance.

In making this radical change, I discovered several things: I was no longer greatly disturbed about failing and being rejected as I had often previously been, though I was still sorry and displeased about these happenings. I still did not *want* to do badly, but I entirely lost my terror of failing. I was no longer uncomfortable about trying to speak in public and approach women, and when I did poorly, I accepted this with equanimity and didn't in any way put myself down for my failures. I began to actually look forward to taking the risks that I previously had been phobic about taking, and actually enjoyed taking them. I knew that my panic about trying to speak and to encounter new women was gone, and that in all probability it would not return. My fear of failing at other pursuits, like interviewing for a job or taking an important test, also almost totally vanished. I had much greater self-efficacy and looked forward to success at ventures at which I previously predicted I would dismally fail. I began to see that practically *nothing* bad that might happen to me, including important failures and rejections of *any* kind, would set me on the downward path to anxiety and avoidance of risk-taking. I became much more adventurous and actually sought out new pursuits that I had previously seen as dangerous but now saw as exciting and inviting.

Because I achieved this elegant solution to my emotional problems, and because I was pretty certain that they would not reoccur even if serious failures and deprivations happened to me, I began to see that the methods that I used to help myself—especially radically changing my philosophy and repetitively doing what I was afraid to do no matter how uncomfortable I was at first in doing it—would most probably work with other neurotic individuals. I also began to believe that in some cases, where people strongly and actively adopted my anxiety-attacking methods, they could make themselves both less disturbed and eventually less disturb*able*. So when I began practicing REBT I included in it what I call the elegant solution to emotional problems—that is, clients quickly and deeply practice undisturbing themselves, and, if they continue to strongly do so, they ultimately bring themselves to the point where they are much less disturbable than they previously were—yes, even though humanity as a whole continues to be highly upsettable!

Although I seem to have been born and reared with a strong propensity to make myself anxious rather than depressed, I have some normal neurotic tendencies to depress myself when things are going unusually badly. Thus, I depressed myself for a while when I was thirty-three years old and I broke up with a woman, Gertrude, whom I had passionately loved for five years and still loved when we parted, because we had radically different ideas about living together. She was much more sociable than I and wanted to be sure, when we were planning to marry, that we lived in a totally open apartment, with no closed doors between the rooms so that neither of us could arrange for any privacy. And she was planning on our having fairly big dinner parties, not to mention other kinds of parties, twice a week. With my own emphasis on seeing many clients and doing quite a bit of reading and writing, this kind of chit-chatty life simply wasn't for me. So we agreed to be friends, and shortly thereafter she got engaged to marry a man who was more social than I.

I felt depressed for a short while, but quickly started to use the methods I had previously used to overcome my feelings of anxiety, and was pleased to see that they worked very well. I strongly convinced myself that I didn't *need* to live with Gertrude, though I very much wanted to do so. I made myself see that she wasn't the only possible mate for me; that I could have a good life without her; that I wasn't a loser for not living up to her highly social standards; and that I would in all probability soon find a more suitable partner. That was pretty good, cognitively. But I also threw myself into more studying and writing; I started building my psychological practice; and I began actively dating, which soon led to my having another steady love relationship.

This experience tended to show me that feelings of depression, like those of severe anxiety, are usually related to demands that I (and other people) *absolutely must* perform well and *must not* be deprived of their important wants. Although I agree with Aaron Beck that specific automatic thoughts that people frequently use to make themselves anxious are somewhat different from those that they use to make themselves depressed, I still think that their underlying musts and demands are similar. Thus, I have said for years: suppose anyone thoroughly believes, "I *prefer* very much to do well and be loved by significant others, but I never, never *have to* perform well or be loved. Too damned bad if I do not! I greatly *desire* to get what I want when I want it and to avoid severe pain and discomfort, but I never *need* what I desire and can always find other enjoyable things. Tough shit if I am deprived! Now let me work like hell to try to get what I want!" If anyone really thinks this way and consistently carries these thoughts into action, would he or she ever become and remain severely anxious or depressed? Yes, perhaps, if their body chemistry was severely awry and they had endogenous anxiety or depression. Otherwise, I doubt it.

Anyway, my belief that both anxiety and depression usually stem from strong absolutist musts, needs, and demands, and that they can mainly be relieved by thoroughly giving up these commands and changing them back into *only* the *preferences* from which they originated, this theory and practice of REBT once again largely stems from my own emotional growth and development. And my use of REBT on myself has, I think, led to further growth and development.

Time is running out, so let me end before I get going on another book. Having presented this lovely paper, I strongly *prefer* that all you listeners see what a brilliant person I am, acknowledge how I have beautifully evolved over the years, and realize that REBT is a marvelous form of therapy that is backed by my personal experience as well as convincing clinical and research findings.

Alas, many of you, for whatever reasons, will not go along with my preferences. Well you obviously don't *have to*. My wish may well *not* be your command. You are entitled to be as stupid as you wish about this. Too damned bad! Tough! By stubbornly refusing to take your objections too seriously, and by refraining from unhealthily upsetting myself about them, I shall once again show how REBT clearly works. At least for a sensible, sane, and—of course—completely rational person like me!

Notes

Editor's Introduction

1. Shawn Blau, "Cognitive Darwinism: Rational Emotive Therapy and the Theory of Neuronal Group Selection," *ETC: A Review of General Semantics,* no. 50 (1993): 403–41.
2. Albert Ellis and Shawn Blau, "Rational Emotive Behavior Therapy," *Directions in Clinical and Counseling Psychology* 4, no. 8 (1998): 41–56.

Introduction to Part I

1. Albert Ellis, *The American Sexual Tragedy.* (New York: Lyle Stuart, 1962), pp. 154–55.
2. Ibid., p. 155.
3. Ibid., p. 157.

Chapter 9: How I Became Interested in Sexology and Sex Therapy

1. Albert Ellis, *The Case for Sexual Liberty.* (Tucson, Ariz.: Seymour Press, 1965).

Introduction to Part II

1. Albert Ellis and Shawn Blau, "Rational Emotive Behavior Therapy," *Directions in Clinical and Counseling Psychology* 18, no. 4 (1998): 41–56.

Chapter 11: Psychotherapy and the Value of a Human Being

1. B. Russell, *The Conquest of Happiness* (New York: New American Library, 1951).
2. J. Henry, *Culture Against Man* (New York: Random House, 1963).
3. G. E. Axtelle, "Effectiveness as a Value Concept," *Journal of Educational Sociology* 29 (1956): 240–46.
4. R. A. Farson, "Praise Reappraised," *Encounter,* no. 1 (1966): 13–21.
5. R. Robertiello, *Sexual Fulfillment and Self-Affirmation* (New York: Larchmont, 1964).

Chapter 15: How to Maintain and Enhance Your Rational-Emotive Behavior Gains

1. I [Albert Ellis] gratefully acknowledge the contributions of the following people at the Albert Ellis Institute for Rational Emotive Behavior Therapy who read this manuscript and who made voluble comments on it: Raymond DiGiuseppe, Mal Holland, Terry London, Leonor Lega, Naomi

McCormıck, Harrıet Mıschel, Beverly Pıeren, Susan Presby, Karın Schlieder, Janet Wolfe, Joe Yankura, and Thea Zeeve. However, I take all responsibility for the views expressed

Chapter 17: Achieving Self-Actualization

1. M. Daniels, "The Myth of Self-Actualization," *Journal of Humanistic Psychology* 28, no. 1 (1988): 13.
2. A. H. Maslow, *Toward a Psychology of Being* (New York: Van Nostrand Reinhold, 1968), p. 97.
3. S. R. Wilson, "The 'Real Self' Controversy: Toward an Integration of Humanistic and Interactionist Theory," *Journal of Humanistic Psychology* 28, no. 1 (1988): 49.
4. T. Crawford and Albert Ellis, "A Dictionary of Rational-Emotive Feelings and Behaviors," *Journal of Rational-Emotive and Cognitive Behavioral Therapy* 1, no. 7 (1989): 3.
5. Ibid., p. 3.
6. Ibid., p. 3.
7. Ibid., p. 3.
8. Ibid., p. 5.
9. S. I. Hayakawa, "The Fully Functioning Personality," *Symbol, Status, and Personality* (New York: Harcourt Brace Jovanovich, 1968), p. 57.
10. Albert Ellis, *The Case Against Religiosity* (New York: Institute for Rational Emotive Therapy, 1983), p. 3.
11. Ibid., p. 4.
12. Ibid., p. 5.
13. Ibid., p. 2.
14. M. J. Mahoney et al., "Psychological Development and Optimal Psychotherapy: Converging Perspectives Among Clinical Psychologists," *Journal of Integrative and Eclectic Psychotherapy* 8 (1989): 251–63.

Chapter 19: Rational Effectiveness Training

1. See L. C. Lyons and P. J. Woods, "The Efficacy of Rational-Emotive Therapy," *Clinical Psychology Review* 11 (1991). See also D. Hajzler and M. E. Bernard, "A Review of Rational-Emotive Outcome Studies," *School Psychology Quarterly* 1, no. 6 (1991): 27–44.
2. S. H. Klarreich, R. DiGiuseppe, and D. DiMattia, "EAP's: Mind Over Myths," *Personal Administrator*, 2, no. 32 (1987).

Chapter 20: The Objectivist View of Self-Esteem

1. N. Branden, *The Psychology of Self-Esteem* (New York: Bantam, 1970).
2. Ibid.
3. N. Branden, "Emotion and Repression," *Objectivist*, August-September 1966.
4. N. Branden, *The Psychology of Self-Esteem*.

5. Ibid.
6. N. Branden in A. Rand, *The Virtue of Selfishness* (New York: New American Library, 1964).
7. N. Branden, *Psychotherapy and the Objectivist Ethics* (New York: Nathaniel Branden Institute, 1965).
8. N. Branden, "Benevolence Versus Altruism," *Objectivist Newsletter,* July 1962.
9. N. Branden, *Who Is Ayn Rand?* (New York: Paperback Library, 1965).
10. Ayn Rand, *Atlas Shrugged* (New York: New American Library, 1957).
11. Ayn Rand, *The Virtue of Selfishness* (New York: New American Library, 1964).
12. N. Branden, *The Psychology of Self-Esteem.*
13. N. Branden, "Self-Esteem," *Objectivist,* March 1–7, April 5–10, May 8–10, June 1–4, September (1967).

Chapter 23: Humanism and Psychotherapy

1. For a review of other CBT outcome studies, see Lyons and Woods, "The Efficacy of Rational-Emotive Therapy." See also S. D. Hollon and A. T. Beck, "Cognitive and Cognitive-Behavior Therapies," in *Handbook of Psychotherapy and Behavior Change,* eds. Bergin and Garfield (1994), p. 428–66.

Chapter 24: The Biological Basis of Human Irrationality

1. R. S. Parker, *Emotional Common Sense* (New York: Harper, 1973), p. 13.
2. G. Ainslie, "Specious Reward: A Behavioral Theory of Impulsiveness and Impulse Control," *Psychological Bulletin* 82 (1974): 463–96.

Chapter 26: General Semantics and Rational Emotive Behavior Therapy

1. A. Korzybski, "The Role of Language in the Perception Processes," in *Perception: An Approach to Personality,* eds. R. R. Blake and G. V. Ramsey (New York: Ronald Press, 1951), p. 170–205.
2. Ibid., p. 187.
3. Ibid., p. 218.
4. Ibid., p. 192.
5. Korzybski, *Science and Sanity* (San Francisco: International Society of General Semantics, 1933), p. 440; Korzybski, "The Role of Language in the Perception Processes," p. 190.
6. Ibid., p. 189.
7. Ibid., p. 192.
8. Ibid., p. 189.
9. Ibid., p. 181.
10. Ibid., p. 184.
11. Ibid., p. 186.
12. Ibid., p. 194.

13. Ibid., p. 177.
14. Ibid., p. 196.
15. Albert Ellis, "Rational Psychotherapy," *Journal of General Psychology* 59 (1958): 35.
16. Korzybski, "The Role of Language in the Perception Processes," p. 193.
17. Ibid., p. 194.
18. Ibid., p. 195.
19. Ibid., p. 172.
20. Ibid., p. 178.

Dates of Original Publication

Part I: Sex, Love, and Marriage

1. "Is the Vaginal Orgasm a Myth?" In *Sex, Society and the Individual*, edited by A. P. Pillay and A. Ellis. Bombay: International Journal of Sexology Press, 1953, pp. 156–163.
2. "Sex Fascism." In *Sex Without Guilt*, by A. Ellis. New York: Lyle Stuart, 1958.
3. "Adventures With Sex Censorship." In *Sex Without Guilt*, by A. Ellis. New York: Lyle Stuart, 1958.
4. "Sexual Intercourse: Psychological Foundations." In *The Art and Science of Love*, by A. Ellis. Secaucus, N.J.: Lyle Stuart, 1960.
5. "The Facts of Female Sexuality As Learned From My Personal Sexual Experiences." In *Suppressed: Seven Key Essays Publishers Dared Not Print*, by A. Ellis. Chicago: New Classics House, 1965.
6. "Unhealthy Love: Its Causes and Treatment." In *Symposium on Love*, edited by M. E. Curtin. New York: Behavioral Publications, 1973, pp. 175–97.
7. "Sex-Love Adventuring and Personal Growth." In *The New Sexuality*, edited by H. Otto. Palo Alto, Calif.: Science and Behavior Books, 1972, pp. 94–108. Original Title: "Sexual Adventuring and Personality Growth."
8. "The Nature of Disturbed Marital Interaction." Paper presented at the Annual Convention of the American Psychological Association, Los Angeles, September 7, 1974.
9. "How I Became Interested in Sexology and Sex Therapy." In *Personal Stories of "How I Got Into Sex,"* edited by B. Bullough, V. L. Bullough, M. A. Fithian, W. E. Hartman, and R. S. Klein. Amherst, N.Y.: Prometheus Books, 1997, pp. 131–48.

Part II: Rational Self-Help

10. "Rational Psychotherapy." Paper presented at the Annual Convention of the American Psychological Association, Chicago, August 31, 1956. Originally published in *Journal of General Psychology* 59 (1958): 35–49.
11. "Psychotherapy and the Value of a Human Being." In *Value and Valuation: Axiological Studies in Honor of Robert S. Hartman*, edited by J. W. Davis. Knoxville: University of Tennessee, 1972.
12. "Techniques for Disputing Irrational Beliefs (DIBS)." New York: Institute for Rational Living, 1974.
13. "Rational Emotive Imagery." Originally published in *Technique for Using Rational-Emotive Imagery (REI)*, by M. Maultsby and A. Ellis. New York: Institute for Rational Living, 1974.

14. "REBT Diminishes Much of the Human Ego." Paper presented at the Annual Convention of the American Psychological Association, Chicago, September 1975. Originally published as "RET Abolishes Most of the Human Ego." *Psychotherapy* 13 (1975): 343–48.

15. "How to Maintain and Enhance Your Rational-Emotive Behavior Gains." *Cognitive Behaviorist* 6, no. 1 (1984): 2–4. Original title: "Maintenance and Generalization in Rational-Emotive Therapy (RET)."

16. "A Dictionary of Rational-Emotive Feelings and Behaviors," by A. Ellis and T. Crawford. *Journal of Rational-Emotive and Cognitive-Behavior Therapy* 7, no. 1 (1989): 3–28.

17. "Achieving Self-Actualization." In *Handbook of Self-Actualization* (Special Issue), edited by A. Jones and R. Crandall. *Journal of Social Behavior and Personality* 6, no. 5 (1991): 1–18.

18. "Using Rational Emotive Behavior Therapy Techniques to Cope With Disability." Paper presented at the Annual Convention of the American Psychological Association, New York, 1997. First published in *Professional Psychology: Research and Practice* 28, no. 1: 17–22.

Part III: Rational Living in an Irrational Society
19. "Rational-Effectiveness Training: A New Method of Facilitating Management and Labor Relations." Originally published as "Rational Training: A New Method of Facilitating Management and Labor Relations," by A. Ellis and M. Blum. *Psychological Reports* 20 (1967): 1267–84.

20. "The Objectivist View of Self-Esteem." In *Is Objectivism a Religion?*, by A. Ellis. New York: Lyle Stuart, 1968, pp. 9–53.

21. "The Case Against Religiosity." *Independent*, no. 126 (1962): pp. 4–5. Original title: "The Case Against Religion: A Psychotherapist's View."

22. "Rational Emotive Behavior Therapy and Its Application to Emotional Education." Paper presented at the Seventeenth International Congress of the International Association of Applied Psychology, Liege, Belgium, July 26, 1971.

23. "Humanism and Psychotherapy: A Revolutionary Approach." *Humanist* 32, no. 1 (1972): 24–28.

24. "The Biological Basis of Human Irrationality." *Journal of Individual Psychology* 32 (1976): 145–68. Adapted from a paper presented at the American Psychological Association annual convention, September 1975.

25. "Addictive Behaviors and Personality Disorders." *Addictions Newsletter* 2, no. 3 (1995): 10–11.

26. "General Semantics and Rational Emotive Behavior Therapy." Paper presented at the Annual Convention of the Institute of General Semantics, Alfred Korzybski Memorial Lecture. Originally published in *More E-Prime: To Be or Not II*, edited by P. D. Johnston, D. D. Bourland Jr., and J. Klien. Concord, Calif.: International Society for General Semantics, 1991, pp. 213–40.

27. "Is Psychoanalysis Harmful?" *Psychiatric Opinion* 5, no. 1 (1968): 16–25.
28. "How I Manage to Be a *Rational* Rational Emotive Behavior Therapist." Paper presented at the Annual Convention of the American Psychological Association, New York, August 14, 1995. First published in *Journal of Rational-Emotive and Cognitive-Behavior Therapy* 14, no. 4 (1996): 211–13.
29. "The Evolution of Albert Ellis and Rational Emotive Behavior Therapy." In *The Evolution of Psychotherapy: The Third Conference*, edited by J. K. Zeig. New York: Brunner/Mazel, 1997, pp. 69–82.

Selected References

The items preceded by an asterisk (*) in the following list are largely self-help books on Rational Emotive Behavior Therapy (REBT) and Cognitive Behavior Therapy (CBT).

Many of these materials may be obtained from the Albert Ellis Institute, 45 East 65th Street, New York, NY 10021-6508. The Institute's free catalogue and the materials it distributes may be ordered on weekdays by phone (212-535-0822) or by FAX (212-249-3582). The Institute will continue to make available these and other materials, and it will offer talks, workshops, and training sessions, as well as other presentations in the area of human growth and healthy living, and list these in its regular free catalogue.

Adler, A. *Understanding Human Nature.* New York: Garden City Publishing Company, 1927.

*————. *What Life Should Mean to You.* New York: Capricorn, 1958.

Ainslie, G. "Specious Reward: A Behavioral Theory of Impulsiveness and Impulse Control," *Psychological Bulletin* 82 (1974).

*Alberti, R. F., and M. L. Emmons. *Your Perfect Right.* 7th rev. ed. San Luis Obispo, Calif.: Impact, 1995.

Anderson, C. "Depression and Suicide Reassessed," *Journal of the American Medicine Woman's Association* (1964).

————. "Depression and Suicide Reassessed," *Rational Living* 1, no. 2 (1966): 31–36.

Axtelle, G. E. "Effectiveness As a Value Concept," *Journal of Educational Sociology 29* (1956).

Baldon, A., and A. Ellis. *RET Problem Solving Workbook.* New York: Institute for Rational-Emotive Therapy, 1993.

Balter, R. "Disabilities Update: What Role Can REBT Play?" *IRET Letter,* spring 1995.

Bartley, W. W. "Theories of Demarcation Between Science and Metaphysics." In *Problems in the Philosophy of Science,* edited by I. Lakatos and A. Musgrave. Amsterdam: North Holland Publishing Company, 1968.

Beck, A. T. *Cognitive Therapy and the Emotional Disorders.* New York: International Universities Press, 1976.

————. "Cognitive Therapy: A Thirty-Year Retrospective," *American Psychologist* 46 (1991).

————. *Depression: Clinical, Experimental, and Theoretical Aspects.* New York: Hoeber-Harper, 1967.

*————. *Love Is Never Enough*. New York: Harper and Row, 1988.

Beck, A. T., and G. Emery. *Anxiety Disorders and Phobias*. New York: Basic Books, 1985.

Beck, A. T., A. J. Rush, B. F. Shaw, and G. Emery. *Cognitive Therapy of Depression*. New York: Guilford, 1979.

Beck, J. S. *Cognitive Therapy: Basics and Beyond*. New York: Guilford, 1995.

Benjamin, H. *The Transsexual Phenomenon*. New York: Julian, 1966.

Benjamin, H., and A. Ellis. "An Objective Examination of Prostitution," *International Journal of Sexology* 8 (1954).

Bergler, E. "Frigidity in the Female—Misconceptions and Facts," *Marriage Hygiene* 1 (1947).

*Bernard, M. E., *Staying Rational in an Irrational World*. New York: Carol Publishing, 1993.

————, ed. *Using Rational-Emotive Therapy Effectively: A Practitioner's Guide*. New York: Plenum, 1991.

Bernard, M. E., and R. DiGiuseppe, eds. *Rational-Emotive Consultation in Applied Settings*. Hillside, N.J.: Erlbaum.

*Bernard, M. E., and J. L. Wolfe, eds. *The RET Resource Book for Practitioners*. New York: Albert Ellis Institute, 1992.

Berscheid, E., and E. Harfield. *Interpersonal Attraction*. Reading, Penn.: Addison Wesley, 1978.

Blau, S. F. "Cognitive Darwinism: Rational-Emotive Therapy and the Theory of Neuronal Group Selection," *ETC: A Review of General Semantics* 50 (1993).

————. "Conspiracy of the 'Musts,'" *Contemporary Psychology* 43, no. 2, (1998).

*Bloomfield, H. H., and P. McWilliams. *How to Heal Depression*. Los Angeles: Prelude Press, 1994.

Boas, C. V. E. "Group Therapy of Anorgasmic Women," *International Journal of Sexology* 4 (1950).

Bond, F. W., and W. Dryden. "Why Two Central REBT Hypotheses Appear Untestable," *Journal of Rational-Emotive and Cognitive-Behavior Therapy* 14 (1986).

Bone, H. "Two Proposed Alternatives to Psychoanalytic Interpreting." In *Use of Interpretation in Treatment*, edited by Emanuel F. Hammer. Northvale, New Jersey: Jason Aronson, 1968.

Bourland, D. D., Jr., and P. D. Johnston, eds. *To Be or Not: An E-Prime Anthology*. San Francisco: International Society for General Semantics, 1991.

Boylan, R. *Infidelity*. New York: Putnam, 1970.

Branden, B. "A Biographical Essay." In *Who Is Ayn Rand?*, by N. Branden. New York: Paperback Library, 1965.

Branden, N. "Benevolence Versus Altruism," *Objectivist Newsletter*, July 1962.

———. "Emotion and Repression," *Objectivist,* August/September 1966.

———. In A. Rand, *The Virtue of Selfishness.* New York: New American Library, 1964.

———. *Judgment Day: My Years With Ayn Rand.* Boston: Houghton Mifflin, 1989.

———. *The Power of Self-Esteem.* Deerfield Beach, Fla.: Health Communications, 1992.

———. *The Psychology of Self-Esteem.* New York: Bantam, 1970.

———. *Psychotherapy and the Objectivist Ethics.* New York: Nathaniel Branden Institute, 1965.

———. "Self-Esteem," *Objectivist,* March 1967.

———. "Self-Esteem," *Objectivist,* April 1967.

———. "Self-Esteem," *Objectivist,* May 1967.

———. "Self-Esteem," *Objectivist,* June 1967.

———. "Self-Esteem," *Objectivist,* September 1967.

———. *Who Is Ayn Rand?* New York: Paperback Library, 1965.

Broder, M. *Overcoming Your Anger in the Shortest Period of Time* (audiotape). New York: Albert Ellis Institute, 1995.

*———. *Overcoming Your Anxiety in the Shortest Period of Time* (Audiotape). New York: Albert Ellis Institute, 1995.

*———. *Overcoming Your Depression in the Shortest Period of Time* (audiotape). New York: Albert Ellis Institute, 1995.

*Burns, D. *Feeling Good: The New Mood Therapy.* New York: Morrow, 1980.

———. *Intimate Connections.* New York: Morrow, 1984.

———. *Ten Days to Self-Esteem.* New York: Morrow, 1993.

Bychowski, G. "Some Aspects of Psychosexuality in Psychoanalytic Experience." In *Psychosexual Development in Health and Disease,* edited by P. H. Hoch and J. Zubin. New York: Grune & Stratton, 1949.

Calabro, L. E. *Living With Disability.* New York: Institute for Rational-Emotive Therapy, 1991.

Cayer, M., D. DiMattia, and J. Wingrove. "Conquering Evaluation Fear," *Personnel Administrator* no. 6 (1988).

Clark, D. A., and D. R. Hemsley. "Individual Differences in the Experience of Depressive and Anxious, Intrusive Thoughts," *Behavior Research and Therapy,* 23 (1984).

Clark, L. "The Psychology of Feminine Sex Experience," *International Journal of Sexology* 2 (1949).

———. "The Role of Urethra in Female Orgasm," *International Journal of Sexology* 4 (1950).

Coopersmith, S. "Studies in Self-Esteem," *Scientific Monthly* 218, no. 2 (1968).

*Covey, S. R. *The Seven Habits of Highly Effective People.* New York: Simon and Schuster, 1992.

Coyne, J. C., and I. H. Gotlib. "The Role of Cognition in Depression: An Appraisal," *Psychological Bulletin* 94 (1983).

Crawford, T. Personal letter to Albert Ellis. September 30, 1989.

Crawford, T., and A. Ellis. "A Dictionary of Rational-Emotive Feelings and Behaviors," *Journal of Rational-Emotive and Cognitive-Behavioral Therapy* 7, no. 1 (1989).

Csikszentmihalyi, M. "The Flow Experience." In *Consciousness*, edited by D. Goleman and R. J. Davidson. New York: Harper and Row, 1979.

*————. *Flow: The Psychology of Optimal Experience.* San Francisco: Harper Perennial, 1990.

Daniels, M. "The Myth of Self-Actualization," *Journal of Humanistic Psychology* 28, no. 1 (1988).

Danielsson, B. *Love in the South Seas.* New York: Reynal, 1956.

————. "Sex Life in Polynesia." In *The Encyclopedia of Sexual Behavior,* edited by Albert Ellis and Albert Abarbanel. New York: Hawthorn, 1967.

De Rougemont, D. *Love in the Western World.* New York: Harcourt Brace, 1940.

DiGiuseppe, R. "The Nature of Irrational and Rational Beliefs," *Journal of Rational-Emotive and Cognitive-Behavior Therapy* 14 (1996).

*————. *What Do I Do With My Anger: Hold It in or Let It Out?* (audiotape). New York: Albert Ellis Institute, 1990.

DiMattia, D. "Using RET Effectively in the Workplace." In *Using RET Effectively,* edited by M. Bernard. New York: Plenum, 1991.

DiMattia, D., and T. Idzermans. *Reaching the Minds: A Trainers Manual for Rational Effectiveness Training.* New York: Albert Ellis Institute, 1996.

DiMattia, D., R. J. Yeager, and I. Dube. "Emotional Barriers to Learning," *Personnel Journal* 68, no. 11 (1989).

DiMattia, D., and L. Lega, eds. *Will the Real Albert Ellis Please Stand Up?: Anecdotes by His Colleagues, Students and Friends Celebrating His Seventy-Fifth Birthday.* New York: Institute for Rational-Emotive Therapy, 1990.

Dorcus, R. M., and G. W. Shaffer. *Textbook of Abnormal Psychology.* Baltimore: Williams and Wilkins, 1950.

Dreikurs, R. *Psychodynamics, Psychotherapy, and Counseling.* Chicago: Alfred Adler Institute, 1974.

Dryden, W. *Brief Rational Emotive Behavior Therapy.* London: Wiley, 1995.

*————. *Dealing With Anger Problems: Rational-Emotive Therapeutic Interventions.* Sarasota, Fla.: Professional Resource Exchange, 1990.

*————. *Overcoming Guilt!* London: Sheldon, 1994.

————. *Rational Emotive Behavior Brief Therapy.* New York: Wiley, 1996.

————. *Rational-Emotive Therapy: Fundamentals and Innovations.* London: Croom Helm, 1984.

*————. *Teaching Self-acceptance.* New York: Wiley, 1998.

Dryden, W., and A. Ellis. *A Dialogue With Albert Ellis: Against Dogma.* Philadelphia: Open University Press, 1991.

*Dryden, W., and J. Gordon. *Think Your Way to Happiness*. London: Sheldon Press, 1991.

Dryden, W., and M. Neeman. *Dictionary of Rational Emotive Behavior Therapy*. London: Whirr Publishers, 1995.

*Dryden, W., and J. Yankura. *Albert Ellis*. London: Sage, 1994.

Elkan, E. "Evolution of Female Orgastic Ability—a Biological Survey," *International Journal of Sexology* 2 (1948).

Ellis, A. Achieving Self-Actualization. In *Handbook of Self-Actualization*, edited by A. Jones and R. Crandall. Corte Madera, Calif.: Select Press, 1991.

*———. *Albert Ellis Live at the Learning Annex* (audiotape, 2 vols.). New York: Institute for Rational-Emotive Therapy, 1990.

———. *The American Sexual Tragedy*. New York: Twayne, 1954.

———. *The American Sexual Tragedy*. Rev. ed. New York: Lyle Stuart, 1962.

*———. *Anger—How to Live With and Without It*. Secaucus, N.J.: Citadel Press, 1977.

———. "Applications of Clinical Psychology to Sexual Disorders." In *Progress in Clinical Psychology*, vol. 1. Edited by D. Brower and L. A. Abt. New York: Grune & Stratton, 1952.

———. *The Art and Science of Love*. Rev. ed. New York: Lyle Stuart, 1969.

*———. *Better, Deeper, and More Enduring Brief Therapy*. New York: Brunner/Mazel, 1996.

———. "The Biological Basis of Human Irrationality," *Journal of Individual Psychology* 32 (1976).

———. *The Case Against Religiosity*. New York: Institute for Rational Emotive Therapy, 1983.

———. "A Case for Polygamy," *Nugget* 5, no. 1 (1960).

———. *The Case for Sexual Liberty*. Tucson, Ariz.: Seymour Press, 1965.

*———. *The Civilized Couples Guide to Extramarital Adventure*. New York: Pinnacle Books, 1972.

———. "A Comparison of the Use of Direct and Indirect Phrasing in Personality Questionnaires," *Psychological Monographs* 61 (1947).

*———. *Conquering the Dire Need for Love* (audiotape). New York: Albert Ellis Institute, 1977.

*———. *Conquering Low Frustration Tolerance* (audiotape). New York: Albert Ellis Institute, 1976.

———. "Discussion of W. Stokes and D. Mace, 'Premarital Sexual Behavior,'" *Marriage and Family Living* 15 (1953).

———. "Do Some Religious Beliefs Help Create Emotional Disturbance?" *Psychotherapy in Private Practice* 4, no. 4 (1986).

*———. *Executive Leadership: The Rational-Emotive Approach*. New York: Albert Ellis Institute, 1972.

———. *The Folklore of Sex*. New York: Boni/Doubleday, 1951.

*————. *A Garland of Rational Humorous Songs* (audiotape and songbook). New York: Albert Ellis Institute, 1977.

————. "Group Marriage: A Possible Alternative?" In *The Family in Search of a Future*, edited by H. A. Otto. New York: Appleton-Century-Crofts, 1970.

*————. *How to Control Your Anxiety Before It Controls You*. Secaucus, N.J.: Birch Lane Press, 1998.

*————. *How to Live With a Neurotic: At Home and at Work*. Hollywood, Calif.: Wilshire Books, 1957. Reprint, rev. ed. New York: Crown, 1975.

*————. *How to Refuse to Be Angry, Vindictive, and Unforgiving* (audiotape). New York: Albert Ellis Institute, 1991.

*————. *How to Stubbornly Refuse to Be Ashamed of Anything* (audiotape). New York: Institute for Rational-Emotive Therapy, 1973.

*————. *How to Stubbornly Refuse to Make Yourself Miserable About Anything— Yes, Anything!* Secaucus, N.J.: Lyle Stuart, 1988.

————. *Humanistic Psychotherapy: The Rational-Emotive Approach*. New York: McGraw-Hill, 1973.

*————. *The Intelligent Woman's Guide to Dating and Mating*. Secaucus, N.J.: Lyle Stuart, 1979.

*————. *The Intelligent Woman's Guide to Manhunting*. Rev. ed. Secaucus, N.J.: Lyle Stuart, 1979.

————. "Introduction." in *The Homosexual in America*, by D. W. Corey. New York: Greenberg, 1951.

————. "Is Psychoanalysis Harmful?" *Psychiatric Opinion* 5, no. 1. Reprint. New York: Institute for Rational-Emotive Therapy, 1963.

————. "Is the Vaginal Orgasm a Myth?" In *Sex, Society, and the Individual*, edited by A. P. Pillay and A. Ellis. Bombay: International Journal of Sexology Press, 1953.

————. "The Issue of Force and Energy in Behavioral Change," *Journal of Contemporary Psychotherapy* 10 (1979).

————. "Love and Family Relationships of American College Girls," *American Journal of Sociology* 55 (1950).

————. "Marriage Counseling With Couples Indicating Sexual Incompatibility," *Marriage and Family Living* 13 (1953).

————. "Masturbation," *Journal of Society Therapy* 1, no. 3 (1955).

————. "My Life in Clinical Psychology." In *History of Clinical Psychology in Autobiography*, edited by C. E. Walker. Homewood, Ill.: Dorsey, 1990.

————. "New Light on Masturbation," *Independent* 51, no. 4 (1956).

————. "On Premarital Sex Relations," *Independent* 58, no. 6 (1956).

*————. "Outcome of Employing Three Techniques of Psychotherapy," *Journal of Clinical Psychology* 13 (1957).

————. *Overcoming Resistance: Rational-Emotive Therapy With Difficult Clients*. New York: Springer, 1985.

————. "Perversions and Neurosis," *International Journal of Sexology* 6 (1952).

————. "Psychosexual and Marital Problems." In *An Introduction to Clinical Psychology*, edited by L. A. Pennington and I. A. Berg, pp. 264–83. New York: Ronald, 1954.

*————. *Psychotherapy and the Value of a Human Being*. New York: Institute for Rational-Emotive Therapy, 1972.

————. "Questionnaire Versus Interview Methods in the Study of Human Love Relationships," *American Sociological Review* 12 (1947).

————. "Questionnaire Versus Interview Methods in the Study of Human Love Relationships, II: Uncategorized Responses," *American Sociological Review* 13 (1948).

————. "Rational-Emotive Therapy Approaches the Problems of Achieving and Maintaining Peace," *Journal of Cognitive Psychotherapy* 6 (1992).

————. "Rational Psychotherapy," *Journal of General Psychology* 59. Reprint. New York: Institute for Rational-Emotive Therapy, 1958.

*————. *Reason and Emotion in Psychotherapy*. Secaucus, N.J.: Citadel, 1962.

*————. *Reason and Emotion in Psychotherapy*, Rev. ed. Secaucus, N.J.: Birch Lane Press, 1994.

————. "Recent Studies on the Sex and Love Relations of Young Girls," *International Journal of Sexology* 6 (1953).

————. "Responses to Criticisms of Rational Emotive Behavior Therapy (REBT) by Ray DiGiuseppe, Frank Bond, Widy Dryden, Steve Weinrach, and Richard Wesseler," *Journal of Rational-Emotive and Cognitive Behavior Therapy* 14 (1997).

————. "Review of 'Sexual Behavior in the Human Male,'" *Journal of General Psychology* 39 (1948).

*————. *Sex and the Liberated Man*. Secaucus, N.J.: Lyle Stuart, 1976.

*————. *Sex and the Single Man*. New York: Lyle Stuart, 1963.

*————. *Sex Without Guilt*. Rev. ed. New York: Lyle Stuart, 1969.

————. "Sexual Problems." In *Progress in Clinical Psychology*, vol. 1. Edited by L. A. Abt and D. Brower. New York: Grune & Stratton, 1952.

————. "The Sexual Psychology of Human Hermaphrodites," *Psychosomatic Medicine* 7 (1945).

————. "Some Significant Correlates of Love and Family Behavior," *Journal of Social Psychology* 30 (1949).

————. "A Study of Human Love Relationships," *Journal of Genetic Psychology* 15 (1949).

————. "A Study of the Love Emotions of American College Girls," *International Journal of Sexology* 3 (1949).

*————. *Twenty-two Ways to Brighten Up Your Love Life* (audiotape). New York: Albert Ellis Institute, 1980.

*————. *Unconditionally Accepting Yourself and Others* (audiotape). New York: Institute for Rational Emotive Therapy, 1988.

————. "What Is Normal Sex Behavior?" *Complex* 8 (1952).

————. "Woman as Sex Aggressor," *Best Year* 1, no. 3 (1955).

————, ed. *Sex Life of the American and the Kinsey Report*. New York: Greenberg, 1954.

*Ellis, A., and M. Abrams. *How to Cope With a Fatal Illness*. New York: Barricade Books, 1994.

*Ellis, A., and I. Becker. *A Guide to Personal Happiness*. North Hollywood, Calif.: Wilshire Books, 1982.

Ellis, A., and S. Blau. Rational Emotive Behavior Therapy. *Directions in Clinical and Counseling Psychology*, 8, no. 4 (1998).

*Ellis, A., and D. DiMattia. *Self-Management: Strategies for Personal Success*. New York: Institute for Rational-Emotive Therapy, 1991.

Ellis, A., and W. Dryden. *A Dialogue With Albert Ellis: Against Dogma*. Stony Stratford, England: Open University Press, 1991.

————. *The Essential Albert Ellis*. New York: Springer, 1990.

————. *The Practice of Rational-Emotive Therapy*. Rev. ed. New York: Springer, 1997.

*Ellis, A., and R. A. Harper. *A Guide to Successful Marriage*. Hollywood, Calif.: Wilshire Books, 1961.

*————. *A Guide to Rational Living*. Rev. ed. North Hollywood, Calif.: Wilshire, 1997.

*————. *A Guide to Rational Living*. 3d ed. North Hollywood, Calif.: Wilshire, 1997.

*————. *A New Guide to Rational Living*. North Hollywood, Calif.: Wilshire, 1975.

*Ellis, A., and W. Knaus. *Overcoming Procrastination*. New York: New American Library, 1977.

*Ellis, A., and A. Lange. *How to Keep People From Pushing Your Buttons*. New York: Carol Publishing, 1994.

Ellis, A., and E. Sagarin. *Nymphomania: A Study of the Oversexed Woman*. New York: Gilbert Press, 1964.

*Ellis, A., and R. C. Tafrate. *How to Control Your Anger Before It Controls You*. Secaucus, N. J.: Carol Publishing Group, 1997.

*Ellis, A., and E. Velten. *Optimal Aging*. Chicago: Open Court, 1998.

*————. *When AA Doesn't Work for You. Rational Steps to Quitting Alcohol*. New York: Barricade Books, 1992.

Ellis, A., and R. Yeager. *Why Some Therapies Don't Work: The Dangers of Transpersonal Psychology*. Buffalo, New York: Prometheus, 1989.

*Ellis, A., M. Abrams, and L. Dengelegi. *The Art and Science of Rational Eating*. New York: Barricade Books, 1992.

*Ellis, A., S. Moseley, and J. L. Wolfe. *How to Raise an Emotionally Healthy, Happy Child*. North Hollywood, Calif.: Wilshire Books, 1966.

Ellis, A., J. Gordon, M. Neenan, and S. Palmer. *Stress Counseling*. New York: Springer, 1997.

Ellis, A., J. Sichel, R. Yeager, D. DiMattia, and R. DiGiuseppe. *Rational-Emotive Couples Therapy*. New York: Pergamon Press, Inc, 1989.

Ellis, A., R. A. Harper, S. Dyer, R. Timmons, R. Hill, and N. Kavinoky. "Premarital Sex Relations," *Marriage and Family Living* 14 (1952).

Ellis, A., and R. Grieger, eds. *Handbook of Rational-Emotive Therapy*. 2 vols. New York: Springer, 1977, 1986.

Ellis, H. *Studies in the Psychology of Sex*. 2 vols. New York: Random House, 1936.

*Epictetus. *The Collected Works of Epictetus*. Boston: Little, Brown, 1890.

*Epicurus. *Letter on Happiness*. San Francisco: Chronicle Books, 1994.

Epstein, S. "Cognitive-Experiential Self Theory." In *Handbook of Personality and Research*, edited by L. Pervin. New York: Guilford, 1990.

Erikson, E.H. *Childhood and Society*. New York: Norton, 1956.

Farson, R. A. "Praise Reappraised." *Encounter*, no. 1, 1966.

FitzMaurice, K. E. *Twelve Steps of Emotional Disturbance*. Omaha, Neb.: Author, 1994.

———. *Attitude Is All You Need*. Omaha, Neb.: Palm Tree Publishers, 1997.

Ford, C. S., and F. Beach. *Patterns of Sexual Behavior*. New York: Harpers, 1951.

Frank, J. Therapeutic Components Shared by All Psychotherapies. In *Cognition and Psychotherapy*, edited by M. J. Mahoney and A. Freedman. New York: Plenum, 1985.

*Frankl, V. *Man's Search for Meaning*. New York: Pocket Books, 1959.

Frazer, J.G. *The New Golden Bough*. New York: Criterion, 1959.

Freud, S. *Standard Edition of The Complete Psychological Works of Sigmund Freud*. New York: Basic Books, 1965.

*Fromm, E. *The Art of Loving*. New York: Harper, 1962.

Gandy, G. L. *Mental Health Rehabilitation: Disputing Irrational Beliefs*. Springfield, Ill.: Thomas, 1995.

Geller, L. Another Look at Self-actualization. *Journal of Humanistic Psychology* 24, no. 2 (1984).

Glasser, W. *Reality Therapy*. New York: Harper and Row, 1965.

———. *Schools Without Failure*. New York: Harper and Row, 1969.

Goldfried, M. R., and G. C. Davison. *Clinical Behavior Therapy*. New York: Holt, Rinehart and Winston, 1976.

Grafenberg, E. The Role of Urethra in Female Orgasm. *International Journal of Sexology* 3(1950).

Grant, V. *Psychology of Sexual Emotion*. New York: Longmans, Green, 1957.

*Grieger, R. M., and P. J. Woods. *The Rational-Emotive Therapy Companion*. Roanoke, Vir.: Scholars Press, 1993.

Guidano, V. F. "A Systems, Process-Oriented Approach to Cognitive Therapy." In *Handbook of Cognitive Behavioral Therapies*, edited by K. S. Dobson. New York: Guilford, 1988.

Hajzler, D., and M. E. Bernard. "A Review of Rational-Emotive Outcome Studies." *School Psychology Quarterly* 6, no. 1 (1991).

Harris, S. J. "A Man's Worth Is Not Relative," *Detroit Free Press,* December 12, 1963.

Hartman, R. S. Letter to Albert Ellis, June 27, 1967.

―――. *The Measurement of Value.* Carbondale, Ill.: University of Southern Illinois Press, 1967.

―――. "Sputnik's Moral Challenge," *Texas Quarterly* 3, no. 3 (Autumn 1960).

*Hauck, P. A. *Overcoming Depression.* Philadelphia: Westminster, 1973.

*―――. *Overcoming Frustration and Anger.* Philadelphia: Westminster, 1974.

*―――. *Overcoming the Rating Game: Beyond Self-Love—Beyond Self-Esteem.* Louisville, Ken.: John Knox, 1991.

Hayakawa, S. I. *Language in Thought and Action.* New York: Harcourt, Brace and World, 1965.

―――. "The Fully Functioning Personality." In *Symbol, Status and Personality,* edited by S. I. Hayakawa. New York: Harcourt Brace Jovanovich, 1968.

Henry, J. *Culture Against Man.* New York: Random House, 1963.

Herschberger, E. *Adam's Rib.* New York: Pellegrini and Cuddahy, 1948.

Herzberg, A. *Active Psychotherapy.* New York: Grune & Stratton, 1945.

Hirsch, E. W. *Modern Sex Life.* New York: Permabooks, 1949.

―――. *Sexual Fear.* New York: Garden City, 1950.

Hitschmann, E., and E. Bergler. "Frigidity in Women: Restatement and Renewed Experiences," *Psychoanalytic Review* 36 (1949).

Hoffer, E. *The True Believer.* New York: Harper, 1951.

Hollon, S. D., and A. T. Beck. "Cognitive and Cognitive-behavior Therapies." In *Handbook of Psychotherapy and Behavior Change,* edited by A. E. Bergin and S. L. Garfield, 1994.

Horney, K. *Collected Works.* New York: Norton, 1965.

―――. *Our Inner Conflicts: A Constructive Theory of Neurosis.* New York: Norton, 1945.

―――. *Neurosis and Human Growth.* New York: Norton, 1950.

Human Development Institute, Inc. *Improving Communication in Marriage.* Atlanta: Human Development Institute, 1964.

Jahoda, M. "What Is Prejudice?" *World Mental Health* 13 (1961).

*Johnson, W. *People in Quandaries.* New York: Harper and Row, 1946.

Johnson, W. R. *So Desperate the Fight.* New York: Institute for Rational-Emotive Therapy, 1981.

Jung, C. G. *The Practice of Psychotherapy.* New York: Pantheon, 1954.

Kelly, G. *Psychology of Personal Constructs.* New York: Norton, 1955.

―――. "Technique of Marriage Relations." In *Successful Marriage,* edited by M. Fishbein and E. W. Burgess. New York: Doubleday, 1947.

Kelly, G. L. *Sex Manual for Those Married or About to Be.* Augusta, Ga.: Southern Medical Supply Company, 1953.

Kinsey, A. C., W. B. Pomeroy, and C. E. Martin. *Sexual Behavior in the Human Male*. Philadelphia: Saunders, 1948.

Kinsey, A. C., W. B. Pomeroy, C. E. Martin, and P. H. Gebhard. *Sexual Behavior in the Human Female*. Philadelphia: Saunders, 1953.

Kirby, P., and D. DiMattia. "A Rational Approach to Emotional Management." *Training and Development Journal* 45, no. 1 (1991).

Klarreich, S. H., R. DiGiuseppe. and D. DiMattia. "EAPs: Mind Over Myths," *Personnel Administrator* 32, no. 2 (1987).

Knaus, W. *Rational-Emotive Education*. New York: Institute for Rational-Emotive Therapy, 1974.

Kobasa, S. C. "Stressful Life Events, Personality and Health. An Inquiry Into Hardness," *Journal of Personality and Social Psychology* 37 (1979).

Korzybski, A. "Fate and Freedom." In *The Language of Wisdom and Folly*, edited by I. J. Lee. San Francisco: International Society for General Semantics, 1923.

———. *Manhood of Humanity*. Lakeville, Conn.: International Non-Aristotelian Library Publishing Co., 1921.

———. "The Role of Language in the Perceptual Processes." In *Perception: An Approach to Personality*, edited by R. R. Blake and G. V. Ramsey. New York: Ronald Press, 1951.

———. *Science and Sanity*. San Francisco: International Society of General Semantics, 1933.

Lasch, C. *The Culture of Narcissism*. New York: Norton, 1978.

Lazarus, A. A. *Behavior Therapy and Beyond*. New York: Hill, 1989.

*———. *Marital Myths*. San Luis Obispi, Calif.: Impact, 1985.

———. *The Practice of Multimodal Therapy*. New York: McGraw-Hill, 1981.

———. *The Practice of Multimodal Therapy*. Baltimore: Johns Hopkins University Press, 1989.

———. "Toward an Egoless State of Being." In *Handbook of Rational-Emotive Therapy*, vol. 1. Edited by A. Ellis and R. Grieger. New York: Springer, 1977.

Lazarus, R. S. *Psychological Stress and the Coping Process*. New York: McGraw-Hill, 1966.

Lazarus, R. S., and S. Folkman. *Stress, Appraisal, and Coping*. New York: Springer, 1984.

Levi-Strauss, C. *Savage Mind*. Chicago: University of Chicago Press, 1970.

Levie, L. H. "Vaginal Orgasm." *International Journal of Sexology* 3 (1949).

Levine, L. "Orgasm Capacity of Women." *Marriage Hygiene* 1 (1948).

Lewinsohn, P. M. "A Behavioral Approach to Depression." In *The Psychology of Depression: Contemporary Theory and Research*, edited by R. M. Friedman and M. M. Katz. New York: Wiley, 1974.

London, T. *REBT Questions: A Study Guide to the General/Clinical Theory, Philosophy, and Techniques of Rational Emotive Behavior Therapy*. Chicago: Garfield Press, 1995.

LoPiccolo, J., R. Stewart, and B. Watkins. "Treatment of Erectile Failure and Ejaculatory Incompetence and Homosexual Etiology," *Behavior Therapy* 3 (1972).

LoPiccolo, J., and L. LoPiccolo, eds. *Handbook of Sex Therapy*. New York: Plenum, 1978.

Lorand, S. *Technique of Psychoanalytic Therapy*. New York: International Universities Press, 1946.

*Low, A. *Lectures to Relatives of Former Patients*. Boston: Christopher, 1967.

*————. *Mental Health Through Will Training*. Boston: Christopher, 1952.

Lucka, E. *Evolution of Love*. London: Allen and Unwin, 1922.

Lundberg, F., and M. F. Farnham. *Modern Woman, the Lost Sex*. New York: Harpers, 1949.

Lyons, L. C., and P. J. Woods. "The Efficacy of Rational-Emotive Therapy," *Clinical Psychology Review* 11 (1991).

Mahoney, M. J. *Scientist as Subject: The Psychological Imperative*. Cambridge, Mass. Ballinger, 1976.

————. *Human Change Processes*. New York: Basic Books, 1991.

Mahoney, M. J., J. C. Norcross, J. O. Prochaska, and C. D. Missar D. "Psychological Development and Optimal Psychotherapy: Converging Perspectives Among Clinical Psychologists." *Journal of Integrative and Eclectic Psychotherapy* 8 (1989).

Malleson, J. "A Criterion for Orgasm in the Female," *Marriage Hygiene* 1 (1949).

————. "The Psychology of Feminine Sex Experience," *International Journal of Sexology* 4 (1949).

*Marcus Aurelius. *Meditations*. Boston: Little, Brown, 1899.

Maslow, A. H. "Love in Healthy People." In *The Meaning of Love*, edited by A. Montagu. New York: Julian Press, 1953.

————. *Motivation and Personality*. Rev. ed. New York: Harper, 1970.

————. *Toward a Psychology of Being*. New York: Van Nostrand Reinhold, 1968.

Masters, W. H., and V. E. Johnson. *Human Sexual Inadequacy*. Boston: Little, Brown, 1970.

————. *Human Sexual Response*. Boston: Little, Brown, 1966.

Maultsby, M. C., Jr. *Rational Behavior Therapy*. Englewood Cliffs, N.J.· Prentice-Hall, 1984.

May, R. *Love and Will*. New York: Norton, 1969.

McGuire, W. J. "Inducing Resistance to Persuasion." In *Advances in Experimental Psychology*, edited by L Berkowitz. New York: Academic Press, 1964.

McIntyre, A. *After Virtue: A Study of Moral Theory*. London: Duckworth, 1981.

McKnight, D. L., R. O. Nelson, S. C. Hayes, and R. B. Jarrett. "Importance of Treating Individually Assessed Response Classes in the Amelioration of Depression," *Behavior Therapy* 15 (1984).

Meichenbaum, D. *Cognitive-behavior Modification*. New York: Plenum, 1977.

*Miller, T. *The Unfair Advantage*. Manlius, N.Y.: Horsesense, Inc., 1986.

*Mills, D. *Overcoming Self-Esteem*. New York: Institute for Rational-Emotive Therapy, 1993.

Mitchell, R. E., R. C. Cronkite, and R. H. Moos. "Stress, Coping and Depression Among Married Couples," *Journal of Abnormal Psychology* 92 (1983).

Montagu, A. (Ed.). *The Meaning of Love*. New York: Julian Press, 1953.

Mowrer, O. H. *The New Group Therapy*. Princeton, N.J.: Van Nostrand, 1964.

*Nottingham, E. *It's Not As Bad As It Seems: A Thinking Approach to Happiness*. Memphis, Tenn.: Castle Books, 1992.

*Nye, B. *Understanding and Managing Your Anger and Aggression*. Federal Way, Wash.: BCA Publishing, 1993.

O'Hare, H. "The Normal Woman," *International Journal of Sexology* 4 (1950).

————. "Vaginal Versus Clitoral Orgasm," *International Journal of Sexology* 4 (1951).

*Oliver, R., and F. A. Bock. *Coping With Alzheimer's*. North Hollywood, Calif.: Melvin Powers, 1987.

Ortega y Gasset, J. *On Love*. New York: Meridian, 1966.

Parker, R. S. *Emotional Common Sense*. New York: Harper, 1973.

Perls, F. *Gestalt Therapy Verbatim*. Lafayette, Calif.: Real People Press, 1969.

Pillay, A. P. "Frigidity in the Female," *Marriage Hygiene* 1 (1947).

Pillay, A. P., and A. Ellis. *Sex, Society, and the Individual*. Bombay: International Journal of Sexology, 1953.

Popper, K. *Objective Knowledge*. London: Oxford, 1972.

Rado, S. "An Adaptational View of Sexual Behavior." In *Psychosexual Development in Health and Disease*, edited by P. H. Hoch and J. Zubinx, eds. New York: Grune & Stratton, 1949.

Raimy, V. *Misunderstandings of the Self*. San Francisco: Jossey-Bass, 1975.

Rand, A. *Atlas Shrugged*. New York: New American Library, 1957.

————. *For the New Intellectual*. New York: New American Library, 1961.

————. "Our Cultural Value Deprivations," *Objectivist*, April/May, 1966.

————. *The Virtue of Selfishness*. New York: New American Library, 1964.

Rehm, L. P. "A Self-control Model of Depression," *Behavior Therapy* 8 (1977).

————, ed. *Behavior Therapy for Depression*. New York: Academic Press, 1981.

Reichenbach, H. "The Verifiability Theory in Meaning." In *Readings in the Philosophy of Science*, edited by H. Feigl and M. Brodbeck. New York: Appleton-Century-Crofts, 1953.

Reik, T. A. *A Psychologist Looks at Love*. New York: Rinehart, 1945.

Robertiello, R. *Sexual Fulfillment and Self-Affirmation*. Larchmont, N.Y., 1964.

*Robin, M. W., and R. Balter. *Performance Anxiety*. Holbrook, Mass.: Adams, 1995.

Rogers, C. R. *On Becoming a Person*. Boston: Houghton-Mifflin, 1961.

Russell, B. *The Basic Writings of Bertrand Russell*. New York: Simon and Schuster, 1965.

*————. *The Conquest of Happiness*. New York: New American Library, 1951.

Sapirstein, M. R. *Emotional Security*. New York: Crown, 1948.

Seligman, M. E. P. *Helplessness: On Depression, Development, and Death*. San Francisco: Freeman, 1975.

*————. *Learned Optimism*. New York: Knopf, 1991.

Seligman, M. E. P., L. Y. Abramson, A. Semmel, and C. vonBaeyer. "Depressive Attribution Style," *Journal of Abnormal Psychology* 88 (1979).

Silverman, J.S., J. A. Silverman, and D. A. Eardley. "Do Maladaptive Attitudes Cause Depression?" *Archives of General Psychiatry* 41 (1984).

Sorokin, P.A. *The Ways and Power of Love*. Boston: Beacon, 1954.

Stendhal. *On Love*. New York: Liveright, 1947.

Stokes, W. *Modern Pattern for Marriage*. New York: Rinehart, 1948.

Sweetland, J. *Cognitive Behavior Therapy and Physical Disability*. Point Lookout, N.Y.: Author, 1991.

Tart, C. ed. *Altered States of Consciousness*. New York: Wiley, 1969.

Thompson, C. *Psychoanalysis: Evolution and Development*. New York: Hermitage House, 1950.

*Tillich, P. *The Courage to Be*. New York: Oxford, 1953.

*Vernon, A. *Thinking, Feeling, Behaving: An Emotional Education Curriculum for Children*. Champaign, Ill.: Research Press, 1989.

Walen, S., R. DiGiuseppe, and W. Dryden. *A Practitioner's Guide to Rational-Emotive Therapy*. New York: Oxford University Press, 1992.

Weinrach, S. G. "Reducing REBT's 'Wince Factor,'" *Journal of Rational-Emotive and Cognitive Behavior Therapy* 14 (1996).

Wessler, R. L. "Idiosyncratic Definitions and Unsupported Hypotheses: Rational-Emotive Behavior Therapy as Pseudoscience," *Journal of Rational-Emotive and Cognitive Behavior Therapy* 14 (1996).

Wicker, A. W. "Getting Out of Our Conceptual Ruts: Strategies for Expanding Conceptual Frameworks." *American Psychologist* 40 (1985).

*Wiener, D. *Albert Ellis: Passionate Skeptic*. New York: Praeger, 1988.

Williams, J. M. G. *The Psychological Treatment of Depression*. New York: Free Press.

Wilson, S. R. "The 'Real Self' Controversy: Toward an Integration of Humanistic and Interactionist Theory," *Journal of Humanistic Psychology* 28, no. 1 (1988).

Wittels, F. *Sex Habits of American Women*. New York: Eton, 1951.

Wittgenstein, L. *Philosophical Investigations*. New York: Macmillan, 1958.

*Wolfe, J. L. *What to Do When He Has a Headache*. New York: Hyperion, 1992.

———. Overcoming Low Frustration Tolerance (video). New York: Albert Ellis Institute, 1993.

———. Woman Assert Yourself (audiotape). New York: Albert Ellis Institute, 1980.

Wolpe, J. *The Practice of Behavior Therapy.* 4th ed. Needham Heights, Mass.: Allyn and Bacon, 1990.

Wright, H. "A Contribution to the Orgasm Problem in Women." *International Journal of Sexology* 3 (1949).

———. *Sex Fulfillment in Married Women.* London: Williams and Norgate, 1947.

*Yankura, J., and W. Dryden. *Albert Ellis.* Thousand Oaks, Calif.: Sage, 1994.

———. *Doing RET: Albert Ellis in Action.* New York: Springer, 1990.

*Young, H. *A Rational Counseling Primer.* New York: Albert Ellis Institute, 1974.

Acknowledgments

We gratefully acknowledge the contributions of Tim Runyon for transcribing the manuscript, and of Ginamarie Zampano for her executive management.

"Achieving Self-Actualization" was originally published in 1991 by Select Press in the *Journal of Social Behavior and Personality* 6 (5), 1–18. It has been reprinted here with the permission of the publishers.

"The Evolution of Albert Ellis and Rational Emotive Behavior Therapy" was originally published in 1997 by Brunner/Mazel in *The Evolution of Psychotherapy: The Third Conference*, edited by J. K. Zeig. It has been reprinted here with the permission of the publishers.

"How I Became Interested in Sexology and Sex Therapy" was originally published in 1997 by Prometheus Books in *Personal Stories of "How I Got Into Sex"*, edited by V. L. Bullough, M. A. Fithian, W. E. Hartman, and R. S. Klein. It has been reprinted here with the permission of the publishers.

"Humanistic Psychotherapy: A Revolutionary Approach" was originally published in 1972 by the American Humanist Association in *The Humanist* 32 (1), 24–28, and has been reprinted here with the permission of the publishers.

"Using Rational Emotive Behavior Therapy Techniques to Cope With Disability" was originally published in 1997 in *Professional Psychology: Research and Practice* 28(1), 17–22. Copyright © 1997 by the American Psychological Association. It has been adapted with permission.

"Addictive Behaviors and Personality Disorders: A Rational Emotive Behavior Therapy Approach" was originally published in 1995 in the journal *Addictions Newsletter* 2(3), 10–11. It has been reprinted here with the permission of the publishers.

"The Biological Basis of Human Irrationality" from the *Journal of Individual Psychology* 32(1), 145–168 is reprinted by permission of the University of Texas Press.

Index

About the Editors

Albert Ellis is the founder of Rational-Emotive Behavior Therapy and president of the Albert Ellis Institute, which has branches throughout the United States and the rest of the world. He has published over 800 articles in psychological, psychiatric, and sociological journals and anthologies, and has authored or edited more than sixty books, including *How to Live with a "Neurotic," Reason and Emotion in Psychotherapy, A Guide to Rational Living, A Guide to Personal Happiness, The Practice of Rational-Emotive Behavior Therapy,* and *How to Stubbornly Refuse to Make Yourself Miserable About Anything—Yes, Anything!*

Shawn Blau is an Associate Fellow and Training Faculty Supervisor of the Albert Ellis Institute in New York City, and Adjunct Professor of Statistics at Fairfield University in Fairfield, Connecticut. He is a member of the American Psychological Society, National Academy of Neuropsychology, American Statistical Association, and the Institute of General Semantics.